BLOOD
DONE SIGN
MY NAME

BLOOD DONE SIGN MY NAME

A TRUE STORY

TIMOTHY B. TYSON

THREE RIVERS PRESS

NEW YORK

Published in the United States by Three Rivers Press, an imprint of the Crown
Publishing Group, a division of Random House, Inc., New York.
www.crownpublishing.com

THREE RIVERS PRESS and the Tugboat design are registered trademarks of
Random House, Inc.

Originally published in hardcover in the United States by Crown Publishers, an
imprint of the Crown Publishing Group, a division of Random House, Inc.,
New York, in 2004.

Library of Congress Cataloging-in-Publication Data

Tyson, Timothy B., 1959–
   Blood done sign my name / Timothy B. Tyson.—1st ed.
Includes bibliographical references
   1. Oxford (N.C.)—Race relations. 2. African Americans—Crimes against—North
Carolina—Oxford—History—20th century.
3. Murder—North Carolina—Oxford—History—20th century.
4. Trials (Murder)—North Carolina—Oxford. 5. Riots—North Carolina—Oxford—
History—20th century. 6. Tyson, Timothy B.—Childhood and youth. 7. Whites—
North Carolina—Oxford—Biography.
8. African Americans—North Carolina—Oxford—Biography.
9. Oxford (N.C.)—Biography. I. Title.
   F264.095T97 2004
   975.6'535'00496073—dc22

                                                                    2003019804

ISBN 1-4000-8311-7

Printed in the United States of America

Design by Lauren Dong

10 9 8 7 6 5 4 3 2 1

First Paperback Edition

to my Mama and Daddy

Contents

"Ain't you glad, ain't you glad,
that the blood done sign your name?"
—AFRICAN AMERICAN SPIRITUAL

BLOOD
DONE SIGN
MY NAME

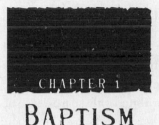

CHAPTER 1

BAPTISM

DADDY AND ROGER and 'em shot 'em a *nigger*." That's what Gerald Teel said to me in my family's driveway in Oxford, North Carolina, on May 12, 1970. We were both ten years old. I was bouncing a basketball. The night before, a black man had "said something" at the store to Judy, his nineteen-year-old sister-in-law, Gerald told me, and his father and two of his brothers had run him out of the store and shot him dead. The man's name was Henry Marrow, I found out later, but his family called him Dickie. He was killed in public as he lay on his back, helpless, begging for his life.

I was stunned and bewildered, as if Gerald had informed me that his family had fried up their house cat and eaten it for breakfast. We did not use *that* word at our house. It was not that I had never heard it or had never used it myself. But somehow the children in my family knew that to utter *that* word in the presence of my father would be to say good-bye to this earthly life. My daddy was a Methodist minister, an "Eleanor Roosevelt liberal," he called himself in later years, and at our house "nigger" was not just naughty, like "hell" or "damn." It was evil, like taking the Lord's name in vain, maybe even worse. And now my friend Gerald was using it while talking about his daddy and his brothers killing a man.

Before Gerald could say anything more, my mother opened the

front door of our house and called me in for supper. "What are we having?" I yelled back at her.

"I am not announcing my menu to the neighborhood," Mama said in a clear but quiet voice. I hurried inside, dumbstruck, wondering what the grown-ups in my world were going to say about Gerald's news. Could this be true? Or was it just a little boy's boasting? Mama and Daddy would know.

Mama wielded an abundantly sharp sense of how things were and were not done. That was why she was "not about to advertise my dinner menu up and down Hancock Street," as she reminded me when I came into the kitchen. Pork chops, mashed potatoes and gravy, peppery cabbage simmered with fatback, and crisp fried cornbread served with sweet iced tea seemed no cause for shame. Mrs. Roseanna Allen, the black woman who worked for us, had also made us a chocolate pie that afternoon, as she often did when I begged her. But the details of our supper were beside Mama's point. Yelling like that was "tacky," a label that applied to a disquieting number of my habits.

I figured that Mama and Daddy would talk to us about what had happened, but instead an eerie hush hung over the supper table. Somewhat oddly, Daddy refrained from his custom of interviewing us one by one about our day. He and Mama exchanged knowing words and weighted glances whose meanings were indecipherable to me. My twelve-year-old brother, Vern, and I talked halfheartedly about something—how fast Dudley Barnes, who pitched for A&W Root Beer's Little League nine, could throw a baseball, something like that. But a deep silence had fallen among us.

After supper, my little sister Boo and I crept out of the house and down to the corner, where we huddled on the sidewalk behind Mrs. Garland's cement wall, across the street from the Teel house. Boo was seven years old, blond and freckly, by turns deferential and officious in the way of little sisters, and she went wherever I did, provided I let her. In the Bible, Ruth tells Naomi, "Entreat me not to leave thee; or to return from following after thee: for whither thou goest I will go; and where thou lodgest, I will lodge," and while this was frequently quoted as a tribute to filial devotion, I always noted that we never heard from Naomi on the point. When I came home from church one Sunday and announced that I was going to become a missionary to Africa, Boo immediately declared her intention to become a nurse and accompany me. I shot back, "What do you think I am going to Africa for?" But truth be told, I was glad to have her with me this particular evening.

We could see the house clearly through the budding crape myrtles that laced the long traffic island in the middle of Main Street. Gerald's family lived in a gracious, older two-story structure with white columns, wide porches, and a carport on one side that must have been built originally for carriages. At least a dozen men with shotguns and rifles stood guard on its porches as Boo and I peered across the corners of Front and Main Streets. A couple of the men were draped in white hoods and robes, but most of them looked for all the world like our own father when he went bird hunting. We did not know exactly how these men pertained to Gerald's announcement, but we knew something perilous was unfolding.

For one thing, neither of us had ever seen anyone who didn't live there go into the Teel house. I played with Gerald Teel practically every day, but the boys in our neighborhood came to my house or we ran the woods and fields that stretched out beyond my backyard. Sometimes we smoked Jeff Daniels's mother's Tareyton cigarettes down by the creek. We played football in the front yard of the old Hancock place, a once palatial but now rotting three-story white structure with huge wooden pillars that stood empty across the street from my house.

Gerald, Jeff, and I wore the same brand of brogans as a kind of uniform—our look was straight-leg blue jeans, army surplus jackets, and those brownish orange work boots—and we fought together in the forbidden BB-gun wars that raged in our neighborhood on Saturday mornings. Gerald was a slight, olive-skinned boy with dark hair and eyes. He rarely talked much. We considered him a respectably tough kid, a member of the gang in good standing, but he also had a kind of whipped-dog manner, a shyness that said something was wrong. You'd say we were friends. But I did not visit in Gerald's house and, as far as I knew, neither did anybody else. All Mama would say, in her offhand, gracious way, was that they weren't really our kind of folks, but it was worse than that. Everybody was afraid of Gerald's daddy, who never spoke in my presence until many years had passed.

That night, after kneeling beside the bed with my father to say my prayers as we usually did, I lay me down to sleep on the cool, clean sheets, wondering about what had happened and fearing, without really knowing what to fear, the things that might happen now. The attic fan in the top of the house pulled the gauzy white curtains inward on a cooling breeze; two weeks into May it was already hot, and not everyone had air-conditioning in those days. From my upstairs window, I could see the blinking red light of Oxford's radio tower. The raspy, playful voice of Julius's Jukebox, WOXF's "Little Round Brown Mound of Sound," beamed from the transistor radio propped in my windowsill, announcing song dedications—"This one goes out from Shirley to S.O.S."—and spinning Otis Redding, James Brown, or Aretha Franklin. Every night that summer, the ominous pulse of Marvin Gaye's "I Heard It Through the Grapevine" pounded on the airwaves, and what may have seemed a haunting anthem of lost love for some listeners sounded a dire warning to me. Sleep was slow to come.

While I slumbered, six blocks away in downtown Oxford hundreds of young blacks exploded into rage. At least half a dozen people had witnessed the murder in Grab-all, the black ghetto where Mr. Teel's store was located. Word traveled fast. "This won't no goddamn murder mystery," one of the young blacks spat, "and the son of a bitch lived three blocks from the police station." Rumors flew through Oxford that the magistrate, J. C. Wheeler, refused to swear out a warrant against the Teels, and that the police were not planning to arrest anyone. This poured the gasoline of indignation onto the flames of vengefulness. "When Dickie was first killed," one black witness to the murder told me years later, "people in Grab-all was talking about 'everything white *dies.*'"

Though neither blood vengeance nor race war ensued, I learned years later that two or three hundred young African Americans ran through the well-ordered streets of downtown Oxford that night, smashing windows and setting fires. The angry throng would assemble in one place, demolish the agreed-upon storefront, and then sprint at breakneck speed through the alleyways to another target. At the American Oil station, some of the insurgents paused to loot beer and cigarettes, also making off with a portable television. The screaming alarm at Edwards Jewelry Store did not deter the mob from emptying the window of wristwatches. Behind the Western Auto hardware store, they stacked up old tires against a heavy door and set them ablaze, trying unsuccessfully to get inside and find guns and ammunition. The rioters retained the presence of mind to distinguish between white-owned property and the handful of establishments owned by blacks; they also pelted passing cars with bricks and bottles, but only those vehicles whose drivers appeared to be white. At one point, a group of the rioters ran to the Confederate monument, threw a length of rope around the old Rebel's neck, and tried to pull him off his granite pedestal, but the bronze infantryman would not budge.

When the first police car arrived, half a dozen bricks smashed the windshield and the mob heaved the car over onto its side. The terrified officer inside clambered out and ran for dear life. Two or three more squad cars screeched up, but there was little they could do against the small, angry army in the streets. Some whites criticized Mayor Currin the next day for not ordering his handful of men to shoot down the rioters. Currin understood his town, knew the limitations of his small and unsophisticated police force, and kept his cool. "With the police department we had," the mayor told me later, "it was no reason to send the officers in there to try and stop it. I didn't do it, and I am glad I didn't do it."

Even those who criticized the mayor's judgment could not fault his courage. During the height of the melee, Currin joined Assistant Chief of Police Doug White in a patrol car downtown. The two men drove to the edge of the riot and watched as dozens of looters sacked the A&P. And then they heard gunfire. "We were sitting in the car at the Esso station about midnight," Currin recalled. "There was a lot of noise, of course, and then we heard this loud report." Someone had fired a large-caliber bullet into one of the rear doors of the car in which Currin and White were sitting. The shot seemed to come from behind a low retaining wall twenty feet away, but the two city officials did not drive away. Mayor Currin later discounted the possibility that anyone had aimed the bullet at either one of them. "I think anyone shooting at that distance that wanted to shoot me, they could have shot me, that close." Currin and White stayed in the car, keeping an eye on things, moving the car only when the epicenter of the violence moved, but not trying to interfere with the riot.

At about two forty-five Wednesday morning, the rioters grew tired and went home. The police had not made a single arrest, and no one had been injured. The mob had destroyed seventeen storefronts, firebombed four buildings, ransacked the grocery store, smashed a police car, and scared the hell out of most of the white people in Oxford, and some of the black ones, too. The next day, every hardware store in town sold out of ammunition. White businessmen who owned stores downtown assessed the damages and started repairs; many of them also moved cots to their stores, and some of them slept there for weeks with shotguns across their laps.

Though things settled down during the day, the rioters awaited news from the courthouse of any possible arrests in the killing. A handful of black Vietnam veterans began to meet down at McCoy's Pool Hall and out at the Soul Kitchen, discussing strategies and plotting tactics. Although their elders generally disapproved, young blacks celebrated the riot gleefully and totted up the financial costs they had inflicted upon whites. At last, they felt, the white people who ran Oxford would have to listen to them, and the sole reason for that was that they had finally resorted to open revolt. For years afterward, the young people of the Black Power generation, the generation for whom the murder of Martin Luther King Jr. spoke more loudly than his message, talked about the riot with pride. "We tried to tear that bitch *up*," one of them boasted. "The only thing I really hate is that we couldn't pull down that damn Confederate monument."

The morning after the riot, Boo and I walked past the Teel house on our way to school. There was no sign of the armed men we had seen the night before. The place looked empty except for an abandoned bicycle in the driveway. If we had gone inside and upstairs, which we certainly never had done before, we would have seen the bullet hole in one of the bedroom walls; someone in a passing car had fired a .30-30 rifle into the house. We did see a note taped to the front door, which we would not have dared walk up and read, not even for a bottomless charge account at Hall's Drugstore. Boo and I hurried toward downtown. There was no sign of Gerald, whom I would not see again for twelve years, not until the afternoon I went to his father's barbershop to ask his father why he and his sons had killed Henry Marrow.

Three blocks past Gerald's house, as we approached Hall's, the sidewalks and streets were sequined with broken glass, glinting in the morning sunlight. Sheets of fresh plywood, with their sharp sawdust-and-glue smell, shielded all the storefronts. Charred wood framed shattered shop windows in black, where firebombs had broken the plate glass the night before. Strapping state troopers, sent by the governor, stood on street corners with their radios and shotguns. Local cops with traffic whistles and big revolvers guarded our route to school. As we passed the Confederate monument in the middle of town, we saw a bandy-legged policeman climbing up to remove a long yellow nylon rope tied in a noose around the tarnished old soldier's greenish neck.

When I walked home that afternoon, the noose no longer dangled from the monument, but violence still hung in the air. "The first thing we did," a young black woman told me years later, when we were both grown, "was we left school." The schools were still segregated in 1970, except for my class at Credle Elementary, which had two black kids, but the school board had finally made plans to comply with the Supreme Court's 1954 ruling and had scheduled full-scale integration for that fall. "And we said the first white child we see we gonna kick their ass," she continued, "and that's what we did." But the violence clearly went both ways. That day I walked home with

Jeff Daniels, the skinny, mischievous eleven-year-old boy who was my friend and protector. Gerald Teel usually accompanied us, but that afternoon Gerald was nowhere to be found. As Jeff and I walked down Main Street, we saw a gang of six or eight black kids slightly older than us walking together on the opposite side of the street. Without saying a word to me, Jeff suddenly winged a small shard of concrete at them, missing one of them narrowly. The black boys scrambled around for rocks, fired off a barrage—one of which whizzed past my head—and then chased us most of the way home. Only a deft bit of footwork along the top of a fence behind Burton Gibbs's house saved us from an ass kicking. Panting in Jeff's garage, terrified but safe at last, I wondered not only why I was walking with a damn fool who would pick a fight with half a dozen older boys, but also what would come of all this enmity and rage.

Even then, I knew that there had been some kind of black uprising in the streets of Oxford the night before. It was neither the first nor the last such upheaval—the black veterans had already been planning what one of them called "a military operation" against white domination—but it was the first one I was aware of. What I could not imagine was how deeply these events and the dramas to come would reshape my life and my world. In the years ahead, I sometimes stood and stared down into the dust behind the old Teel store, along Highway 158, and thought about the blood that had soaked that soil in 1970. I pondered, too, the blood that beat in my own veins and the ways in which my family's history was implicated in Henry Marrow's killing—and perhaps even redeemed, since by the end of things, if anything ever really ends, his killing set our faces toward a strange new Jerusalem. It was the blood, to paraphrase the old spiritual, that signed our names.

Before I could grasp what had happened in my hometown, I had to root through the basement of the courthouse, ransack the state archives, read a hundred years of old newspapers, and kneel beside the graves of blood kin and strangers. I had to get to know my own father and mother as real human beings, and to understand that the Lord works through deeply flawed people, since He made so few of the other kind. I had to listen to the ghost of my old friend Thad Stem, who taught me that it is better to understand a little than to misunderstand a lot. Above all, perhaps, I had to listen carefully to the stories of black men who had referred to one another fondly as "bloods" in Vietnam and ponder why they had returned to Oxford ready to burn it down, if that was what it took to end the racial caste system. Like generations of black veterans before them, who had come home from France or the Philippines insisting that their sacrifices had bought them full citizenship, the Vietnam generation demanded justice. Though they had paid the price, more would be required. "They didn't just open the door up and say, 'Y'all come in, integration done come,' " Eddie McCoy instructed me. "It didn't happen that way in Oxford. Somebody was bruised and kicked and knocked around—you better believe it."

The stories of freedom-movement veterans like Eddie McCoy and twenty years of research in dusty archives and around dozens of kitchen tables taught me that the life-and-death struggle in Oxford that summer was inextricably bound up with much larger and more enduring conflicts about the meanings of race and nation and freedom. Only a week before Henry Marrow's brains were blown out, National Guard troops fired into a crowd of antiwar protestors at Kent State University in Ohio, killing four students and wounding eleven. The day after Marrow died, a mentally retarded black teenager was beaten to death in an Augusta, Georgia, jail, setting off riots in which white law enforcement officers killed six blacks and wounded dozens more. On May 16, 1970, five days after the killing in my hometown, Mississippi state troopers fired 350 rounds into a women's dormitory at historically black Jackson State University, killing two students and wounding twelve. In Vietnam, racial clashes in the U.S. Army made America's misbegotten war almost impossible to pursue. The country seemed to teeter on the brink of apocalypse. "This is a dangerous situation,", the editors of *BusinessWeek* declared. "It threatens the whole economic and social structure of the nation."

So while this is the story of a small boy in a small town one hot

Southern summer, it is also the story of a nation torn apart by racial, political, social, and cultural clashes so deep that they echo in our lives to this day. The cheerful and cherished lies we tell ourselves about those years—that the black freedom movement was largely a nonviolent call on America's conscience, which America answered, to cite the most glaring fiction—do little to repair the breach. There are many things we never learned about the civil rights struggle, and many others things we have tried hard to forget. The United States could find work for a national Truth and Reconciliation Commission like the one that has tried to mend the scars of apartheid in South Africa; any psychiatrist can tell you that genuine healing requires a candid confrontation with our past. In any case, if there is to be reconciliation, first there must be truth.

The truth will set us free, so the Bible says, and my own experience bears witness. This story has carved changes in my life as deep as the enduring chasm of race in this country, but far more fortuitous. My search for the meaning of the troubles in Oxford launched me toward a life of learning, across lines of color and caste, out of my little boy's vision of my family's well-lighted place in the world and into the shadows where histories and memories and hopes abide.

CHAPTER 2

ORIGINAL SINS

M Y FAMILY WAS as Southern as fried okra and sweet tea. Because my father was a Methodist minister, we moved from town to town every few years. But we always stayed in eastern North Carolina, where my father's father, grandfather, and great-grandfather before him had planted tobacco and preached the gospel. We ate collards and cornbread, pork barbecue and banana pudding. On car trips, Mama and Daddy taught us to sing "Dixie"—though mostly we sang spirituals like "'Trampin'" and "Michael, Row the Boat Ashore." Tyson children often had double names—I had cousins called "Thomas Earl" and "George Hart" and so on. We called my sister Martha Buie "Boo," and everybody referred to my uncle Charles as "Bubba," even though his mama had never been in prison and he did not even drive a truck. We called my father "Daddy," which rhymes with "ready." When we said we were going to do something "directly," which is pronounced "dreckly," we meant we were going to do it sooner or later, one of these days, maybe never, and please don't ask again. If I hadn't learned to read, I might never have found out that "damn Yankee" was two words. But I already knew how to read pretty well by the time the big green-and-yellow Mayflower moving truck carried our household belongings to Oxford late in the summer of 1966.

We followed the moving vans in "Chief Pontiac," Daddy's old

gray sedan with the webbed seat covers and the musty smell and the Indian's head symbol on the center of the steering wheel, singing our car songs and pestering Daddy to tell us when we were going to be there. Coming into town, I greatly admired the old Confederate soldier that stood guard atop a high granite pedestal in the center of the main intersection; my friends and I played "Civil War" just like we did "cowboys and Indians," and we were always the Rebels. All the Yankees were imaginary. I mean, somebody might want to be a cowboy, but there were limits. Oxford was as drenched in Dixie as we were, just about as Southern a town as you would ever hope to find, which generally was a good thing, because that meant that the weather was nice, except when it was hot enough to fry pork chops on the pavement, and the food was delicious, though it would thicken the walls of your arteries and kill you deader than Stonewall Jackson, and the people were bighearted and friendly, though it was not the hardest place in the world to get murdered for having bad manners. Even our main crop would kill you.

Every fall, the sharp, sweet smell of brightleaf tobacco wafted through the wide streets of Oxford as the farmers brought their crops to market. Trucks piled high with great burlap bundles rumbled in and out of the massive warehouses in the middle of town. This tobacco market town was the county seat of Granville County, which lay sleeping in the sun just south of the Virginia border. Oxford was home to about eight thousand people, roughly half of them descended from the slaves who had been brought there two hundred years earlier to cultivate the precious leaf. Tobacco farming was a job of many hands, which was why Granville had had the highest slave population of any county in North Carolina. Throughout the antebellum period, and often afterward, it was said, Granville County produced more tobacco than any other county in the nation. Inside those capacious wooden warehouses, the auctioneers still chanted their singsong staccato of profit and loss.

Millions of dollars changed hands on the spit-stained pine floors of the warehouses. And when the harvest was over and the auctioneers fell silent, black and white alike—but rarely together—celebrated with eastern North Carolina barbecue, marinated in red pepper vinegar and smoked with hickory wood in greasy pits beside the empty barns. Tobacco put food on our tables, steeples on our churches, stains on our fingers, spots on our lungs, and contradictions in our hearts.

A hundred years after the fall of slavery, C. G. Credle Elementary School still didn't open until mid-September, after the farm children were finished "priming" and "putting in" tobacco—picking the leaves and hanging them in wood-fired barns to cure. Bright golden leaves blew off the trucks and littered the streets every autumn. My friends and I would pick them up and tie them in bunches and hang them from the ceiling of our lean-to forts in the woods. When we played baseball, we chewed the dark, acrid stems and pretended not to get queasy. We forever tried to devise ways to smoke the fragrant leaves, without much success. Mostly we puffed store-bought cigarettes, not being adept enough to roll our own or to manage the corncob pipes that sounded so good when Huck Finn and Tom Sawyer talked about them, though we tried. When Gerald and Jeff and I rode with Jeb Stuart's cavalry, we were Rebel soldiers smoking around the campfire.

Smoking cigarettes, much like the racial slavery that had originally made tobacco profitable, was regarded as sinful by a substantial minority of folks, even though the entire economy rested upon it. Sin or no sin, anybody tall enough to see over the counter at Monk's Grocery could buy a pack for thirty-five cents. Me and my brother, Vern, bought them regularly, though we lived in terror of getting caught. "I need a pack of Tareyton's for my mama," I would say to the man at the register, as if my mother would be caught dead sending a child out for cigarettes. The lie was superfluous. Monk probably would have sold me the smokes if I had said they were for the little baby Jesus. I would stuff the pack into the pockets of my cutoffs and light out for the woods, where neither my mama nor the lie seemed likely to catch up with me.

Since Mama and Daddy had not grown up in Oxford but had only just brought us to town, many people seemed to regard us as "not *from* here." That was part of being a Methodist preacher's family in those days, because it was an itinerant system, but Granville County was a harder place to belong than the others we had known. "Oxford," my mother remembered, "was sort of a little blue-blood town and it was hard to really get *in* it." People whose families had been in the county for anything less than several generations remained forever outsiders. The chamber of commerce erected a sign at the city limits that read WELCOME TO GRANVILLE COUNTY— OUR HOME, YOUR OPPORTUNITY, as if to say that outsiders with money to invest were welcome, but they should understand from the outset that they would never be *from* here.

And then there was the race thing. The color line in Oxford was as bright as blood. Though I had no way to know it at the time, the birth pangs of the black freedom struggle were terrifying whites everywhere. And even most grown-ups did not realize that neither these fears nor the African American self-assertions that provoked them were new.

In the late 1880s, after the fall of slavery but before African Americans lost their voting rights, white conservatives had felt similarly threatened by an earlier freedom movement. The Knights of Labor had organized both black and white workers in Granville County to support child labor laws, a shorter workweek, and federal funding for public schools; Democrats responded by denouncing whites who voted with blacks as "traitors to their race and color."

In the spring of 1887, when a white woman accused a local black man, Albert Taborn, of attempted rape, a charge many questioned, a white mob threatened to lynch him. Armed black men surrounded the jail to prevent the lynching; others vowed to burn the town. When it became clear the local authorities remained determined to see Taborn hanged, someone torched the tobacco warehouses downtown. Taborn was hanged nonetheless, and soon what remained of interracial political action was equally dead. Yet when similar events occurred in 1970—challenges to the color line, a controversial trial, and tobacco warehouses going up in flames—white people seemed amazed. "We always had good race relations here," they said to any-one who would listen.

Maybe it was misplaced nostalgia, or maybe it was because the town was half black, but white folks in Oxford seemed especially determined not to relinquish any part of what they thought of as "the Southern way of life." White people who sympathized with the movement could either keep quiet or risk being seen as traitors.

Even as a little boy, I already knew somehow that the Tysons were not always part of what white newspaper editors of the day called "the South," as in "*the South* will not submit to forcible destruction of its customs and its culture." I suppose they never stopped to con-sider that black people might be Southerners, too, or that people like my parents might love the South and hate segregation. But most of the time I did not think about those things and, unlike my parents, perhaps, I quickly adopted Oxford as my hometown.

When I was a little boy in Oxford, I am told, our friend Thad Stem asked me if I knew what my father did. "He goes to meetings," I answered. My parents repeated the remark, maybe bragging side-ways that Daddy worked so hard, but perhaps with a twinge of guilt that he was not home as much as the children wanted him to be. My father tended his flock at Oxford United Methodist Church with pas-sionate attentiveness. He learned the names of his parishioners and their children, polished his sermons into the wee hours, burned up yards of shoe leather visiting the sick and the elderly, and did attend meetings several nights a week. Daddy was always a curious mixture of personal ambition and deep spirituality, though he leaned more and more to the latter. "I want to be and do what an ideal minister would be and do," he wrote in his diary, "the Lord being my helper." But even though Daddy felt that the Lord had called him to sow the seeds of the Spirit in Oxford, he did not hesitate to acknowledge that it was a tough row to hoe. He told me years later that serving the church in Oxford reminded him of driving an old Model T Ford on a muddy country road; the steering column had so much play in it that turning the wheel didn't do much good and the car just followed the ruts anyway.

"This is not an easy church to serve," my father confided to his diary soon after we moved there. "I have visited in the homes and preached but it has been difficult. There is little spiritual vitality in this church that I can discern. The leadership is staid and conservative." Every minister worthy of the name has to walk the line between prophetic vision and spiritual sustenance, between telling people the comforting things they want to hear and challenging them with the difficult things they need to hear. In Oxford, Daddy began to feel as though all the members wanted him to do was to marry them and bury them and stay away from their souls. The first time Daddy mentioned the race issue in a sermon, one of the church elders accosted him at the door. "I'm accustomed to being served barbecue after a political speech," the man growled, refusing to shake Daddy's hand.

"Most of the people are reluctant about church work. No one is willing to keep the nursery," Daddy complained to his diary. "No counselors for Methodist Youth Fellowship. I am reminded of St. Paul, who once wrote that a large door of opportunity had been opened but that there were many adversaries."

When Daddy did finally find a young married couple to lead the Methodist Youth Fellowship, trouble immediately ensued. The young people swept out the boarded-up former parsonage next door to the church and opened Wesley House, a meeting place and recreation center. Its pool table and old overstuffed furniture soon made it a haven for Oxford's youthful counterculture, such as it was. "I thought all the hippies came out of New York City and San Francisco," my father said later, "but here they were. They were our children, and they began to show up with their long hair and strumming their guitars." And a few of them, oddly enough, had black friends. Soon Wesley House became the only voluntarily integrated social space in Granville County, a fact that pleased my father.

"And then some of my members came in and asked me to keep the blacks out," Daddy recalled. One man kept trying to persuade everyone that the Santa Claus figure hanging in the window, which had a red light bulb for a nose, was the drug signal—if there was dope available, he conjectured, the bulb in Santa's nose was lighted. But the whole uproar was really about the handful of black teenagers who came into Wesley House from time to time. "I was so afraid my daughter was going to come home from there holding hands with a black boy," one woman explained to me years later, shaking her head as though she no longer understood what she had meant back then, exactly. "Race mixing" at the church was creating a problem, a number of the men in the church told Daddy, demanding that he put a stop to it. "I told them, 'I will just ask one thing of you,' " Daddy said. " 'Just find me a racial formula from the New Testament and we'll follow that, if you find one.' " Well, that was pretty much the end of that, but his adversaries neither forgave nor forgot that he had betrayed his race.

The power of white skin in the South of my childhood was both stark and subtle. White supremacy permeated daily life so deeply that most people could no more ponder it than a fish might discuss the wetness of water. Our racial etiquette was at once bizarre and arbitrary, seemingly natural and utterly confusing, inscribed in what W. E. B. Du Bois termed "the cake of custom." White people regarded "Negroes"—they often pronounced the word as "nigrahs"—as inherently lazy and shiftless, but when a white man said that his employer worked him "like a nigger," he meant that he had been engaged in dirty, backbreaking labor to the point of collapse. Nearly all jobs were either "black" or "white," though no one said so. To say "black maid" or "black janitor" would have been entirely redundant; there were no other kinds. Black people did not work at the bank or at the stores downtown, nor anywhere where they might have direct contact with white customers. Restaurants did not hire blacks to wait tables—and white diners would not have wanted black hands to bring them their meals, although everyone knew that black hands in the kitchen had patted out the biscuit dough and fried the chicken.

In Oxford, black people lived in several distinct neighborhoods, all of which came under the rubric of "niggertown," as my playmates on Hancock Street called it. The older boys and even some of the younger ones on our street knew about that side of town because they had visited uninvited many times. On warm nights, they would pile into the back of a pickup truck and go "nigger knocking." The teenaged boys filled the truck bed with Coca-Cola bottles and rocks, then roared through the African American neighborhoods hurling them at pedestrians, windshields, and windows. I heard secondhand tales of these vicious adventures many times from Jeff Daniels, who was my age and lived across the street from me. Neighborhood boys older than us were a regular part of these attacks. And then one Christmas, when I saw my cousins from Laurinburg at my grandmother's house, they told me about some white high school boys near Maxton who had thrown a beer bottle out of a moving car and hit an elderly black man in the head, killing him. It seemed so awful. But I knew exactly what had happened. It didn't matter that it wasn't our town or our boys who had killed someone. I knew even as a little boy that it was all part of the same ordinary evil that divided us into separate and unequal worlds.

The Orpheum Theater, where my friends and I went to the movies on Saturday mornings, was segregated, and black customers sat in "the buzzard's roost"—the balcony upstairs. We often slipped up through the ratty seats and sticky aisles to throw popcorn over the railing onto the white children below. To transgress the color line was disreputable and therefore periodically irresistible for otherwise respectable white boys such as ourselves. White girls would have been much more carefully policed. And for blacks to challenge that line was not only criminal but mortally dangerous; when they did, white policemen—virtually all police officers were white men—punished them for breaking custom as well as law.

The law meant little in Oxford. Many people nowadays think that after the U.S. Congress passed the Civil Rights Act of 1964, which outlawed racial discrimination in public accommodations, café owners and city officials read the news in the morning paper and took down all those WHITE ONLY and COLORED signs by lunchtime. But this landmark legislation did not make a dent in Oxford. The town's leaders immediately elected to close most city parks, the municipal baseball diamond, and the public swimming pool. Rucker Pool, a fine structure built by the Works Progress Administration in the 1030s with tax dollars and local fieldstone, had been "public, yes," explained Mayor Hugh Currin, "but whites only." Rather than obey federal law, Oxford chose to sell Rucker Pool to some local white businessmen for pocket change. These men operated the pool as a whites-only "private club." Dues were not prohibitive, but the board barred all blacks. Neither the chamber of commerce nor the local Merchants Association opened their ranks to black members. "There's no question about it," Mayor Currin explained years later, when I asked him about how blacks and whites got along in Oxford. "By and large the larger portion of white people looked down on black people. I don't think there was any hostility between the races—it was just an accepted way of life."

Though black citizens had their own lives, families, churches, and social institutions, which they had little desire to abandon, they did not accept this "way of life" that relegated them to a lower caste. In the spring of 1070, blacks in Oxford complained bitterly about the lack of parks. Most of the parks in white neighborhoods had been closed to avoid integration, while the city had never built one single park in a black neighborhood. Mayor Currin explained that most of the land for Oxford's city parks had been bequeathed to the city with legal clauses that would rescind the gift should the parks ever be opened to black people. The United States Supreme Court had ruled in the late 1940s that such restrictive covenants were unenforceable, but the law did not matter. In any case, the city government ignored several offers from private citizens of free land for public parks. It rejected an offer from Carolina Power and Light Company to provide free basketball goals. The town's Recreation Committee never drew a quorum for meetings, said local blacks, because there was a tacit understanding that no recreational facilities would be provided so that none would have to be integrated.

A few weeks before the killing of Henry Marrow, city workers closed one of Oxford's few remaining public parks in a white residential area and removed the basketball goals, alleging that "noise" bothered the neighbors. According to local blacks, however, the reason the city closed the park was because it had begun to draw interracial basketball games—playing "salt and pepper," the boys called it. During one such game, a white man had emerged from one of the nearby houses and told the boys, "Niggers can't play here—y'all got to leave." One of the black youths talked back to him and he slapped the young man hard across the face. Two days later, the city truck arrived and workmen uprooted the basketball goals. Years afterward, one of the neighbors admitted to me, "The grown-ups were all scared. We should have listened to the children."

If my own mother, Martha Buie Tyson, ever sought the guidance of her children on racial matters or anything else, I do not remember it. She stood along the banks of our lives like a tree. What she believed and what she did was between her and the Lord, and what we believed and what we did was between us and the Lord and Martha Buie Tyson. Mama was a quietly beautiful woman with pretty brown hair, cream-colored skin that deepened past beige in the summertime, and rich brown eyes. She'd grown up in a big white house, the oldest daughter of the leading family of a small mill town not far from Oxford. "The bell cow of Biscoe," my father sometimes called her, although he only said that when she was visibly sunny; one did not trifle with my mother.

Her telephone voice sang in that sweet lilt of the Southern belle, but there was nothing merely ornamental about her. She wore a gold charm bracelet that jingled decorously when she walked. It had one charm for each of her children, a little brass schoolhouse, my father's high school ring, and a small gold medal she had won in a county-wide speaking contest in high school for her oration on world peace. She had been the president of the senior class at Greensboro College and was brilliant, too, I realize now. When I was ten, women could be virtuous and kind, but who knew they could be brilliant?

Mama read constantly, and her first visit to the local public library gave her a taste of the embattled racial atmosphere in Oxford. She picked up a copy of *Jubilee,* by Margaret Walker, a black novelist and poet from Jackson, Mississippi. Everyone who worked in the public library was white in those days, except the janitor, and it was segregated, although there were no signs to that effect. When Mama handed *Jubilee* to the librarian behind the counter, the woman peered over her glasses and said, "You don't want to read that," setting the book aside as though my mother were a little child who'd found a poisonous mushroom. "I *do* want to read it, actually," my mother insisted, reaching past the librarian for the book. The librarian reluctantly handed over the novel, shaking her head at Mama's disreputable choice. "They tried to segregate your mind," my mother recalled of the incident, looking like she wanted to spit.

If Mama's mind was flint and steel, her hands were soap and sympathy. I loved to share a hymnal with her at church. She always held the red leather book low so that I could read it, and her soprano was sweet milk to me. Her mothering style was quickstep and unwavering. Chicken noodle soup and grilled cheese sandwiches materialized as if she had summoned them by sorcery; heads were patted, cheeks were kissed. In love and work, her household moved at a brisk and consistent pace. Though she resisted playing any set role as "the preacher's wife," Mama also took care of dozens of other people, in ways large and small, without any fanfare. "I do the preaching, she does the practicing," Daddy liked to say, though she preached and he practiced more than the joke acknowledged.

Mama's congregation was a classroom of third graders at C. G. Credle Elementary School. In those days some people at church considered it somewhat disgraceful for a white woman—especially the preacher's wife—to work after she got married. But Mama paid them no mind and remained a consummate professional. She wore long skirts, practical shoes, and cotton sweaters with things stitched onto them—ribbons, bells, wreaths, one-room schoolhouses. It did not bother me that she taught right down the hall from the classroom where Miss Sue Bryan ruled me with an iron hand. Mama belonged at school. Every time the bishop appointed my father to a new church—my baby sister Julie once pointed to the bishop's name on a church bulletin and muttered bitterly, "I do not like that man"—we would cart dozens of boxes of her teaching supplies out to her station wagon and into her new school. It never struck me as odd that Mama was at Credle Elementary, nor did I notice that it conferred certain advantages when I got in trouble with Miss Bryan, as I often did.

Miss Bryan had been teaching the fourth grade at Credle since large reptiles walked the earth. She was an utterly unreconstructed Confederate. When she talked about the Civil War, which she firmly insisted that we refer to as "the War Between the States," I was pretty sure that she had marched up Cemetery Ridge with Pickett, though this could not have been true or the Yankees never would have won at Gettysburg. I had run afoul of Miss Bryan early in fourth grade, when she gave a true-false quiz on North Carolina history, the final question of which was "Granville County is the best place to live on earth." Methodist ministers moved every few years, and so I considered myself a man of the world. My grandmother's house, for example, was only eighty miles from Oxford, and anything that I wanted at her local drugstore lunch counter—fresh-squeezed orangeades and limeades, a "cherry smash"—was charged to "Miz Buie" without my even asking. And so I naturally marked the statement false, a mistake that Miss Bryan designated with a big red X and for which she deducted ten points. No discussion. As far as she was concerned, this was a simple point of historical fact.

My ardor for books did not impress Miss Bryan. I think my mother and Mrs. Patsy Montague, the rosy-cheeked woman with white hair and pink suits who served as principal, both realized that the less time Miss Bryan and I spent together, the better off everyone would be. For the rest of the year, "Miz Patsy" would periodically summon me out of Miss Bryan's class and wave me on into the library, where my mother conducted storytime with her pupils. Her students considered me something of an honorary classmate, since they knew I was her subject, too, even though I was never in her class. (Once, when she pressed one of her slower pupils for the answer to a social studies question, he scratched his head and finally said, "I reckon Tim would know.") I loved the sound of Mama's resonant reading voice and her deep brown eyes, even though she could seem mighty proper at times.

My mother had been raised by lovely people who believed that white people belonged on top and that white people, especially the better classes, had an obligation to treat blacks charitably and help lift them up, though not to the point of "social equality." But Mama had grown out of this mold long before the spring of 1970. When she'd attended Greensboro College in the early 1950s, her professors had quietly organized interracial meetings with African American coeds from Bennett College, a historically black institution, which had helped to open her eyes to certain realities on the other side of the color line. Over the years, she'd continued to peel back the white supremacist assumptions of her well-kept world and to throw them off layer by layer. She never shook her mother's convictions about our responsibilities to "those less fortunate than ourselves," but Mama went far beyond her own mother's worldview. It was not that she was untainted by the white supremacy that marked her world and all the people she knew, black and white. All of us breathed it in unconsciously, like we did the smell of curing tobacco. But like her mother, if not in precisely the same ways, Mama was an independent thinker who was never content to tack her thoughts to the prevailing winds and declined to let the world dictate her opinions.

Her own mother, Jessie Thomas, a shrewd and lovely sharecropper's daughter, never went to college, even though she followed her father's plow down the furrows of spindly cotton and begged him to send her to Women's College so she could become a teacher. But there was not enough money for that, and even if there had been cash stacked up like stove wood, most farmers in those days would have been reluctant to spend it educating a girl. What seemed much more likely was that Jessie would end up working in the textile mill. As willful as her daddy, Jessie Thomas refused to yield herself to the mill. Instead, she found a clerical job at Efird's Department Store in Charlotte and began saving her pennies. Impressed with her wit and presence, Mr. Efird spoke highly of her to Charles Buie, the bright and amiable bookkeeper at the textile mill in Biscoe. Buie began by asking her parents if he could drive Miss Thomas back to Charlotte one Sunday and ended by marrying her. Soon afterward, the mill owners selected Charles Buie as general manager, offered him a handsome salary, and gave Mr. and Mrs. Buie a big white house in the middle of town.

By December 7, 1941, when President Franklin D. Roosevelt told Americans that the Japanese had bombed the American fleet at Pearl Harbor, Jessie Thomas Buie had already saved enough money to open the Biscoe Sandwich Shop, which sat right beside the bus station in the little mill town. Those years were the heyday of bus travel, and tiny Biscoe was situated at the intersection of the major routes connecting Charlotte to Raleigh and Greensboro to Wilmington. As the country mobilized for war, soldiers, draftees, and workers poured through the bus station, hundreds and hundreds each day. Many of them bought Jessie's yeast rolls stuffed with pimento cheese, chicken salad, or egg salad, each one carefully wrapped in wax paper with a napkin tucked into the fold. Though she never went to college, Jessie paid college tuition for both of her sisters, partly out of generosity and partly, perhaps, to spite her father. The first time Jessie set foot in the textile mill, she wore a plumed hat and handed out free ham biscuits.

Black soldiers who stopped in at the Biscoe Sandwich Shop, of course, bought their food to go and ate it standing outside, while whites could enjoy the red-checked tablecloths and comfortable chairs inside. My uncle Bubba, thinking back and asking for a fair-minded understanding of Grandmother Buie's segregationist ways, called his mother "a woman of her time and place," but Jessie both defied and defined her time and place. Though she refused the place that society had set for her, the presumptions of white paternalism seemed as natural to her as segregation itself. She clearly did not consider any black person in the world to be her social equal, but she took seriously her responsibility to "those less fortunate than ourselves."

Paternalism was like a dance whose steps required my grandmother to provide charity to black people, as long as they followed the prescribed routine—that is, coming to the back door, hat in hand; accepting whatever largesse was offered; furnishing effusive expressions of gratitude; and at least pretending to accept their subordinate position in the social hierarchy. For white people, paternalism provided a self-congratulatory sense of generosity and superiority; for blacks, it supplied dribs and drabs of material sustenance—shoes and books and hand-me-down clothes for their children. Paternalism strengthened the system of white supremacy by softening its sharper edges and covering its patent injustices with a patina of friendship. Accepting black expressions of gratitude at face value, whites congratulated themselves on their friendly relations with "their" Negroes. But paternalism rendered the candor that real friendships require virtually impossible. Grandmother Jessie did not invent or even endorse paternalism. When she and Mr. Buie moved into the big white house that the mill gave them, she merely assumed its privileges and rituals.

It was more a matter of privilege than responsibility that Grandmother Jessie employed five local blacks at her house. Betty Clegg cooked everyday meals, polished the silver, and prepared the tables for fancy dinners when Mr. Brooks, who owned the mill, came to visit or when "Miz Buie" held a family wedding or hosted Thanksgiving dinner. Mary Alston scrubbed the family's clothes, first on a tin washboard and later in the electric tub with its hand-cranked, roller-style wringing attachment. Ida Jowers dissolved gluey starch in water and sprinkled Mr. Buie's shirts with it before the iron hissed over the cotton cloth, creating a wonderful pasty smell. Charlie Ledbetter mowed the grass, scrubbed and waxed the wide porches, washed Mr. Buie's Lincoln Continental, and trimmed the ivy that lined Mrs. Buie's brick walkways. Joe Dunlap, who also worked as a handyman at the mill, tended my grandmother's rose garden.

One day when my mother was perhaps twelve or thirteen, she was in the laundry room helping Mary Alston, the middle-aged black woman who came every Monday to wash the family's clothes by hand. As young Martha sorted the clothing into piles, the white girl idly sang, "When the roll is called up yonder I'll be there," from a familiar hymn. Her hands plunged deep into a galvanized tin tub filled with hot, soapy water, Mary Alston said in a low voice, "Do you really think you will be?"

The white girl who would grow up to be my mother looked at Mrs. Alston in surprise, thinking she must be joking. "It just kind of shocked me," Mama explained to me many years later. "I didn't know what to say." There was no sign of mirth in Mrs. Alston's dark face; she had asked a serious question, and she would neither back off nor discuss it further. The tremor was sufficient that Mama always remembered the moment and wondered exactly what Mary Alston had been thinking. This was the first sign for Mama that there existed a world on yonder side of the color line, where white eyes and ears could not readily penetrate and where black people did not necessarily accept white valuations of moral worth.

From the early days of slavery, in fact, African Americans had forged a Christian faith that affirmed their own humanity and sometimes called their masters to judgment: "Everybody talkin' 'bout heaven ain't a-goin' there," the unknown poets of the spirituals observed. This was the faith that rejected what Dr. King called the "thingification" of human beings, and that he evoked for the world when my mother became Mary Alston's age. By that time, Mama would be ready to hear and understand it.

I never knew my mother's father, Charles Buie, who died when I was an infant. But I grew up knowing that Grandmother Jessie was a woman of vast and immeasurable wealth. Stacked in her basement, for example, stood eight or ten wooden crates of small, seven-ounce Coca-Cola bottles and taller, light-green Frescas. To a small boy, these seemed like riches that Arab oil sheikhs and European monarchs could only envy.

When I was seven or eight, I saw Mr. Dunlap sweating in the sun amid Jessie's rosebushes, and I carried him one of the Coca-Colas and a glass of ice. "You're just like your grandfather," he said, smiling at me. And then his face became grave. "I want you to know something, son," he told me. "Back during the Depression, when nobody had any money, Mr. Buie kept me working at the mill when he didn't have anything for me to do. They weren't selling any cloth, but he would have me out there planting flowers or working over here in Miz Buie's garden so my children would have something to eat." As he sipped his Coca-Cola, Mr. Dunlap's eyes began to water. "Your granddaddy put shoes on my children's feet, and they wouldn't have had any to wear to school if he hadn't done it." Mr. Dunlap pulled out his handkerchief, swabbed his eyes, and handed me the empty glass. "You ought to be proud of your granddaddy, son."

The Buies bought truckloads of shoes, "seconds," at cut-rate prices and gave them away. Even after my grandfather died, Jessie Buie kept the trunk of her car filled with shoes and clothes, which she handed out to poor families, most of them black. Many years later, when I was cleaning out her garage so that we could move Jessie to a nursing home, I found an enormous pile of what once had been shoes. There must have been several hundred pairs of them, their laces knotted together, but they were molded and matted into a thick mulch, rotting into their original elements, and I had to toss them into the dumpster with a pitchfork. But "Miz Buie," teetering around behind me, her mind wandering back through nine decades, kept repeating, "I do wish we could find some nice colored people who might like to have those shoes."

Their ethos of paternalism gave my grandparents a sense of doing what was good and right, a feeling far more luxurious than the crisp, clean sheets, "angel biscuits," and tomato-asparagus aspic that Betty Clegg made for them. I have never doubted the sincerity of Joe Dunlap's gratitude to my grandfather, and I am proud of the Buies, and of course I love them. But the hierarchy of white supremacy, at its heart, was as rotten as that pile of old shoes, and the generations that follow will be many years cleaning it up.

One way my grandmother Jessie instructed me in the obligations and rewards of racial paternalism was through her favorite story about the Civil War. Many times over the years she told me that our family had always treated their slaves like family members. In fact, she always said, our slaves had loved us so much that they'd hidden the family silver from General Sherman's Yankee marauders. When I got old enough to research the history myself, I discovered that we'd owned no slaves, no silver, and that General Sherman's army hadn't come within a hundred miles of the family homeplace. But I know in my heart that she believed this to be the unvarnished truth, and that it had come to her from people she loved and admired.

In Oxford, white children often grew up with family stories about the antebellum South, like my grandmother's gentle hand-me-down fiction, stories that portrayed slavery as a largely benign and sometimes even beneficial social order. "My mama told me that our slaves were just like family to us," one local white woman recounted, "and that after the war they didn't want to leave. And my father always said [slavery] was the first chance they got to experience anything like civilization or to learn anything."

African Americans in Granville County grew up with a set of slavery stories that reflected a wholly different view of what was civilized. Black people old enough to have heard tales of slavery from their grandparents told their own children and grandchildren stories about families being broken up and sold, black women used by white men as concubines, and slaves whipped mercilessly. Novella Allen, whose grandparents had been slaves, grew up hearing her grandfather recount how their master had announced his intention to sell their family. "His daddy and his mama was going to be sold from the Lawsons to the Thorpes," she said. But her grandfather's father had refused to accept the sale, and tried to thwart his master by mutilating himself with an axe. "His daddy went and cut his hand off," she said, "because he didn't want to be sold. Papa said that's what he cut it off for, because he didn't want to be sold from the people he had been with all his life. But they took his wife and child on anyway."

Annie Bell Cheatham, born in 1891, learned from her grandfather about his despair at being sold away from his mother as a boy and having his name forcibly changed to Cheatham, the name of his new owner. "That child crying, him looking back and wanting to go with his mama," she recounted, "and the mama crying, too, but she couldn't do nothing. Yeah, we have been through something in this world. Not just me and you," she said, "but just think about the black folks—Lord, have mercy." Even though he had been young, her grandfather never forgot the agony of losing his mother and his name, and repeated the story often when Annie Bell Cheatham was growing up. "He told us, he said, 'We are not Cheathams, we ain't no Cheathams.' And then he would tell how they sold him and everything."

Judge Chavis, a local black man born in 1898, was raised on his grandmother's stories about having her brothers sold away from her family. "My grandmother on my mama's side," Chavis recalled, "she said there were eight of them. Said she had seven brothers, you know. And they had a sale and they sold all seven of them to a man down east somewhere, bought all seven of them, but didn't want the girl, and she never did see them no more." Johnny Crews had been told as a youngster that his family name had been Mayhew and that they had lived in Wendell, North Carolina, but that the family had been separated and some of them sold to a white farmer named Crews in Granville County. "So colored people do not know what they is," Crews said.

But enslaved African American families in Granville County remembered who they were, and whose they were, through the distinctive Afro-Christian faith they adapted from the religion their masters sought to impose on them. To the South's four million slaves, W. E. B. Du Bois wrote, "God was real. They knew Him. They had met Him personally in many a wild orgy of religious frenzy, or in the black stillness of the night." And in that stillness and tumult, the enslaved sons and daughters of Africa met their God and their neighbors, and affirmed that they were all children of the same Lord who'd brought the Israelites out of bondage, the same Lord who'd rescued Daniel from the lion's den, the same Lord who'd given a little shepherd boy a slingshot to bring down mighty Goliath. In the "brush arbor," as some called their invisible church, they sang their own songs, drawn from the Scripture and from the lives of their slave ancestors. They knew that God, in His grace, had sent Jesus to be nailed to the cross to raise them up, and that their names were written in the Lamb's Book of Life: "Ain't you glad, ain't you glad, that the blood done sign my name," they would sing.

"You got a right to the tree of life," their voices would ring out. "I got shoes, you got shoes, all God's children got shoes," slaves and descendants of slaves would sing, standing together, often barefoot, in the woods. "When I get to heaven gonna put on my shoes and gonna walk all over God's heaven." And of course they sang some of the songs they learned from white Christians, too. According to Judge Chavis, his father's mother, Lou Chavis, born in bondage, explained carefully the sharp difference between the religion the masters taught and the faith the slaves practiced. Though the slaves had no formal church of their own, she told him, their masters would cart them to the white church and have a separate meeting for them. "And that white preacher would preach at them, 'Now, y'all obey y'all masters, like the Bible says.'"

But the slaves' own secret church meetings had nothing to do with obedience. Lou Chavis told her grandson that the slaves would pass the word that there was going to be a meeting; they'd "just notify one another when they get a chance in the daytime, and then what they done was meet at one another's shack, and had their singing." If they did not meet in a slave cabin, they would meet in the woods. "They would do their praying and singing while [the whites] was asleep—they better not catch them singing." Elders in the community still remembered how their ancestors would place a cooking pot on the ground outside the meeting place in the folk belief that it would keep whites from hearing their songs and prayers. "Sometimes they would turn a pot down at the door," Judge Chavis said his grandmother told him, "to catch the sound."

Though whites typically grew up hearing that their slaves had been treated kindly, the inherited memory among African Americans included many stories of brutality and abuse. Lou Chavis told her grandson that their white master would fasten disobedient slaves to a tree using a wide leather belt, then whip them. Chavis never forgot his grandmother's account of having seen a fellow slave beaten to death. "She said she had seen them do that, and they unbuckle the man, and him fall dead and die." Chapel Royster, born a slave, told his granddaughter Mary Thomas Hobgood that he had wanted to learn to read but had been too terrified of the punishments. "My grandfather lived with us," Hobgood said. "His master told him if he tried to read and study, [the master would] cut his hands off, cut his fingers off. And when he died he was ninety years old, and he couldn't read a line."

Despite the bitter memory of slavery, some black people in Oxford always enjoyed fairly good relationships with whites. Mary Catherine Chavis, who took Henry Marrow into her house when he was a teenager and acted as a mother to him, grew up around white people in the 1930s and 1940s and had very little trouble from them. Her maternal ancestors had been free blacks and well educated. Her mother attended North Carolina College for Negroes in Durham and then came back to Oxford to teach school, and Mary Catherine followed in her footsteps, graduating from Shaw University and then coming home to teach at Mary Potter High School. "We really didn't have a lot of problems with white people when I was growing up," she recalled. William Baskerville, born at the turn of the century in a small, racially mixed neighborhood near the railroad tracks, had close attachments to his white neighbors. "I would go over there and they would say, 'Come on in here, William, and get you some dinner.' They would invite us in and we would sit down and eat together."

While very few whites during the Jim Crow era invited black people to sit at their dinner tables, leading whites in Oxford invoked warm memories of their paternalistic relationships with African Americans in defense of the "good race relations" that they insisted had forever prevailed. "A black man was my hunting partner," explained Billy Watkins, Oxford's leading attorney and a representative to the General Assembly. "He kept the dogs and fed them, and I bought the feed." In his mind, this proved that "relations were always good here," he told me. "A black man keeps my horses now. I've got horses, and was raised on a farm, and we had some blacks out there who stayed on our farm for fifty years and more." This was undoubtedly a sincere description of Watkins's vision of his relationships with the loyal family retainers who worked on his family's plantation. But these ties, even when the affection was genuine on both sides, were like a clay pot that had to be shattered for the tree inside to grow. What kind of fruit that tree would yield, in the long run, remained an open question.

My mother grew up in the shade of that spreading paternalist oak of "good race relations," but she herself broke free of it. By the time I had children of my own, I saw what a fearlessly self-reliant person she was. And if Mama sometimes seemed a little starchy to me when I was growing up, this was not the case with my father, partly because she married so far beneath herself. Jack Tyson, my father's father, was a fiery New Dealer with unconventional views on race, and had only recently left tenant farming when he moved his family to Biscoe. "I don't have but three cents," Granddaddy Tyson would laugh, "and I got to mail a letter with that." In 1946, Mama was fourteen when she saw Daddy, a sixteen-year-old, ride into town sitting in a chair in the back of the truck. "I thought he was the best-looking thing I had ever seen," she laughed later.

Her diary from the late 1940s confirms her opinion. "Vernon sat with me in the picture show," she wrote a few months later, "winked at me, held my hand, and wore my hat. I LOVE him!" At fourteen and fifteen, she wrote about him in her diary nearly every day, even when there was not much to say: "Saw Vernon today," or "Vernon wasn't there," or less persuasively, "Vernon is dating Betty Charles but I don't care!" When she turned fifteen, her parents reluctantly permitted her to begin dating, and she never dated anyone else, at least not seriously. On the flyleaf of her diary, "Vernon Tyson" is scribbled over and over, in different versions of the same hand, and then the words "I do," and then in the same handwriting but much older, "You bet I do."

In the spring of 1948, when it became clear that the young couple was pointed toward the altar, the Buies tried to send Martha to Europe for the summer, hoping to derail their romance. "Mother said she wished I would get over my 'Vernon' crush," Mama confided to her diary that year. "That hurt me so much." Several weeks later, on May 17, it looked like Jessie Buie was out of luck with respect to her love-smitten teenaged daughter. "Dear Diary," Martha wrote, "Vernon said he was gonna hit a home run for me in the baseball game, and sure enough he did. I love him! I love him!" On May 28, however, things were looking up for Jessie's campaign. "Vernon makes me sick," Martha wrote. "He can't be decent."

But opposites attract, so they say, and my mother's cleaned and pressed upbringing may have made my father seem all the more appealing to her. "I just can't help liking Vernon," she wrote soon afterward. "Sometimes I wonder if it is right to feel this way or not. We're so very different. But I love him so much I just don't think anyone else will do. I love every inch of that fine boy." And so it was that when I was growing up, my mother loomed as the guardian of manners, while my father's eyes laughed as he drank out of the milk jug — when she wasn't looking.

When my father walked through the door in the evening, his children jumped on him and held on tight, laughing and squealing. No one was more fun than Daddy, and when he turned his charm on a child, the effect was as powerful as a narcotic. If you stayed home sick from school, Daddy was likely to show up and take you out to lunch, a gesture that all of the children interpreted as a sign of his special pleasure in our delightful company. His presence in the house was raucous, rollicking, warm, and attentive, except on those frequent occasions when it was cloudy, oblivious, foreboding, or even threatening.

That fact, in itself, was not strange. In the small-town South where I grew up, we children were afraid of *everybody's* daddy. Vernon Tyson's rich baritone was the voice of God. The only problem was that you never knew if you were going to get the Old or the New Testament. Six feet tall with shoulders seemingly half that wide, Daddy could be tender and impish, and he plainly loved my mother like a hound dog loves a bone. I remember lying beside him in their bed, his massive arm under my neck. My brother, Vern, lay on the other side of Daddy, but with my father's chest between us, heaving up and down as he snored softly, Vern might as well have been on the yonder side of the Blue Ridge Mountains. Daddy's hands seemed roughly the size of chuck roasts. Those meaty paws tenderly stroked our faces and patted our backs and tousled our hair whenever we went near him. But on those rare occasions when he roared into a room in anger, we froze in terror. "Child abuse" had not yet been invented, and every father I knew obeyed the biblical injunction not to "spare the rod and spoil the child." Not all of them, however, were built like a freight car and wired like a bomb.

Though he seemed to us an iron-fisted disciplinarian, he was also remarkably gentle and intuitive for a man of the John Wayne generation. One Saturday morning when I was seven, Vern, Gerald, Jeff Daniels, Burton Gibbs, and I were secretly smoking cigarettes down by the creek. We perched on the muddy bank, cupping our palms and fumbling with the matches. Jeff had stolen a pack of Tareytons from his mother and on that authority, presumably, commanded everyone not to "nigger-lip," an admonition that meant we must not suck the cigarette too far into our mouths and get the filter soggy. My brother was twelve years old and took charge in his capacity as the senior member of the expedition. Certain rules were necessary, even here in the wilderness. It was permissible to cuss and talk "dirty," Vern said, since we were smoking cigarettes anyway. When men were smoking cigarettes and cussing, we reckoned, they could talk about anything they damn well pleased. After all, since the penalty for smoking cigarettes was undoubtedly death and then hell, talking about "you-know-what" couldn't make things much worse.

We had been down by the creek smoking when Gerald had first told me about sexual intercourse, though he'd used another word. *That* was when a man "puts his you-know-what between a woman's you-know-whats," he'd said in a tone of grave authority. Gerald's account of coitus, which had seemed to draw on direct observation, explains how I'd come to think that a woman's private parts resided between her breasts. This tantalizing misunderstanding had prevailed for several weeks, fascinating my seven-year-old mind until the fateful day that we got caught smoking cigarettes.

One of the neighbors saw us down by the creek and called each of our parents. When we came home for supper, Daddy solemnly ushered us into the living room and left us there on the couch for what seemed like several months. No one ever used the living room at our house. We'd always thought it had been reserved for Sunday afternoon company, but now it appeared that it had actually been set aside for executions. Death Row at Central Prison would have been more cheerful. Vern whispered something to me along the lines of

"We're dead," but otherwise we sat silently, huddled under a cloud of iniquity darker than the grave, pondering our demise.

We could hear Mama and Daddy talking in hushed tones in the kitchen. And then suddenly that huge bear of a man lumbered into the room, sat down in front of us, and so began the sermon. The voice was calm but the content was indecipherable. They knew, of course, exactly what boys talk about while smoking cigarettes down by the creek. Rather than punishing us, Daddy and Mama had decided that it was time for him to tell us about the birds and the bees. Daddy's lips continued to move, but I had no idea what he was saying. He never even mentioned cigarettes. It seemed cruel, in a way, to burden condemned men with this prattle about God's plan for Creation.

Our one comfort was that as long as Daddy kept talking, he was not whipping us to death. Maybe our reprieve would last for only a few minutes, but why not make the most of it? So I nodded at what seemed appropriate times, and tried to appear alert and attentive, even as I peered into the abyss. The whole idea was to keep him talking. Daddy still hadn't said one word about cigarettes. And then suddenly, without my having apprehended a single sentence, Daddy's momentous speech ended. Did we have any questions? he asked us. Any questions at all? Was there anything we wanted to know about anything?

The moment of death drew nigh. I tried to telepathically urge my brother to ask Daddy *something, anything* to save our lives for another few minutes. Perilous silence gripped the room. Seconds ticked by. If I'd only had the remotest idea what Daddy had been talking about, I would have asked him a hundred questions, as slowly as possible, like that woman in my "Arabian Nights" book who told the sultan long, interwoven stories to keep him from chopping off her head. But I couldn't even identify the topic, let alone ask a pertinent question. Why didn't my stupid older brother think of *something, anything,* to ask Daddy? Finally, positive that further delay would move us straight to the End, I blurted out, "What is my front tooth made of?"

Daddy laughed out loud and long, shook his head, and handed each of us a Christian book about where babies come from. Late that night, with a flashlight under the covers, I read both my book, which was called *Wonderfully Made,* and then Vern's book, which I was not supposed to see until I got older, read them cover to cover and still never found out that a woman's vagina was between her legs. Apparently, while a man and wife lay sleeping, something horrible crawled out of him and into her—into her ear, for all I knew. Anyway, right after he gave us our books, Daddy took the whole family out for dinner at the new Hardee's drive-in. Sucking on a chocolate milkshake, I contemplated the mysterious grace of God.

Neither Divine mercy nor threat of punishment actually made us stop smoking cigarettes, in part because this taboo was inextricably linked with our haunting prepubescent sense of ourselves as sinners in the hands of an angry God. If we couldn't smoke the whole pack in one sitting, we'd hide them under a fallen tree, just like the dirty magazines we sometimes found there. We would repent predictably and promise God never to do it again, though we knew we would be back. But you couldn't be taking that kind of stuff home with you, and it was hard to escape the deep uneasiness that it might somehow follow you and disrupt the warm goodness of family dinners, saying grace and singing hymns and hugging Mama good night. It was no accident that our father had made the leap from cigarettes to sex. This seemed appropriate—sin was sin, whether you smoked it or just peered at it with the fearful awe that gives way to the dry tightness in your throat and the strange stiffening in your pants.

Sex was sinful. And sin was sexual. Both of them were inextricably bound up with race, which was something we all knew, the way we knew that Robert E. Lee was a hero and North Carolina was the basketball capital of the world. I could not help but notice that grown-ups always talked about both race and sex in exactly the same whispered tones. Hymns we sang in church promised that the blood of Jesus would wash our sins "as white as snow," cleanse our souls of "one dark blot," or help our "dark passions to subdue." And I knew, without knowing how I knew, without ever being told, that the color line throbbed with sexual taboo.

Segregation, I understood without ever having been told, existed to protect white womanhood from the abomination of contact with uncontrollable black men. Whites who questioned segregation confronted the inevitable and, for most people, conclusive cross-examination: Would you want your daughter to marry one? The answer never came, and it never had to come. Everybody knew that would be the most horrible thing imaginable, because interracial sex was inherently pornographic, unnatural, and perverted. If sex was sinful, interracial sex was the most sinful—and therefore the most sexual that sex could get. And the worst abomination of all, of course, was sex between a black man and a white woman. It was that sin—or the faint hint of it—that got Dickie Marrow murdered.

It took me many years and a Ph.D. in American history to find my way toward the roots of this strange folkway. The sexual obsessions of white supremacy, which were so evident to the children of Jim Crow, had their origins in the fundamental structure of the colonial economy three hundred years earlier. In 1662, the Virginia legislature passed a statute that read, "Children got by an Englishman upon a Negro woman shall be bond or free according to the condition of the mother." This reversed English common law, under which the status of a child followed that of the father.

The new statute meant that white men who fathered children by their slave women increased their own material worth. Violating their own deeply held beliefs, they sired offspring that would work in their houses and fields without fee and care for them in their old age without fail. Children born of white fathers and black mothers became black, not white, and remained slave, not free. Without that provision, growing numbers of apparently "black" people who were legally "white" would have populated the American colonies. The whole system of racial bondage rested upon the fact that free white men could father "black" slave children, while black men could never father "white" children. The children of slave mothers or fathers must always inherit that status. If large numbers of white women had birthed mulatto children by black fathers, the system of slavery based on racial caste would have been undermined and might have been rendered unworkable. Some form of unfree labor would have persisted for a time, but racialized slavery, justified in the name of white supremacy, might well have never evolved the way that it did. "Race" itself could have meant something entirely different without these rules about sex.

It was a different thing, of course, for a white man to father "black" children. Annie Bell Cheatham remembered her grandfather, born a slave in Granville County, telling her that white men would often have sexual relations with the slave women who worked in their houses, even if the woman had a black husband. "They would keep the woman in the house," Cheatham said, "and she would do the cooking, and the white men would go with the black women. They didn't have no choice." The slave husband, her grandfather explained, "better not say anything about it—they will hang him." Some white men who had black families on the side chose to free their black children, who were often called "free-issue Negroes." " 'Free-issue' people was white men taking black women and them having children," Rachel Blackwell, born in Oxford in 1891, remembered. "And they would call them 'issued free.' The white man would help support that old colored woman and them children, and they would be real light-skinned but the other children would be black. My mother told me about this," Blackwell continued, "but she couldn't say or do anything about it."

The sex and race taboo that grew from these roots in slavery remained a mighty oak in my boyhood. The challenge to segregation that arose in those years shook that tree like a hurricane, and the white supremacists clung to its trunk for dear life. "What the white man fears and what the white man is fighting to prevent at any cost," the editor of the *Warren Record* wrote in 1955, "is the destruction of the purity of his race. He believes that integration would lead to miscegenation, and there is some basis for his fears." Of course, "miscegenation" was not the real concern; a system that gave all the power to the men in one group and virtually no power to the women in another group made "race mixing" in one direction almost inevitable, as many African Americans in Granville County could attest. The social order permitted white men in the South, by virtue of their position atop the race and gender hierarchy, to take their liberties with black women, while white women and black men remained strictly off-limits to each other. The much traveled sexual back road between the races was clearly marked "one way."

When I was growing up, many whites assumed that "race mixing" in schools would lead to rampant interracial sexual activity and that the "death of the white race" would inevitably follow. White purity and white power were imperative, all things good and decent hung in the balance, and sex was the critical battleground. Mainstream white conservative James J. Kilpatrick, whose national influence would persist well into the Reagan era, declared that white Southerners had every right "to preserve the predominately racial characteristics that have contributed to Western civilization over the past two hundred years." William F. Buckley's *National Review* agreed, and justified not merely segregation but disfranchisement for blacks, arguing that "the White community in the South is entitled to take such measures as are necessary to prevail, politically and culturally, in those areas where it does not predominate numerically." The race-sex complex, with all its hypocrisies and contradictions, underlay the entire struggle. James Baldwin's was one of the few public voices that could pierce the fog of "miscegenation" rhetoric, and he offered a timeless retort to the question "Would you want your daughter to marry one?" In a television debate with Kilpatrick, he explained, "You're not worried about me marrying *your* daughter—you're worried about me marrying *your wife's* daughter. I've been marrying *your* daughter since the days of slavery."

The fall of Jim Crow tested these deeply rooted taboos. In 1970, for example, when I was eleven years old, the county fair just up the road in Yanceyville began to admit black people on the same day as whites; in the old days, the fair in Oxford and other towns nearby had set aside a day or two for "Negroes," and whites otherwise had their run of the place. The new arrangements may have seemed unthreatening; black and white Southerners, after all, lived and worked in close proximity to one another, and it was only the county fair, for goodness sake. Why couldn't black and white shuffle through the turnstiles together, munch cotton candy, and throw up on the Tilt-A-Whirl? What the authorities had failed to consider were the "girlie shows," carnival burlesque performances in which pale white girls from somewhere else danced out of their skimpy clothing and bumped and grinded for a hooting tent full of men. When the ticket taker admitted a group of young African Americans to the show, things inside the tent got tense. After one of the black men yelled out his appreciation for the white dancers, a white man behind him smashed a wooden folding chair across the black man's head. Fists flew, knives flashed, and blood flowed both ways across the color line. The fighting spread from the fairgrounds to the streets of Yanceyville, and the mayor had to call a curfew and bring in state troopers for several days to stop the violence.

The central political fact that hung over the spring and summer of 1970 in Oxford, rooted in four hundred years of history, was that the Granville County schools were scheduled to undergo full-blown racial integration that fall. Three years earlier, Oxford had taken the first ineffectual and involuntary steps toward desegregation. Two African American children had left Orange Street School, the segregated all-black elementary school, to enroll at previously all-white C. G. Credle Elementary. The school board had carefully selected two middle-class black boys and assigned them, just like me, to Mrs. Emily Montague's third-grade class at Credle, where they said the Pledge of Allegiance every morning like the rest of us.

Thirty years later, when my own children were learning the Pledge of Allegiance, I suddenly remembered another set of words that schoolkids had chanted in unison at my elementary school: "Go back, go back, go back to Orange Street." It just came to me in the shower, a singsong echo in my mind, like a forgotten football cheer or an unwelcome snatch of music that would neither finish nor stop: "Go back, go back, go back to Orange Street." At first I had no idea where it came from—my first theory was that it was from "Goin' Back to Indiana," an old pop tune by the Jackson Five. I called my sister Boo, who reminded me that Orange Street was the black school in Oxford, the school that those black children at Credle would have attended had the Supreme Court held its tongue. And then, of course, I knew very well where I had learned the words. I have no clear recollection of any protests against integration at Credle Elementary. But standing in the shower, thirty years later and a thousand miles away, I could still hear a chorus of schoolchildren chanting, "Go back, go back, go back to Orange Street," and I cannot help but ponder how those two brave and unfortunate black children must have felt as they made their way up the sidewalk to a school where they were not wanted.

My first memory of being in school with black children was standing behind one of the two black boys at the water fountain on the playground at Credle. It was an old cast-iron fountain with a foot pedal, and a couple of seconds after you stepped hard on the pedal, bitter-smelling water gurgled up from the primordial depths of the earth, tasting like iron. I hadn't noticed the black boy in the line, and suddenly there he was in front of me, bent over the old iron spout. Deep down, I did not want to drink after him. Without really understanding why, and even though I knew better, somewhere inside I had accepted white supremacy. The world had kenneled a vicious lie in my brain, at the core of the lie a crucial silence, since there was no *why*. Black was filthy, black was bad, I had somehow managed to learn. Many of my white classmates turned away from the fountain in disgust rather than drink after a black child. And even at that moment, because I had been taught to know better, I knew that my revulsion was a lie, someone else's lie, and an evil thing. This time, I decided not to give the lie the power it demanded. I suppose I was both resistant and complicit, in the same moment. I could not turn away—I lowered my head and drank after him. But I succumbed slightly; when he moved, I took my turn and pressed the pedal down, and let the water run for a few seconds before I drank, bending over the arc of cool water but pausing for a moment to let the water rinse the spout before I touched my lips to the acrid stream. I guess that made me a "moderate."

It was the logic of moderation that permitted schools across the nation to evade the Supreme Court's 1954 ruling for almost twenty years, but when defiance and evasion finally became untenable, "seg academies" sprouted across the landscape. Fearful white parents flocked to the all-white Christian academies, abandoning the public schools in the hour of their deepest need so that their children would not have to attend school with black children. This set a terrible and enduring example and undid any possibility that integration might work. At the molten core in the very center of white fears of school integration was the specter of sex between black males and white females. That simmering sexual subtext overwhelmed the feeble official efforts to ease racial tensions in Oxford after the killing.

"We had tried to do everything we could to get things quieted down after the riot," said Mayor Currin, "and finally we decided, 'Let's get the ministers together.' " Reverend Don Price, a white Baptist minister, recalled that the mayor "was trying to say, 'Hey, we've had enough violence in this community, let's talk to our congregations and try to be peacemakers.' " Currin contacted most of the ministers in the county, black and white, and invited them all to meet at my father's church. "We were talking about the situation," the mayor remembered, "and we got back to what had brought on the trouble at Teel's place, and somebody said something about the black man saying something to a white woman, and that was all she wrote."

The visceral reaction among some of the white ministers was so strong, Currin recounted, that "I will never forget this as long as I live. I will never forget this. This white preacher rears up in his chair and yells, '*What* did you say, brother? *What* did you say?' And then he made his little speech about race mixing." According to the mayor, his official efforts to turn preachers into peacemakers "ended right then and there, as soon as he made that statement." For many whites, the allegation that Henry Marrow had made a lewd remark to a white woman turned public murder into justifiable homicide, transforming a crime of passion into a late-model lynching that fateful May.

CHAPTER 3

"TOO CLOSE NOT TO TOUCH"

T HE FORCE THAT drove the bullet through Henry Marrow's brain, if you were searching for something more explosive than gunpowder and more specific than that Cain slew Abel, was white people's deep, irrational fear of sex between black men and white women, any single instance of which was supposed to abolish the republic, desecrate the Bible, and ring in the Planet of the Apes. But we should also consider the strange and nearly inexplicable fact that a man like Robert Teel had decided to open a store in Grab-all, a black neighborhood nestled on the northwest edge of town.

My boyhood image of Teel is of how he walked into his house: eyes locked ahead, his gait more like that of a man the power company had sent to disconnect the electricity than a man coming home for dinner, his shoulders braced as if he were going to walk through the side of the house instead of the door. In four years of playing with his son nearly every day, I never heard his voice. And now I realize that the white supremacy that clouded all of our minds back then must have raged like a tornado in his. Looking back, I cannot imagine what he might have thought it would be like to run a store on the busiest corner of a black shantytown.

There were some tidy middle-class homes in Grab-all—the neighborhood was mixed. Both segregation and strong community ties kept the black middle class rooted there. "We were all like family in

Grab-all," Nelda Webb recalled. But some parts, like the area behind Teel's store, called Around the Bend, were hard scrabble and hand-to-mouth. "Those were some of the poorest people in the world," a local black man explained. And everybody knew "Lynching Hill" near the Browntown section of Grab-all, a hill whose bloody history haunted the area.

Some of the roads were unpaved, and car wheels churned clouds of dust in the summer and muddy ruts in the winter. Streetlights and sidewalks were few. Some of the houses in Grab-all were ramshackle wooden frame structures with swaybacked porches, most of them dilapidated and many of them painted the same rusty shade of red. "Those rental houses all belonged to one person, Mr. Bennie Watkins," Mayor Currin explained to me, "and he got hold of a lot of red paint one year, I reckon, and just painted them all red." It was a rough territory in spots. "It was hard even for a black to walk in Grab-all that didn't live there," William A. "Boo" Chavis told me years later, "much less white folks. The cops didn't want to go out there no way."

When Robert Teel opened his store at Four Corners, the main intersection in the neighborhood, it is fair to say that Grab-all did not welcome him. "When he first come out there," said Chavis, "didn't nobody like the idea." When I asked Teel about it years later, he freely admitted that "sometimes there was a little violence, sometimes there was some ugly words said," but he maintained that accounts of the clashes were always exaggerated. "Sure, I had some trouble with a few blacks come up," he conceded, "but when you're running four or five businesses, you're gonna have a percentage. If you have one place of business, and you have trouble with one person a year," Teel argued, "then if you have five businesses, and you have trouble with one person per business per year, then that's five per year. And it looks like you're getting a black eye, when you're not having trouble but with one person per business per year."

If anyone was getting a black eye at the Teel place, it certainly was not Teel. The establishment became known as a place where conflict was common and where Teel settled disputes in a brisk and direct fashion. "I have never been used to taking foolishness from people,"

Teel told me a dozen years later. A local black political leader put it differently, though how accurately I do not know: "Didn't nobody want to mess with him because the Klan was backing him."

Herman Cozart, a dark-skinned black man who hauled pulpwood for a living, often stopped by the store at Four Corners in the early days, and he developed a low opinion of Robert Teel. Cozart recalled that Teel denied him change for a dollar on two separate occasions and cussed him for asking the second time—an odd posture for a man who owned a coin-operated laundry. Cozart, though he was an affable, easygoing fellow, could have passed for an NFL lineman. A massive, thick-chested hombre who spent his days handling huge timbers, Cozart was known to carry at least one gun almost everywhere he went. He was not afraid of Teel, but he watched him carefully.

Cozart's account of one encounter he had with Teel in the barbershop revealed the degree of racial tension down on the corner. "One Saturday evening we were coming through there after I had got off work," Cozart recounted, "and I figured, you know, I got to go to church tomorrow, and the boy in there was shining shoes." Taking his dress shoes off the seat of his truck, Cozart walked into the barbershop. "I said, 'I need a shoe shine here,' and the head man looked at me and said, 'We don't shine y'all's shoes in here.'" Miffed, Cozart pushed Teel a little. "Well, how about a haircut? You got a barbershop." The black man flashed a roll of bills.

And Teel glared at him, saying, "We don't cut *y'all's* hair." Cozart was slow to anger, but he wasn't afraid, and he made his point before leaving.

"No problem," he said, slipping the bankroll back into his pocket. "I got plenty of money and I can take it someplace else. Cutting hair ain't nothing noways. I cut hair myself, and I've cut black hair and white hair. What's the difference? Clippers ain't gonna catch no germs, is they?"

Teel bristled. "He turned all red," Cozart recalled, "and said, 'I DON'T cut y'all's hair!' And I said, 'All right, then,' and I looked at him and I thought, 'This booger-bear ain't gon' be up at *this* corner very long.' " Cozart strolled calmly out of the barbershop, feeling no need to prove himself in a fight with a little bantam rooster of a white man whom he regarded as a dangerous idiot. "I knowed Teel was a tough hog," Cozart said, "and I knowed somebody was gon' have to hurt him one day, or he was gon' hurt somebody, one."

It had taken Teel more than fifteen years to open the place at Four Corners. Arriving in town on a rainy Wednesday morning in 1953, Teel remembered, he had not known "one soul in Granville County." In a town organically suspicious of outsiders, Teel had been determined to make good as a barber. He had not had much luck before he came to Oxford. He'd enlisted in the army just after World War II, but had left the service after a fellow soldier had knocked out all his front teeth with a rifle butt. Returning to eastern North Carolina in 1946 with a medical discharge and disability benefits, Teel got married and worked hard, first in a lumberyard at Mount Olive and then in a textile mill in Carrboro. These jobs paid little and did not satisfy Teel in any case. His first marriage fell apart quickly, and in an arrangement most unusual at the time, Teel retained custody of his toddler son, Larry Teel. After a few years, he used his G.I. Bill benefits to attend the Durham Institute of Barbering. Upon his graduation in 1953, an elderly bachelor from Oxford named C. R. Wells offered him a job cutting hair. "I had never heard tell of Oxford before," Teel recalled. (Everyone called him Teel, even his wife and children.) "But my instructor and the state examiner both told me it was one of the best jobs in the state, and that Mr. Wells would do right by me." Teel and his little boy moved to Oxford on March 11, 1953.

Wells, an elderly, effeminate bachelor, apparently fell in love with Teel and did everything he could to help the young man establish himself in Oxford. "Teel had a power over Mr. Wells," recalled the gracious older woman in whose home Wells boarded. "It was like he wanted so badly for Teel to love him."

The relationship paid off handsomely for the ambitious newcomer. Teel performed his duties well, attracted considerable business and eventually, with a coworker, bought the older man's business. "We sort of more or less pressured him," Teel said. The pair informed Mr. Wells that they were planning to open a barbershop down the street. "He said, 'I won't be no good without you at my age, and I'd rather sell to you than have you competitive against me.' That's how we done it." Whatever Teel lacked in polish of education, he made up for in crude charm and raw cunning. He built up a reputation as a talented barber and began to cut the hair of Granville County's economic and political elite at his shop downtown. "He cut my hair many times," Mayor Hugh Currin recalled. "Good barber, and a right good fellow, too, though I would not advise you to cross him."

Others saw Teel as "a man very much out for his own personal gain," which rubbed some of the more traditional Southerners the wrong way. If grasping ambition ran against the grain of Granville County's rickety agricultural elite, however, it was perfectly acceptable to the rising class of merchants and lawyers who had begun to lure industry into the county. The 1960s were boom years for Oxford. Despite some resistance from old planter families, who feared wages going up and Yankees coming down, Granville Developers Inc. recruited roughly 4,000 new manufacturing jobs to the county during the decade. Not quite all of the new jobs were reserved for whites. Teel fit into the new spirit well, his conversation ambling in the old tobacco-farming style but his aspirations honed to "New South" boosterism. "I've always had the ambition to want a nice home," said Teel, "a ten-thousand-dollar brick home, a nice, big Cadillac, at least one boy, things like that."

Having gotten a good start financially, Teel met and married Colleen Oakley, a high-strung widow from the nearby township of Berea. Oakley's first husband had died in an industrial accident, leaving her with three children—Elbert, Jerry, and Roger Oakley. The first children Colleen and Teel had together were twins born prematurely; one of them, Alton, died almost immediately. The other twin, Alvin, Teel explained, "always had some hearing problems, and eye problems, and an allergy-type thing." Two healthy boys followed the twins: Jesse and then Gerald, the last one born, like me, in 1959. Half of them were Teels and half of them were Oakleys, but they all seemed to be young men with dark hair, olive skin, and a reputation, deserved or not, for a bad temper.

It wasn't just the men. Colleen Oakley Teel could cut quite a shine herself. When I was in the fourth grade at Credle Elementary, one of my mother's fellow teachers gave one of the children a bad grade, and his mama reportedly came to school and beat the teacher over the head with a pocketbook. Black children who grew up in Oxford remembered Mrs. Teel chasing them after a disagreement over a tricycle. "Y'all black niggers!" they said she yelled. "I'm gonna kill every last one of you!" One of Teel's lawyers, thinking back on the family twenty years later, considered the problem to be congenital. "I guess it just runs in the family," the attorney told me. "He was hotheaded, his wife was hotheaded, and the children were hotheaded. I think it was just in their blood to be hotheaded. I mean, you just didn't need to be messing with the Teels."

As the Teel family grew, they also became quite prosperous. Teel bought a big, gracious home on the corner of Front and Main. It was a white two-story house with ample porches held up by carved pillars. Magnolias and crape myrtles perfumed Front Street in the summer, and the Victorian-era homes on the broad, tree-lined avenue—one or two of them literally mansions—belonged to some of the county's wealthiest families. Front Street was only one block over from Hancock, where we lived, but I realize now that it was a long way socially; houses on Hancock were far more humble, though I'd never even noticed when I was growing up. But while the Teels had the money to live on Front Street, they lacked what their more aristocratic neighbors would have thought of as "background." They were still uneducated and, like my family, they were still from somewhere else. And so perhaps it is not surprising that, apart from the youngest children, they kept to themselves. Besides, Robert Teel was too busy for social climbing, even if he had entertained such aspirations. He made his money not from an inherited plantation or a position at the bank, but with his own hands.

In fifteen years cutting hair downtown near the courthouse, Teel won the trust of a number of Oxford's bankers and landowners. In

1969, these connections helped him buy the large lot at Four Corners, literally across the tracks from the rest of Oxford, in the heart of Grab-all. Beside the roughest part of Grab-all, "around the bend," where many houses did not even have indoor plumbing, let alone washing machines, Teel erected four cinder-block storefronts. Before he knew it, Teel had managed to install what amounted to a little shopping center without investing a nickel of his own money.

The coin laundry was the most lucrative of Teel's businesses. His convenience store offered his African American customers basic groceries at high prices, but within walking distance. Besides these, gas pumps, a car wash, a Yamaha motorcycle dealership, and a barbershop kept the Teel and Oakley boys busy and the money rolling in. "Out there it was a percentage black and a percentage white, it was near about a fifty-fifty deal, and people could decide whether they wanted to go all-black or all-white," Teel recalled. The neighborhood was all black, of course, and so the walk-in customers were black, but the store's location at the intersection meant that perhaps half his customers were white.

The grocery store and the coin laundry were open to anybody, but the barbershop was whites only. "And the races were mixing some out there," Teel said, "and I figured I could just stand there and take up the money." Before the killing occurred, Teel said, "Mr. Roger Page had told me he'd help me put in Volkswagens to sell on that lot next door, and that would have been another business over there." Even without the car dealership, Teel claimed, his road to becoming a millionaire was clear to him within the first year. Richard Shepard, the owner of a funeral home in the black community, felt that Teel was not exaggerating: "He would have been rich if he had stayed out of trouble." But trouble always found its way to Teel's door.

Between 1969 and 1977, Teel was arrested many times, charged with at least a dozen different offenses, including driving under the influence of alcohol; two separate counts of assault on a police officer; assault by pointing a gun; assault and battery; aiding and abetting murder; assault with a deadly weapon; assault on a female; and assault with a deadly weapon with intent to kill, inflicting serious bodily injury. Judges dismissed eight of these charges, and the other four netted Teel only suspended sentences and small fines. "It always seemed like there was some kind of loophole," said one court official who had been present at most of the proceedings. "I don't think it was by design, I just think that was how things worked out." A local African American businessman saw things differently: "Had Teel been a black man, he would have been in jail after his first assault. There would have been no suspended sentences."

Not all of the clashes at Teel's place involved race. "He didn't care who it was," observed one young black man who frequented the abandoned Tidewater Seafood Market next door. "He was a mean person—to anybody. Didn't make no difference who, black or white." Other observers noted that Teel didn't seem to like the poor whites that used his washing machines any more than the blacks. Boo Chavis claimed to have seen Teel bodily remove a troublesome white customer from the laundry. Herman Cozart, who knew something about physical labor, generously speculated that one reason Teel was testy was because he had to work so hard. "He had to pump gas and cut hair and run all them washers and take care of everything," he noted. "He had to work like a man, I could see that much."

Two notorious brawls exploded between Teel and Archie Wilkins, the white police lieutenant who later became Oxford's chief of police. These fistfights, both of which Teel won handily, created bad blood between Teel and the police department. The first time, Wilkins pulled Teel over for drunken driving and quickly ended up on his back in the street, Teel standing over him with his fists cocked, asking did he want some more. Another time, Wilkins took a second officer along with him and went to the store to hassle Teel about something. "I saw the cops go over there," Boo Chavis said later, "two of them, and he beat 'em up, both of 'em, beat both of 'em up pretty bad." A state trooper came to the store and arrested Teel that time. "He didn't respect the cops," Chavis recalled. "He *was* his own law, as far as he was concerned." After he beat up Officer Wilkins, Teel said later, he "couldn't get no police protection for my busi-

nesses, no matter what." It was certainly true that the police were not
eager to come to Grab-all for any reason. Other blacks speculated
that the police steered clear simply because they were afraid of Teel.

Each time there was violence, Teel called upon Billy Watkins, the
powerful local attorney who served in the state legislature. "I think
he had good legal representation," one of the local courthouse gang
sniffed when I asked him how Teel had managed to draw only small
fines and suspended sentences for these clashes. Some local blacks
believed that the police let Teel alone because many of them were his
fellow Klan members.

The evidence seems strong that at some point Teel joined the
Granville County klavern of the Ku Klux Klan. Though the membership lists have never been public and I cannot prove he was a
Klansman, the KKK held fish fries, barbecues, and square dances at
which Teel was seen on any number of occasions by people who were
loath to admit having attended themselves. "It was just how we rallied around in those days," one local woman admitted, echoing a
local refrain of remorse, "because of all the race trouble. I was afraid
my daughter was going to bring home a black boy. My impression
was that Teel was one of the leading people in the Klan. He asked me
to dance one time, but I didn't do it. I never went back to that thing
again, either." While remarks like these could be dismissed as
hearsay, it is true that when Teel got in trouble in 1970, the Klan held
rallies for him and protected his house and his place of business with
armed guards. If he was not a member, he certainly had no trouble
calling upon the organization's resources when he needed them.

That was why Boo and I had seen the crowd of Klansmen all over
the Teel family's front porch the evening after the murder. We knew
all too well what those robes and hoods were intended to say to the
world: that Gerald's daddy belonged to the evil order that our father
had taught us was a force of pure hatred in this world. But Daddy had
also taught us to confront hatred with love, and that some people you
just had to leave in the hands of the Lord. "We just have to let God
handle that one," Daddy would say. "The Lord isn't quite finished

with him yet, or you either." I knew that the Klan wanted people to fear them, but I never saw any evidence that my daddy was afraid of anyone or anything, and I walked through the world blanketed by his protection. Daddy didn't tremble at a bunch of pointy hats and what my uncle Bobby laughingly called "those reversible choir robes." If they were so dangerous, why did Daddy take us to one of their meetings?

I reckon we were not the first white Southerners whose daddy took them to a Klan rally, but our visit was probably different than most. One evening when I was about six, the year before we moved to Oxford, Daddy trundled my brother, Vern, and me into "Chief Pontiac." Vern, who was almost ten, sat in the front seat and I perched in the back, my arms hooked over the seat between him and Daddy; back then, nobody wore safety belts. We rattled down Highway 87 through the peach orchards of the Sandhills, across Little River, to the county line where Lee meets Cumberland, near Peggy's Fish House. Daddy stopped the car on a dirt road uphill from a big, grassy field. We watched the carloads of people arriving and looked down as they used cables to erect a giant wooden cross. Chief Pontiac was parked close enough so that we could hear the fiery speeches and see the fiery cross, a scene that took on the air of some kind of strange county fair. But as the flames flickered below, Daddy told us about racism and hatred and evil. Riding home together in the darkness, we sang "Jesus loves the little children, all the children of the world / Red and yellow, black and white, they are precious in His sight / Jesus loves the little children of the world." At some point, one of us asked Daddy exactly why he had taken us to see the cross burning. "I wanted you to know what hate looks like," he said.

In those days, the hooded order was having a revival in eastern North Carolina, barnstorming the countryside night after night. "North Carolina is by far the most active state for the United Klans of America," a congressional investigation reported in 1965, listing 112 local klaverns. Taking advantage of the fear and resentment aroused by the civil rights movement, the Klan plunged for the mainstream. At their almost nightly gatherings across the state, the KKK served barbecue and fried fish plates. They raffled off cases of motor oil, coconut cakes, and trips to Myrtle Beach. Hooded Klansmen staffed a booth at the state fair, and the head of the Johnston County klavern, Billy Flowers, was invited to speak on "Today's Problems" at a Methodist church in Smithfield, alongside the chair of the local Republican Women's Club. Five thousand attended a 1965 Klan wedding in a cornfield near Farmville. A rally near Fayetteville drew almost fifteen thousand people in November. Speakers railed against "burr-headed niggers" who aspired to "sit beside our sweet little white girls in school." The chair of the state Republican Party, Jim Gardner, attributed the Klan's success to "a general dissatisfaction with the Johnson administration," especially on matters of civil rights. But he warned against believing Klan claims to having members in the state legislature and against taking the huge rallies in eastern North Carolina as indications of the Klan's actual size. "I believe there are many persons sympathetic to the Klan," Gardner said, "who do not belong to it."

Though the Klan that supported Robert Teel made a bid for mainstream acceptance, they remained openly committed to terrorism and launched a statewide campaign of violence in 1965. Klansmen tried to assassinate attorney James Ferguson, who would later help prosecute Teel for the death of Henry Marrow. They bombed a black-owned funeral home in New Bern and a black migrant labor camp near Swansboro, and they dynamited the cars of several New Bern civil rights activists. Klansmen torched two barns owned by the white mayor of Vanceboro, Royce Jordan, because he also directed a job training program that helped poor blacks. Night riders fired dozens of shotgun blasts into a house where ten college student volunteers were sleeping as part of an antipoverty program in Craven County. In Harnett County, two Klan terrorists held a white man and a black man at gunpoint and tortured them with knives for being friends too conspicuously and "frequenting Negro houses and drinking whisky together," the Klan's attorney explained. Klan terrorists burned a black school in Mars Hill and another in Johnston County. On May 28, 1965, the Klan burned a cross on the courthouse lawn in

Oxford, and also on the grounds of courthouses or city halls in Currie, Ward's Corner, Burgaw, Roxboro, Salisbury, Henderson, Statesville, Tarboro, Whiteville, Elizabethtown, Southport, and Wilmington, all on the same day.

Judge Pretlow Winborne of Raleigh won my daddy's heart on November 2, 1965, with his response to a Klan cross burning at his home. The white jurist had lashed out at the KKK and at "bigots" generally when he sentenced a seventeen-year-old Klan member to jail for a random assault on an elderly black man. A few nights later, Judge Winborne said, "I had gone to take the maid home that night, and when I returned I saw a fire on my lawn. The least they could have done was burn the damn thing while I was home and could enjoy the full effect." But the judge's family responded quickly and effectively. Winborne and his brother-in-law invited several neighbors over, and they all roasted wieners over the dying flames of the cross in their yard. "We just had a good old time," the undaunted Judge Winborne laughed. But he knew as well as anyone that the Klan's rampage was no laughing matter.

The Klan revival of the mid-1960s was actually the third since World War II. In the late 1940s, a cigar-chomping wholesale grocer named Thomas Hamilton had become Grand Dragon in the Carolinas and launched a reign of terror aimed at stamping out the gains that black Carolinians had made during the war and its aftermath. According to the Southern Regional Council, white terrorists bombed the homes of more than forty black families in eastern North Carolina in 1951 and 1952, and dozens of similar attacks were not reported. In one notorious incident near Tabor City, fifty Klansmen fired more than one hundred shots into the home of a black family and dragged the woman of the house outside and whipped her. More than five thousand people attended a rally halfway between Tabor City and Whiteville in 1951, hearing Hamilton bellow, "Do you want some burr-headed nigra to come up on your porch and ask for your daughter's hand in marriage?" The Grand Dragon, who claimed to be a devout Christian above all else, warned especially against white ministers like my father, whom he said advocated "mongrelization, which God never intended. If your preacher is telling you that," the Grand Dragon ranted, "then he needs a special thermometer in hell to burn him with."

Though the first postwar Klan faded somewhat in the early 1950s, white reaction to the 1954 *Brown v. Board of Education* decision injected the bedsheet brigade with new life. Reverend James "Catfish" Cole, a former carnival barker and Free Will Baptist tent evangelist from Marion, South Carolina, tried to bring together all the splinter Klan groups and disaffected whites in the Carolinas under his charismatic leadership. The Reverend Dr. Cole, as the rabble-rousing racist billed himself, hosted the *Free Will Hour* radio show on WFMO in Kinston, peddled spurious diplomas from "Southern Bible College," and whipped crowds into a frenzy with his diatribes against "race mixing" and communism. Like my daddy, who'd grown up in the same mudhole, ol' Catfish had formidable oratorical gifts, and did well for himself; newspaper accounts report as many as fifteen thousand people at some of his rallies in 1956 and 1957.

Cole's rabid rhetoric was not just empty talk. On November 18, 1957, Mr. and Mrs. Frank Clay, an African American couple in East Flat Rock, North Carolina, were found shot and slashed to death in their home after a series of telephone threats from callers claiming to represent the Klan; neighbors found a cross smoldering in their yard. A few days after the Clays were murdered, Klan terrorists hurled what the local chief of police called "enough dynamite to blow the place to Kingdom Come" into the Temple Beth-El synagogue in Charlotte. The only thing that spared the lives of the forty Jewish clubwomen inside was that the lighted fuse fell out of the bomb.

When Cole's Klan attacked blacks in Monroe, North Carolina, a local NAACP president named Robert F. Williams organized black military veterans to meet Klan gunfire with gunfire of their own. After Williams began to pressure city officials to let African Americans use the tax-supported municipal swimming pool, Catfish Cole came to town with his Klan organizers. "A nigger who wants to go to a white swimming pool is not looking for a bath," Cole told a crowd of two thousand local whites. "He is looking for a funeral." On October 7, 1957, Cole led a heavily armed Klan motorcade in an attack on the home of Dr. A. E. Perry, the vice president of the NAACP. Firing their guns into Dr. Perry's house and howling at the top of their lungs, the Klansmen ran head-on into a hail of disciplined gunfire. Williams and his friends fired from behind earthen entrenchments and sandbag fortifications, and sent the Klan fleeing for their lives. "When we started firing, they run," one of the black men recalled. "Them Klans hauled it and never did come back to our place."

His manly honor in tatters, Reverend Cole retreated to southeastern North Carolina to rebuild his following. In Robeson County, which had a history of strong support for the Klan, the evangelist of hate hoped to rally his forces among a population divided almost evenly among African Americans, whites, and Lumbee Indians. On January 13, 1959, the Klan burned a cross on the lawn of an Indian woman in the town of St. Pauls as "a warning" because, Cole claimed, she was "having an affair" with a white man. The cross burnings continued, with Reverend Cole ranting at each gathering about the terrible evils of "mongrelization," the loose morals of Lumbee women, and the manly duties of white men "to fight [America's] enemies anywhere, anytime." Cole's favorite subject at the time was Ava Gardner, eastern North Carolina's own homegrown movie star, born in Grabtown, near Smithfield, and in the late 1950s said to be having a Hollywood affair with Sammy Davis Jr., whom Cole contemptuously referred to as "that one-eyed nigger."

The climax of the Klan's Robeson County campaign was to be a heavily armed rally on January 18 near Maxton, North Carolina, at which, Cole predicted, five thousand Klansmen would remind Indians of "their place" in the racial order. "He said that, did he?" asked Simeon Oxendine, who had flown more than thirty missions against the Germans in World War II and now headed the Lumbee chapter of the Veterans of Foreign Wars. "Well, we'll just wait and see."

That Friday night, as a few dozen Klansmen gathered in a roadside field in darkness lit only by a single hanging bulb powered by a portable generator, more than five hundred Lumbee men assembled across the road with rifles and shotguns. The Lumbees fanned out across the highway to encircle the Klansmen. When Cole began to speak, a Lumbee dashed up and smashed the light with his rifle barrel; then hundreds of Indians let out a thunderous whoop and fired their weapons repeatedly into the air. Only four people were injured, none seriously, all but one apparently hit by falling bullets. The Klansmen dropped their guns and scrambled for their cars, abandoning the unlit cross, their public address system, and an array of KKK paraphernalia. Magnanimous in victory, the Lumbees even helped push Cole's Cadillac out of the ditch where his wife, Carolyn, had driven in her panic; the Grand Wizard himself had abandoned "white womanhood" and fled on foot into the swamps. Laughing, the Lumbees set fire to the cross, hanged Catfish Cole in effigy, and had a rollicking victory bash. Draped in captured Klan regalia, they celebrated into the night. The cover of *Life* magazine featured a playful photograph of a beaming Simeon Oxendine wrapped in a confiscated Ku Klux Klan banner.

Faced with escalating terrorism, black Southerners who remained politically active in those days generally armed themselves. Medgar Evers, the NAACP leader from Jackson, Mississippi, who was assassinated in 1963, seriously pondered the possibility of launching a guerrilla war in the Delta. *The Eagle Eye: The Woman's Voice*, a black women's newsletter in Jackson, argued in 1955 that "the Negro must protect himself" because "no law enforcement body in ignorant Miss. will protect any Negro who is a member of the NAACP" and warned "the white hoodlums who are now parading around the premises" of the publisher that the editors were "protected by armed guard." Daisy Bates, the black heroine of Little Rock, Arkansas, wrote to Thurgood Marshall in 1959 that she and her husband were under constant attack and "keep 'Old Betsy' well-oiled and the guards are always on the alert." Even Martin Luther King Jr. relied on guns and guards in the late 1950s. Reverend Glenn Smiley, who visited Dr. King's home in 1956, reported back to his employer, the

Fellowship of Reconciliation, that "the place is an arsenal." If nonviolence now seems the inevitable or even the most likely strategy for black Southerners, no one could be sure of that in the late 1950s.

The Klan's resurgence in the mid-1960s, when Robert Teel seems to have joined, gave white Southerners a voice for their fears and resentments about the gains of the civil rights movement. The Klan in North Carolina "had long lived in shadows," historian David Cecelski writes, "but between 1964 and 1967 it rose out of its obscurity and walked in broad daylight." The Democratic Party, which had once called itself "the party of white supremacy" and which still included people like Jesse Helms and Strom Thurmond, seemed to have deserted *their* South. President Johnson, a white Southerner himself, had signed the Civil Rights Act and the Voting Rights Act, and the entire North Carolina congressional delegation opposed the Voting Rights Act. Many white people in eastern North Carolina felt that they had nowhere to go—and so they ran to the Klan. A few years later, Helms and Thurmond helped Richard Nixon push his "Southern strategy" and led white Southerners into a new, Southern-based Republican Party that railed against "forced bussing" and the intrusions of the "feddle gubment," and the Klan faded again. But Robert Teel had no patience with just talk. Though he claimed to have harbored no resentments against blacks, he ruled his little empire in Grab-all with an iron hand, and black people who crossed him usually regretted it.

The worst incident at Four Corners came in late April 1970, only about two weeks before the killing and the conflagrations of that fateful summer. Clyde Harding, a local black schoolteacher, was washing his car at the self-service car wash that Teel had built across the street from his store and his barbershop. "Jerry Oakley, my stepson," Teel recounted, "came out there on his lunch hour and wanted to vacuum out his car, and he came running in and said he'd had some trouble with a black guy over there." According to witnesses, Jerry Oakley had roared up in his car and demanded that Mr. Harding move his vehicle immediately. Harding continued to wash his car, and Oakley ran across the street and into the barbershop. A few seconds later, Robert Teel emerged from his place with a pistol tucked into the front of his belt and stomped across to the car wash. Teel told me, "I pulled out the gun with one hand and slapped him upside the head with the other hand." Medical and court records, however, indicated that Teel pointed the gun at the black schoolteacher and then pistol-whipped him, breaking several teeth and cutting his face.

The magistrate in the Harding case, J. C. Wheeler, charged Teel with assault by pointing a gun and assault and battery. Despite the fact that Teel was already serving *two* suspended sentences for crimes of violence—in both instances, beating up police officers—Billy Watkins was able to persuade the judge to acquit Teel on the first count and issue a prayer-for-judgment continuance on the second charge. The court did require Teel to pay the schoolteacher's hefty medical and dental bills. Lacking any semblance of equal justice, young blacks in Grab-all went to Clyde Harding and offered to avenge the beating; the black schoolteacher firmly discouraged them. "If Clyde had wanted us to do something," Boo Chavis speculated, "we would have burned Teel up, ain't no probably about it. But Clyde didn't want to push the issue."

The Clyde Harding incident and the court's apparent lack of concern about it hardened resentments toward the Teel family in Grab-all and smoothed a pathway for the destruction soon to follow. Blacks began to boycott the little shopping center, which infuriated Teel. Some black parents forbade their children to go to the store because it was a dangerous place, while other local blacks organized an informal protest boycott. Teel complained later that his business dropped by half almost immediately. "This is when my windows started getting knocked out," he added. "They were boycotting my place. I had other people in here washing and then people come in there and help people get their clothes out the washers, get them off the yard, and cross the road hollering, 'Don't trade with him, he's a black hater!'" Years later, Teel resisted the description: "I've had colored people come in and brag on what a nice place I had put up for them to shop, and how much they liked me, and things like that. Eighty-five percent of my business was black."

Teel had always kept a pistol handy, but after the Harding incident, the black boycott, and the breaking of his store windows, he and his sons moved two more guns to the barbershop: a 12-gauge pump shotgun and a .410-gauge shotgun with a .22-caliber rifle barrel attached in the over-and-under style. Teel and his boys began to spend nights in the barbershop with their guns, hoping to catch whoever had shattered the windows. There was an atmosphere of war around the place. It remains a matter of curiosity for some people in Oxford as to why Teel, a man known to dislike black people and widely rumored to be a leader in the Ku Klux Klan, would set up shop in Grab-all. His attorney, Billy Watkins, wondered the same thing. "It was bound to happen," he said, referring to the imminent racial tragedy. "With his temper and his attitudes, it was like two naked electrical wires, that if they ever touched, all hell would break loose—and they were too close not to touch."

CHAPTER 4

MISS AMY'S WITNESS

I DON'T KNOW WHEN or how I first became infected with white supremacy. But when I was no more than six years old, I discovered within myself both that monstrous lie and the moral cowardice necessary to its preservation. Though only a first grader, I was forced to confront what James Baldwin called "the realization that a civilization is not destroyed by wicked people; it is not necessary that people be wicked, but only that they be spineless." I wished then and I wish now that this was not the truth, and that I had no part in it, but it is and I did.

At that time, we were living in Sanford, North Carolina, a little town where my father served as minister of Jonesboro Heights Methodist Church. My mother had stopped teaching when I was born, but she had taken up her chalkboards and construction paper again as soon as I started kindergarten. Mama had hired a black woman, Mrs. Fanny Mae McIver, to keep house and tend to my brother and me. "She got her right out of the cotton field," Sarah Godfrey, our neighbor and friend, told me later. "That was Fanny Mae's first job working indoors, working in white people's houses. She was a fine woman," Sarah continued. "All three of her boys ended up with good jobs in New York and bought her a new home here, and were always good to her. They all turned out real nice."

Ironically, perhaps typically, my spineless act of cruelty was rooted in love. That first year in kindergarten, when I was not quite six, I befriended David Barrett, a towheaded boy with a crooked grin, a zany laugh, and a big heart. We quickly became infatuated in the way of preadolescent boys, organizing the "Rat Fink Club" together, playing Davy Crockett and Daniel Boone in the woods, and taking turns sleeping over at each other's houses. I especially loved to stay at David's house on Saturdays, when his father grilled steaks and his mother made blueberry pie.

At bedtime, we developed a ritual that David dubbed "Tim's Tall Tales." We would lie there in the dark in the twin beds, and I would tell him stories, making them up as I went. His fierce and unfeigned enthusiasm for these rambling odysseys was like a drug to me. I loved him unreservedly, and preferred his company to anything else in the world. The year I turned seven, when my family moved to Oxford, David and I pledged to meet at the Washington Monument when we turned twenty-one. That we did not keep the appointment takes nothing away from the depth of our attachment.

One day David and I were playing at my house, and Mrs. McIver brought her little boy to work with her. I can't remember his name, though I recall that he was smaller than David and me, and perfectly nice. But no one could penetrate the fog of infatuation that enveloped David and me in those days, and anyone else's presence would have constituted an intrusion. The little black boy was a pest, we concluded, and we shunned him. He followed us from room to room, imploring our acceptance, no doubt adhering to his mother's instructions to be nice to her employers' children. But we shut him out, quite literally, closing a door in his face. And when we were safely on the other side of that door, holding it closed, David began to taunt him in the singsong rebuke that children around the world still sling at one another. You can hear the tune in your own mind's ear, where it may sting even now: "nah-nah-nah-nah-naaaaaah-nah." But the words to David's rendition must have burned in that boy's brain: "Nigger-nigger-niiiiiii-ger, nigger-nigger-niiiiiii-ger." And the blood ran hot to my face, as it must have run much hotter to the face on the other side of the door.

I wanted this terrible thing to stop, but I didn't have the courage to risk alienating my best friend. Like many people who fail to live up to their best lights, I found that my deep sense of belonging and my tenacious desire for acceptance trumped my moral judgment. I joined in the song.

I knew that we were being cruel, though I had no way to understand how cruel, and I knew that what I was doing was wrong. I wasn't punished for it, however. Surely the little boy told his mother, but she must not have felt at liberty to tell mine. Afterward, David and I simply pretended it hadn't happened, and no one ever said a word to us about it. But the episode violated everything that I had been taught—nearly everything, that is. Obviously, if someone had taught me that it was wrong to call another person *that* word, someone else had taught me that there was such a category. Still, I knew that it was my solemn duty to be kind to our guests, to see that anyone who came into our home was treated graciously and warmly. Color was not at issue in that sense. Beyond that, however, I knew that it was not only evil to *say* that word, of course, but that it was unspeakably wicked even to *think* that word, to place another human into a category separate from our own.

The very *idea* of "nigger," quite apart from the specific racial context of our particular lives, was the heart of human evil, the avenue down which the Nazis had marched into Poland, and David and I, like some of the Poles, had somehow welcomed them. The fact that this cruelty violated my relationship with Mrs. McIver, whom I called Fanny Mae, of course, was only the top layer of the sin that we had committed. The thick bottom layer was the whole idea that another child of God could belong to a category less than human. My father had explained much of this to Vern and me at the Ku Klux Klan meeting, and that was far from the last lesson.

Daddy had observed the escalating violence of the black freedom movement of the 1960s with growing uneasiness. Yet he knew that remaining silent about race would betray his calling. Born in 1959, I don't remember learning that race was *the* issue for my father and my five uncles who were Methodist ministers, or for any white preacher in the South. That's just the way it was. In our family, at least, if you didn't take a stand at all, you weren't much of a man or much of a preacher; the "race question" was the acid test of integrity. At the same time, it could destroy your ministry, and the point was to lead the people as far as you could without losing influence or your livelihood. You wanted to remain true to your lights and yet avoid the fate of the irrelevant crusader. If the people in the pew were ever going to imagine a new world, beyond the boundaries of white supremacy, someone they respected had to make the case.

If he hoped to stay in the conversation, a preacher who believed in racial equality could never afford to neglect to shine his shoes or forget to visit a parishioner in the hospital. "It forced me to be a better pastor than I probably would have been," my father explained later, "because I found that people who opposed me on race would often attack me on other issues, because I hadn't been to see their grandmama. And sometimes, if I had been to see Grandmama in the nursing home even more than they had, it made it hard for them to oppose me on race, and they'd stand with me even when they didn't agree with me."

My father's commitment to civil rights grew over the same years that the Ku Klux Klan went through its series of revivals and as black Southerners pushed the issue of racial justice to the forefront of American life. Daddy's beliefs came in part from his own family heritage, but his moral and intellectual world had expanded a good deal when he was an undergraduate at Guilford College, a Quaker school in Greensboro with a liberal social vision. From its founding in the 1830s, Guilford had been coeducational, advocating an unusual egalitarianism between the sexes. There Daddy had read the work of Southern dissidents, like Lillian Smith's *Killers of the Dream* and Stetson Kennedy's *Southern Exposure*. He'd studied with Gordon Lovejoy, who'd preached racial equality for the National Conference of Christians and Jews. Charlotte Hawkins Brown, the great African American educator, had come to speak at Guilford from Palmer Memorial Institute in Sedalia, just down the road, and made quite an impression on him.

In about 1950, early in his college days, my father went home to Biscoe and attended a meeting of the Lions Club with Charles Buie, the father of the girl he intended to marry. Mr. Buie liked young Vernon, though the prosperous Buies were uneasy at the prospect of their daughter marrying a poor preacher's son. What happened next could not have helped matters. When the meeting opened with everyone standing for the Pledge of Allegiance, my father would not say the words. "It said 'liberty and justice for all,' and I knew that was a lie, and just not true," Daddy told me years later. "I knew it ought to be true, but it was no more true than the tooth fairy. I couldn't say it." The troubling thing, however, was that his wealthy and imposing prospective father-in-law, whom he greatly admired, was standing beside him. But Daddy wasn't going to say that pledge. "Mr. Buie flashed his eyes at me and he realized that I wasn't going to say it," my father said. "It was a hard thing. I don't think he really understood why I wouldn't say it. We didn't speak of it again."

He clashed more openly with his own father in those years when his mind was growing in all directions like ten acres of kudzu. One day, overtaken by the powerful logic of A. J. Muste, the dean of American pacifism, Vernon called his father on the telephone to tell him that he'd decided to register as a conscientious objector. In the days after World War II, as the McCarthy era opened in all its repression and conformity, announcing one's unwillingness to fight for one's country was not especially fashionable. In the small-town South, particularly, this was not how to win friends and influence people. Jack Tyson told his son to come home and talk it over with him. "I told him I hadn't called to discuss it, I had called to tell him what I was going to do," Daddy remembered. "He said I was making a big mistake. And when I went down to the draft board to register as a conscientious objector, my best friend's mother was working at the desk. For the rest of my life, she never spoke to me again." That hurt, but what really hurt was to break with his father on an important issue. "I went in my room and laid down on the bed and cried," he recalled. "I'd never parted with him on anything serious before. And the funny thing was that within a year reading Reinhold

Niebuhr shot my pacifism all full of holes." Like his father before him, Daddy became a growing person who felt the call of conscience and frequently acted on it. And the most important issue, of course, was race.

In 1952, when my father took his first appointment as the student pastor at Oak Ridge Military Institute, Zack Whitaker, one of the officials at Oak Ridge, took him aside and urged him to go easy about racial matters. "I don't know how you feel about things, Vernon," Whitaker said, "But I know you're a young man. And I know we haven't treated the nigrahs right. But this is not the time and Oak Ridge is not the place to talk about things like that." My father hadn't even delivered his first sermon, but he'd grown up in a preacher's house and knew exactly what was happening.

"He was trying to put his hand over my mouth before I had even opened it," Daddy remembered. On the second Sunday in February—"Race Relations Sunday," the Methodist church hierarchy had designated it—Daddy preached about the inevitable crisis of race that faced the church, advocating a new openness to equality for all Americans, and led his congregation in singing "In Christ There Is No East or West." The great hymn reads, in part, "Join hands, then, brothers of the faith / Whate'er your race may be. / Who serves my Father as a son / Is surely kin to me." Later in the spring, he took the church youth group to hear Marian Anderson, the famous African American contralto whose historic defiance of segregation in 1939 had echoed from the steps of the Lincoln Memorial to the palaces of Europe. Daddy made sure that Mr. Whitaker's daughter was on the bus.

The 1950s marked a lonely vigil for Southern liberals like my father, who operated under galling strictures that made it hard to take a meaningful stand. In 1955–56, however, the patient toil of generations of black Southerners in Montgomery, Alabama, lifted up a stirring young preacher named Martin Luther King Jr., whose vision gave voice to a prophetic tradition nurtured since the days of slavery. Knowing white Americans better than they knew themselves, King did nothing to stanch the rivers of ink that described him as a

Southern black Gandhi, "the little brown saint" of Alabama. King blended the nonviolence of Gandhi with the political realism of Reinhold Niebuhr, who had taught a generation of theologians, including my father, that good intentions were not good enough. In a fallen world marked by human depravity and deep-seated sin, in a world where Hitler and Stalin had recruited millions of followers to commit mass murder, love must harness power and seek justice in order to have moral meaning. Love without power remained impotent, and power without love was bankrupt.

No dreamer at all, King understood the world that confronted black Southerners as they called for their freedom. The Cold War competition between the United States and the Soviet Union offered African Americans the unique leverage to redeem or repudiate American democracy in the eyes of the world. The demonstrations in the streets of the civil rights–era South were carefully staged dramas that forced the contradictions of American democracy to the surface. The street-theater morality plays that King and his organizers presented in Montgomery, Albany, Birmingham, and Selma captured in almost poetic fashion both the brutal social order of Jim Crow and the obvious justice of black demands. But their audience included a mostly dark-skinned world torn apart by the Cold War, and their intention was to force the federal government to intervene on behalf of black Southerners. Once the campaign began, King made no secret of his strategy. "Mr. Kennedy is battling for the minds and the hearts of men in Asia and Africa," he told a crowd in Birmingham, "and they aren't gonna respect the United States of America if she deprives men and women of the basic rights of life because of the color of their skin."

Though the crusades in Alabama received more press coverage, North Carolina had provided no hiding place from the civil rights movement. On February 1, 1960, four black college students from North Carolina Agricultural and Technical College sat down at the segregated Woolworth's lunch counter in Greensboro, where my mother and father had both attended college a decade earlier, and asked to be served. The next day twenty-three classmates joined them; the next day, there were sixty-six; the day after, one hundred. When white hoodlums with Confederate flags blocked the doors, players from the North Carolina A & T football team formed a flying wedge that broke through the hostile crowd, each player carrying a little American flag. The wedge of big bodies permitted demonstrators to reach the lunch counter. One of the hoodlums demanded to know just who they thought they were, and one of the black football players replied, "We're the Union Army." Within two months, there *was* an army of sorts; the nonviolent warriors carried the sit-in campaign to fifty-four towns and cities across nine of the eleven states of the old Confederacy.

The battalions of nonviolence eventually overran segregation, and they also helped free white Southerners who felt the way my father did. After the sit-ins opened a new, more aggressive phase of the freedom movement, Daddy began to press the Methodist Church to live up to the inclusive vision of the gospel. "Since 1960, I have increasingly become associated with those who fight for social reform and renewal in our state," an entry in his diary revealed. Mama wrote on February 10, 1962: "Beautiful Sunday. Vernon preached on race relations. He really 'laid it on the line.' It was real good." That was when we were living in Sanford and he was serving Jonesboro Heights Methodist Church. He persuaded the administrative board of his local congregation to vote to seat anyone who came to church, regardless of color. He chaired the Commission on Social Action of the North Carolina Council of Churches and sat on the executive committee of the North Carolina Council on Human Relations. "I believe that the Church must relate itself to this struggle for racial equality," his diary said in 1962. "It is doing so in spots and these spots are increasing. I hope it is not too late." In later years, I would come to understand what he meant by that.

On April 3, 1963, Martin Luther King Jr. and the Southern Christian Leadership Conference (SCLC) launched their Birmingham campaign with sit-ins at the city's segregated lunch counters. The movement initially found it hard to recruit supporters, with large elements of the black community still reluctant and many of King's supporters in jail. Slapped with a court injunction to cease the demonstrations, King decided to go to jail himself on the same day that a group of "moderate" white clergymen pronounced the campaign "unwise and untimely." During eight days of confinement, King penned his famous "Letter from Birmingham Jail," an eloquent critique of "the white moderate who is more devoted to 'order' than to 'justice.'"

It is easy, King wrote, for those who had not suffered the violence and the indignity of segregation to advise patience. But it was excruciating, he said, to "see the vast majority of your twenty million Negro brothers smothering in an air-tight cage of poverty in the midst of an affluent society." King described the agony of finding "your tongue twisted and your speech stammering as you seek to explain to your six-year-old daughter why she can't go to the public amusement park that has just been advertised on television, and see tears welling up in her little eyes when she is told that Funtown is closed to colored children, and see the depressing clouds of inferiority begin to form in her little mental sky." Black Americans find themselves "living constantly at tip-toe stance never quite knowing what to expect next, and plagued with inner fears and outer resentments; when you are forever fighting a degenerating sense of 'nobodiness,'" King wrote. And the biggest obstacle, King argued, was the sympathetic white liberal who wanted to preserve peace and civility.

The effect of King's words on my father was electric. He was already committed to racial equality, but Dr. King hit him with the conviction that he needed to do something. "When I began to read his 'Letter from Birmingham Jail,'" Daddy recounted, "I wept while I was reading it and got down on my knees, because it was the best thing outside Scripture that I had ever found."

As his rhetoric galvanized liberals like my father, Dr. King's organizers located the perfect adversary in Birmingham's Public Safety Commissioner Eugene "Bull" Connor. Knowing that the television cameras followed Dr. King, they also knew they could count on the volatile Connor for a dramatic display of brutality; though the SCLC organizers did not know it, Connor longed to be governor of Alabama

and believed that becoming the state's leading segregationist firebrand was his ticket. Sure enough, whether it was temper or ambition, Connor ordered his officers to use police dogs and fire hoses. In
resorting to open violence, Connor stepped right into King's trap.
"The ball game was over, once the hoses and the dogs were brought
in," former city official David Vann recalled. "In marching only one
block, they could get enough news film to fill all the newscasts of all
the television stations in the United States." The images of violence
in Birmingham echoed around the world: "Sensational aspects of the
Birmingham crisis including arrests of children and use of dogs and
hoses have received widespread play," one diplomat reported to the
White House.

While the televised drama played out perfectly, Birmingham
could not be reduced to an epic struggle between pure nonviolence
and bare-fanged evil. King and his organizers were committed to
nonviolence, but their strategy depended on provoking violence
against demonstrators. And though the SCLC taught nonviolence
and begged those who could not accept nonviolent discipline to stay
home, black bystanders often pelted police with "nonviolent" rocks,
bricks, and bottles, which helped prod Connor's cops into stupid
overreactions that played to King's advantage in the media.

Beyond the chaos in the streets, white terrorism, especially dynamite bombings, had long plagued Birmingham's black community.
But Klan terrorists who wanted to kill the leaders of the freedom
movement knew that they themselves might die in the attempt.
Colonel "Stone" Johnson, a black labor union representative, organized the Civil Rights Guards, who armed themselves to protect the
movement and sometimes exchanged fire with the Klan. Asked many
years later how he'd managed to protect civil rights leaders in
Birmingham, given his commitment to nonviolence, Johnson
grinned and said, "With my nonviolent .38 police special."

Armed self-defense was nothing new. But black Birmingham
responded to the bombings in a new way during the SCLC's 1963
campaign. After white terrorists bombed King's motel room, poor

blacks whose commitment to nonviolence was negligible took to the streets, ravaging nine blocks of Birmingham, overturning cars, shattering storefronts, and burning buildings. It was in large measure the prospect of race war in the streets, with the whole world watching, that forced President Kennedy to respond. Kennedy, a devoted Cold Warrior, lobbied white business leaders in Birmingham to reach an agreement with the freedom movement, ending what he called "a spectacle which was seriously damaging the reputation of both Birmingham and the country." Birmingham was a decisive triumph for nonviolent direct action, but violence and nonviolence were both more ethically complicated and more tightly intertwined than they appeared in most media accounts and history books.

Across the South, the news from Birmingham inspired dozens of similar campaigns. In cities, hamlets, small towns, and rural crossroads far beyond the scope of television camera crews and civil rights celebrities, black Southerners pushed hard for their freedom. In a ten-week period, African Americans launched at least 758 demonstrations in 186 cities and towns, yielding 14,733 arrests.

Sanford, North Carolina, was no exception. As in Birmingham, violence and nonviolence lived side by side, working in tension and in tandem with each other; the jails filled with nonviolent demonstrators, but riots in the streets left many people injured and one man shot through the leg. The tension in the streets made its way into the pages of my parents' diaries, which they let me read almost forty years later. "I returned from Biscoe," my father wrote in his diary, "to find that racial demonstrations had been held on our streets and 52 Negro youths had been arrested. I visited the jail and talked and prayed with some of those who had demonstrated." On December 28, 1963, Mama noted tersely in her own diary, "Much stir over Negro demonstrations."

The next day, Daddy wrote a letter to the editor of the *Sanford Herald,* not from jail but from the confines of his conscience in a community of white Christians that did not want to hear him. His letter clearly drew on the tone of King's Birmingham missive. "Last night, a 14-year-old boy spent his first night in jail," Daddy wrote. "He was one of the more than 50 young people who were arrested yesterday in our city. His only real crime is that he had the wrong mother.

"A moment of truth has arrived for Sanford," he asserted. "Our Negro neighbors are no longer able to accept indignities imposed upon them. They are asking for centuries-long delayed justice. They have been charged with 'trespassing.' Indeed, they have trespassed, not so much upon our restaurants as upon our consciences." Daddy went on to make some specific proposals for negotiation and recon- ciliation, employing King's own phrasing to suggest that "our churches ought to open their doors to every person for whom Jesus Christ died and thus become the headlights of our community rather than the tail-lights," and advocating "that our School Board ought to make plans now to voluntarily desegregate our schools next fall." He saw no reason "to force our Negro neighbors to haul us into court."

"That 14-year-old boy who spent last night in our jail is going to win," Daddy declared. "The highest we know of Democracy and Christianity is on his side. He wants to be free. Our community now has the opportunity finally to become true sons and daughters of one who once said, 'Give me liberty or give me death.' " He signed the letter "A fellow sinner, Vernon Tyson."

The newspaper editor wrote my father a scolding reply, remind- ing him that leaders who went "too far, too fast" ended up without any followers, and maybe without a job, too. Other people signaled their disapproval with lowered eyes, resentful stares, or anonymous hate mail. The editor was right that people in the pews at most white churches resisted the news that God called them to love their black neighbors as themselves—and to accept them as civic and social equals. My father needed no reminder that he was walking through a minefield. The editor had no way of knowing, of course, that my father drew on a deep well of spiritual strength, and was a Tyson from eastern North Carolina and therefore half crazy besides. It was not a bad trait for a man facing what was about to happen to my father in the perilous historical moment of 1963 and 1964.

In the months after the Birmingham crusade, the fixed stars and immovable pillars of American history began to reel and rock. On June 11, 1963, fearing that Birmingham might soon ignite a local race war, President Kennedy made a historic address on national television, describing civil rights as "a moral issue" that was "as old as the Scriptures" and "as clear as the American Constitution" and calling for new civil rights legislation. Later that night, a member of the White Citizens Council in Jackson, Mississippi, took a high-powered rifle and assassinated NAACP leader Medgar Evers. On August 28, Dr. King spoke to 250,000 people in front of the Lincoln Memorial and delivered his famous "I Have a Dream" speech; this brought him wide admiration but caused the Federal Bureau of Investigation to "mark him now, if we have not done so before, as the most dangerous Negro of the future in this nation from the standpoint of communism, the Negro, and national security." On September 16, Klan members in Birmingham bombed the Sixteenth Street Baptist Church, killing four little black girls and maiming many others. And before Thanksgiving, sniper fire in Dallas took the life of President Kennedy, a death that seemed inextricably bound up with the momentous racial challenges confronting the nation.

Amid these perilous hopes and agonizing tragedies, my father met Dr. Samuel Proctor at a statewide meeting of the North Carolina Council of Churches. Dr. Proctor was the president of North Carolina Agricultural and Technical College, where the sit-ins had been born, and one of the leading black preachers of his generation. Proctor gave a majestic speech at the council meeting, and Daddy stood patiently in line to speak to him afterward. Without thinking about it much, Daddy asked Dr. Proctor to come preach on February 2, 1964, Race Relations Sunday. Dr. Proctor accepted immediately, smiled warmly as he shook my father's hand, and said, "Yes, and we'll get run out of town together."

Proctor probably knew just how close to the bone of truth he was cutting with that prediction. As Dr. King liked to remind people, eleven o'clock on Sunday morning was the most segregated hour in America, and our all-white churches did not welcome black preachers to the pulpit. Daddy had extended the invitation in the fall of 1963, when things were fairly calm in Sanford, but when we came back from my grandmother's house in Biscoe after Christmas, the jails in Sanford were filled with black teenagers, the police had shot one of them, the Klan was on the rampage, and the whole community was in an uproar. Daddy's timing could have been better. And he had neglected to tell anyone, even his allies, that he had invited a black preacher to come only a month later.

Dr. Proctor was not just any black preacher, either; he was one of the leading black educators in the country and one of the most prominent African American ministers of his generation. In the decades to come, Ivy League universities would pay thousands of dollars to have Dr. Samuel Proctor deliver their commencement addresses. In late 1963 and early 1964, however, Jonesboro Heights Methodist Church rocked on its foundations at the thought of having a black man in their pulpit. When church members began to hear about Dr. Proctor's proposed visit, the telephone started to ring incessantly. Fifty church members called a protest meeting in the fellowship hall and insisted that my father rescind the invitation. He was shocked at the outcry. "We are really having fireworks in our church concerning Dr. Proctor's coming," Mama scrawled in her diary. "I have hardly slept at all."

As the word filtered out into the community, Daddy began to receive a steady stream of death threats on the telephone. "I called the police station and told them that I wouldn't mind a bit if they would bring a squad car by the house every once in a while," my father recalled. "I really thought they were going to kill him," Mama said later.

My father found himself under enormous pressure from within and without. Not only was he afraid that someone might make good on the threats and dynamite the house; he was also afraid that he would lose his job. "I had badly miscalculated my position with the congregation," he admitted years later. "If I had known how upset people were going to get, I might not have invited Dr. Proctor in the first place." His own feelings were even harder to confront. He was an ambitious man of immense talents, a handsome preacher with gifts of eloquence. He had grown up poor and married a rich man's daughter, and he had always wanted to give her things that he could not afford. Daddy's generation was not given to admiration for noble failures; they wanted nice cars, brick houses, and all the accoutrements of success. One suspects, too, that he felt his in-laws looking over his shoulder; Martha's younger sister had married a surgeon, and her brother now owned a textile mill. Being a preacher carried some small status, but it did not pay much. And being an unemployed preacher was a different matter altogether.

The paycheck must have felt nearly as important as the pulpit that winter. Mama was pregnant again and money was tight. "Went to fit maternity dresses and get groceries," Mama wrote in January. "We are very hungry these days." But even though she was "kinda blue about finances," as she noted, Mama kept on taking care of people. "I have been in kitchen most all day," she wrote a few days later. "Mr. Caddell died. Made chicken tetrazzinni and baked cake. I fried chicken and made pimento cheese to carry to his family." The next day she noted, "Vernon had two weddings tonight. He got $20. We certainly can use it!"

Daddy was not much interested in money, but he had a driving need to succeed as a minister. "I was overly ambitious," he admitted. "I don't know where I got such ambition, but I had it bad. Ambition was one of those demons in the dark that came to me again and again. I was wanting people to like me and wanting to succeed, but knowing that I needed to stand in the fire, too." Daddy's closest friend in those days, Jack Crum, was a maverick Methodist preacher who had been run out of a church in Raleigh over the race issue and worked in constant threat of losing his job. But Crum kept on pushing, though not always gracefully. "Jack and I were different," Daddy laughed. "He was a social prophet—a social firebug, some might say. He put it on the line. I was a politician, trying to lead people and preserve my influence and do my job as best I could. Jack was one of the farmers of my soul. He was my conscience. But I didn't want to be like him, exactly. I wanted to do the right thing, but I didn't want to pay that kind of price. I never wanted to lose." And now Daddy felt like the mob was upon him.

The day his parishioners held the protest meeting to oppose Daddy's invitation to Dr. Proctor was the worst day of all. He strode into the fellowship hall, all shoeshine and handshakes, confident that he could win them over and carry the day, and found instead that he'd walked into a hornet's nest. Daddy was stunned by the hostile reception and disappointed in his own performance. "Our faith is really being <u>stretched</u>," Mama wrote in her diary on January 31. "At the meeting tonight Vernon was hurt to the core. Several made terribly cutting remarks to him. He just took it, but afterwards shed tears." When Daddy came back to the house, there was more bad news.

"Things were just about as bad as they were going to get," Daddy recalled, thinking about that awful day, "and when I got home, someone had just called and said they were going to blow up my house and do harm to my children, and Martha was very much afraid." Daddy walked quickly upstairs, tears welling in his eyes, wondering what on earth he would do.

"Truth is," he told me later, "I might have backed down if it hadn't been for your mother. I didn't want to lose. I just could not think about losing." The main thing he did not want to do was to disappoint Mama. But she followed him upstairs. "Martha grabbed me from behind and squeezed me tight, and said she had rather live on a five-point circuit on minimum salary for the rest of her life than to see me sell my soul. She gave me permission to fail. If she hadn't done that, our marriage could have fallen apart, or I might have turned tail and run. But she grabbed me from behind and told me to stand my ground."

The segregationists put their own kind of squeeze on Daddy, though, and some of my father's supporters began to back off. The weak tea of moderation flowed freely and went like this: "Vernon might be right, but it isn't worth tearing the church apart over." At six o'clock the night before Dr. Proctor was scheduled to preach, Daddy called an emergency meeting of the church's administrative board in an effort to ease the controversy. It may have been a tactical error. Some of the board members angrily demanded that my father cancel Dr. Proctor's appearance the next morning. One of his adversaries kept pushing the telephone on the desk toward him, saying, "You can end all this with one phone call." Others began to ask Daddy why he thought this one service was really worth the painful breach that loomed in front of them. "This thing is going to tear this church apart," one man insisted. Just as the meeting threatened to dissolve in an uproar, a quiet, dignified older woman rose to speak.

"Miss Amy" Womble was sixty, an "old-maid schoolteacher," her neighbors would have said in those days. She walked with a limp. Miss Womble had been a first-grade teacher to most of the people in that room. The community honored her, but nobody had any idea what she thought about the burning social issues of the day. "I've been just sitting here sort of listening," Miss Amy said. "And I hear one of us saying this is going to tear this church apart." She looked directly at the man who had said it. "Now, I don't know the man who is coming very much. I know he is the president of A & T, that's all I know. But I know our pastor, and you know him, too, and he's not going to tear anything apart. And I don't suppose Dr. Proctor is going to tear anything apart, either. If there is going to be any tearing done, we're going to do the tearing apart ourselves."

Miss Amy slowly hobbled to the front of the room and told the silent group of her former students a story. "There was a case up near Chapel Hill recently," she said, "where a teenage boy went around a curve too fast and was killed in a car crash. So they thought. He was down there by the side of the road and they were just waiting for the ambulance to come and take him to the funeral home. There wasn't any signs of life.

"But then an airman from Pope Air Force Base stopped. He was home on furlough, and he saw the boy lying down there and he scrambled down the embankment and opened that boy's mouth," she continued. "And he saw the boy's tongue stuck back in his throat, and he ran his finger back there and pulled out that tongue, and then

gave that boy mouth-to-mouth resuscitation. By the time that ambulance got there," Miss Amy said, "that boy was walking around alive
as you or me. And the next week they had a big dinner up at the fire
station out in Orange County for that airman, celebrating how he had
saved that boy's life." She paused once more.

"What I haven't told you is that the boy who had the wreck was
white, and that airman that saved him was a black man. But that's the
truth," she said, "and I want all of you fathers to tell me something."
She looked searchingly around the room. "Now, which one of you
fathers would have said to that airman, 'Now, don't you run your
black fingers down my boy's white throat'? Which of y'all would have
told that airman, 'Don't you dare put your black lips on my boy's
mouth'?"

My father, who retold the story in later years, including the day he
preached Miss Amy Womble's funeral, said, "I have never heard the
voice of the Lord with such thunder, such wisdom, such love." And
something slightly miraculous occurred. "The board voted 25 to 14
to stand with Vernon and welcome Dr. Proctor," my mother wrote in
her diary. "We feel so blessed." Afterward, several of my father's
friends and allies took him out for a quiet steak dinner. It was the
fourth anniversary of the first sit-ins at Woolworth's in Greensboro.
Blood was still flowing but barriers were still falling, although Dr.
Proctor could not have joined them at the restaurant even if he had
been present. And that was just the beginning.

When Daddy got home, my mother met him at the door with a
bemused expression on her face. "Grayson Bryan came by," she said,
"and he was crying." Bryan was from South Carolina and had come
to Sanford to work in the local textile mill and live with what my
daddy generously called "his poor sainted mother," whom my father
visited regularly. But Bryan had been one of my father's most ardent
adversaries on the issue of race, and had angrily condemned Daddy
for inviting "that nigger preacher" to our church. My father did not
even come in the house, just turned around and drove straight to
Grayson Bryan's place.

Mr. Bryan, his face still wet with tears, met Daddy at the door, welcomed him inside, and poured him a glass of iced tea. "I want to tell you, Preacher, something happened to me tonight. When Miss Amy was talking, something happened that ain't ever happened before. Old Love just come up in my heart," Bryan sobbed, "and I want to tell you that I love you, I love Dr. Proctor, I love everybody." And then Mr. Bryan fell to his knees beside his chair, and Daddy knelt beside him and said a short prayer, and went on home.

It wasn't over yet. When Daddy got back to the house, Mama met him at the door again. "I don't know what you are doing," she said with a smile, "but you must be serving liquor up there at the church because James Stephens came by here, and he was crying, too." By that time, it was ten o'clock at night, but Daddy turned around again and got back into his old gray Pontiac and headed out to the Stephens place. Stephens was a member of the board, a man of some wealth, and profoundly conservative.

"I went up there ready to vote against you tonight," Stephens told my father, "but after Miss Amy talked I gave it some more thought, and I want you to know that it's all right with me. I will be there in the morning and I will be glad to welcome Dr. Proctor as our guest."

The next morning was a beautiful sunny day, the kind of harbinger of spring that can come to the Carolinas in late winter. We looked out the windows and saw bumper-to-bumper traffic pouring into the church parking lot. Dr. Proctor turned out to be a tall, handsome man who radiated warmth and dignity. Though I was only five years old, I can still remember his soaring sermon, though I don't know what he said, exactly. "We sang Fosdick's great hymn, 'God of grace and God of glory / On Thy people pour Thy power,'" Daddy recalled, quoting the old classic. "'Grant us wisdom, grant us courage, for the facing of this hour.' I looked up and the sanctuary was slam full, no visitors that I could see—these were our people. The ushers had flat run out of bulletins. It was our folks who had come."

Everyone probably expected Dr. Proctor to deliver nostrums on race relations, but he didn't preach on race at all. Instead, he preached on Jacob wrestling with the angel. The only mention of race was in an opening story that Dr. Proctor deftly deployed in order to cross the chasm that lay before him that morning. He was the president of North Carolina A & T, he reminded them, and he faced a problem of enormous magnitude this morning. Everyone knew that, of course, and steeled themselves for an integrationist harangue.

"My football coach came in to see me the other day," Proctor said, "and he told me that the finest running back he had ever seen is down at New Bern, and his daddy and his brother both went to A & T. But when my coach went down there to recruit him, he says, the boy says he ain't coming to A & T, he is going to school over in Chapel Hill, going to play for the Tarheels. They've got the big school over there, and the big money, and he going to play for them. And then," Proctor said, "that poor man drove over to Kinston to see this three-hundred-pound defensive tackle they got at the Negro high school there, and he says he ain't coming to A & T, his mama wants him to play for N.C. State"—the other huge state school that had been all-white until just recently. "And after Coach finished complaining, you know, I just had to tell him, 'That's the problem with all this integration, Coach, that's just the price we're going to have to pay!'"

The congregation, divided just about evenly between UNC and N.C. State fans, roared with laughter. That was the last mention of race that morning—once he had vaulted the racial divide, Dr. Proctor didn't look back. And then the brilliant theologian proceeded to deliver the most elegant sermon on Jacob and the angel that you could ever want to hear.

When I met him after church, Dr. Proctor squatted to shake my hand, looking me in the eye as if I were a man and a brother. "Beautiful Sunday," Mama wrote that night. "The Lord has been with us. Had over 200 at church—good service. We are filled with God's joy and peace. Several of the opposed were truly converted at church. Dr. Proctor ate lunch with us." To get around the restaurant problem, we all enjoyed fried chicken and deviled eggs and all kinds of Methodist church dinner-on-the-grounds casseroles at Margie Mann's house; Margie, one of my father's favorite people, was not afraid of anything. All through lunch, I could not stop staring at this graceful brown-skinned man with the beautiful voice. He was almost as good as my daddy, I thought. In fact, he seemed a lot like my daddy, and that made me proud of both of them.

My father's lay leader, a wholesale grocery salesman named Carl, had come into Daddy's study in the middle of the controversy about Dr. Proctor. He'd been crying, too. It was that kind of year. When my father asked him why, he said, "I went to see one of my merchants this morning, and he said, 'Carl, you go up there to that church, don't you?' I said, 'Yeah, I go up there. I'm the lay leader.' And he said, 'Are you going to support your preacher having that nigger up there?' And I said, 'Yeah, I am going to support him.' And that merchant told me to get the hell out of his store and never to set foot in there again." Carl looked at my father and smiled through his tears. "Preacher," he said, "I've heard all my life about witnessing, but until this morning I didn't know a damn thing about it."

CHAPTER 5

KING JESUS AND DR. KING

IN THE BEGINNING, the Bible says, was the Word. And Oxford's leading man of the Word became my father's friend and ally as soon as we arrived. "You've got great gifts, Vernon," Thad Stem, Oxford, North Carolina's only known author, once told my daddy, "and people love you, too, even if you are a dupe of the international communist conspiracy." Thad grinned. There was a conspiracy, all right, and they were both members of it, but it had precious little assistance from Moscow or anywhere else, and could have held its meetings in a booth down at the Three-Way Diner. Not that Thad would have made a very good liberal crusader: "I really dig sharks," the poet once wrote, "because when they bite your goddamn head off, they never say it was for a good cause."

The ever-irascible Thad must have been around fifty when I met him. He had silver hair and wore black turtlenecks and blue jeans, tweed jackets and white Converse All-Stars, strange attire for a grown-up. (I had never heard of bohemians or intellectuals. There were only grown-ups and kids, near as I could tell, and I knew who was in charge. But this man seemed to belong to neither category.) Thad, who called himself "a militant, if not particularly sophisticated, New Dealer," soon visited Daddy's office regularly to rail against the "tithing racists" and "mealy-mouthed miscreants" who beset them both and to remind his new friend to keep the faith.

The real problem with most liberals and do-gooders in general, Thad thought, was that they were faint of will and fuzzy of purpose. "You're going to win if you don't weaken, Vernon," Thad liked to say, grinning at his preacher pal as he turned to leave. "Just stick to your guns and keep preaching like the angel Gabriel and kissing up on everybody's grandmama, and you're gonna win." And with that, our writer friend, who once signed a letter, "Thad Stem, Jr. If Not The Best Poet in Granville County, Certainly The Best On Gilliam Street," would take his ambling leave.

Our own pathway from Sanford, where Miss Amy and Dr. Proctor had rescued my father from his good intentions, to Oxford, where Thad gave us aid and comfort, ambled in its own way. Even though Miss Amy had won the day, and Dr. Proctor had mopped them up from the pulpit, Daddy had paid a price. "There's still so much talk about Vernon having Dr. Proctor here," Mama wrote a month later. "I hear a lot of catty remarks. Vernon seems a little discouraged, though he has not said it." But Daddy did not back off. On July 19, she observed, "Vernon preached a very good sermon on race relations but strong. I am so proud of him." Later that summer, my father confided in his diary, "Since February, I have had my most trouble-some time in the ministry. Some stopped giving to the church. Some stopped attending worship. One man moved his membership. I have tried to weather the storm, but the 'Dr. Proctor' episode has taken its toll."

Within a few months, however, the dust of battle settled and the landscape of victory became clear. Even though many people had been upset, in the end only one man actually left our church in Sanford over the race issue. "He was a tobacco farmer, hadn't really been in the church since I had been there," Daddy said, "but if I would show up in the fall after he'd sold tobacco, he would give me a check for two hundred dollars." When Daddy went to see him that fall, the farmer said he wasn't going to be a part of any church mixed up in that integration mess. But another woman, an unmarried schoolteacher, showed up at Daddy's study one day. "She told me, 'I know what this church is standing for in this community and I want to move my membership here,' " Daddy recalled. "And she did some church work and was a tither," he added, meaning that she gave 10 percent of her income to the church. Daddy grinned. "I traded a two-hundred-dollar farmer for a tithing schoolteacher."

More happiness arrived at the end of the Freedom Summer of 1964. On the morning of August 12, Mama "woke up having some pretty hard pains," she scribbled. "Got to hospital at 12:00. Our lovely little Julie born at 3:00. Am so happy to have another girl. Got along fine. Vernon sent red roses. We love each other so all is well." Though I am tempted to high-hat Daddy about this—my generation of fathers was expected to do a lot more than send flowers—I can't say I was paying much attention at the time. I was too absorbed in my duties as Daniel Boone, friend to the Indians and enemy to the redcoats, to pay very much attention to the arrival of a new sister. Daddy brought Vern and me to see Mama in the hospital, and Grandmother Jessie brought three-year-old Martha Buie. "She is so precious," Mama noted. Julie would be her last child, and somehow seemed a signal that the storm clouds had passed.

Daddy had not only weathered the gale over Dr. Proctor's visit; he had come out of it strong enough to build a new sanctuary and fill its pews. Curiously, he thought, no one had asked the bishop to move him away from Sanford. In fact, the bishop told him that his office had received a number of letters asking him to keep Daddy in his pulpit—probably from parishioners who assumed that our enemies would try to be rid of us. But apparently there was nothing to fear. "I am definitely returning to Sanford for my sixth year," Daddy noted in his diary in June 1966. "I am as happy in my ministry here as I ever hope to be. The longer I stay the more I appreciate this congregation."

Apparently the Lord had other plans.

One Sunday that fall, my father looked out over his congregation and noticed four or five strangers sitting together near the back of the church. After the service, they quietly let him know that they were the pastor-parish relations committee from the Oxford United Methodist Church, and that they were shopping urgently for a new minister.

Their previous minister—the Reverend Smith, as I shall call him—apparently had become spiritually and perhaps otherwise entangled with one of the more prominent women in his congregation. Counseling the good sister on matters of the Spirit, alas, Reverend Smith had wandered into the realm of the flesh. And the poor fool, intoxicated by love, had written Herself an amorous and wistful letter, which had fallen into the hands of her husband. Mr. Jones, as I shall call him, was a shopkeeper in a nearby town who sold, among other things, shotguns and pistols.

While Mr. Jones's response to the illicit overture is perfectly understandable, we should not rush to harsh judgment of the unfortunate pastor. Falling into such a dalliance, if that is what it was, is common enough among preachers to constitute a professional liability. Of course, not all hatters are mad, and not all preachers run off with the church organist. But ministers tend to be impassioned men of the Word, large of ego, expansive of spirit, persuasive by profession, and admired by their flocks. Their status and their gifts offer them many temptations, and theological training does not transform a man into an angel.

Preachers counsel with their congregants, more of them women than men, on personal matters and in intimate settings. People pour out their souls to the preacher, and attachments develop easily. And if a lonely woman hankers to have an affair, the minister is the safest object in town. The minister is one fellow whom a woman can be certain won't kiss and tell, since he is very likely to lose everything should the matter become public. As Martin Luther King Jr. himself wrote in his "Advice for Living" column in *Ebony* magazine, "almost every minister has the problem of confronting women in his congregation whose interests are not entirely spiritual." But if we should not be shocked that a man of the cloth can have feet of clay, neither should we expect Mr. Jones to have taken these mitigating factors into account when he found the minister's love letter among his wife's things.

Selecting a large and compelling revolver, Mr. Jones called upon the improvident parson, not so much to seek Divine guidance, but to

deliver a sermon of his own. His homily has come down to me ver-
batim, at least third-hand, and hence the language may be mere legend, though it carries the ring of veracity. "You sorry son of a bitch,"
the merchant is said to have said. "You have been loving up on my
wife." When impassioned denials were offered, Jones waved his text
for the morning, written in the minister's own hand, and lifted his
.357-magnum. "You Bible-thumping bastard," Jones continued. "You
are going to stay the hell away from my wife." On this point, the
brothers in Christ appeared to be reaching a spirit of unity. "And
there you are standing up in there in that pulpit, passing yourself off
as a man of God, lifting up prayers to the Lord, and then trying to
persuade a good woman to leave her husband."

Cocking the pistol and pressing the barrel against Reverend
Smith's forehead, Mr. Jones outlined the conditions under which the
improvident parson might live to preach another day. "This is my
church," the merchant said. "My mama went to this church, I was
baptized here, and I am not leaving. But if I go to church Sunday
morning and see you standing in that pulpit, I am going to kill you
right then and there. In fact," Jones asserted, "if you ever set foot in
that pulpit again, I am going to blow your brains out and watch you
bleed to death right there between the pulpit and the altar." After
prayerful consideration, the Reverend Smith decided it might be
time for him to take that late-summer vacation he had been consid-
ering. He spent the next week or two sleeping in a tent up near Kerr
Lake, slipping into town from time to time to help his own wife pack
their household belongings. It is hard to say, of course, whether or
not his impassioned parishioner would have carried out the threat,
but Reverend Smith lit out for parts unknown without offering
any final wisdom to his Oxford congregation except, perhaps, by
example.

And so the committee had come to see Vernon Tyson, a promising
minister whom they hoped to lure into the pulpit that Reverend
Smith had vacated so hastily. Daddy came highly recommended, the
Oxford pastor-parish relations committee told him, and now that they
had heard him preach they certainly understood why. Would he con-

sider moving to Oxford, if the bishop would send him? My father thanked them for coming but told them that he thought the Lord had called him to remain in Sanford.

The thing you have to understand about Daddy is that he wasn't just saying that stuff about the Lord. His God was a God who had a plan for your life, but who left you room to make your own mistakes. Your job was to watch for signs and to listen for guidance. What others might dismiss as the vagaries of fate, my father interpreted as dancing lessons from the Divine. Every step was part of a ballet too large for you to see it all, a provisional choreography perhaps not even intended for you to understand, and the key was to move into its rhythms with both humility and boldness, never mistaking yourself for the director. When he found himself in a car headed straight for Oxford a few days later, he felt a strong premonition that maybe the Lord had changed His mind. "Lord, I've got no business in Oxford, but I am here, and I am trying to cooperate with your leading," as he wrote in his diary later, recounting his prayer. "If you have any leadership for me, send someone who can guide me."

Daddy could literally inhale Oxford's history as he rolled into town that afternoon. The strong, sweet aroma of the world's finest cigarette tobacco filled his nostrils as he passed the wooden warehouses stacked with brightleaf gold. He drove past McCoy's Pool Hall and the Moonlight Cab Stand, where black men stood around on the corner, talking and telling jokes. At the center of town, in front of the courthouse, Daddy circled the bronze Confederate soldier in the middle of the intersection. Much like his comrades in nearly every town in the South, the old Rebel sentry had stood at the center of Oxford since 1909, when the Granville Grays chapter of the United Daughters of the Confederacy had erected the monument *To Our Confederate Dead*. Turning back at the monument, Daddy passed the Orpheum Theater, where black moviegoers were relegated to the segregated balcony.

On College Street, he drove past the gracious old homes that were their own kind of monument to Southern grace and tobacco money. Shaded with magnolias, maples, and dogwood trees, College

Street was picturesque in the antebellum style. Some houses looked like Tara in *Gone With the Wind*, with the white columns and brick walkways. More recent Victorian homes, with their wraparound porches, gingerbread woodwork, and beveled-glass windows, also lined the broad avenue. As Daddy passed the Oxford orphanage on the edge of town, he turned back through a more modest neighborhood and saw the dull orange bricks of Timothy Darling Presbyterian Church, where Reverend Roscoe "Rock" Walls preached the ancient faith to the grandchildren and great-grandchildren of slaves. And then he pulled up in front of Oxford United Methodist Church at the corner of McClanahan and College Streets.

Daddy got out of his car and paused beneath the stained-glass windows. Oxford Methodist was a beautiful old brick church. Some parts of the building were older than others, and the brick did not quite match up, so the administrative board had decided to paint the whole thing a dull red. Sandblasting would fix that, he thought to himself, and make this a truly pretty church, with its quaint slate roof and gracious shade trees. He had a compelling, almost overwhelming sense that the Lord was telling him to come here, even though it made no practical sense. "I don't know when I have ever heard the voice of God so clearly," he told me years later.

As Daddy stood in the churchyard wondering if he had really heard the Lord right, a car pulled up over the curb and parked in the grass right in front of the church office. A primly dressed woman stepped out of the car and started briskly inside. It was Frances Talton, the church secretary, although Vernon did not know that at the time. "Can I help you?" she asked, looking a bit uneasy. He explained who he was and told her that he had just come down to see the church. "There's nobody here," she stammered. "We don't have a preacher right now. And I don't like to come down here during the tobacco market, not without a preacher here. The whole town is full of nigger men and I just don't feel safe down here by myself."

That was why she had parked on the grass—she hadn't even wanted to walk the fifteen yards from the street to the office door, even in the middle of the afternoon. My father, who would have slapped one of his children into perdition for saying *that* word, did not scold the woman. His view was that you needed to have a relationship with someone before you could hope to change that person's habits, let alone her heart, and he wasn't even her minister yet. "I don't know why I came down here," she told him. "I just felt that I ought to come here." That was good enough for Daddy, who had no problem believing that God sends messengers, few of them angels.

By any conventional measure—size, salary, prospects, and so on—the church in Oxford was not quite as promising as our church in Sanford. But Daddy rattled down the highway home with the very strong sense that the Lord wanted him in Oxford. "It was as strong a sense of Divine guidance as I have ever felt about anything," he said. Ten days later we were unpacking boxes at 415 Hancock Street, Oxford, North Carolina.

Mr. Jones, the homicidal shopkeeper who had held a pistol to the head of the previous pastor, was out in the driveway with a posthole digger, putting up a basketball goal. Women from the church showed up with heaping platters of chicken, steaming casseroles, brimming pots of collard greens, and homemade pies—chocolate, lemon chess, and apple. After lunch, when Mama put away the leftovers, she discovered that they had stocked the refrigerator with bacon, eggs, bread, milk, and juice, so that she wouldn't have to go to the grocery store in the morning. And the neighbors came to greet us. I still remember Daddy and Thad Stem sitting on the back porch that first day, sipping coffee and telling each other stories. They were only having coffee, not whiskey—Daddy was a teetotaler, not a drinking man like Thad—but you'd have never known it to watch them throwing back their heads and laughing. That was the day that I first met Gerald Teel. Four years later, underneath that basketball goal, he would tell me that his father and his brothers had killed a black man.

We arrived in Oxford at a moment when African American freedom movements across the region had begun to galvanize black folks in Oxford to press harder for equal citizenship. There had been little in the way of visible victories, although the movement had begun stirring twenty-five years earlier. Resistance to white supremacy went back to slavery days, but the black South's longstanding protest traditions emerged full-blown during World War II because international politics gave black Americans fresh perspectives and new leverage. "The problem of the Negro in the United States is no longer a purely domestic question," A. Philip Randolph observed in 1943. "We have become the barometer of democracy to the colored peoples of the world."

African Americans wielded these contradictions as weapons in their own war on the home front. Randolph, a crucial link between the "New Negro" militants of the 1920s and 1930s, the civil rights generation of Martin Luther King Jr., and the Black Power rebels that followed, argued during World War II that there was "no difference between Hitler of Germany and Talmadge of Georgia or Tojo of Japan and Bilbo of Mississippi." NAACP membership grew nearly tenfold during the war years, and the number of branches tripled, three-quarters of the new branches arising in the South. CORE organized nonviolent direct-action campaigns against segregation in northern cities that laid the groundwork for its important Southern campaigns in the 1960s. Circulation of black newspapers increased by 40 percent during wartime, and the black press kept the pressure on the federal government by publicizing the widespread violence that occurred around military bases across the South.

These same tensions and transformations came to Granville County during the war. Camp Butner, a large training camp, brought thousands of black soldiers from across the country, many of them "not familiar with the laws and customs of this section," the editors of the *Oxford Public Ledger* complained. In fact, most of the black soldiers were quite familiar with the rules of segregation, but their refusal to obey them made enforcement "utterly impossible," officials at the North Carolina Utilities Commission protested in 1943. When white bus drivers attempted to enforce the segregation ordinances, black soldiers at Camp Butner overturned the buses. The Oxford Police Department purchased tear gas, riot equipment, and a tripod-mounted .50-caliber machine gun.

That machine gun came in handy one Saturday night in June

1944. A black private named Wilson stationed at Camp Butner had accompanied a fellow soldier into Oxford. Walking into a downtown café, the two black GIs asked for a beer. Told that there was no beer, Private Wilson tried to buy a package of Lucky Strike cigarettes. The white proprietor claimed that he told the black soldiers, "We only serve white patrons," an unlikely choice of words if I ever heard one. As Wilson and his comrade stalked out the door, one of them muttered that the proprietor was a "poor white son of a bitch." Chief of Police H. J. Jackson, who'd been eating meat loaf in one of the booths, ran outside, collared Private Wilson from behind, and clubbed him to the sidewalk with his pistol. Wilson's friend escaped back to Camp Butner while Chief Jackson dragged the black private to the jail in the basement at the rear of the courthouse.

Less than an hour later, sixty black men from Camp Butner launched what the Raleigh *News and Observer* called "an unsuccessful effort by a squad of Negro soldiers to storm the Oxford jail and release one of their number." Huddling in the shadow of the Confederate monument, the soldiers sent two representatives toward the double front doors of the courthouse to negotiate Private Wilson's release.

Chief Jackson met the two black soldiers on the steps, pistol-whipped one of them to the concrete, and jabbed the barrel of the gun hard into the face of the other. The two men retreated into the crowd of black enlisted men. Chief Jackson loudly ordered the troops to disperse, and police fired tear-gas grenades into the crowd, but the black soldiers decided to rush the courthouse doors. Swinging the doors wide, Assistant Chief J. L. Cash confronted the oncoming phalanx with the large, tripod-mounted machine gun Oxford had purchased "expressly for such a purpose," according to the *Oxford Public Ledger*. Only in the face of certain annihilation did the black soldiers scatter and flee, thus averting another tragedy of the kind that was all too common around Southern training camps during the war. Across the World War II–era South, dozens of black G.I.s died in uniform at the hands of their own countrymen.

Racial clashes, though frequent, did not entirely define the wartime experience in Granville County. During the war, a sewing room operated by the Works Progress Administration in Oxford quietly employed white and black women alike, and they worked side by side in apparent harmony. White men went before the county commission in 1941 to insist that the sewing room comply with the segregation statutes. The men insisted that the room be segregated, if only by having a curtain hung down its center. But the women who worked there enjoyed their subversive camaraderie. The white woman who supervised the sewing room firmly resisted the men's segregation proposal, arguing that the white women really did not mind and that the black women especially needed the work. Finally, the county commission let the matter drop. In an all-female space, "race mixing" did not threaten to become "amalgamation," apparently; in any case, the women simply would not comply.

After the war, local black veterans came home determined that the war for democracy abroad would expand democracy at home. Randolph Johnson and James Gregory, two black veterans, organized voter-registration drives in the late 1940s and early 1950s. Though some whites recognized the contradictions in denying the ballot to black men who had risked their lives for democracy, they remained silent. Black registration drives met with considerable resistance. "Out in the county," recalled Richard C. Shepard, a local black funeral home director, "you had to go to some of these stores to get registered. A lot of them was Klansmen, and they would give you the long way around to get registered." The black freedom movement had never confined itself to mere citizenship rights, however, but also sought to bolster a new black sense of self. Randolph Johnson, who had "nothing *but* brains," in the words of a former employer, not only tried to register votes but also broadcast a local weekly radio program entitled *Negroes in the News,* in which he featured both local and national achievements by African Americans. Like the Black Power militants who came afterward, black World War II veterans struggled against internalized white supremacy, defeatism, and apathy in their own communities.

During the late 1950s and early 1960s, black churchwomen in

Oxford rallied against that apathy in a series of church meetings and soon affiliated themselves with the Southern Christian Leadership Conference led by Martin Luther King Jr. Elizabeth Chavis, Helen Amis, and quite a few others met regularly and supported the movement in Oxford and across North Carolina. "They believed in the civil rights," SCLC field secretary Golden Frinks recalled. "Some of them had come out, had gone to other demonstrations in places like Ayden and Edenton, had come way down there in eastern North Carolina, wherever we was needing them to demonstrate or cook or whatever needed doing. Elizabeth Chavis was very strong. These were some strong women."

Young black people in Oxford also responded to news of the growing movement in the South. "Yeah, we was listening to TV, that's how we got involved in the first sit-ins in Oxford, because we saw on TV they was doing it up in Greensboro," Eddie McCoy recalled. Soon afterward, he and two friends went to a local department store and sat down at the segregated counter. "We told them we wanted to be served," he said, "but they didn't pay no attention to you. And we said again we wanted to be served, and they said we don't serve no niggers here.

"The funny thing," McCoy continued, "is that if they had served us, we didn't have no money. If it had been fifty cents, we would have been in trouble." McCoy and his friends knew that the police would arrive soon. "We even knew who would come," McCoy recounted. "They gonna send Nathan White. He's one of those white guys that's like a diplomat, he want to work with everybody, he don't mean no harm, that's just his nature." The police officer's response was classic small-town South. "When he come in he looked at us and asked who our parents are," McCoy said, "and then we told him, and that rang a bell, so he said come on outside and work this thing out." They walked out to the sidewalk, where White told the young men to go home and warned that he would contact their parents, whereupon they left. "But when we went back again, they decided they just didn't serve anything in the afternoon to anybody. They started taking up the stools."

Soon afterward, a group of young black high school athletes in Oxford organized a sit-in at Herring's Drugstore, right next door to the barbershop where Robert Teel worked. After asking to be served, the young black men were shocked to see the white proprietor quietly drop their hamburgers onto the flat grill and their french fries into the deep-fat fryer. Again, McCoy wondered how they would pay for the food if the manager actually served them. But as they sat watching their lunch sizzling on the grill and wondering what might happen, the proprietor made a short series of telephone calls. "We knew damn well he wasn't calling up people to tell them he done seen the light of integration," McCoy laughed. A large group of Klansmen began to arrive in the drugstore and gather around the seated young men, making menacing remarks. "They was getting ready to flat kick our ass," said McCoy, who told his teammates that when he gave the signal, they should all dash out the door. As they fled, the white men gave chase.

Most of the young black men easily outran their pursuers, but James Lyons found himself cornered in an alley and was forced to take cover in the back entrance to the Oxford Police Department. Needless to say, in 1960 this was not widely considered a safe haven for black revolutionaries. As Lyons careened through the back door, he lost his footing and landed at the feet of the desk officer, panting, "Please don't let them kill me, please don't let them kill me." In seconds, the mob crowded into the room around the prostrate young black man. The police officer began kicking and stomping Lyons in full view of the crowd, but using the flat side of his foot and making only light contact; even at that terrifying moment, the young black man realized that the officer was putting on a show for the crowd so that they would not kill him. "Y'all go on, now," the white cop told the angry mob, kicking the fallen black man again. "I can take care of this black bastard." When the men had all filed out the back door, the policeman looked down at Lyons and spat, "I ought to have let them kill you." Such was the strange debut of nonviolent direct action in Granville County, North Carolina.

James Lyons, Eddie McCoy, and quite a few of the other young

African American men joined the sporadic campaigns of picketing and boycotting against segregated businesses in downtown Oxford in the early 1960s. In fact, their efforts closed the lunch counters for a time. "We shut down the lunch counters," McCoy said. "And we was happy with that. Everybody was treated equal." In the wake of that limited success, a group of the young men tried to desegregate the Orpheum Theater and the police took them into the alley and beat them with nightsticks. "I knew that won't gon' work," McCoy recalled. "It's an alley, blacks had go down the alley to go upstairs. Whites went in the front door. But when my friends bought tickets and tried to go in like the white people, the police came and beat them up."

But the young men were not alone. Local women of their mothers' generation formed the backbone of the early movement in Oxford. "Ben Chavis's mama, Mrs. Elizabeth Chavis, she got out there, and her sister Eunice and all of them, and her other sister Helen, and some of their friends, they was up on it," Golden Frinks recalled. "They was up on what was happening." These movements, which were not directly linked to efforts by national organizations like the SCLC and the Student Nonviolent Coordinating Committee (SNCC), met with occasional and sometimes temporary success. In June 1963, inspired by the SCLC's campaign in Birmingham, hundreds of black citizens in Oxford took to the streets in a series of protests aimed at segregation at local restaurants, lunch counters, and the Orpheum Theater. Many of the demonstrators confronted violence at the hands of local whites, including the Oxford Police Department. When the police attacked protestors in 1963, blacks fought them in the streets and the demonstration "became a riot," according to a report from the governor's office.

Tom Ragland, the city manager of Oxford and a lifelong resident, considered his hometown fairly typical. "Oxford was like most Southern towns in 1963 and 1964," he said a few years later. "We had demonstrations and boycotts by the Negroes against segregation in stores, restaurants, theaters. We set up a Human Relations Commission to try and set up some communication between the races. And I think there was some communication." The problem, of course, was that white Southerners may have needed "communication" as a way of congratulating themselves on their paternalistic generosity toward "the Negro," but black Southerners needed what amounted to a whole new social structure, one that did not stigmatize and impoverish them. "We had changed it some," Eddie McCoy reflected. "But then they messed it up and went back to how it was. They just went back to the old ways again."

Whether or not there had been any real "communication," the local Good Neighbor Council, the Bi-Racial Commission, and the Human Relations Council—it is hard to distinguish among these overlapping and evanescent committees—accomplished almost nothing. The Good Neighbor Council, with four black and four white members, focused on creating jobs for blacks, but managed to come up with less than a dozen. The Bi-Racial Commission, with five whites and five blacks, approached one hotel and three motels, asking them to drop the color bar; the establishments agreed to integrate, but withdrew their commitments when demonstrations failed to cease immediately. One drive-in restaurant undertook a thirty-day trial period of integration but discontinued the process after two days; three other drive-ins committed to thirty-day trials that never even began. None of the sit-down restaurants in Oxford would consider opening their doors to black customers. Segregation persisted not only at restaurants and hotels, but also in the local hospitals, the all-white chamber of commerce, and the all-white Merchants Association. So much for committees.

On our first Race Relations Sunday in Oxford, Daddy invited the head of the state Good Neighbor Council, Dr. David Coltrane, to speak at our church. Thad was not impressed. Coltrane was a distinguished gray-haired financier who worked for Governor Terry Sanford, the most progressive white liberal politician in the South. Coltrane traveled the state, putting out political fires and making pleasant noises about "good race relations" while trying not to rub anybody the wrong way. A moderate by temperament and inclination, Coltrane tended to stress the importance of "communication" between the races, as if slavery and segregation had been some terrible misunderstanding. The "race problem," his calm words suggested, could be solved if the right people were on the committee. "Best damn sermon I ever heard in this church," Thad whispered playfully as he walked past Daddy on his way.

In fact, according to Daddy, Coltrane's complacent pronouncements about racial "progress" troubled Thad deeply. That night, Coltrane spoke again at Methodist Men; Thad didn't show up. At about nine-thirty, my father cut out the lights in the fellowship hall and headed home. Driving down College Street toward the monument, Daddy saw Thad shuffling down the sidewalk. It was February and a little nippy, and Daddy stopped to offer him a ride home.

"Where you been this evening, Preacher?" Thad asked, getting into the Pontiac. Daddy could smell the whiskey.

"I've been down at Methodist Men," Daddy replied, still delighted with the evening. "You should have come, Thad. Dave Coltrane had a good word for us, and the Methodist Women served pecan pie."

"He ain't nothing but a damn fool," Thad growled, shaking his head. "Terry Sanford, Dave Coltrane, and all them political do-gooders are off on another fool's errand. What he and all the rest of them need to understand is that we were wrong about the Negroes, and I don't mean mistaken. I mean we were wrong, as wrong as David was when he sent Uriah off to be killed so he could take Bathsheba for himself, and there ain't a committee or a commission in the world that is going to change that. We're about three hundred years late for the goddamn 'Good Neighbor Council.' " The two men rode home for three blocks of awkward silence, and my father dropped Thad off in front of his house.

Daddy went home, got out of his suit and tie, and read the newspaper at the kitchen table in his underwear by himself. Everyone else was already asleep. At around eleven o'clock he went upstairs and crawled into bed beside my mother. Just as he started to close his eyes, Daddy heard a knock on the front door. Putting on his old purple bathrobe, Daddy clambered back down the stairs and opened the front door. There stood Thad Stem. "Come in, Thad, come on in," Daddy said.

"No, I won't come in, thanks," Thad said.

"What is it, Thad?" my father asked. "What's wrong?"

"I'm the damn fool," Thad muttered. "The truth is, *I'm* the damn fool. Good night, Preacher." And then Oxford's illustrious man of letters turned and headed back out into the night.

Thad still lived on the street where he was born, and wrote his books in a dusty office above Hall's Drugstore. He was the prodigal son of the late Major Thaddeus Stem, a lawyer and then judge who had been an almost legendary figure in the state's Democratic Party. He taught me, with his unforgettable stories, that the poet and the preacher—if they're both doing their jobs—are only working different sides of the same street, even if Thad was pretty sure that his side was more fun.

Educated at Duke University, Thaddeus Garland Stem Jr. came home from postgraduate wanderings in Florida in the late 1930s and gave himself to the serious pursuit of whiskey and women and verse. Although he held a sinecure as the Veterans Administration representative in Oxford, which occupied him for two or three hours a week, he spent the rest of his hours reading and writing. His regular "Rock Wall Editorial" for the Raleigh *News and Observer* was renowned for many years for its erudition and wit. He published two novels and a whole shelf of poetry.

The self-appointed singer of rainstorms and pretty girls on bicycles, Thad had taken Chesterton's advice to learn to love the world without trusting it. He detested sham and loved flowers; Thad would have plowed up his lovely yard and planted corn before he'd let the Junior League's "Yard of the Month" sign pop up on his property. Thad was proud of his position on the margins of small-town Southern life. Asked to join anything, Thad always gave the same reply. "I don't belong to but two things," he'd say, "the Methodist

Church and the Democratic Party, and I am thinking about quitting both of 'em."

Thad inherited at least some of his racial progressivism from his father, Major Stem, an unlikely egalitarian, who died the year I was born. Back in the 1930s, when Thad was a teenager, Major Stem was leaving Hall's Drugstore with his son and they passed Mrs. G. C. Shaw, the wife of the principal at Mary Potter High, the local Negro high school. "Good afternoon, Mrs. Shaw," the major said, tipping his hat.

A local white bootlegger, idling under the store awning, accosted Major Stem. "Why'd you call that damned nigger woman 'Mrs. Shaw'?" he demanded. In those days, white Southerners did not use courtesy titles for their black neighbors. While it was permissible to call a favored black man "Uncle" or "Professor"—a mixture of affection and mockery—he must never hear the words "mister" or "sir." Black women were "girls" until they were old enough to be called "auntie," but they could never hear a white person, regardless of age, address them as "Mrs." or "Miss" or "Ma'am." But Major Stem made his own rules.

"Well, Mrs. Shaw's older than I am," he began softly. "She's better educated than I am, and she has more money." Then, thrusting the bootlegger away from him, the major exploded: "But more to the point, what I call Mrs. Shaw is none of your goddamned business, you low-life taxidermist, you two-for-a-nickel jackal, you knee-crawling son of a bitch, net." These were the days when people really knew how to cuss.

Back then, the appendage "net" meant a *real* son of a bitch, doubled and in spades. Thad knew that, and he understood what the rest of the words meant, but on the way home he asked his father why on earth he had called the bootlegger a "taxidermist." The major said quietly that a taxidermist is a man who mounts animals. Thad told me it took him about five years to figure that one out, and he reckoned the bootlegger never did. In any case, whether it was nature or nurture, Thad clearly acquired some of his father's freethinking ways.

Raised on the concept of original sin, too, Thad knew that human beings not only *had* problems but *were* problems. What was different about Thad was that he did not permit his pessimism about human possibility to translate into an easy defense of the status quo. Things *could* be done, and ought to be done to make the world work better. But Thad could never be persuaded, however, that any amount of reform or education would ring in the Kingdom of Heaven here on earth. One day he was strolling down Front Street and came to a group of sweaty workmen leaning on their picks and shovels under a shade tree, taking a break from their toil. They had removed several slabs of sidewalk and had dug a deep trench, which Thad was stepping around when he spoke.

"That is a right good-sized hole you're digging, brethren," he said, smiling as he stepped past them.

"Yeah," one of the workmen replied. "We're digging a hole big enough so we can bury every sorry sumbitch in Oxford."

"Who's going to be left to cover us all up?" Thad responded.

Renegade though he was, Thad had a full set of keys to the library at Duke University, that great seat of learning forty miles south of Oxford, down the Jefferson Davis Highway. If he got curious about something, he would get in the car and ride down there, day or night, and roam the stacks. Thad would quote Cicero, Browning, Wilde, Housman, Frost, and Whitman as though he'd run into them at Hall's Drugstore that morning on his way to work. Listeners unfamiliar with the poetry of Edna St. Vincent Millay might have adjudged by Thad's tone of voice that he was dating her. He could rattle off Lord Tennyson's "Ulysses" faster than a cat licks cream.

His own words ambled in the salty, succulent patois of Southern courthouses and roadside taverns of a distant day, before television had drained the life out of regional dialect, back when people told stories to pass their evenings. One local politician "wasn't worth hell room in August," Thad would growl. "Anybody could take a Barlow knife and a wooden shingle and fashion a better specimen of humanity." One of my father's fellow preachers in Oxford was a man of some vanity and bombast. "The sumbitch sends his mama a congratulatory telegram every year on his own birthday," Thad would say whenever the good reverend's name came up. "He is the only man I ever saw who can strut sitting down."

Thad had strong views about liquor—that is, he held a solemn conviction that there were only two occasions when drinking was appropriate: one, when a fellow was thirsty, obviously, and, two, when he wasn't, as a preventative measure. Thad loved Jack Daniel's sour mash whiskey and made no secret of it, though he certainly was not what people used to call "the town drunk," as if it were an elected position and singular, too. It is true, however, that Thad's last will and testament stipulated that "good liquor" be served after his funeral. And he loved to quote a bit of doggerel that he attributed to Dean Samuel Fox Mordecai: "Not drunk is he who from the floor / Can rise again and drink once more. / But drunk is he who prostrate lies / Without the will to drink or rise."

Most of Thad's intoxication stemmed from the English language. He was literally a man of letters, and the archives in North Carolina are jeweled with his hilarious and insightful correspondence. When a man from Bunnlevel wrote to Thad in the late 1950s to ask advice about his own "poetry career" and to find out "how one goes about getting the most from a poem financially," the salty writer replied that "the Deity probably knows, but I am not aware that He has told any poet." Stem's advice reveals both his joy in his work and his sense of isolation in Oxford. "I suppose," he wrote, "that only a damn fool is a poet. God knows, he will be personally misjudged, socially mismatched, virtually unpaid, and worse than all of that misquoted." Stem wondered whether his questioner had the "guts" to be "lonesome, out of step, often out of tune and soon out of time. Can you look the world in the teeth and tell it to go to hell and continue to stitch the dawn with gleaming words as if doing so is the only decent thing left in the world?"

Poetry did not pay, Thad regretted to tell his correspondent, and it was hard work, too. "If you subsequently improve upon the Psalms and upon *Leaves of Grass* you will still need a paying job," Thad told him. "And if poetry isn't as thrilling as making love—that is, if it can

be successfully replaced with anything else, give it up." He realized
that he had been discouraging, Thad added, but the rewards of the
writing life for those crazy enough and disciplined enough to follow
it were immense: "I have never been a Kipling adherent, but if you
do what I have told you, you will be a MAN, and what Ike, or Billy
Graham, or Mr. Du Pont think about it will not matter a two-penny
damn."

That self-willed style of manhood was one important thing that
Daddy shared with Thad, although the preacher was inevitably more
politic than the poet. In between his periodic assaults on their sense
of racial superiority, Daddy took such good care of his flock's families
and delivered such soul-soothing sermons that many of them were
inclined to overlook his race-traitor tendencies. In response to the
inevitable "n-lover" epithet, I recall hearing him telling a hostile
caller, "Yes, I guess you've got a point there, because I do *try* to love
everybody." Thad probably would have added "even stupid
sumbitches like you." But Daddy was more patient, and rarely
showed anger toward his adversaries, even though he had inherited
a full measure of the Tyson temper. He held his ground like a sweet-
gum stump, trying hard to live in a spirit of love and action, not anger
and reaction. Oxford might be a little spiritually arid, but Daddy
wasn't drawing his water from an empty well.

He went back to the well in 1967 and once again invited a black
preacher into his pulpit, thinking that things had probably eased up
a little since the Dr. Proctor episode in Sanford. He had survived that
one and, after the waves of race riots in the intervening years, Daddy
probably figured that a black man in the pulpit would not seem so
revolutionary. In any case, when Daddy told Eli Regan, his powerful
lay leader, that he was planning to invite Reverend Gil Gillespie, a
noted black Methodist preacher, to deliver a sermon at our church,
Regan asked why Daddy wanted to do a thing like that. Racism was
an important moral issue, Daddy replied, an issue that the church
needed to confront. Putting a black man in a position of honor and
authority in front of a white congregation was a good thing, and if

there was controversy over it, that was not a bad thing, either. People needed to work through these things, and not just in the abstract.

The wizened old conservative responded that he didn't think racism was a problem in our church at all, that he'd never heard anything that suggested any antipathy toward "our nigrah brothers and sisters." Had Vernon asked anyone on the administrative board whether they thought this was a good idea? No, Daddy told him, the Methodist *Book of Discipline* stated clearly that the minister shall determine the number and nature of services. And he didn't need to take a poll to know how people felt about these things. Nor did he think that a minister was bound by the principle of majority rule in all cases. Did the preacher mind, Regan wanted to know, if he asked around a little bit? Daddy told his lay leader that he didn't mind him asking around, as long as Regan understood that as a preacher he had to do what the Lord called him to do.

Regan dropped by the office the following day. "Vernon, you've only been here a year and you know us better than we know ourselves," he said. "I asked almost everyone on the administrative board, and you don't have one bit of support for bringing in that nigrah preacher. I don't think you have one vote, if it came to that," Regan said. For a moment, it seemed as though the conservative elder was preparing to warn Daddy not to invite Reverend Gillespie to speak. "We need him a lot worse than I thought we did," Regan went on. "You bring him on. And don't you back down on it, either. I'm not going to say a damn word about it unless you get in trouble," he said. "I might even oppose you a little bit. But if they come after you, they'll have to come through me first." And then the red-faced old man winked at him and ambled out the door and back down to the orphanage.

When the news of Reverend Gillespie's coming filtered out to the congregation, there was a fair amount of low grumbling, but nothing approaching the protests in Sanford before Dr. Proctor came. And while Reverend Gillespie never became a nationally known orator and intellectual like Dr. Proctor, he was steeped in a black Southern homiletic tradition and was one hell of a preacher. Reverend Gillespie had all the traditional strengths and the polish of a good education, too, and a smile that would melt glass. His personality was so forceful, as folks back home say, that if he'd drowned in the river, folks would have looked for the body upstream. He was the genuine article, a first-class, grade A "pulpit peacock," as my father and his five preacher brothers would put it.

WOXF routinely broadcast my father's sermons locally, so that shut-ins, the elderly, and those members whose Sunday morning could not transcend their Saturday night could hear the Word nonetheless. That morning, Daddy hadn't notified WOXF that he would not be preaching. And so when Reverend Gillespie climbed into the pulpit, he was unfurling his words not merely for the white congregation in front of him, but for all of Granville County. Otto von Bismarck had a point when he warned the Reichstag that conquering armies were not halted by the power of eloquence, but he had never heard Gil Gillespie. That morning, my father's controversial guest was like the minister who, as the poet Richard Baxter once wrote, "preached as never to preach again, and as a dying man to dying men." Gillespie simply mesmerized everyone in the congregation and, for all we knew, everyone in the county who had a radio.

Daddy's most implacable adversary on the question of inviting Reverend Gillespie had come to Sunday school earlier that morning. But the fellow made a point of letting my father know that, as "a matter of principle," he was not staying for the eleven o'clock worship service. The next week, however, the man dropped by the church office with a confession. "Vernon," he laughed, "I started on home, but I reckon I have more curiosity than I do principles, because I could not keep myself from turning on the radio in my car just to see what the man was going to say." As he drove along, the fellow told Daddy, he became more and more intrigued by the sermon and almost forgot who was giving it. "When I got to the house," he said, "I couldn't get out of the car because he was still going at it. My wife just brought me out a sandwich and laughed at me." The man threw back his head and squealed at his own silliness. "I'll tell you, Vernon," he said, "the longer that feller preached, the whiter he got."

Even though Reverend Gillespie's 1967 visit caused less trouble for my father than Dr. Proctor's had in 1964, it would be a mistake to assume that the racial chasm in American life had narrowed. In fact, few white people, North or South, were comfortable with the notion of racial equality in the early 1960s, and the victories that black Southerners finally won—the Civil Rights Act of 1964 and the Voting Rights Act of 1965, principally—recruited legions of opponents. As the Democrats increasingly became identified with the black freedom movement, white Southerners poured out of the party. Senator Josiah Bailey of North Carolina had predicted this thirty years earlier as he'd filibustered against a 1938 anti-lynching bill: if national Democrats "come down to North Carolina and try to impose your will upon us about the Negro, so help me God, you are going to learn a lesson which no political party will ever again forget."

Bailey's prophecy came true. In the presidential election of 1964, five states from "the Solid South" went to the Republican candidate, Barry Goldwater, who had opposed the Civil Rights Act of 1964; Republican organizers in Dixie traded almost exclusively in racial fear and white resentment. Political developments in the North reflected the same racial impetus; in the Democratic primaries of 1964, a third of the Democrats in Wisconsin and Indiana voted for Alabama's Governor George Wallace, the bellowing, slick-haired icon of Southern white supremacy. That summer when President Lyndon Johnson signed the Civil Rights Act of 1964, he is said to have handed a souvenir pen to aide Bill Moyers, remarking, "Bill, I think we just gave the South to the Republican Party for your lifetime and mine." Johnson turned out to be an optimist. Two traditional Democratic constituencies, white Southerners in Dixie and "white ethnics" in the northern suburbs, now stampeded out of the Democratic Party, launching an enduring and racially driven realignment in American politics that would eventually put determined opponents of the early 1960s freedom movement into the highest offices in the land.

It is important to note that the "white backlash" that fueled this realignment, fed Richard Nixon's "Southern strategy," and created the Republican Party of Strom Thurmond, Jesse Helms, Trent Lott, and Newt Gingrich began with the Civil Rights Act of 1964, not the riots of the late 1960s. The reaction against the African American freedom movement began much earlier, and rejected not only black militancy but also simple justice. National opinion polls taken in 1963, only weeks after Dr. King told America about his dream "that one day on the red hills of Georgia, the sons of former slaves and the sons of former slave owners will be able to sit down together at the table of brotherhood," documented that "anti-Negro prejudice is widespread and deeply rooted in the U.S., extending to the vast majority of ordinary, well-meaning Americans" in all parts of the country. In truth, Dr. King had many admirers, but he was also one of the most widely and deeply hated men in the United States.

The sugar-coated confections that pass for the popular history of the civil rights movement offer outright lies about most white Americans' responses to the freedom movement instead of reminding us how profoundly it challenged American practices of justice and democracy. No one, in the rosy glow of our hindsight, was opposed to this movement except potbellied, tobacco-chewing racist rednecks in Mississippi. And thank God for the federal government, who in these fantasies rode over the hill like the cavalry to iron out these little difficulties on the frontier of American society. Polling data revealed that the majority of white Americans *in 1963*, prior to the Civil Rights and Voting Rights Acts, believed that the movement for racial equality had already proceeded "too far and too fast." North and south, whites avoided social contact with black people and strongly objected to integrated housing and schools. Agents for the Federal Bureau of Investigation, hearing Dr. King's dream of racial reconciliation and equal citizenship, launched a calculated effort to destroy King's personal life and tried to blackmail the eloquent young preacher into committing suicide.

While most Americans would not have approved of the FBI's secret campaign to bring about King's suicide, we should not forget that comparatively few of them applauded Dr. King while he lived. In the years since his murder, we have transformed King into a kind of innocuous black Santa Claus, genial and vacant, a benign vessel that can be filled with whatever generic good wishes the occasion dictates. Politicians who oppose everything King worked for now jostle their way onto podiums to honor his memory. Many of them quote Dr. King out of context as they denounce "affirmative action," despite the fact that King repeatedly, publicly, and passionately supported that principle. In his 1964 book, *Why We Can't Wait,* King called for "compensatory consideration for the handicaps [American Negroes] have inherited from the past. It is impossible to create a formula for the future which does not take into account that our society has been doing something special *against* the Negro for hundreds of years." But our memories about what actually happened in the civil rights era are so faulty that Dr. King's enemies can safely use his words to thwart his goals.

There remains no place in American memory for the economic vision of King, who said in 1957, "I never intend to accommodate myself to the tragic inequalities of an economic system which takes necessities from the many in order to give luxuries to the few." Not many people today recall the King who died in an attempt to organize the downtrodden of America into a nonviolent revolution to take political and economic power from the rich. "We are called upon to raise certain basic questions about the whole society," King declared just before his assassination. "We must recognize that we can't solve our problem now until there is a radical redistribution of economic and political power." The radicalism of Dr. King's thought, the militancy of his methods, and the rebuke that he offered to American capitalism have given way to depictions of a man who never existed, caricatures invented after his death. The real Martin Luther King Jr. went to Memphis in 1968 calling for "the dispossessed of our nation" to "organize a revolution." There he told the nation that "the whole structure of American life must be changed"—just before somebody killed him.

The assassination of Dr. King set off a racial crisis across the nation that spread into our church. "You can't have it here," the man snapped at my father as we walked toward his study at the church on Sunday morning. "This is *our* church, and you cannot have it here. This ain't your church, Vernon, this is our church. And I am telling you right now, you ain't having no Martin Luther King service in our church." As the door to the small room swung open, I could see that Daddy's office was literally full of angry men. The pastor's study couldn't have been much more than fifteen feet square, and there were about twenty-five men packed in there. We could hardly get in the door for all the red-faced men in their Sunday suits. And I had never heard anyone address my father in that tone of voice.

"Little Buck," my father said, turning the broad barrel of his body to face me, "you run on up to Sunday school now. Your mother will be along to get you before church." I turned and scampered down the hall into the education building and then upstairs to my class. I don't remember being worried in the least about the men in Daddy's study. I knew that something odd was going on, but I figured it had to be some kind of misunderstanding among grown-ups. Everybody loved my father, for one thing, besides which nobody in their right mind would attack *my* daddy in a small room with only two dozen men.

Daddy hadn't been expecting anyone to find out about the memorial service until he announced it at church that morning. Dr. King had been killed on Thursday in Memphis. More than a hundred cities had exploded overnight into the flames King had worked so hard to forestall. Rioters and revolutionaries set more than seven hundred fires in the nation's capital alone. Army units in full combat gear took battle positions around the White House and ringed the Capitol building with machine-gun nests. Into the weekend, violent clashes occurred in cities and towns across the country, including rock throwing and street fights in our own little town. Saturday, as the smoke from the riots lingered from sea to shining sea, black and white ministers from Oxford convened an emergency meeting in my father's small study.

The preachers quickly agreed that there should be an interracial memorial service for Dr. King the following day, Sunday afternoon, at five o'clock. White people weren't going to attend a black church, it seemed pretty clear, and it appeared pointless to have an all-black service, given that their purpose was to nurture some sense of community across racial lines. But any white preacher who sponsored a memorial service for Dr. King was putting his job on the line. "The Baptist minister said, 'Well, we sure can't have it at my place. I have a Board of Deacons, and they'd have to approve it, and I don't think I'd get a single vote,' " Daddy recalled.

"And finally I pulled the *Book of Discipline* down, and looked it up. So I said, 'The book says I have the authority to do this, and I want to invite you all to come and meet here.' " The ministers agreed to meet there at Oxford United Methodist Church the next afternoon at five, and to say nothing about it until the following morning at church. They would announce the five o'clock memorial service for Dr. King simultaneously, at the eleven o'clock morning worship service. That way the opposition would have little time to mobilize.

The roomful of indignant men that met us the next morning clearly revealed that someone had failed to keep the agreement. "This ain't your church, Vernon, it's our church," the spokesman repeated. "You can't have a church full of niggers in here. This is our church." An angry clamor of assent echoed around the cool, white plaster of the walls lined with books, and now also lined with churchmen young and old. Eli Regan stood silently near the back, letting this younger fellow do the talking.

"The last time I checked, it was God's church," my father replied. "I think it probably still is." He made his way around the desk and took the robe that his daddy had given him off the coat rack. Nestling it around his shoulders, he straightened his tie in the small mirror in the corner and ran a comb through his hair.

"Well, you can say whatever you want, Vernon, but you can't do it," the man replied. "You are not having any damn Martin Luther King service in our church, and that's a fact. You can't do it. We're not going to let you do it. So you may as well get on the telephone right now and tell them it is not happening in our church."

My father again plucked his copy of the Methodist *Book of Discipline* from the shelf behind his desk, opening it to the page he had marked the day before. "I don't mean to be arrogant, you understand," Daddy said, "and I understand that you're not happy about it, I hear that, and I am not saying that you have to come to the service. But we're all Methodists here, and part of that is having methods, you might say, for doing certain things. This book lists them, and it says right here"—he opened to the page, holding the book out toward his interrogator—"that the pastor of this church can determine the number and nature of services held in the sanctuary. And for the moment, at least, I believe I am still the pastor of this church." He scribbled a number on the back of his business card and handed it to the speechless spokesman. "And here's the bishop's phone number. If he says I am not the pastor of this church, I can't do it. Otherwise, I plan to proceed."

Daddy started rummaging through his satchel for his sermon notes. There was a stunned silence. Nobody knew quite what to do or say. The study was so packed that it was literally hard for the men to leave. But Eli Regan shuffled around to the front of Daddy's desk, stepping in front of the man who had been speaking. Regan was probably as conservative a man as you could have found in the state of North Carolina, and he spoke with great authority in this group as the lay leader and as one of the senior men in the church. "Well, Preacher," he said, "I have two things to say about all this. The first thing is that I believe in my heart that Martin Luther King is the worst enemy that America has had in my lifetime—the very worst. You don't think so, but that's what I think, and I think most of these men agree with me." There were nods of assent all around the small room. "And the second thing I want to tell you," Regan continued, "is that if anybody in this room knocks you down, Preacher, I'm gonna pick you back up again. You're still *my* preacher."

"That's all it took," my father recalled. "They all left, and nothing else was said about it." Half an hour later, Daddy announced from his pulpit that there would be a community-wide memorial service in honor of Dr. Martin Luther King Jr. at the church at five o'clock that evening. When the hour came, people attended from all over the county. "The people came interracially, more folks from the black churches than from our church, maybe, but some of our folks, too, and they filled up that sanctuary that afternoon," he recalled. "We had everyone sign a registry that we mailed to Mrs. Coretta Scott King, along with a program from the service."

Despite the Martin Luther King Jr. Day celebrations we now hold nationally every January, many white people at the time celebrated the murder of Dr. King. Ronald Reagan, then governor of California, blamed Dr. King's assassination on King himself and the politics of nonviolent direct action, calling it "a great tragedy that began when we started compromising with law and order, and people started choosing which laws they'd break." Reagan also suggested that the murder was probably committed by antiwar protestors, who "will do anything to further their own ends." But hundreds of churches across the nation held services similar to the one at our church, mourning a loss so deep as to defy easy assessment, even at a distance of decades. And I would wager that Eli Regan was one of the very few ushers at any of those services in the spring of 1968 who had favored Strom Thurmond for president in 1948 and was fixing to vote for George Wallace that coming fall. Richard Wright wrote of black Southerners in the Jim Crow era that other Americans "think you know us, but our history is far stranger than you suspect, and we are not what we seem." He could have just as easily been talking about all of us.

THE KING ASSASSINATION also marked my experiences of race in an indelible way. In the year or so leading up to his killing, with direct exposure to black children at school—even if there were only two of them—I began to notice and confront my own received assumptions that white people were somehow better than black people. It wasn't that I had been taught that explicitly, mind you—my parents *told* me quite the opposite—and yet white supremacy was like the water and we were like the fish, and of course we were all drenched to the skin. All the social signposts of American life taught me that white people were superior in some vague and undefined way, but my particular world instructed me that nice white people must try to help blacks become more like white people. The astonishing arrogance and ignorance of these assumptions would be funny if those attitudes were not still fairly prevalent. The truth is, I was probably more fortunate than most. When I study old photographs of Klan rallies now, I find my eyes turning to the children in the pictures, and wondering what they think about all that stuff today.

When I ponder the origins of that ingrained sense of white supremacy that I found inside myself, I have to consider the fact that nearly all of the African Americans with whom I had intimate contact were servants. I never once saw a white grown-up who did house-work or yard work for a living; black adults who performed those labors worked at houses all around me. I knew, of course, that there were other black people—college presidents, funeral directors, educators, and so on. I saw such people from time to time, carrying out their warm but somewhat formal dealings with my father, whom they seemed to regard with great affection. Dr. Proctor had dined with us, and Reverend James Hampton, an easygoing black preacher in Sanford, sometimes enjoyed a sandwich with Daddy at the house while they talked about local civil rights politics. But I never saw any real degree of ease with any of the other black people in our lives—except the African American women who worked in our house.

For readers born later or elsewhere, it may come as a surprise to know that even white people of modest means employed black household help in the South where I grew up. In large measure, this reflected a racial and gender caste system that denied most other opportunities to African American women. That system was designed to ensure a ready supply of cheap black labor, especially for the Southern ruling classes that emerged out of slavery's old planter class. But the privilege of exploiting black labor extended even to fairly lowly whites; textile mill hands and poor farmers, for example, frequently employed their black neighbors to do laundry.

Middle-class white liberals like my parents understood all of this to be part of a misbegotten and unjust system. But they needed the labor, they could easily afford it, and many of them assuaged their consciences by treating "their" help better than the market dictated. "Why, she's just like family to us" was the paternalist explanation. In truth, to refuse to employ black household help would not have liberated anyone, and having a maid, ironically, freed up my mother to teach school. The federal government was entirely complicit. When President Roosevelt passed the Social Security Act of 1935, Southern conservatives and their Northern Republican allies forced the New Deal legislation to exclude domestic workers and farmworkers from all of its employment provisions. That shielded people like us from having to pay retirement or unemployment insurance for the people who scrubbed the toilets and tended the tobacco. There was nothing clean about the way white people's houses got cleaned in Oxford, North Carolina, including our own house.

I don't know how my first black friend, Mrs. Roseanna Allen, would have felt about all this. We certainly did not discuss it. Mrs. Allen was a tall woman with chocolate brown skin and moist, beautiful eyes. Like Mrs. Fanny Mae McIver in Sanford, she kept house for our family so that my mother could teach school. In her starched white work dresses and rubber-soled canvas shoes, Mrs. Allen was quite imposing. By 1966, I had two little sisters, Boo and Julie, and Julie was only two. Mrs. Allen cleaned the house and washed the clothes and cooked our supper, while she took care of Julie and waited for the rest of us to get home from school.

Mrs. Allen respected my father for his well-known positions on racial issues. Reverend Tyson was *somebody* in her world, and she was intent on making certain that we understood why. "Your father believes in what is *right*," she told us over and over again. I did not fully understand what she meant, and she did not go into the details, but I knew even then that what was *right* was connected to the race issue. Mrs. Allen had full adult authority in our household; I remember her chasing me down the brick walkway one morning when she saw that I was wearing jeans with both knees kicked out. "Your mama is a teacher and your daddy is a preacher," she huffed, turning me around forcefully, "and you *ain't* going to school dressed like *that*." In spite of her firm hand, I loved Mrs. Allen truly. Her skill, her grace, and her good spirits fascinated me. It was also obvious from my mother's warnings and inflections that Mama greatly respected her abilities and her character.

Mrs. Allen had what seemed to the Tyson children an exotic secret life. Her husband, Fred Allen, ran a taxicab service. If he got more than one call at a time, he might telephone his wife at our house and ask her to pick up someone on the far side of town. She would herd whatever children were in her care into my mother's station wagon, and off we would go. Since white people did not ride in "black" taxi-cabs, we were always off to pick up an African American who needed a ride from someplace we might never have seen otherwise to the hospital to visit a relative or to the post office to pick up a package. We literally saw the color line between our neighborhood and the black side of town—neighborhoods without sidewalks, pavement, or streetlights, poor people living in run-down houses.

But until the day Gerald told me about the murder of Dickie Marrow, the sharpest sense of the color line I had was from a spring day in 1968, when I was almost nine. Mrs. Allen stood at the ironing board in between the twin beds where my brother and I slept, which she used as laundry tables on washday. I remember the smell of starch and the hissing of steam, and then the sudden realization that Mrs. Allen was crying. Silent streams of tears trickled onto my father's white shirts. When I asked her what was wrong, she almost bellowed: "What's wrong? What's *wrong?*" She seemed desperate and almost out of control. "They gone and killed Martin Luther King, *that's* what's wrong!" She choked hard on her sobs and buried her face in the laundry.

I knew vaguely who Dr. King was, and I knew that my father admired him greatly, but I was too young to understand even a little of the magnitude of that murder in Memphis. All I knew was that I wanted to comfort my beloved Roseanna. I don't think I had ever seen a grown-up crying like that. And so I said the only thing I could think of to say: "Maybe it will be all right, Roseanna, maybe somehow it will work out for the best."

She lifted her head and almost roared at the obscenity of the thought. "Work out for the *best?* How could it possibly work out for the best?" Mrs. Allen's face, contorted with tears and anger, looked at me with a stunned expression of rage. "How could it work out for the best that the man that God lifted up to save my people has been shot down like a dog in the streets? Did it work out for the best that Hitler killed six million Jews? Would it work out for the best if somebody burned your house down to the ground? Did it work out for the best that they took King Jesus out and nailed him to the cross?" She sobbed into the laundry.

Somehow I managed to whisper, "We think it did, don't we?"

"What?" she said, raising her red-rimmed eyes toward me.

"We think it worked out for the best that they hung Jesus on the cross, don't we, Roseanna? Jesus died on the cross to save us all from sin, didn't he?" I asked her.

"Oh, child," she cried, moving toward me on her knees. "Oh, baby." Reduced to roughly my height by her kneeling, she squeezed me tight, rocking me back and forth in a muttered mixture of tears and prayers, and she held on to me for what seemed a long, long time. Afterward, she rounded up my brother and my sisters and gave everybody their own little bottle of Coca-Cola, and we took the thick green bottles out to the back steps, where we sat together for what seemed like the rest of that terrible day. Just how terrible it was I simply had no way to know at nine years old.

For years, I have told myself the story of Mrs. Allen and me on the day Dr. King died. Without thinking about it much, I have remembered it as a story of how, even at one of the worst moments in our nation's racial history, the color line could dissolve in redemptive love. Even now, the memory brings tears to my eyes. And yet I have to confess that my account erases some of the important truths about my relationship with Mrs. Allen and the moment. In a society where white men made decisions and black women made dinners, she was a black woman who worked for my white parents. Even if those barriers had not governed everything that passed between us, I was nine years old. Mrs. Allen, who understood her world clearly enough, did not need explanations about the power of redemptive suffering from me. She had a church, a family, and a whole life of her own of which I knew almost nothing. And she had already realized, as I would come to understand only many years later, that what had happened on that bloody balcony in Memphis threatened to destroy any path that could ever connect us. As I look back at the story, I still feel the enveloping love that she gave me. But what strikes me most is the soothing and self-congratulatory way that I interpreted the moment in my memory, and how much greater was the distance between us than I could possibly comprehend.

ONE SUNNY DAY in the terrible spring of 1968, the poet laureate of Oxford accosted me on the sidewalk. I was nine years old and had recently written my first poem, which I'd showed to my mother, who had immediately showed it to Thad without telling me. It is possible that I had not yet fully comprehended that adults are engaged in a relentless conspiracy against the privacy and dignity of their offspring. Thad was smoking an unfiltered Camel cigarette, about half of which seemed to fester into smoke with every deep drag. The smoke swirled around his head and sometimes shot out his nostrils suddenly, which scared me a little. "I hear you wrote a poem, boy," he growled at me. "I want to hear it."

Terrified, I reluctantly admitted authorship but firmly denied any memory of the text itself. "Don't lie to me, boy," Thad spat. "You remember every goddamn word you ever wrote." I was stunned to hear an adult use the g-d word right there on the sidewalk, where lightning could strike at any second. But the language had the desired effect. After I stammered through all three stanzas of "March Winds Blow and Kites Fly High," which I will spare the reader here, Thad walked me up to Hall's Drugstore and bought me an Eskimo

Pie. Afterward, he escorted me up creaky stairs that smelled like an old trunk to his office above the drugstore, where his heavy black Underwood typewriter perched on a cluttered altar of books and papers. He pulled down several volumes and enchanted me with snatches of Edwin Arlington Robinson and Walt Whitman. His office charmed me utterly. Thad's musty sanctuary, like Dostoevski's Grand Inquisitor, had improved upon God's work and given it miracle, mystery, and authority. I became a frequent visitor.

From that day forward, a writer was something you could be, like a plumber or a teacher. In order to preserve my standing in this secret fraternal order of the Word, I read all of Mr. Stem's published poetry and wrote more poems of my own to show him. Not long afterward, I penned something fanciful—a boy's romantic ditty about a distant war and a gallant soldier. In the late 1960s, as the Vietnam War made more and more corpses and less and less sense, distant wars and gallant soldiers were considerably less romantic to Thad than to his young admirer. He praised my eloquence, but gently suggested that I write instead about the things that I knew—the people around me, what he called my own "little postage stamp of soil," a phrase I would locate decades later in the works of William Faulkner. My next poem about a distant war was about dear Chuck Rose, the lifeguard at Green Acres swimming pool, who stayed after hours one summer evening to teach a nine-year-old boy to dive and came home in a coffin the following Christmas from a place called Vietnam. But three years after I met Thad, my own little postage stamp of soil yielded up a story that changed my life forever. And I promised him that I would write it someday.

CHAPTER 6

THE DEATH OF HENRY MARROW

Henry D. Marrow Jr. did not normally go to Teel's place. "I never seen him before in my life," Teel later told me, "until the day he come in here. I didn't really see him until I rolled him over with the butt of the gun." Marrow was about five feet, nine inches tall and weighed 140 pounds. His family and friends called him Dickie. Soft-spoken and sweet natured, he was not a physically imposing twenty-three-year-old. "He would fight," said one of his close companions, "but he won't no bully." His friends thought of Marrow as quiet and reserved, though he liked to drink beer and laugh sometimes. "He was just a regular guy," said Herman Cozart. "I knowed him right good, and I liked him all right. He didn't hurt nobody."

Dickie Marrow's mother and father had separated when he was young. His father, Henry D. Marrow Sr., had moved to South Carolina, where he'd been killed in an altercation. His mother, Ivey Hunt Marrow, had gone to New Jersey to find work, leaving her son with her parents in Grab-all. As a teenager, Dickie had moved in with the Chavis family on West College Street, about a block from where Robert Teel would soon build his storefronts. After he'd finished at Mary Potter High, Marrow had attended Kittrell College in Kittrell, North Carolina, for a year or so, and had then come back to live with the Chavis family, although he still stayed with his grandparents some nights, and he saw his mother whenever she visited. Jimmy and William Chavis were both about his age, and the boys were all close friends. "We slept in the same room," said William. "We wore each other's clothes. He was wearing my hat the night he died."

The Chavis home was orderly. The Bible, good manners, and formal education were all highly valued. "They would lay that religion down," said William, whom they called "Boo." "They didn't play no mess." Mary Catherine Chavis taught at Mary Potter High School and knew something about authority. "Mary Catherine and them was strict—they will tell you that," Boo Chavis remembered. Mary Catherine Chavis developed a firm maternal attachment to Marrow. Beatrice and Roberta, her sisters, the other two adults in the household, were also fond of Dickie. Beatrice, whom they called "Fannie" or "Bee," loved him with what seemed a special understanding of both his mischief and his merit. Marrow was the most reliable babysitter of all the older children, Mary Catherine thought, and helped out around the house more than the other boys.

"Dickie just adopted us," said Mary Catherine Chavis. "We loved him."

Like many teenagers, Marrow was restless and aimless, but he stayed out of trouble. At nineteen, he joined the army. Stationed at Fort Bragg, Marrow was less than a hundred miles from home—perhaps not far enough, Mary Catherine Chavis believed. He came to dislike military life and often visited home, sometimes slipping away without permission to court a young woman in Oxford. In the late 1960s, racial brawls involving hundreds of black and white soldiers occurred both in Vietnam and at U.S. military bases around the country. The mostly white officers corps at Fort Bragg tried to maintain control, but the racial situation was extremely tense and volatile. Sometimes Marrow would overstay his leaves of absence and get in trouble with his superiors. And he did not want to go to Vietnam; like most young African Americans of his generation, he considered this fiasco in Southeast Asia a white man's war and a black man's fight. Dickie's commanding officer took a personal interest in him, however, and did not throw the book at the young soldier. Discharged in 1968, having managed to avoid service in Southeast Asia, Dickie came straight home to Oxford.

Upon his return, Marrow resumed his life with the Chavis family. But even before he had left the army, the romance he had started with a local young woman named Willie Mae Sidney had blossomed, and by the time he moved back home they were on their way to the altar. Marrow landed a job as an orderly at Umstead Hospital in nearby Butner and settled into married life. Willie Mae gave birth to a daughter, Tammy, right after Dickie came home from the army and another girl, Tasha, a year later. Late in 1969, Willie Mae Marrow became pregnant again with a third daughter, whom Dickie Marrow would never live to see. Though he'd had a somewhat bumpy young life, Mary Catherine Chavis believed he was finding his way and had settled down to be a good father. "I thought he had picked up the pieces and was doing well," she said.

On Monday, May 11, 1970, Marrow had dropped by the Chavis home after work to chat with Fannie, who was laid up on the couch after a minor surgery and wanted a cold drink. "I was sitting right out there on that porch, and he came through, messing with me, and playing, and I said, 'Go on, Dickie, run up there and get a big Pepsi-Cola for me, and don't be all day getting back,'" Fannie recounted. "When he got up there on the hill, halfway up to the Teel place, he called to me, and he waved to me, and I said, 'You hurry back, now,' and he was gone."

The old Tidewater Seafood Market sat on the corner beside the Teel place at Four Corners. Before the Teels had arrived, the old white wooden frame structure had been a service station, then a fish market, and by 1970 it stood empty. Its front overhang sheltered a Coca-Cola machine that still worked sometimes, and empty bottles were stacked in crates beside the machine. Young blacks sat on the curb where the gas tanks used to be or perched on the crates in the evening and talked. Cars would pull up and the drivers would roll down their windows and banter with anybody who might be around. When it was raining, the Tidewater provided shelter. A bottle of wine or a quart of malt liquor might make the rounds. "We stayed up on that corner all of the time," Boo Chavis recalled. "We'd just sit up there chitchatting until two or three in the morning sometimes, if nobody didn't want to go home."

A few minutes before nine o'clock that evening, Boo Chavis finished a hand of bid whist at a friend's house down the street and walked up toward the Tidewater. Dickie Marrow told the other young men under the awning that he was going over to Teel's store to get something to eat and to buy Fannie Chavis her big Pepsi-Cola. Dickie strolled unhurriedly across the thirty yards or so of gravel between Tidewater and the Teel place, past a cabin cruiser boat parked beside the store. Hidden from view, Robert Teel and his twenty-one-year-old stepson, Roger Oakley, were working inside the boat's cabin. As he continued toward the store, Marrow passed eighteen-year-old Larry Teel and his wife, Judy, who were in the parking lot near the shop, uncrating motorcycles that had been delivered that afternoon.

Rumor had it that Judy secretly enjoyed the company of young black men. "Everybody knew that," one local black woman told me. Some people even claimed, after the fact, that she was involved with Henry Marrow. These rumors shaped the controversy that came afterward, but I have never found evidence that either of them was true. I personally don't believe she had ever laid eyes, let alone hands, on Henry Marrow before that day. Maybe her husband had heard the rumors, but it is just as likely that they were invented after the fact, in an effort to explain the inexplicable brutality that followed. But when Marrow violated a time-honored Southern taboo and appeared to make a flirtatious remark to Judy, Larry responded with instant rage. What Marrow actually said remains a matter of dispute and is probably unknowable. But it is clear that Larry Teel interpreted Marrow's words as a sexual remark from a black man to a white woman who belonged to him. "That's my wife you're talking to," Larry yelled, reaching for a heavy length of wooden motorcycle crate that was lying on the gravel. Judy screamed, and Robert Teel and Roger Oakley clambered out of the boat and ran inside.

"We knew they was going for the guns," said one onlooker.

Marrow tried to explain to Larry that he had not been talking to the white woman at all. "I was talking to the sisters," he said, gesturing toward two young black women standing nearby. The young Teel did not accept the explanation and rushed at Marrow, swinging the heavy piece of wood. Marrow stumbled backward, dodging, and then snatched up a handful of rocks from the parking lot and hurled it into Larry's face. Behind the blast of gravel, Marrow quickly pulled a knife from his pocket. It was a folding pocketknife with an imitation bone handle and a four-inch blade. He opened it and held it forward menacingly, backing up slowly. "He didn't believe in running," Boo Chavis explained. "And that's probably why he's dead."

When the other young black men at Tidewater heard the commotion between Larry and Dickie, they came running with drink bottles. "We didn't like that goddamn Larry worth a damn," one of them recalled. But when they saw the Teel boys racing into the barbershop, no one had to tell them what the white men were running to get. "We all said, 'Hey, come on, Dickie, man,' but he just stood there," Edward Webb recalled. The rest of the young black men fled just as fast as their legs would carry them. Robert Teel bolted out of the barbershop with a 12-gauge shotgun, and Roger Oakley was right on his heels with another gun, a combination .410-gauge shotgun and .22-caliber rifle, with the two barrels arranged over-and-under style.

Marrow finally fled, following the path his friends had taken around the fish market, running under the awning and starting toward the highway and the houses beyond. About half a dozen young black men were running full tilt well ahead of Dickie. Boo Chavis, however, knew nothing about what was happening and saw the first of them pass him on the other side of the highway as he strolled up to the Tidewater. They did not see him, and he crossed the road as they went by. "I thought they were racing, you know, sometimes we used to do that," he recalled. "I didn't know where they were going so fast."

Dickie ran for his life while all three of the white men gave chase, Teel with the 12-gauge, Roger with the other gun, and Larry still wielding the section of crate. Boo Chavis wandered directly into their path under the awning at the Tidewater, caught completely unawares, just as one of the pursuers opened fire. Two shotgun blasts in rapid succession splintered the air, and Boo felt a sharp burning on his face. Although the main force of the shot missed him, shotgun pellets peppered Chavis's head and face. "I put my hand up like this," he said, touching his palm to his upper face and his forehead, "and it come down all bloody." As the speechless Chavis brought his bloody hand down from his face, Robert Teel stopped three feet in front of him, staring with a vacant, animal gaze. They stood under the awning at the old seafood market perhaps twenty or thirty feet from where Marrow was stumbling, wounded in the buttocks. "What are you shooting me for?" Boo screamed at him. "I didn't do nothing!"

Teel made no reply, but simply aimed the gun at Boo's head. The red-faced barber "put a shotgun barrel in my face," Boo testified later in court. It may be that Teel had simply mistaken Chavis for Marrow; the two men were roughly the same size and complexion, and Chavis was standing in exactly the wrong place. Why Teel didn't kill Chavis is hard to say. He had already fired the shotgun, for one thing, and even if he had pulled the trigger, it would have clicked on an empty chamber. Larry Teel, who ran up and swung the stick at Boo Chavis, may have interrupted his father before he pulled the trigger. In any case, Teel apparently saw Marrow, his intended target, running or perhaps already fallen face down in the dust and gravel on the other side of the Tidewater.

Saying nothing else to Boo Chavis, Teel dashed through the Tidewater's overhang, lowering the barrel of the shotgun and shooting again. "After I fired the twelve-gauge," Teel told me many years later, "then Roger, he fires." Roger emptied the upper shotgun barrel. Marrow had probably been hit by Robert Teel's first blast from the 12-gauge, though Roger's fusillade may have knocked him down. Boo Chavis could see what was happening as if it were in slow motion, but he could not make it stop. "I saw Dickie coming," he told me years later, "and I heard the shots, and I saw him fall." The young black veteran skidded onto his face in the dirt and gravel beside Highway 158.

Larry Teel, meanwhile, still swinging the stick, accosted the bleeding Boo Chavis, who had been trying to leave the scene, under the awning of the market. His face pouring blood, Boo wanted no part of whatever was happening. And Larry, too, may have mistaken Chavis for Marrow for a moment. But then Larry left Boo Chavis, threw down the stick, and ran to where his father and stepbrother stood over Dickie Marrow. Stunned, Chavis turned and watched the white men accost Marrow. "When we run around the building," Robert Teel told me, "the boy was laying flat on his stomach."

Dickie began to plead for his life, according to several witnesses. "Okay, okay, man, you got me," he wept. "Let's just forget it, you got me."

"He started getting up on his elbows," recounted Teel matter-of-factly, "and I had taken the gun and hit him with the butt across his head. Broke the gun butt half in two, and it wheeled him over on his back." The blow fractured Marrow's skull and flipped his body like a pancake.

Larry Teel dived onto Marrow and began pounding him with his fists. "Larry jumped on him and hit him one or two licks," said Teel. "Larry was hitting him and Teel and me was kicking him," Roger Oakley testified later. "Larry got hold of the knife, and he told us he had it, and he got up." They continued to beat the limp body beneath them.

"They kicked him in the head, and when it hit his head it sounded like knocking on wood," said Boo Chavis, who was watching from under the awning. "They took the butt of the shotgun and started beating him in the face. I guess they did that for about five minutes."

The three white men stood above the prostrate Marrow, kicking him. The barrel of the over-and-under rifle pointed toward Dickie's head. "They were right down on top of him," recalled Boo Chavis. "The barrel was down on his head, touching it."

"Shoot the son of a bitch," said Robert Teel, according to two different witnesses. Mrs. Evelyn Downey, watching from across the street, claimed that the father yelled at his sons a second time: "Shoot the son of a bitch nigger." Teel himself maintained that he said, "*Don't* shoot the son of a bitch." The reader can judge which of those bits of dialogue seems more plausible. Nor can I tell the reader, for a petrified fact, whether it was Larry Teel or Roger Oakley holding the rifle; Roger had brought the gun out, but Larry may well have taken it from him in order to kill the man who had affronted his wife. In any case, the .22 made a popping sound, no louder than a firecracker, and a small piece of lead drilled a hole in Henry Marrow's brain. As William Burgwyn, the prosecutor in the case, told me at a booth in his favorite restaurant twenty years later, "They shot him like a hog. They shot him like you or I would kill a snake."

After the fatal shot, there was silence. And then Robert Teel quickly locked up the businesses and went home with his family. After the Teels left Four Corners, Boo Chavis knelt in the dirt behind the Tidewater Seafood Market, holding the battered body of Dickie Marrow in his arms. Through his own blood and tears, Boo could see that Marrow was only semiconscious. "Dickie wasn't right, he was all messed up and couldn't talk," Jimmy Chavis recalled. Jimmy and the others had fled down the road and dived under porches or hidden under cars when the Teels had run out with the rifle and shotgun. But slowly they'd returned to the place where Dickie lay bleeding into the dust and gravel. Sobbing convulsively, Boo called out to Jimmy and to Edward Webb when he saw them trotting warily back up Highway 158. It was roughly nine o'clock in the evening.

"Jimmy and Bab-bro"—Webb's nickname, short for baby brother—"was coming back. It took all of us to pick him up," said Boo. "His brains was hanging out—I didn't know what it was at the time—and it looked like scrambled eggs." The young men gently lifted Marrow into the back seat of Willie T. Harris's car. Bab-bro and Boo sped to Granville Hospital, which was only about a mile and a half away. Boo wept as Marrow made hoarse, half-conscious gasping noises. When they got to the hospital, doctors whisked Marrow into one operating room and Boo Chavis into another. Though Marrow was far more badly wounded, Chavis was such a bloody mess that it was hard to tell. "Boo looked terrible," Fannie Chavis recalled.

Fannie, who had sent Dickie Marrow to get her a big Pepsi-Cola a few hours earlier, was lying on a sofa in the Chavis home on West College Street when Jimmy Chavis ran breathlessly into the house. "Bee," he cried, "Bee, get up, get up—Dickie, Dickie—Teel done shot Dickie and I believe he dead." Fannie, who was recuperating from surgery and confined to the couch, sprang to her feet like a sprinter.

"Go over there and get Clyde or somebody to run me to the hospital," she snapped at Jimmy. "Roberta! Roberta! Dickie's been shot! Come on!" Fannie and Roberta Chavis raced to the hospital in a neighbor's car. When they arrived, they were told that they could not see either of the young men, whom doctors were treating in adjacent rooms with swinging doors. "I just pushed that door open anyway," said Fannie Chavis, "and there was Boo. He was just bleeding, bleeding, and it scared me so bad. I heard Roberta, she kicked open the other door, and we could just hear groaning, and that was Dickie." The surgeons never had much hope for Marrow but, after their failed attempts to stabilize him, an ambulance sped him toward Duke University Medical Center in Durham, forty miles away. Marrow died before he got out of the county.

Boo Chavis stayed at the hospital for less than an hour. The doctors picked the shotgun pellets from his face and neck, cleaned his wounds, wiped the blood from his forehead, gave him a tetanus shot, and sent him home. There were, however, much deeper and less visible wounds.

Back at the house on West College Street, the Chavis women asked a family friend, Mr. Yancey, to drive Boo to the police station to tell the investigators about the murder. "I told them I won't going to the damn police station, they won't gon' listen to a word I said," Boo recalled. All he could think about was the empty malice in Robert Teel's eyes as the white man had tried to kill him. Yancey, a deeply religious man, had been a kind of surrogate father to Boo for some years. "They got him 'cause I used to listen to him, so I listened to him. 'Come on, Boo, I'll take you,' he told me, and I just said, 'Naw, man. I ain't going up there.' "

Seeing the terror in Boo's eyes, Yancey pulled the young man aside and opened a paper sack he had brought with him. A heavy .357 magnum revolver rested at the bottom of the bag. "Come on, Boo," said the older black man, "ain't nobody gonna mess with us."

Yancey drove Boo Chavis to the police station shortly after ten o'clock. As they turned onto Williamsboro Street and headed past the Confederate monument and the courthouse, Yancey and Chavis could see that the streets downtown were lined with cars. "Along beside the movie [theater] and where the jail at, too," Boo Chavis recalled. Teel must have made some phone calls, and the people he called must have made some phone calls; less than an hour after Marrow had been killed, crowds of white people had begun to gather, anticipating violence, some of them Ku Klux Klan members from Granville County and elsewhere. "Tallyho was really where the klavern was in Granville County," said Mayor Currin, "out at Tallyho and Shoo-fly and Providence. And we had people from outside the county who came in to provide protection for [Teel], so I understand. I've been told that certain people who were thought to be Klansmen from Johnston County went to his house and protected him."

"As we were getting to the police station," recalled Boo Chavis, "you should have seen the white people lined up on the sidewalk. It was at least a good two hundred of them—Klansmen, I guess." Yancey walked the young man through the mob and into the police station, where they told the officer at the desk why they had come. And then they huddled in the waiting room for roughly four hours, waiting for the Oxford Police Department to interview Boo. Several other blacks who had seen at least part of what happened also went to the police station but, surprisingly, the police interviewed none of them that night. "We went down there and sat down there—we stayed until two in the morning," Chavis recalled. "Mr. Yancey stayed with me the whole time. They didn't even try to talk to me, they didn't try to do nothing." Finally, Mr. Yancey picked up his paper sack and beckoned to young Chavis, and they drove back to the house on

West College. Boo Chavis was angry and devastated, but he was not surprised. "I didn't think they was gon' listen to me no way," he concluded, perhaps thinking about how Teel had pistol-whipped the black schoolteacher two weeks earlier and barely even been punished. "I was thinking about revenge."

Word raced through black Oxford the next morning that Teel and his boys had killed Henry Marrow in front of several people and that the police had neither arrested Teel nor shown any interest in talking to the witnesses; it was several days later before the police finally got around to talking to Boo Chavis. If black folks in Oxford were talking about little else except the killing, my parents avoided the topic, at least with their children. That Tuesday evening was when Gerald told me about the murder, and when the strange silence fell over our dinner, and when my sister and I saw armed men all over the porches at the Teel house.

Boo Chavis and many of his friends joined the hundreds of young blacks who ran through the streets of downtown Oxford that night, leaving the wreckage that my sister and I witnessed the next morning on our way to school and leaving white people in Oxford reeling. Blacks and whites had fought in the streets of Oxford in the summer of 1963—scuffles and fistfights during civil rights demonstrations, mostly. The riot that Tuesday night went far beyond the scale of those conflicts. Oxford police sat helpless as bricks shattered plate glass, bottles smashed windshields, and flames crackled in storefronts. Much of the damage was to white property in or near the black neighborhoods. Here "you could hide, you know," Carolyn Thorpe, one of the rioters recalled. "Like if a police car come down Granville Street, we could duck into an alley or anybody's house, 'cause they gon' let us in."

The anger in the black community that Tuesday night reflected a common belief that Teel and his sons were literally going to get away with murder. "It was Wednesday before anyone even knew that they had been arrested," city attorney Dan Finch told newspaper reporters. Many did not believe it even Thursday or Friday. It speaks volumes about the racial situation in the United States in 1970 that virtually every African American in the county believed that white men could butcher a black man in public and not even face arrest and prosecution, let alone conviction. And, in fact, the police had not jailed the Teels immediately; the arrest warrant showed a time of 8:30 the morning after the murder, but even that much information was not public knowledge. Herman Cozart, the stocky black truck driver who knew Teel from his own experiences at the store, learned about the killing late that week in another store in the black community. "They said, 'He ran and the man killed him up by the oil tanks.' Said, 'They ain't locked him up *yet,* 'cause they say it was on his property.' And I said, 'That ain't his property all the way down 158.' " Cozart felt cold, bitter anger rising in his massive chest. "I told them, 'They ought to locked him up for *something.*' "

Faced with the riot of the night before and a mounting sense of black rage, Mayor Currin dispatched a telegram on Wednesday morning to Governor Robert Scott, a white "law and order" moderate, informing the governor's office of his intention to declare a curfew and requesting state troopers to help enforce it. In a telephone conversation around lunchtime, David Murray, an aide to Governor Scott, told Mayor Currin that the governor was in Europe but assured him that the state would provide all the manpower necessary to keep the peace. Lieutenant Governor Pat Taylor ordered fifty highway patrol officers and a large contingent of State Bureau of Investigation agents into Oxford that afternoon. Mayor Currin called an emergency session of the city council, which immediately passed "an ordinance authorizing the mayor to proclaim the existence of a state of emergency and impose a curfew during same." Currin then immediately announced a curfew for all citizens from 7:30 in the evening until 6:00 in the morning. The SBI agents who arrived Wednesday afternoon assessed the situation in Oxford as "extremely tense." Noting that District Court Judge Linwood Peoples had announced a preliminary hearing in the Teel case for that afternoon, the agents suggested that the outcome of that proceeding might determine the extent of the violence in Oxford.

While they waited for the hearing, local authorities decided to keep the schools in session. In May 1970, only a handful of black kids attended the previously all-white schools, and no white kids were enrolled in the black schools. So the Granville County schools conducted classes as usual, and our teachers and principals said nothing about the murder or the riot. Given that many of the rioters had been school age, I suppose that the authorities felt that calling off classes would simply leave the young people free to fight in the streets. In an aside that reflected the mind-set of most white officials, the SBI report stated that, regardless of what happened at the hearing, "young blacks are likely to be looking for trouble anyway."

That description was perhaps only a negative phrasing of something positively true, which was that Dickie Marrow's close family friend twenty-two-year-old Ben Chavis was already plotting a massive revolt of young black people in Granville County. There would have been upheavals in the streets of Oxford in any case. And Chavis, a charismatic firebrand and a gifted leader, would have been battling white supremacy in some fashion even if the Teels hadn't killed anyone at all. But Ben Chavis was a relative of Boo Chavis, Jimmy Chavis, and Mary Catherine, Roberta, and Fannie Chavis. When the bullet tore through Dickie Marrow's brain, it killed a young man whom Ben Chavis had known for years. And although Ben Chavis was already a bright young radical, that bullet also launched a political career that would take him to national notoriety in the waning days of the African American freedom struggle.

One of the first telephones that rang in Granville County after that gunshot was in the Satterwhite home of Mrs. Elizabeth Ridley Chavis, Ben's mother and the widowed matron of the county's most illustrious African American family. As Golden Frinks, an activist for the Southern Christian Leadership Conference, put it, "They didn't even know who they was killing."

Ben Chavis, a teacher at all-black Mary Potter High School when that telephone rang, was said to be the great-great-grandson of John Chavis, during his lifetime probably the most learned black man in the United States. "In my family," Helen Chavis Othow, Ben's sister, writes, "the tradition that we are descendants of John Chavis has been passed down from generation to generation. My father and many of our elders informed us at an early age of this revered connection."

Born free in 1763, John Chavis is said to have begun his education as part of a wager between two wealthy white men about the innate capacities of the sons of Africa. Though that debate would persist, whoever bet against Chavis lost badly. Chavis studied to become a minister under John Witherspoon, a signer of the Declaration of Independence and the president of what would become Princeton University. He completed his training at Washington Academy in Lexington, Virginia. During the American Revolution, Chavis fought against the British for three years with the Fifth Regiment of Virginia. After the war ended, the Presbyterian Church licensed him "to preach the Gospel of Christ as a probationer for the holy ministry within the bounds of this Presbytery wherever he shall be orderly called, hoping as he is a man of colour, he may be peculiarly useful to those of his complexion." Chavis became a missionary and stumped Maryland, Virginia, and North Carolina on horseback for several years, becoming one of the leading preachers in the South, preaching to enslaved blacks and white congregations alike.

An educator as well as a minister, John Chavis founded a school in Raleigh in the early 1800s, where he taught Latin and Greek to the sons of the state's most influential white families. This was a most unusual achievement. His pupils included two sons of a Supreme Court justice, a future United States senator, and a future governor of the state. Chavis was determined to educate African Americans and early in his enterprise apparently taught black and white pupils together, a practice that offended some whites; in 1809, he advertised that he would "open an EVENING SCHOOL for the purpose of educating Children of Colour, as he intends, for the accommodation of some of his Employers, to exclude all Children of Colour from his Day School." For twenty years Chavis taught the children of North Carolina's landed gentry by day and "when the white children leave the house," the clergyman wrote, "those of colour will take their places, and continue until ten o'clock." He became prosperous and well respected, buying several choice lots in Raleigh, a large house outside of town, and one hundred acres of land in northern Wake County. Historian John Hope Franklin has called John Chavis "the most prominent free black in North Carolina."

In 1831, however, Nat Turner and his band of slave rebels cut a swath through the southern Virginia countryside, coming very close to Oxford and slaughtering fifty-seven white men, women, and children in their messianic march against slavery. Whites put down the rebellion, killing hundreds of blacks and impaling the severed heads of suspected rebels on pikes as a warning. Across the South, white authorities moved to strengthen the racial caste system. The North Carolina legislature voted in 1832 to outlaw preaching and teaching by African Americans, free or slave, and took the vote from free blacks soon afterward. The state's "Act for the better regulation of the conduct of Negroes, slaves and free persons of colour" barred blacks from preaching or exhorting in public "under any pretense." The legislation prohibited blacks from "acting in any manner as preacher or teacher," under penalty of public whipping "not to exceed 39 lashes on his bare back." Three years later, when the legislature took the vote from free blacks, John Chavis was no longer even a citizen.

Despite his political connections, John Chavis was forced to sell his property, close his illustrious academy in Raleigh, and move to the Mangum farm in Granville County. Though the new law pressed Chavis into poverty, he quietly persisted in teaching black children, and his posture remained defiant. After he was "charged with going to Raleigh to teach the children of free people of colour," Chavis wrote to a prominent former pupil to complain about his treatment. "Tell them that if I am black," he wrote to Senator Willie P. Mangum in 1837, "that I am free born American & a revolutionary soldier & therefore ought not be thrown entirely out of the scale of notice." The following summer, when John Chavis was seventy-five, legend has it that somebody clubbed the old man to death at his home in Granville County. According to Helen Chavis Othow, his biographer, it is possible that "he was killed because he didn't stop teaching or preaching." The Chavis children grew up hearing that white opponents bashed in his skull because he refused to stop educating black children.

The legacy of John Chavis was a controlling influence in the life of succeeding generations of the Chavis family. Both of Ben Chavis's parents, Benjamin Chavis Sr. and Elizabeth Ridley Chavis, taught school in the county and served the local branch of the NAACP. "Major Chavis," as the senior Benjamin Chavis was known around town, had fought in World War I, then traveled home on a segregated troopship, bitterly angry at how little the war to "make the world safe for democracy" had done to free black Americans. Racial politics and African American history were mainstays of the dinner-table conversation at the Chavis home. The younger Ben recalled lengthy family discussions of the Supreme Court's 1954 *Brown* decision and the 1955 murder of Emmett Till, a fourteen-year-old black boy butchered by two white men in Mississippi for allegedly flirting with a white cashier. After the Till murder, the seven-year-old Chavis "didn't want to go out of the house for two weeks," he remembered. The Chavis family taught their children to read the newspaper every day and imposed high standards of academic performance. One of Ben's sisters, Helen Chavis Othow, received her doctorate, chaired the English Department at St. Augustine's College in Raleigh, and published a biography of Reverend John Chavis. June Chavis Davenport became a supervisor in the Charlotte-Mecklenburg school system. Another sister, Francine Chavis, graduated from medical school and came home to practice medicine in Oxford.

Born in 1948, Ben Chavis was an intensely aware and articulate young man who had led an effort to desegregate Oxford's public library while still a student at Mary Potter High School. Chestnut skinned and small of frame, Chavis attended St. Augustine's College for a year but transferred to the University of North Carolina at Charlotte in 1966 after the death of his father, becoming one of the first African American students to enroll there. Active in student politics, Chavis won election as president of the UNCC Student Union, campaigning against the Vietnam War and inviting renowned black militant Stokely Carmichael to campus. He worked in the 1968 presidential campaign of Robert F.

Kennedy, switching to Eugene McCarthy's crusade after Kennedy was assassinated.

The searing events of the spring and summer of 1968 radicalized Ben Chavis as they did thousands of other young Americans. A natural leader, Chavis helped create the Black Cultural Association, whose "Black House" in Charlotte became a local center for black radical politics. Chavis and his associates sought to organize a Charlotte chapter of the Black Panther Party, modeling their approach on the Panthers' "Ten Point Program" and setting up a free breakfast program for poor black children. The national Panther organization, however, was in a period of turmoil that would not permit them to charter new groups, and was beset from coast to coast with paid infiltrators and assorted idiots who called themselves Panthers and acted in ways that embarrassed the party. Factional disputes among the would-be Panthers in Charlotte earned Chavis and his accomplices denunciation from the *Black Panther*, the official newspaper of the Oakland-based Black Panthers. Two of Chavis's Black Cultural Association colleagues in Charlotte, Theodore Hood and David Washington, tallied long police records and were suspected of a number of violent crimes. Chavis was also close to James Grant, a radical chemistry professor at UNCC and a black Vietnam veteran turned full-time revolutionary.

Having earned his undergraduate degree in chemistry, Chavis came home to Oxford and reopened the old Ridley Drive-In, a defunct restaurant owned by his family and adjacent to their family homeplace, renaming it the Soul Kitchen. The establishment became a focal point for young blacks in the county, providing space for both partying and politics. Soon after opening the Soul Kitchen, Ben Chavis accepted a substitute-teaching position at Mary Potter High School. He taught the last classes of students to attend the all-black high school; in the fall of 1970, several months after the murder and the conflagration that followed, Granville County would finally integrate its school system. But among the last students at Mary Potter High, Chavis quickly put his organizing experience to good use. "I was trying to raise the black consciousness of the students," he explained. "In the English class I was teaching, I had them write black poetry. In the journalism class I totally transformed the school paper in terms of articles—they had articles against the Vietnam War, raising political consciousness."

Chavis also helped form a group called the Granville County Steering Committee for Black Progress, composed largely of students from Mary Potter, which built upon earlier activist efforts and focused largely on the lack of recreational facilities for young people. In early 1970, Chavis addressed the city council with a recreation proposal that would have forced the recreation committee to hold meetings and open all existing recreational facilities to the public; six years earlier, after the Civil Rights Act of 1964, the city's white leadership had secretly committed itself to providing no public recreational facilities so that they would not have to integrate them. The main impact of these organizing efforts was that, as Chavis said, "We already had a sense of a communications network, but it was mainly on the issue of recreation—nobody knew that a tragedy like this was going to happen."

After the murder, despite Mayor Currin's curfew and the presence of dozens of state troopers, Oxford was a tinderbox and matches were not in short supply. A bomb threat interrupted classes at predominantly white D. N. Hix School that Wednesday morning; a similar threat disrupted all-black Orange Street Elementary. The schools were not that far apart. After classes let out for the day, groups of white and black young people engaged in rock-throwing battles and group fistfights. "We'd catch 'em coming up that hill by D. N. Hix," one young black woman recalled, "and we used to flat kick their ass. It was like that for a long time." Despite the presence of local police and state troopers, these clashes continued for months after the murder. Young blacks would gather at one end of Hillsboro Street, near the poolroom and the corner of Granville Street, and white teenagers would assemble at a gas station near Hix School. "Literally, around ten o'clock at night," one recalled, "the two groups would march toward one another and there would be fighting all up and down the street." The street battles became an almost nightly occurrence. "We was throwing bricks at car windows, all like that," one black woman confessed, "but they be doing the same thing to us."

Oxford was not the only place where street battles raged; in fact, dozens of communities in the United States saw violent racial clashes in May. That same Tuesday of the riots in Oxford, a sixteen-year-old black boy named Charles Oatman was beaten to death in a jail cell in Augusta, Georgia. Oatman was mentally retarded and weighed only 104 pounds. "He had been beaten something awful," said the wife of the undertaker who prepared his body. "There were cigarette burns on his hands and feet and—well, there were burns on his buttocks, too." Sheriff E. F. Atkins in Augusta told black leaders that the frail boy had fallen out of his bed and struck his head on the concrete. But few black people believed that Oatman could have fallen out of his bed twenty or thirty times, sometimes onto burning cigarettes, and the white coroner refused to issue a report. Young blacks began to burn white-owned businesses in the black community. Governor Lester Maddox blamed the violence on "a Communist conspiracy" and ordered state troopers into the city, warning the rioters that they had "better prepare to meet their maker." The troopers fired into the crowds, killing six blacks and wounding dozens more. According to national wire service reports, all six of the dead had been hit multiple times in the back at close range.

Four days later, on May 16, eighty Mississippi state troopers fired at least 350 rounds into a women's dormitory at Jackson State University, killing two students and wounding at least twelve more. In the presence of a national wire service reporter, one of the troopers radioed back to headquarters, "You'd better send some ambulances. We've killed some niggers out here." Governor John Bell Williams claimed that snipers inside had fired hundreds of shots at police, but a Justice Department investigation revealed no evidence of any shots fired from the dorm whatsoever—not a shell casing, not a bullet hole, not one witness. Local black leaders announced the formation of a black self-defense organization. "We are determined," Dr. Aaron Shirley, a prominent black physician, told reporters, "that from now on when we suspect that law enforcement officers are hell bent on killing some black folks, they'll be doing it at their own risk."

In Oxford, at least, the police held their fire. But the firebombing, which had damaged seventeen downtown stores during the first night of rioting, persisted on Wednesday night. At about ten-thirty, someone hurled a small, ineffectual gasoline bomb through the window of the Tiny Tote, a convenience grocery store on Lanier Street; this appears to have been a diversionary attack. Ten minutes later, three firebombs landed on the roof of James Rudder's house in a quiet, all-white, middle-class housing development called Green Acres. Two of the bottle bombs, failing to shatter, bounced onto the lawn and flamed out. The third burned out on the asphalt shingles, but failed to ignite the roof and caused only minor damage. Perhaps the arsonists had selected the home at random, wishing only to take the battle to a white suburban area; perhaps Rudder was a target for some specific reason. Though the physical destruction was slight, the psychological effect of a bombing attempt in a white residential area heightened many white people's sense that this was a war in which they could choose only one side. Many whites, and not just Klan members, began muttering about retaliatory violence. Granville County had become an armed camp. "People didn't know when something might happen out their way," Mayor Currin explained. "Folks were just scared half to death."

Heavily armed state troopers ringed Oxford with roadblocks. In their gray uniforms and military-style hats, pump shotguns at the ready, backed up at many of the checkpoints by local police, the highway patrol garrison presented an imposing presence—one that blacks saw as a militia for white political power. The highway patrol had not employed its first black officer until 1967; most people in the state had never seen one of the handful of black troopers. Even black North Carolinians who wanted no part of radical politics tended to view the patrolmen as storm troopers for white supremacy. On May 30, two weeks after the murder, the *Carolina Times*, a fairly conservative black newspaper at the time, warned African American drivers in North Carolina "to be on their guard and take care not to encounter a member of the North Carolina Highway Patrol." The editors, noting several beatings and killings by state troopers, reported dozens of complaints about "brutality committed against blacks by Highway patrolmen." Middle-class white people, on the other hand, generally regarded the highway patrol as nice men who issued traffic tickets, which could be thrown out if you knew the right lawyer.

The emergency curfew ordinance under which they operated gave law enforcement officers tremendous leeway; it forbade anyone to "travel upon public roads, streets, alleys, or any public property" during the hours stipulated by the mayor, "unless in search of medical assistance, food, or other commodity or service necessary to sustain the well-being of himself or his family or some member thereof." In practice, this large loophole permitted the white authorities to allow anyone they deemed trustworthy to move freely and to arrest anyone on the streets whom they deemed untrustworthy.

Children may not fully understand the social order, but they learn it easily enough when it gets acted out in front of them. I remember riding in Chief Pontiac with my father at the wheel, and how terrified I was when the men with guns stopped our car at the roadblock. But Daddy pulled up to the blockades of troopers and smiled fearlessly. I recall feeling as though Daddy must be important, a man well known to the troopers, since they simply waved him right on through the barriers. I realized years later that the state troopers were not even from Oxford and had no idea who he was, beyond the crucial fact that he was a white man wearing a tie. Blacks had a completely different experience at the roadblocks.

Herman Cozart, who was easily as large as my father but many shades darker, found out about the curfew by driving up to a roadblock manned by the state troopers. "They didn't just look in there and say, 'Get out of the car,' " Cozart recalled. "They snatched the driver right out." No one snatched Herman Cozart easily; the pulpwood hauler had arms like legs and legs like tree stumps. "And I said, 'Hold it, now, I ain't handicapped,' " he recounted, and he lumbered down from the cab of his truck. The troopers leveled their shotguns at his chest. "I said, 'What the hell—did somebody done hold up a bank or something?' And they said, 'No, it's a curfew,' and that was the first I heard of the damn thing." Cozart, who rarely went anywhere without a gun, became one of twenty black men arrested on the first night of the curfew, charged both with violating the emergency statute and with carrying a concealed weapon. "I didn't really think it was concealed," said Cozart. "It was laying right there on the seat."

Despite the almost nightly Ku Klux Klan gatherings that summer, every one of the roughly one hundred persons arrested for violation of the curfew was black. Young blacks derided the curfew measure as "the No-Niggers-after-Nightfall Act." Mayor Currin, who did not approve of the Klan, nonetheless found the highway patrol's immense display of force comforting: "The pistol on the belt, that's one thing, but the big shotgun, that's something else."

NO AMOUNT OF military force could have made the district court preliminary hearing on Wednesday afternoon a soothing experience for Mayor Currin or the rest of the white power structure in Oxford. Ben Chavis led Mary Potter High School in a massive walkout and herded black students into the courthouse by the dozens. "When it came time for the preliminary hearing," Chavis said, "I took the class I had to court, and when my class left the school, the whole school walked out behind us. I looked around and saw the whole school coming. I thought, 'Well, maybe this will be good for everybody.'" Walking several blocks to the courthouse without a permit, the large group filed into the courtroom, filling nearly every available seat. "We had all four grades, ninth, tenth, eleventh, and twelfth grades, in the Granville County courthouse. Even the teachers came. Of course, the judge and everybody was shocked." Judge Linwood Peoples kept strict order, but the presence of two hundred young blacks clearly unnerved the white people who worked in the courtroom.

The young blacks listened quietly as Boo Chavis told the court how he had watched the Teels kill Henry Marrow. According to a report in the *Pittsburgh Courier*, Chavis testified that *three* white men stood over the fallen Marrow: Robert Teel with a shotgun, Larry Teel with a rifle, and a third man with a stick. Only the first two sat before the court charged in the killing; it is not clear why the third man was not identified and arrested. The third man had been Roger Oakley, of course—the fact that this seems not to have occurred to the police is beyond explanation. That Boo Chavis and the others who hung around near the store did not recognize Roger immediately is less mysterious; Roger worked at the Bandag rubber plant, not at his father's store, and was not a familiar figure at Four Corners the way Teel and Larry were.

Some of the confusion about who stood over Henry Marrow's body may have been by design. According to local courthouse legend, Billy Watkins instructed Larry to put on Roger's clothes before Larry and Teel went to the police station, in order to confuse the witnesses. None of the Teel family had said anything about Roger's presence whatsoever. His wife, Betsey, was pregnant and had reportedly suffered a series of miscarriages, and the family is said to have thought that he should stay out of the legal proceedings if possible. Whether the rumored clothing swap occurred or whether it influenced the accounts of the witnesses is hard to say.

All of them had partaken in the violence against Marrow, Boo Chavis testified, but he identified Larry Teel, now sitting at the defense table, as the one who'd fired the fatal shot, after his father had ordered him to "shoot the son of a bitch." Of course, all three of them had been engaged in the killing of Henry Marrow—stomping him, kicking him, smashing his skull with the stocks of the guns. In both moral and legal terms, the specific one who fired the final shot through his brain seems almost beside the point.

Despite some fogginess about the details of the killing, one thing became crystal clear to the blacks who attended the preliminary hearing: there were powerful white people who did not want to see Robert and Larry Teel go to jail. Lonnie Breedlove, a city commissioner, attested to the good character of the defendants. Basil N. Hart, a wealthy landowner, offered to put his property up to ensure that the Teels would appear for trial. Vassar Surratt, a prosperous lumberman, offered to post bond and swore that Robert Teel was a reliable and civic-minded citizen of excellent repute, as did a number of other prominent whites. "It was shocking," recalled Ben Chavis, "to see some of the presidents of local banks getting up and testifying as character witnesses for [Teel]." Judge Peoples found probable cause to charge each of the two defendants with first-degree murder in the death of Henry Marrow. He also charged Robert Teel with assault with a deadly weapon with intent to kill, inflicting serious bodily harm, for having shot Boo Chavis. Persuaded that no amount of money would be enough to keep Teel and his son in jail, given the combined wealth of their backers, the judge ordered them held without bond. Wednesday night, sheriff's deputies whisked the two men to Raleigh for safekeeping in the Wake County jail at Central Prison.

The following morning, the Human Relations Council, set up in Oxford several years earlier, met at the courthouse. My father and Thad Stem, who had both joined the committee recently, walked to the meeting together. "I was just trying to get the young man buried without having a race war," Daddy told me later. "I didn't worry much about the trial, because it seemed to me that the murder had been committed in a public place, and there wasn't much mystery about who had done it. And so my immediate concern was that people of goodwill on both sides come together and try to prevent further violence. And I wasn't sure that most of the whites knew how dangerous the situation was. I mean, I had church members sleeping in their stores downtown with guns. And I knew that the blacks were fed up, especially some of the young people. I worried that many white people didn't comprehend the level of anger and mistrust, and of course there were many others who didn't much care how black people felt."

Dan Finch, the white liberal attorney who chaired the committee, called the meeting to order, describing it as "an open forum for discussion in an atmosphere of mutual respect." According to newspaper accounts of the meeting, roughly 120 people came to discuss the racial situation, only fourteen of whom were African Americans. The black people who did come to the meeting were "respectable Negroes"—teachers, ministers, and businesspersons. They were angry at the racial injustice in Oxford, but they were not the same people rioting in the streets and making firebombs. Their critique of the problem and their anger at what had happened, however, were much the same. Sam Cox, the principal spokesperson for the African American contingent, charged that "there is no justice in the judicial system in Granville County." Authorities had to act to change things, Cox said. "I'm not going to call names," he continued, referring to Magistrate J. C. Wheeler, "but there is a magistrate who refuses to serve a warrant against whites who commit crimes against blacks." The black schoolteacher also reminded the group that the courts in Oxford had recently convicted a young black woman of first-degree murder after a white salesman had driven her, against her will, to a remote wooded area and had been shot with his own pistol. "We have not had justice," Cox declared, "and we are trying to do something about it."

The handful of people like Cox who had come to speak for "the black community" had an agenda of grievances that amounted to a brief against the whole racial caste system. One man called the attention of the white officials to the obvious: the city did not pave the streets where black people lived. Landlords who rented to African Americans in these places could safely ignore health and housing codes. Some of the houses rented to blacks had smelly, illegal outhouses that would not have been permitted in white neighborhoods. Neither the sheriff's department nor the fire department had any black employees. Neither of the two black policemen had ever been promoted above patrol officer. The health department, the welfare department, the public library, and the board of education were lily-white. Stores downtown did not hire blacks in anything but the most menial positions. The city had closed recreational facilities rather than integrate them.

The African Americans who attended the hearing did not approve of violence in the streets, they reminded the whites on the committee, but no one should be surprised at what was happening. My father agreed completely: "The shooting and the burning and the destruction which followed it are only the fever, not the disease," the newspapers quoted him as saying. "The disease has been around for three hundred years." The sound of hundreds of angry black people milling around in front of the building underlined the point.

"You've got our attention," city manager Tom Ragland told the black people at the meeting, unwittingly affirming that rioting and firebombs had succeeded where patience and petitions had always failed. But Mayor Hugh Currin then went on to explain the procedures for getting a street paved or making a complaint about building code enforcement, as though virtually all the white-owned rental housing in black neighborhoods was either substandard or dilapidated merely because no one had filed the proper paperwork. Finch, the committee chair, conceded that the Civil Rights Act's requirement that whites share public recreational facilities with blacks *might* have something to do with the city Recreation Committee's failure to have a quorum since 1964. Some of the blacks started to leave the meeting in disgust.

Ragland, apparently sensing that the white officials were not getting over with the dwindling black contingent, pledged that things would change: "We're not going to sit dumb as we have in the past. I think that something will be done now." In an effort to dampen black anger, the city manager even incorporated a little New Left lingo into his speech: "The judicial system must serve the people, not the system."

Most of the anger focused on the police department's inexplicable treatment of the Teel family after the killing of Henry Marrow. "Two or three blacks at the meeting Thursday indicated there were rumors that the arrests had been deliberately delayed," the Raleigh *News and Observer* reported. Assistant Chief of Police Doug White claimed that the Teels had come to the station voluntarily and turned themselves in on Monday night at about ten, roughly an hour after the shooting. Not one of the African Americans present accepted this account. One black woman confronted White, saying that she herself had seen Robert Teel loading ice onto a truck at seven o'clock Tuesday morning. Others chimed in with similar evidence. Eventually, Officer White retreated from the official story by thirty-six hours: "White told the group that the Teels had definitely been sent to jail before 7 A.M. *Wednesday*," the *News and Observer* reported. But by that time, whatever credibility the acknowledgment might have earned was lost. Almost half of the African Americans present walked out of the Human Relations Council meeting before it ended.

Those who remained could not help but hear the thunderous chants from outside. The Granville County Steering Committee for Black Progress, which had been organized at the Soul Kitchen the day before, had called earlier that day for a march to the courthouse. "We called that day 'Black Thursday,' " recounted Ben Chavis, "and we assembled at First Baptist Church." More than a thousand African American schoolchildren boycotted classes; two-thirds of the students at Mary Potter High and Orange Street Elementary, the all-black schools, were absent. Hundreds of them joined a large number of adults for the march to the courthouse. "We decided when we left the First Baptist Church that we were going to have a silent march, that if somebody shouted something derogatory that we would not respond, eyes straight ahead, because we were marching in memorial to Henry Marrow and out of our respect for him and for our own self-dignity," Chavis said. The march proceeded wordlessly out of First Baptist and down Granville Street, turned right on Hillsboro, and into the shadow of the Confederate monument in front of the courthouse. Willie Mae Marrow, Henry Marrow's young widow, visibly pregnant with the dead man's third daughter, marched at the head of the procession. At the courthouse, organizers used the back of a pickup truck as a podium and Chavis "spoke to the crowd, just to get the spirit of the thing together," he recalled.

Boo Chavis did not make a speech, but he marched with the protestors that day and wanted to get a good seat from which to hear his eloquent kinsman's oratory. "Me and a guy named Ronald Jordan, me and him climbed up on the Confederate soldier, and we had a fist up," Boo said years later. "But the policeman out there told me that I had to get down." Boo crawled down and joined the angry and high-spirited throng on the streets and sidewalks below. Newspaper photographs of the crowd show dozens of fists raised in the Black Power salute. The tone of the rally could not have been a comfort to the people who heard it from inside the courthouse. My father and Thad Stem found nothing to say and no place to go, and walked home from the courthouse in silence. "We're going back to our own community and we ain't going to let no white folks in," one speaker told the cheering crowd as Daddy and Thad strode pensively down Main Street. Another young black boy, defying the police, climbed up the Confederate monument with a large placard that warned, BLACK POWER STRIKES WITH THE POWER OF A PANTHER.

CHAPTER 7

DRINKIN'
THAT FREEDOM WINE

A T A ROADBLOCK on the southern outskirts of town, two highway patrolmen and a local police officer squinted into the headlights of an oncoming car. Whatever else the occupants of the automobile were doing here, they were violating the city council's emergency curfew. At other checkpoints around the city, law enforcement officers had already arrested twenty-five black men that night, ten of them carrying concealed weapons. As the aging green Buick slowed to a stop, the local cop stepped forward and both state troopers loudly cocked shells into the chambers of their Browning automatic shotguns. The driver, an African American named Walter David Washington, handed over his license and then his keys, keeping his hands up in plain view. Opening the trunk, the police officer found a case of dynamite and a stack of high-powered rifles.

If most white people in Oxford did not know what to make of "Black Power," many had their worst fears confirmed when they read the *News and Observer* the following morning. After the fruitless meeting of the Human Relations Commission and the fiery rally at the courthouse, readers learned, the police arrested a wave of black men trying to enter the town with weapons. The carload of dynamite and rifles made folks wonder if they were about to have a war on their hands.

Two of the men, Washington and Theodore Albert Hood, had police records of staggering dimensions; Washington was under lengthy suspended sentence for armed robbery and under investigation for five separate murders, while Hood had been convicted of assault with a deadly weapon with intent to kill and was facing an armed robbery charge, too. Both men had worked closely with Ben Chavis's would-be Black Panther chapter in Charlotte. Joseph Preston Goins, the third man in the car, was apparently a friend of black radical Jim Grant's, Ben Chavis's former chemistry teacher and political ally from UNC at Charlotte. Years later, FBI files and their own courtroom testimony revealed Washington and Hood to be police informants, and each received thousands of dollars and legal immunity from the U.S. Treasury and Justice Departments as part of the FBI's notorious Counter Intelligence Program—COINTELPRO—in exchange for testimony against Ben Chavis and Jim Grant. "Later," Chavis claimed, "we found out that the guys that came from Charlotte with the dynamite were actually working for the government at the time."

The three men carried a hand-lettered map that suggested that they had intended to bomb J. F. Webb, the local white high school. Black activists in Oxford believed that on their way to the school the three men tried to go see some local girls on Highway 15 and got their directions mixed up. "They was running with those Smith girls," Eddie McCoy asserted. "That was what messed them up. That's how they got caught with all that dynamite." Although it is impossible to know for certain, it seems just as likely that government informants Washington and Hood drove into the roadblock on purpose, snaring the third man, Goins, and implicating Ben Chavis and Jim Grant—prominent COINTELPRO targets—on related charges. In any case, whether it was COINTELPRO or the Smith girls, Washington and Hood escaped prosecution entirely. The *Oxford Public Ledger* had not heard about the Smith girls, but it revealed other information: "In possession of one of the trio was a slip of paper bearing the name of Mary Frances Thornton," the editors noted, "and giving the address of Rt. 5, Oxford, Box 355-B, Salem Rd, Huntsboro community." The editors, who routinely printed announcements for the Ku Klux Klan, also included her telephone number, presumably printing this information just in case any of their readers wanted to visit or call upon the woman in question.

Whatever the reason for their wrong turn—whether they were working for the FBI's notorious COINTELPRO operation, which secretly promoted divisive and especially criminal activity in an effort to undermine the black freedom movement, or whether they lost their way while returning from a social call—the heavily armed trio from Charlotte drove straight into a roadblock that was not on their way to the high school. "We had the map over at City Hall," Mayor Currin said years later, referring to the map the police had captured from the three black men. "They were going to Webb High School, evidently to bomb it, and they made the wrong turnoff, right into the middle of this roadblock."

To hear that police had stopped a carload of black men with dynamite and firearms was hardly a comfort to white people in Oxford. It got worse. At around eleven o'clock, a firebomb landed on the roof of the Oakes Motor Company on Lewis Street, but it rolled onto the ground and burned out without causing much damage. Around midnight, oil torches ignited a serious blaze in the A&P grocery store on Hillsboro Street. Police had been guarding the store and believed that whoever lit the blaze had been monitoring police activity on a minute-by-minute basis. The "military operation" swung into action. In Grab-all, young blacks torched an unoccupied hovel, creating a dramatic blaze that drew police and firefighters away from a much bigger target, a tobacco warehouse on Goshen Street. "We burned one house up, trying to get a diversion," one of the arsonists recalled. "The diversion we had set over on Hicks Mill Road, a little house there, didn't nobody live in it. We wanted the cops to go there while we hit the warehouse on Goshen Street." The incendiaries set firebombs in the flues beneath the large wooden building, but the homemade fuses failed. Nonetheless, the events of Thursday night— twenty-eight arrests, the seizure of dynamite and high-powered rifles, several firebombings and attempted firebombings—suggested the possibility of a small-scale guerrilla war. "It just literally scared the hell out of us," the mayor admitted.

If my parents were frightened, they never told their children. My memories of these days and nights are strangely blurry. Mostly, we stayed home. One night my father came home with a watermelon and sat it in a tub of ice on the back porch, and we ate the cool, pink flesh slathered with salt, a summer treat. Another night we made homemade vanilla ice cream, and Daddy let me and Vern take turns at the crank and then lick the paddles when it was done. Mama and Daddy seemed pensive, but they never talked to us about the atmosphere of war that grew steadily that week. And we lived happily enough inside the cocoon of their calm and loving manner.

But they felt the tension in ways large and small. One of Daddy's parishioners, a man who managed a department store downtown and slept in the store that week with a shotgun, was furious when he saw his minister walking into the courthouse wearing an Irish cap that Thad Stem had given him. Something about the hat just set him off. Like the mother in Ohio who told a journalist that same week, after the National Guard had killed four student protestors, "Anybody who appears on the streets of a city like Kent with long hair . . . deserves to be shot," the department store manager apparently cared more about what was on Daddy's head than what was in it. To him, the cap represented an act of rebellion that my baffled father had not intended at all. "I saw you walking in the courthouse with your little 'go to hell' cap on," he growled at Daddy after church the next Sunday, refusing to talk further and walking away in anger.

On Friday night, arrests were up slightly. The police and the highway patrol arrested twenty-seven more black men, most of them for simple curfew violations but quite a few for carrying concealed weapons into Oxford. White merchants hired armed guards or slept in their own stores, shotguns at the ready. Hardware stores sold guns and ammunition nearly as fast as the Orpheum Theater sold popcorn and Coca-Cola. Mayor Currin, Police Chief Nathan White, Assistant Chief Doug White, and several other city officials began spending their nights at City Hall, drinking bad coffee and wondering what would happen next. "We were pretty much on pins and needles," Currin recalled. The mayor did not want liquor added to the things that inflamed Granville County's population, and persuaded the county Alcoholic Beverage Control board to close the county's liquor stores early that Friday and to keep them closed all weekend. One reason was that Henry Marrow's family had scheduled his funeral for the following day.

The murder of Henry Marrow had attracted the attention of the larger civil rights movement. Golden Frinks, a native of North Carolina, heard about Marrow's funeral when he picked up the telephone in Canton, Mississippi, where the Southern Christian Leadership Conference had sent him temporarily. He says that Hosea Williams, the SCLC's fiery field director, "done told me about, 'Hey, man, they done killed somebody down there in your town.' Say, 'Abernathy wants you to go down there and take a look at it.' That's how I got in there. I called, and they said the funeral gon' be Saturday." Oxford was not his town, exactly, but Frinks was the most important black activist in eastern North Carolina and knew people in Granville County. A former nightclub owner from Edenton, North Carolina, Frinks had entered the freedom struggle with great vigor in the late 1950s, patching together a strong local organization and taking on the air, if not the piety, of a Southern black preacher. Some folks seemed to think his "nightclub" catered to sins of the flesh beyond dancing and drinking. Frinks was far from saintly. He could preach and pray with the best of them, though, and he worked well with most of the black women and young people who made up the rank and file of the movement.

A big, broad-shouldered, dark-skinned man whose speech rambled in the pungent language of the black South, Frinks was brave almost to a fault. His friends called him "Goldie." The Southern Christian Leadership Conference hired Frinks because of his success as a local organizer in Edenton and Williamston, and he had marched across the South with King and his lieutenants. Frinks was a kind of bridge figure between Martin Luther King's generation and the

Black Power rebels, and with a job like that, it probably helped that he was something of a snake oil salesman. An instinctive politician and a sharply analytical organizer, Frinks also leaned toward Christian mysticism, believing that "the Spirit" would guide him. His vibrant speeches could bring a crowd to tears of grief or cries of outrage. "Back then I was hot as pepper," Frinks remembered. "I was either gonna get it now or I couldn't wait. I was restless because I had been introduced to a type of freedom that the truth was in." Frinks knew his role. "I was the stoker," he laughed, "that kept the fire burning. I would stick that fire to it and shake it and keep it hot."

Whites widely regarded Frinks as a wild-eyed militant, partly because in his speeches he sometimes ranted about whites being "devils" and he'd once released dozens of live chickens to stop traffic at a protest march. But Frinks betrayed no hatred for white people as such. Flashing a broad smile, he would reach across the color line even to proven enemies, and try to exploit divisions among whites. In his early days in Edenton, when the local mayor led police officers on a raid against a mass meeting in a local church, Frinks walked down the aisle, embraced the white leader, brought him down front, praised him warmly, and introduced him to the cheering crowd in a way that induced the amazed mayor to make friendly remarks. Frinks never gave up in his efforts to sway his opponents. After a protest rally, Frinks would typically walk up and down the line of highway patrol officers and SBI agents, shaking hands and making jokes. "What I would do, as I'd leave, was thank 'em, say I certainly appreciate this, and then create a handshake with 'em, especially the commander or the sergeant or whoever," Frinks recalled.

As he explained to me at his home in Edenton two decades later, Frinks understood that Southern whites could hardly present a united front. Few whites truly backed the movement, especially in their own communities, but there were many shades of weak support, moral queasiness, deep misgivings, and reluctant opposition, in addition to the fire-eating racists. "You couldn't forget that you had some good white folks, and even the other ones wasn't necessarily all bad. There was some Methodists, there was some Presbyterians, and a few Episcopalians that weren't against you. They were cramped because of the age-old mores of time," Frinks asserted. The old freedom fighter knew that many whites, though they benefited from white domination, did not wholeheartedly support it, even if most of the dissenters were afraid to say anything. Dr. King, in his "Letter from Birmingham Jail," argued that such people were often worse than outright opponents. But Frinks saw them as an opportunity. "A lot of the good whites couldn't just come down here and speak. 'You're wrong, Mr. Teel,' they couldn't say that, but they had what you might call a silence that I could hear. If you forgot that, you wouldn't be nowhere. A man like Teel, getting his badge of honor from the murder of a man who had no cause to be put to death, that man was somewhat out of place. Lots of them supported him, but lots of them didn't, and some that did was ashamed of themselves. You couldn't forget that."

Frinks tried to nurture a similarly pragmatic and expansive vision inside the ranks of the freedom movement at a historical moment when its forces had fragmented. Deeply committed to nonviolence, Golden Frinks's aggressive organizing style sought to bridge the gap between civil rights preachers and Black Power militants. Though he had worked for Dr. King's SCLC for many years and walked faithfully in the path of nonviolent interracialism, no one could question his mettle or call him an Uncle Tom. Frinks remained close to Floyd McKissick of the Congress of Racial Equality, a fellow North Carolinian, a lawyer and World War II veteran who had helped lead the mid-1960s revival of black nationalism.

The Black Power generation, some of whom like McKissick were not so young, rejected interracialism, often to the point of dogma; Frinks did not think that there was so much white support that there was any reason to bicker about it, but that eventually everyone would have to learn to live together. While Frinks knew plenty about guns, he tended to think the youthful embrace of armed self-defense provided more political problems than physical security; he and many other members of the older civil rights generation were also well armed but felt no need to talk about it. Racial separatism, as a philosophical position, made no sense to Frinks at all. But he shared the Black Power cohort's militant opposition to white domination, their sensible emphasis on economic uplift, and especially their fiery assertion of African American pride. He knew that much of the old order's power to oppress black folk came from the lingering self-loathing bred by white supremacy, and he said it loud, black, and proud, nearly as often as James Brown.

For that reason, and because he was an extremely engaging person, the Black Power militants respected Frinks. He befriended Stokely Carmichael, Howard Fuller, Ben Chavis, and the other young black radicals who chanted "Black Power" and often denounced their elders, taking them into his home and feeding them good counsel and collard greens. The young firebrands listened to him, even though they did not always agree. "Whether they admit it or not," he reflected in later years, "they were stealing, getting ideas, replenishing their aggressiveness. And then they went and killed the movement." In the late 1960s, Goldie Frinks donned a golden dashiki in the manner of the Black Power crowd, but he always wore a good-sized cross around his neck, too. And in Oxford, Frinks detected a moment of Divine purpose and historic opportunity for the shaken movement to pick up the disparate threads of protest and restitch freedom's quilt.

"This was at a period when sacrifices had to be made," Frinks reflected, "and everybody has a purpose for being born." Though the murder of Henry Marrow was a tragedy, he said, the sorrow "was supposed to bring that kind of feeling to his daughters, that kind of showing of the weeping of his wife, until a reconnection among the people come. And I was—some kind of way—I was destined to go in there and raise the devil and dust it up and move on. I was supposed to go in there and leave the community but dust it up a little bit so they would have the memory." It may seem ludicrous to suggest that Marrow, who was not even an activist himself, died in order to energize the movement. But Frinks saw himself as a man of history caught up in a moment of destiny. "And after Oxford, we could all look back and say, 'You gonna be a symbol to us for a long time.'" Opponents of the movement had moved the nation into a reactionary posture, and the movement's most important voice and symbol, Dr. King, had fallen to an assassin's bullet. "If Oxford had not been protested," said Frinks, "it would have given legitimacy to stay with the backlash. This was going to revive us and bring us together and get us moving again in North Carolina, was the way I saw it unfolding."

Frinks hurried to town at the invitation of Elizabeth Chavis, Helen Amis, and other African American women in Oxford. "Those women had got together down in Oxford, don't you know," Frinks recalled. "They were some mighty tough black women down there. They believed in the civil rights." Those women must have been slightly dismayed Saturday afternoon, however, when the hour for Henry Marrow's funeral had arrived but the illustrious Golden Frinks had not. Hundreds of mourners overflowed the New Light Baptist Church and crowded the grounds, where latecomers could listen to the service through loudspeakers. "I think near about all of black Granville County attended the funeral," Ben Chavis recalled.

My father and Thad Stem appear to have been the only white people who came to the service. "There may have been another member of the Human Relations Council there," Chavis speculated to me years later. "But the only white people I remember was your daddy and Thad Stem." In any case, neither the city nor the county government dispatched a representative, sent flowers, or shared a word of condolence, a fact that did not go unnoticed among African Americans in Oxford. Daddy thought this was not only wrong but criminally stupid. With the entire community teetering on the brink of racial cataclysm, not one leader of the white-controlled political and economic system of Granville County had the foresight to show his face at the funeral—unless Thad's familial ties in the Democratic Party qualify him. I personally don't think anyone over fifty who wears tennis shoes to church counts as an elite.

Golden Frinks, on the other hand, was a kind of North Carolina civil rights celebrity. When Frinks finally arrived at New Light Baptist, a cordon of state highway patrol cars and officers had already surrounded the church and denied him and his entourage of young people entrance to the grounds. Over the loudspeakers, Frinks could hear the service commencing without him. To Frinks's frustration, the minister who was speaking was "less than impressive," and he was desperate to get inside the barricade and take the pulpit himself. "It seemed like that preacher was restraining himself," Frinks recalled, "trying to say, 'Well, I don't want to upset the white folks, don't want to stir up the black folks, I just want to get this thing over with and get this young man in the earth.'" Frinks sidled up to a white trooper with a crew cut and grumbled, "That's a sorry sermon that man is preaching."

The trooper shook his head in agreement but averred that the preaching should "pick up right much directly" because "they're expecting Golden Frinks to come in here and stir this thing up. That's why all of us are here, because they think Frinks is going to show up and get this thing on the move." Laughing, Frinks identified himself and shook the officer's hand warmly. "Well, I guess you're supposed to be over in there," the trooper said with a grin, waving him through the barrier. It was like a drama in which everyone played a part, but not all of the characters were as predictable as Hollywood and history books usually suggest. Ducking under the barricade, Frinks hustled to the church, where he did not disappoint his new friend the state trooper.

At the end of the service, people started getting in cars to go to the graveside, but Frinks held up his hands and stopped them. "I said, 'Now, wait, we don't want to ride here, we want to march. Ben, Leon, all of y'all come up here.'" He gestured to Ben Chavis and Reverend Leon White, a United Church of Christ minister and another leading activist in eastern North Carolina, then beckoned to Thad Stem and Daddy. The black activists spread the word through the crowd that they planned to march to the cemetery. "They just gave over to me," Frinks said. The black firebrand, who knew the small-town South like Ray Charles knows the keyboard, asked Thad and my father to talk to the police and get their approval for the march.

Daddy and Thad strolled over to the captain of the state highway patrol and Chief of Police Nathan White, who were standing by the rope barrier around the cemetery smoking cigarettes. Hands stuffed deep in his pockets, Thad greeted everybody, introducing my father all around. He wasn't Major Stem's boy for nothing, and he knew local politics. After he'd made a couple of pleasant inquiries about the health of Chief White's family and that sort of thing, Thad lit a Camel, lowered his voice, and got down to business. "Nathan, they want to march downtown," Thad said, snorting tobacco smoke. "I believe you ought to lead them down there. Seems to me we'd rather have this thing official than unofficial."

"They're going to have to get a permit," White answered. "They can't have a march without a permit. I don't have enough men on duty to handle that kind of thing. The captain here would have to bring in some state troopers. It might take a couple of days to handle the paperwork."

"They didn't have a permit to break every goddamn window in Oxford the other night, either," Thad said bluntly. "If you let them march, maybe they won't burn the place down tonight. You know as well as I do that tightening the valve ain't gonna keep the boiler from blowing. If they let off a little steam, we might just get past this thing and everybody keep their job." This last point, no doubt rendered with a certain class condescension, seemed to focus Chief White's attention, and the sweet light of reason descended upon him.

"Tell 'em they can march, but they have to keep it orderly and they have to stay in the right-hand lane," White growled. "I am going to need a few minutes to put up some roadblocks." He spat on the ground. "You tell Frinks they can go ahead on to the cemetery any time they want, we already got that covered, but he better not take one goddamn step past there until I give the go-head." Having routed Chief White while permitting him to preserve some semblance of authority, Thad walked with my father back over to where Frinks and his lieutenants were huddled, let them know that the police had okayed the march, and then joined the mourners.

The hearse drove slowly as the wet-eyed throng plodded the several blocks to the graveyard. My father walked alongside Thad, neither of them quite knowing what their part might be at such a moment. All around them the tone of the funeral was shifting from mourning to protest, and the days of white clergymen marching across the Selma bridge with Dr. King were over. For my father, like for most white liberals, his marching days had ended before they had really begun. Most white advocates of civil rights were, as Daddy had feared they would be, too late. The tragic irony was that by the time mainstream white liberals had mastered a few verses to "We Shall Overcome," the young Black Power insurgents had begun to sneer that the lyrics should be changed to "we shall overrun." Daddy walked uncomfortably, though no one tried to make him feel unwelcome. "We were glad to be there, but it was a little awkward," Daddy recalled.

"We walked slow, you know, impressive," Frinks said. "The hearse going along slow, here we come right behind it, walking strong. Got to the cemetery, let the preacher say 'ashes to ashes,' and bam-bam. But then I said, 'Hold up, now.' " Frinks stepped up beside Henry Marrow's grave, alongside Willie Mae Marrow, the weeping widow, and he climbed onto the pile of earth that would soon cover the casket. Calling on the black community to make this tragedy meaningful by uniting in a campaign for justice, Frinks summoned the deep emotions of the moment. "Back then you played on the feelings to bond people together," he recalled decades later. "You had to create such an emotional, sad moment in your delivery, in your oratory, act like you were gonna cry, and then they'd be ready to go again."

Frinks reminded the crowd of their loss and its meaning. "This young man was a husband, he was a daddy," he said, gesturing toward the pregnant Willie Mae Marrow and her two children. "And he was a son, an uncle, and a cousin." Stressing the word "cousin," Frinks looked directly at Ben Chavis, the handsome young leader, knowing that Ben had taken a new level of leadership among the young people in recent days and mindful of the Chavis family's friendship to Marrow and their historic prominence in the African American community. "I had to do that because Ben was kind of a cousin to the young man, and Ben was coming on up," Frinks recalled. "And then I said, 'Come around here hand in hand, and sing

"We Shall Overcome."' That was an impressive thing. And I knew my thing was working." When Golden Frinks called for the crowd to sing "We Shall Overcome," Daddy and Thad crossed their arms like everyone else, reached for the nearest black hand, and sang along. "And I said, 'All right, now you can go ahead and cover him up,'" Frinks told me. "'And we're going on uptown. Now, we ain't got no permit, ain't got nothing. But we're going to march on.' The thing I wanted was to go back down to that big old Confederate monument, you see. That's what I knew we needed to do."

Daddy and Thad, on the other hand, had come to pay their respects and to try to get Henry Marrow buried without further bloodshed. If it had been 1963 instead of 1970, it is possible that Daddy and Thad both would have made their debut that day as civil rights marchers. That would have been unusual, even in the early years of the movement. Most of the white people who appear in film footage of civil rights marches were brave followers of Leon Trotsky or radical Catholic sisters or saintly kooks of one description or another, and almost all of them were from somewhere else. Very few whites actually joined their own local civil rights demonstrations; local whites never thought the protests were well timed or appropriately organized. Daddy hadn't been there, either. But if he had found himself thrust into the march like this, he probably would have been crazy enough to pay the price. Thad was a federal employee, belonged to an affluent, old-line Oxford family, was on speaking terms with many of the state's most powerful Democrats, and did not give a damn what people thought anyway. Daddy would have been risking his pulpit, of course, but he was used to that. In 1970, however, with young black people chanting "Umgawa, Black Power" all around them, finding themselves walking in a sea of black fists bristling upward in the Black Power salute, neither the white man of letters nor the white man of the cloth knew quite what to do.

As the flow of black marchers poured into the street and headed toward the Confederate monument downtown, Thad muttered to Daddy that he felt "like the one-legged man at a public tail-kicking."

When the march neared the corner of Front Street, where both men would have turned to walk home, Thad asked if Daddy might like to stop by the house for a sandwich and a bowl of soup. The two of them ducked out of the march and turned toward home, and out of history, for there was nowhere else to go. One problem was that they had not had the experiences in interracial coalition politics that would have enabled them to disagree with some parts of a black political agenda and support other parts, for example, and hammer out their differences while finding common ground. Nor was there anything like a ready welcome from blacks. Not knowing about the real history of the South, few blacks and even fewer whites knew that these problems had been confronted before, and with some success. In some respects, the split between white liberals and black radicals was a failure of memory. This tragic parting of the ways occurred across the country. That may have been inevitable, but it would have mixed and enduring consequences for American history.

As Daddy and Thad split off from the procession, the marchers continued toward the Confederate monument. The old Rebel soldier in the town's main intersection was more a monument to white supremacy than to the Confederacy and in 1970 most whites either liked it or simply did not think about it. But neither white supremacy nor the Confederacy had always unified the white population. The monument's appearance in 1909 had marked the consolidation of the new social order of segregation and the establishment of a new degree of racial solidarity among whites, who had been deeply divided by the Populist upheavals of the late nineteenth century and the changing politics of race in the decades after the Civil War.

Before the war, Granville County had 1,348 farms, with an average size of 327 acres. Virtually all of the men who owned these farms lived on them and managed them, though many of them enslaved other people to work the fields. By 1890, however, the size of a farm in the county had dropped to 119 acres and most of the land had changed hands; the majority of farmers, black and white, were now sharecroppers. White farmers, their land forfeited to falling prices and rapacious banks, became so desperate that they began to see their black neighbors as potential allies—and to contemplate leaving the Democratic Party, "the party of the fathers," the party of the Confederacy, the party of "the South" as they had always known it.

Hundreds of these dispossessed white farmers joined the Populist movement in the 1890s, established their own newspaper, the *Granville County Reformer*, and founded an Alliance cooperative tobacco warehouse. They even made common cause with African American farmers, though most white Populists were reluctant to accept the former slaves as civic equals, a tragic failure that led to their defeat. Black and white farmers came to this Fusion coalition for different reasons: the white dissidents focused more on economics, while black men sought access to the ballot box and protection from terrorism. Despite these persistent differences and their enduring prejudices, white Populists helped elect a number of black Republicans to office in Granville County in the Fusion coalitions of 1894 and 1896. The most famous of these, Henry Plummer Cheatham, was the only African American to serve in the Fifty-second Congress; the interracial coalition held on longer in Granville County than anywhere else in the South. "For a time," write two local historians, "the politics of economic interests and universal rights took the place of the politics of race in the county." In a sense, my father and Thad Stem were the political heirs of this Fusionist inter-racialism; seventy years earlier, they would have had little trouble finding a political home for themselves. But the problem was that the Fusion coalition was defeated so utterly at the turn of the century, crushed by violence and fraud, and then blotted out of the history books, that seventy years later, most North Carolinians could not remember their interracial past and found it hard even to imagine a realistic interracial coalition. In the case of white liberals, this amnesia meant they could only imagine themselves as paternalists, not authentic little-*d* democrats.

In the 1890s, however, when black and white North Carolinians managed to set aside some of their differences, their combined forces routed corporate domination, returned power to local governments, reformed election laws, and regulated some of the worst excesses of monopoly capitalism. Though whites kept most of the higher offices for themselves, the coalition elected a number of African Americans, especially in sixteen eastern North Carolina counties where blacks held a majority. And they won, despite the fact that they confronted the entrenched power of wealth and privilege. Whatever the limits of their racial egalitarianism, in 1896 the Fusionists captured the governorship, the state legislature, every single statewide race, and helped refashion race relations at the street level.

In 1898, however, white conservatives, unwilling to live with the consequences of universal male suffrage, overthrew the state government, employing violence, fraud, and demagoguery. White Democrats in Granville County joined Red Shirt clubs, whose leaders urged them to "defend white womanhood" by killing any black man who insisted on voting—and any white man who advocated equal citizenship. White solidarity, when lashed together with the powerful language of sex and manhood, proved stronger than philosophical commitments to democracy. In Oxford, clashes between vindictive white Democrats and the Fusionists saw widespread arson, violence, and upheaval. After the Democratic Party seized power in the white supremacy campaigns of 1898, black men lost the vote. The whites that had been their allies were forced to slink back into the Democratic Party.

In the early years of the twentieth century, after black disfranchisement was an established fact and the race and class conflicts died down, Oxford's erection of the monument *To Our Confederate Dead* buried the bitter divisions of the 1890s among whites in a glow of nostalgia for the Lost Cause. Only two generations later, the fact that the Confederacy itself had divided whites was now lost to popular memory, as were the interracial political movements of the decades after the Civil War. In North Carolina as elsewhere, black and white farmers had fitfully but repeatedly sought to make alliance with each other. It was not until the violent overthrow of their dem-

ocratically elected coalition government in the last years of the nineteenth century that Confederate monuments rose in every Southern
town.

This was the point when white supremacy, formerly the slogan of
one faction of whites in the county, became the insoluble glue of civic
life, and inseparable from the legacy of the Confederacy. In 1909, the
Granville Grays chapter of the United Daughters of the Confederacy
purchased the thirty-foot bronze statue of a Confederate soldier and
planted his feet atop a high pedestal of local granite in the center of
Oxford. City officials placed it in the middle of the town's busiest
intersection, even though some critics pronounced it an inconven-
ience and an eyesore. The monument faced forever north, the majority of whites believed, because the boys who'd worn the gray had
never run from the damn Yankees. Elderly Confederate veterans,
cadets from the local white-only military academy, children from the
segregated Oxford orphanage, and young women from Oxford
Seminary were among the thousands who gathered to hear Governor
W. W. Kitchen render a high-flown paean to the Lost Cause, which
"brought tears to many an eye," reported the *Oxford Public Ledger*.
This tall bronze figure testified to the entrenched power of the new
social order, standing guard in front of the courthouse for the next
sixty-five years—until the next revolution in racial politics came to
town.

That latest revolution marched with Golden Frinks from the
graveyard to the courthouse in 1970 on that sunny Saturday afternoon after Henry Marrow's burial. "I saw that Confederate monument," Frinks said, "and I thought it was a good time for this. There
was something in the core of these black people's psyche that carried
a little racism that is still there, but they can't see it." To confront
white supremacy was not just about confronting white people, Frinks
believed, but also a matter of stamping out internalized feelings of
inferiority among blacks. "I looked out at all the light-skinned blacks
and the dark-skinned blacks, and I knew we needed to go down to
that Confederate monument." For hundreds of black citizens in
Granville County, this was a moment of healing, a moment when they

stood up for themselves, defying subjugation with such force that centuries of fear evaporated like spilled lemonade on hot pavement. Freedom pounded in their hearts. Several hundred black citizens marched silently to the courthouse, spirits soaring with possibility despite the sadness of the occasion. "We was drinkin' that freedom wine," Frinks liked to say.

The crowd came together all around the much-loathed monument and heard Ben Chavis, the leader of the young folks and grieving for his slain contemporary, address the crowd in the fiery style of a new generation of Black Power militants. Frinks, the veteran SCLC warrior, spoke about the meaning of the old Confederate's vigil in the center of town. The monument needed to be moved, he said, "because it's a stigma, because it stands for hundreds of years of a repressive period slavery, segregation, Jim Crow, discrimination, bigotry, and all of that complicity of keeping a people down. But we ain't staying down no more," he declared. Years later, Frinks told me how he had waved his broad hands to the assemblage and leavened the fiery rhetoric with humor: "I talked about that man, this old Confederate soldier, how he hadn't been to the bathroom since 1865, and it was time for him to come on down now and get some relief." But Frinks ended the rally by reminding his listeners of the unconscionable brutality of the murder, how Robert Teel and his sons had butchered Henry Marrow as he lay helpless and pleading for his life. He closed his speech with a bitter attack on the white power structure in Oxford: "To them it's just another nigger dead," he said, "but it ain't gonna stay that way. What's going to be dead here soon is old Jim Crow."

Frinks, with his cross and his dashiki, looked like neither an old civil rights veteran nor like a candidate for membership in the Black Panthers. Younger black insurgents, sometimes quick to play "blacker than thou" politics, could not dismiss Frinks as an Uncle Tom. For one thing, they had a fair amount of common ground. Although "Black Power" was a murky slogan that seemed to invite clashing interpretations, most of the elements that have become associated with Black Power—black self-affirmation, international analy-

ses of white supremacy, an interest in Africa and things African, independent black political action, a willingness to employ armed self-
defense when necessary—were already present in the small towns
and rural communities where the freedom movement was born. A
distinct strain of homegrown African American radicalism can be
traced back to slave revolts and Reconstruction-era militants. The
Black Power generation, often portrayed as a sharp break with the
past, drew on long-standing political traditions in the black South.

"I didn't need the sixties or the civil rights movement to make me
angry," Eddie McCoy, one of the most forceful of the young African
American militants in Oxford, explained to my father and a roomful
of students during a class we taught at the University of North
Carolina at Chapel Hill in 2003. "I didn't need that."

McCoy was a graceful, broad-shouldered man, born in 1942 in a
shotgun house across from the jail. His mother, Lucille McCoy,
labored as a maid and cook in white people's houses to support six
children. James McCoy, Eddie's father, worked three jobs as a janitor until he saved up enough money to open a pool hall in 1960. "The
floor in our house had gaps in it, you could feed the chickens through
the cracks in the floor," Eddie recalled bitterly. "And it snowed in the
house and it rained in the house. And it was hot—you didn't have no
fans. There was one plug in the whole house, you run everything off
a drop-cord."

McCoy traced his rage in 1970 to the ordinary, day-to-day humil-
iations that white supremacy imposed on his childhood. "When my
grandmother used to take us to the five-and-ten-cent store, we would
want water, and she would say wait until you get home. Because you
can't drink out of that water fountain, we couldn't read, and she'd say
it was for white people and we couldn't have any." Until he and his
brothers and sisters got old enough to read, McCoy recalled, laughing softly, "We thought the *water* was white. And we wanted some of
that white water because we never had white water. The things we
couldn't do, I always thought 'Why can't we do this?' and the things
white people had that we didn't have, I always wanted to know why
I couldn't have those things."

The signs that whites relegated black people to a separate, inferior caste were glaringly obvious, as they were intended to be. "You had to go to the back of a restaurant to get food," McCoy said. "The blacks called the restaurant downtown 'hole in the wall' because you couldn't go in the door, you had to go down the alley. The restaurant had a real name on the front, but they had a hole in the wall in the alleyway where the blacks would go pick up their food."

When black children walked to school, school buses filled with white children often passed them by. "When you saw a bus of white kids coming you had to get back," recounted McCoy. "You get back as far from that bus as you can, because they gon' spit at you or throw something at you, because they're in a bus and you can't get at 'em."

And when they got to school, said McCoy, all they had to do was open a book to be reminded of their status. "We never got new books," he told me. "All our ratty old books came from the white schools, after they were done with them. When I got a book it was four or five years old, you had three or four more spellers by the time I got your old one. And everybody didn't get one, we had to share. You'd share it with someone else and if they took it home and forgot it, you'd be out of luck for the next two or three days until that kid remembered to bring it back."

The black children whose parents managed to provide them something like a middle-class existence, McCoy explained to my father and the college students, might embrace nonviolence. But the poor, to whom the system had been brutally indifferent, were faster to grab a brick or a fire bomb. "It was always poor children," McCoy observed, "people that didn't have nothing to lose, and their parents were poor and didn't have nothing to lose, so do I paint the picture? We was dispensable, we could see that. I was a write-off kid from the time I was born. I won't gon' be nothing, won't nothing gon' become of me, I won't gon' finish school, I was supposed to go to jail, am I right, Reverend Tyson?"

"A riot is at bottom the language of the unheard," Dr. King told America, but it was far easier for people like my father to hear Dr. King's words about love than to heed his counsel about the young people rioting in the streets. The Black Power insurgents of the late 1960s, disillusioned by the assassination of Dr. King, and keenly aware of themselves as a new generation, rejected interracial approaches and nonviolent direct action. "We wanted the whole system to change," Eddie McCoy explained. "Those civil rights Negroes, the professional people, they was nice, they talked to white people. I didn't think that would work. Martin Luther King was never my favorite. I admired him, I liked what he stood for," McCoy said, "but I didn't think it would work. When nonviolence did work, mostly it was because white people were afraid we was gon' burn the place down."

In the years since the freedom movement ended, the memory of what had been required of people faded, McCoy explained to me, and people no longer appreciated the sacrifices that had been made regardless of methods. "I was doing that stuff back then, sit-ins and marches and all the rest and nowadays nobody even knows what it was like. People right now think that the white man opened up his drugstore and said, 'Y'all come on in now, integration done come.' But every time a door opened, somebody was kicked in the butt; somebody was knocked down and refused and spit on before you went in them places. It wasn't no nonviolence in Oxford. Somebody was bruised and kicked and knocked around—you better believe it. You didn't get it for free." The Civil Rights Act of 1964 had been a good thing, McCoy conceded, but it was the determination of local citizens, not the legislation itself, that made the new law meaningful. "Law or no law," McCoy spat, "somebody still had to go in there and get kicked in the ass. And by the time they killed Dickie Marrow nobody was having that shit anymore. We was about ready to kick some ass our own selves."

CHAPTER 8

OUR "OTHER SOUTH"

NOTHING IN MY family's history—nothing in American history, for that matter—prepared my father for Black Power in the manner of Eddie McCoy. In that regard, Daddy was like most white liberals of his generation. His family background did, in fact, make him unusually receptive to certain aspects of the African American freedom struggle; to the redemptive rhetoric of Martin Luther King Jr., for example. His independent cast of mind allowed him to defy conventional wisdoms of various kinds, and he admired, if he did not always emulate, iconoclastic Southerners like Thad Stem and Charlotte Hawkins Brown who chopped with a big ax and cut their own path. He probably had enough Christian millennialism in him to imagine a whole new social order, though his theologically conservative view of human nature made him doubt that one was on the way. Daddy was a Methodist preacher first and foremost, tending to the living and burying the dead, and he saw his civil rights duties as a matter of persuading the fearful folks in the pew to accept all human beings as children of God and equal in His eyes. But even if Daddy had not been a preacher above all else, he was not hard-edged enough to make sense to someone like Eddie McCoy.

Where Eddie McCoy simply demanded respect—and back in 1970, at least, really saw little reason to talk to white people at all—Daddy wanted a new heaven and a new earth, where the lion would lie down with the lamb. Daddy liked to joke that the lion had always been willing, especially around lunchtime, but the lamb needed more assurance that the Kingdom was at hand. The Black Power generation's vision of social change, though it was often portrayed as radical, and thought of itself as radical, was actually in some ways a deeply traditional and even conservative assessment: you could have whatever you could take, and you could keep whatever you could hold. Power conceded nothing without a demand, as Frederick Douglass had pointed out a century earlier; it never had and it never would. But my daddy longed for justice to roll down like waters, for the crooked places to be made straight and the rough places to be made smooth, and for all flesh to see it together. Neither his view nor McCoy's involved a pragmatic understanding of coalition politics—how we would get there from here. But both Daddy's committed Christian faith and his Eleanor Roosevelt liberalism led him to yearn that white people would concede power rather than black people merely seize it.

There were other white Southerners with broader visions, I realize now, but few of them had the ear of any appreciable white congregation. I now know that there was a Southern left populated by radicals and prophets, people like Myles Horton, who founded the Highlander Folk School in Tennessee in 1932, where a generation later Rosa Parks became acquainted with other people like herself from across the South, whose defiant stories inspired her famous one-woman sit-in on the bus in Montgomery; Anne and Carl Braden, called "dedicated Communists" by Kentucky's attorney general, whose *Southern Patriot* kept dissidents in Dixie informed of one another's existence in the 1950s and 1960s; Virginia Durr, an Alabama belle whose antiracist activism over the decades placed her *Outside the Magic Circle*, as she titled her autobiography; and Lillian Smith, the Georgia-born lesbian writer whose *Killers of the Dream* inspired generations of Southern dissidents, including my father. But while Daddy had stumbled upon Smith's classic in a course that he took at Guilford College, most of the Tysons had never heard of her or these other radical folks. I came to know their stories much later, as a historian, and wished that I had grown up knowing them.

Southerners like the Tysons did not write for radical magazines or get investigated by the House Un-American Activities Committee, though we sometimes got run out of town all by ourselves. The truth is that neither ideology nor sociology moved my family; instead, we found our footing in the Scriptures we were raised on and in the church that sometimes broke our hearts.

Some people criticized my father and some of his brothers for being "fanatics," and it would be soothing and self-congratulatory now, after the fact, to accept that critique and portray my kinfolks as the kind of saints and heroes that populate many conventional narratives about the civil rights movement. But the truth is that the Tysons got embroiled in this mess out of decidedly mixed motives. It was not that they were crusading heroes or political leaders so much as that they were passionate, willful, stubborn Christians responding to the world around them. They heard the Spirit of God within them and tried to obey—that was *part* of it. But they also drank deeply from that uncompromising and rebellious pride that moves in the hearts of both ruthless tyrants and saintly visionaries.

As the Lord had revealed it to the Tyson boys, they were smarter than you were and better looking than you were, and they could preach rings around anybody you knew, and could not only stomp a mudhole in you and kick it dry, if it came to that, but had their finger on the pulse of the Holy Spirit besides. They took their orders directly from the Lord, and lesser authorities could kiss their asses. Consequently, nobody had any business telling them what to do or say, nor did any of the principalities and powers of this world. In fact, the more power you had, the less likely the Tysons were to take dictation from you. That isn't a saintly orientation toward the world, exactly, but saints who share it probably swim farther upstream than the timorous angels my daddy derided as "little tailor-made Jesus boys." If, as one of the better-known humorists of my granddaddy's day speculated, a fanatic is a person who does just what the Lord would do if He knew the actual facts of the case, then the Tysons probably were fanatics. But before we give them credit as social prophets, we do well to remember that they rebelled not only against an unjust social order but sometimes against their own best lights, too.

However we assess them, certainly the Tysons were not part of the South that U. B. Phillips, one of the leading historians of his day, described in 1928 as "a people with a common resolve, indomitably maintained—that it shall be and remain a white man's country." Mistakenly, in my view, Phillips called this determination for white supremacy "the cardinal test of a Southerner and the central theme of Southern history." But the Tyson family's less common resolve, maintained as indomitably as any that Phillips could have described, reflected a vision of the love of Jesus that emphatically included everyone of whatever color. This did not mean that we were somehow untainted by white supremacy. We breathed it in with the tobacco smoke that wafted through every restaurant back in those days. But we were dissenters from the majority opinion among whites on the matter of race. Carl Degler, a historian of antislavery dissenters in the region, called people like us "the Other South." The Tysons did not know there was an other South, and probably never heard the phrase. Like our ancestors, we took our stand in the only Dixieland we had ever known. If history had seen us defeated again and again, did that make the dissidents any *less* Southern than the slaveholders and segregationists? Lost causes ran in our blood.

Not necessarily *the* Lost Cause, though; my great-great-grandfather William Tyson, who was born in 1835 in Pitt County, North Carolina, bitterly opposed secession in 1860 and never believed in slavery. Early that year, as hotheaded secessionists in the Carolinas worked to foment a revolution against the United States, William Tyson sired a son and named him George Washington, after the founder of American nationalism. In 1862, a year after secessionist troops had surrounded the state capital, shoved the state out of the Union at gunpoint, and hitched North Carolina to the caboose of the Confederacy, William Tyson fathered another son. This time my great-great-grandfather looked to the more recent past for a name that would signal his disapproval. As Union troops overran New Bern, only a few miles away, William Tyson named the boy Henry

Clay Tyson, after the Great Compromiser, who had sought to hold the Union together and favored gradual emancipation of slaves. My father once claimed that this was a little like a white Southerner naming his son Muhammad Ali at the height of the Vietnam War, but that may have been an exaggeration. Henry Clay was not a black liberationist by any stretch, though his political creed—Whig nationalism—got drowned out in the crisis of the 1850s and 1860s, much as my father's liberalism got drowned out in the wake of the Black Power era. In any case, like thousands of his neighbors, William Tyson remained a Unionist like Clay, even while the Civil War engulfed his home, and refused to support the Confederacy.

In 1864, General George E. Pickett, who had led the famous Pickett's Charge at the Battle of Gettysburg, ordered twenty-two local boys in Kinston hanged in public for their loyalty to the United States. On a hastily constructed gallows at the Lenoir County courthouse, eastern North Carolina saw what the Confederacy was willing to do to its dissenters. After the mass hangings, Confederate soldiers went to the homes of the wives and children of the executed men, confiscated all their property, and forbade their friends and neighbors to help them. The Confederates would have hanged William Tyson, too, but he hid in people's barns and in an underground passageway down by the Neuse River at Maple Cypress. From his secret sanctuary, William Tyson would slip out only at night to see his family, eluding the Confederate "recruiters" who roamed the roads. At the end of the war, he was forced into the Confederate "Home Guard" for a short time, then almost immediately captured by Union troops and sent to a prison camp up North. Things had been so hard for working people in eastern North Carolina under the Confederates, he liked to joke in later years, that he actually gained weight as a Union prisoner of war.

My ancestor's experience was quite typical in eastern North Carolina. Too little evidence of William Tyson survives to say for certain, but it would not surprise me if he had been a member of the Heroes of America, known informally as "the Red Strings," a secret society of anti-Confederate guerrillas and saboteurs across the state. There were roughly ten thousand of them, although you would never know it to hear the Sons of Confederate Veterans talk these days. Some were motivated by religious objections to slavery. Many others believed that this war was "a rich man's war and a poor man's fight," and that they themselves had no stake in the system of slavery. Still others objected to the tyranny of the Confederate government, which they had never consented to support. Poor whites resented Confederate impressment and taxation policies, but hated Confederate conscription laws that conveniently exempted wealthy slave-holders and their sons, one exemption for every twenty slaves owned. In 1861, one Rebel loyalist complained to the Confederate secretary of war that eastern North Carolina was "infested by Tories and disloyal persons." When federal troops captured the northeastern North Carolina coast in 1862, almost a thousand white men volunteered for service in the Union armies. In 1864, Zebulon Vance, the widely admired Confederate governor of North Carolina, conceded that "the great popular heart is not now and never has been in this war. It was a revolution of the politicians and not the people."

Ignoring all evidence to the contrary, white supremacists and neo-Confederates have made enthusiasm for the Confederacy posthumously unanimous. Some of them will even try to tell you that the slaves loyally supported the Confederacy, which is just a damn lie. In fact, as soon as federal troops under General Ambrose E. Burnside, guided by runaway slaves, invaded eastern North Carolina, thousands of those "loyal darkies" fled straight to the Union encampments. "It would be utterly impossible to keep them outside of our lines," the perplexed General Burnside reported to the secretary of war, "as they find their way to us through woods and swamps from every side."

The actual history of the South too often rests in an unmarked grave, while the celebratory lies and politically convenient distortions march into immortality. In the 1990s, my father and I drove down to eastern North Carolina and plodded across a plowed field near Friendship Church to a small family graveyard that is William Tyson's final resting place. The stone reads: WILLIAM TYSON, 1835–1916. IN HONEST MAN IS THE NOBLEST WORK OF GOD—illiterate stonemasons had turned "an" to "in." Ironically, given his Unionist politics, which he never recanted, we found a brand-new Sons of Confederate Veterans marker on his grave. My great-great-grandfather hid from the Confederates in life, but their descendants caught him after death, when he could no longer flee, and claimed him as a Confederate veteran, violating his memory in order to polish up the Lost Cause. Daddy pulled up the marker and gently tossed it into the weeds, shaking his head. When we went back ten years later, the marker had returned, and I yanked up the iron stob and pitched it a long, long way into the nearby tobacco field.

That Southern dissenting tradition, however embattled, persisted in the life of my grandfather Marvin Earl Tyson, as well. He was a handsome string bean of a man with an insatiable intellect, born in 1901 near Friendship Free Will Baptist Church in Greene County, North Carolina. No one really knows exactly when or where Jack, as they called him, rejected white supremacy and began to preach a strange new gospel of equality; he came to it by degrees. Raised a fundamentalist, Jack was independent by nature, and as his mind grew he began more and more to live by his own reckoning. "My father was a kind of growing person," Vernon recalled. "He didn't come out of that root," he said, referring to Jack's evolving ideas about racial equality, "but those branches came out of his life, and he just let them flower as they would." Even when nearly everyone around him felt differently, Jack kept his own counsel and trusted his own interpretations of the world. "He didn't give a damn what other people thought about him," my uncle Dewey said, "at least not about theological or philosophical questions, or how he was going to do things. If he did, anyway, we couldn't tell."

Jack was the oldest of the seven children of Willie and Patty Mae Tyson, a farming family. They were poor as Job's turkey. Willie broke his leg one spring when the boy was in the eighth grade, and Jack quit school to plow and plant his daddy's tobacco crop. He and his uncle Alonzo Tyson, who was a Free Will Baptist preacher, farmed side by side and never tired of talking about the things of the Spirit. Early one morning Jack went over to borrow a wrench to reset the sweep of his plow, and they got to talking about God, and when the dinner bell rang at noon, the two men were still standing out in the unplowed tobacco field, discussing the meaning of salvation and the doctrine of original sin. No wonder they stayed poor.

Free Will Baptists had abandoned the old Calvinist belief in pre-destination and believed in "free will, free grace and free salvation." A morally meaningful decision had to be taken freely, and humanity must choose its path to God. In those days, the generic term *Baptist* in eastern North Carolina generally meant Free Will Baptist. They did not get so far in the towns and cities, but out along the rural roads and up at the branch heads, country folk flocked in to hear the fiery sermons and sing the ancient hymns. Free Will Baptists displayed more emotion in church than Methodists and would have made an Episcopalian squirm, but they did not "speak in tongues" and cavort like the Pentecostal holy rollers. Some called them "foot-washing Baptists," and Free Willers did hold quarterly meetings during which they washed one another's feet. Jesus had washed feet, and that was good enough for them. At the end of the service, they would file up, row by row, and take turns kneeling before one another with tin basins and clean towels in a quiet drama of tender humility. This sacramental act underlined the fact that Jesus had called his follow-ers to the way of humble service. Men washed the feet of men and women washed the feet of women; there was a clear understanding that young men and women washing one another's bare feet were unlikely to keep their minds on the things of the Spirit.

Jack attended these services a good deal, but his thoughts seem to have wandered from the things of the Spirit pretty regularly. When he was about eighteen, he was standing with some boys beneath the oaks at Friendship Free Will Baptist Church and saw a pretty girl walking across the yard. He asked who she was, and someone told him that she was one of the daughters of Reverend Willie Hart, the new preacher. "Well," he announced to his companions, "I believe I am going to give that preacher a hard time."

Eighteen months later, when Willie Hart came home one Saturday afternoon, his five-year-old son met him at the road. "Daddy, Daddy, you better come quick," the youngster yelled. "Irene has run off and married Jack Tyson, and Bessie thinks *she* is about grown!" Bessie was Willie's fourteen-year-old girl and, according to family lore, she had rouged her cheeks with brick dust and steadfastly insisted that Irene, who was only two years older, was *plenty* old enough to get married.

Jack had taken Irene to Greenville, the county seat of Pitt County, to get the marriage license, and then he'd driven to his uncle Alonzo's house three miles outside Farmville, in Greene County, to get married. But Alonzo said that he couldn't perform a wedding in Greene County; the ceremony wouldn't be valid, since it was a Pitt County license. And so they all got in the Model T Ford and drove just across the county line at Middle Swamp in the rain, where Jack and Irene said their vows in the back seat of the car. Lots of folks back then got *engaged* in the back seat of a car, though sometimes they did not realize it right away, but Jack and Irene actually got married there. In later years, Irene liked to joke that only the front end of the car was in Pitt County, but that the back seat was still in Greene County and therefore she wasn't legally obligated to honor or obey.

In the early 1920s, Jack Tyson joined the Ku Klux Klan. My grandfather's cousin Henry recruited him into the brotherhood of the bedsheet and sold him his first and only robe and hood. We should never forget that the Klan was about as mainstream as the Rotary club in the 1920s; membership nationally soared into the millions and included U.S. senators and, for example, the entire state legislature of Indiana. The mayor of Madison, Wisconsin, where I live now, openly endorsed the Klan. The Klan pumped its own muscular brand of Protestant morality; Cousin Henry had described it as a Christian men's group devoted to providing cornmeal and sweet potatoes for widows and buying shoes and school books for orphans. If some sorry sumbitch was laying up drunk and his pregnant wife was out in the yard splitting wood, Cousin Henry told Jack, the Klan would drop by in their sheets and tell that man to sober up and that if there wasn't a big pile of stove wood on the porch by the next evening, they would tan his hide but good. My grandfather joined the KKK out of both misguided piety and ignorant bigotry. I find it fascinating, and even hopeful, that Jack could go from klansman to race rebel. But it must have embarrassed my family because I learned about Jack's later racial egalitarianism decades before I heard that he had been in the KKK. Most of us would rather claim to have always been perfect than admit how much we have grown. It occurs to me that my grandfather's turn against white supremacy may have had something to do with his Klan experience, but apparently he never explained. Jack quickly discovered that the Klan was more com-mitted to prejudice than piety, and he left after only a few weeks. Wearing the mask encouraged good people to do bad things, Jack told his children in later years, and the Klan's obsession with white supremacy would not stand up to the injunctions of the New Testament.

Growing up the daughter of a preacher, Irene was neither sur-prised nor dismayed when her young husband began to feel that the Lord was calling him to the ministry. In those days, Jack was an evan-gelical fundamentalist. He led the singing at camp meetings, held prayer meetings at their house, and began "exhorting" a little at Friendship Church. But his great shame was that he had no educa-tion beyond eighth grade, and he was sharp enough to know his own limitations. One day while he was teaching Sunday school, the prin-cipal of the local high school walked in and sat down. Jack was mor-tified that this man of learning was sitting before him, ignorant as he was, and later Jack told his children that he'd wished the floor would open up and let him through. But a few days later, John Holmes, the owner of the John Deere tractor dealership in Farmville, sent for Jack. "The school man told me he heard you at Friendship Church the other day," Holmes told my young grandfather, "and he says you have great gifts for preaching but that you could use a little educa-tion." Jack thanked him and conceded that he sorely lacked book learning. Mr. Holmes then offered to place fifty dollars a month in a bank account for Jack if he'd go to school. At the time, grown men cut timber all day long for a dollar, and fifty dollars a month was good money. And so Jack went first to Eureka College, the Free Will Baptist school in Ayden, and then moved down to Buies Creek and attended Campbell College, which also offered high school courses.

Through this almost bizarre gesture of Christian fellowship from a near stranger, Jack Tyson got his high school diploma and acquired a little polish of learning when he was thirty and the father of seven children. He continued to take correspondence courses. Though he could only dream of graduating from college, he became a voracious reader and dedicated biblical scholar, and his mind ranged freely. His gifts made him a renowned Free Will Baptist preacher, and he conducted revivals all over eastern North Carolina. Jack Tyson had grown up in a world where preachers didn't admit to preparing sermons; you just opened your mouth and God filled it. That kind of preacher would just "beat the Book and holler," Jack liked to say derisively. But his reading and writing, combined with the evangelical style that he had learned growing up among fundamentalists, gave him a striking combination of preparation and passion. ("You read yourself full, you pray yourself hot, and then you turn yourself loose," he taught my daddy.) His inclination to study, undoubtedly a good thing, nevertheless encouraged his persistent temptation to regard his own views as divine writ; he did not think that he was God—that would have been blasphemy—but he sometimes seemed to think that God agreed with him on a pretty regular basis.

Education also encouraged Jack Tyson to break the shackles of fundamentalism. The Bible is not a history text or a biology book, he said. It is the highest that we know of God, but we do not know everything about God, nor are we likely to understand Him fully on this side of the river Jordan. He didn't need a Divine blueprint; a God small enough for him to understand, Jack Tyson liked to say, would not have been big enough for him to worship. As he pondered the Scriptures and the world around him, his social views became increasingly liberal. He kept company with New Dealer sociologists and social prophets, and ran with radicals and renegades of various stripes. He became fast friends with a left-wing Methodist preacher named Key Taylor, a wild-eyed populist who supported cotton mill strikers and treated "colored people" exactly as if they were white. In 1943, when the Free Will Baptist convention voted down a proposal that the denomination move toward having a formally educated clergy, Jack Tyson left the Free Will Baptists and became a Methodist preacher.

Our family's religious journey seems to ratify the old joke that a Methodist was just a Baptist who had learned to read and write. The rumor among resentful Baptists was that Jack had sold out for filthy lucre, that the Methodists had bought him by promising to send his children to college. That was not true, in any literal way, but all six of his sons became Methodist ministers and most of them attended Duke Divinity School; unlike the Free Will Baptists, the Methodists required an educated clergy. That denominational switch changed the whole history of our family. The Methodists were a more middle-class denomination, and Methodist preachers had minimum salary protection and a retirement plan. If I grew up with a carpet on the floor and a picture on the wall and books in the house, it was partly because we became Methodists.

Jack served small-town and country churches, and he never made any money. But life was a little easier. "When my daddy was driving the car and he was dressed up," my own father remembered, "I thought he was so handsome. He had store-bought clothes on, nice suits, and his shoes were shined. He had Palmolive shaving lotion on and Vitalis hair stuff, and I thought his hat smelled good. I thought that any wind that went by him and came in my nostril was a sweet wind."

Life in eastern North Carolina did not always smell so sweet. Though people tend to think of poor, rural white Southerners as the worst racists in the country, these were not the people who redlined black folks out of their neighborhoods, the way northern bankers and real estate agents did. They were hardly in a position to keep blacks out of America's most elite schools, the way northeastern aca-demics did. And white country people in the South often lived right alongside blacks, in similar material conditions, which both softened and sharpened racial clashes. Karl Marx exaggerated only slightly in pointing out that poor whites had nothing to lose but their chains. But Marx couldn't have known that the links that white supremacy and the Civil War had hammered into those chains gave white working people in Dixie a bone-deep sense of themselves as white Southerners, tied to a bloody history that usually pitted them against African Americans, even in opposition to their own interests.

The landscape poor whites shared with blacks, in rough and unequal fashion, was a hardhanded world of hog killing, hookworm, and backbreaking labor, where the Great Depression came early and stayed late. Indoor plumbing was practically unknown; the outhouse, with its Sears Roebuck catalog, and the slop jar under the bed were standard equipment. Kerosene lamps provided what little light was needed, since men and women who had worked from dawn until dusk rarely sat up late reading. The Tyson boys shared shoes when one of them needed to look nice, and cardboard patches made shoe leather walk a little farther. Irene Hart Tyson stitched pajamas and underwear for the children out of flour sacks. Her boys bickered over socks; after my father grew up, his sock drawer was always brimming with new socks, neatly rolled in homage to the painful memory of having had so few to wear when he was a boy.

When there was no meat and not enough eggs in Irene's larder, she would make egg gravy and biscuits. Or else she would fry out a little fatback pork, add flour, and make thin gravy with black pepper, Tabasco sauce, salt, and water. She would slice leftover biscuits into the gravy and simmer them, a dish she called "stewed biscuits." On cold winter mornings, she would break up kindling and light a fire in the stove, and serve fried dough with homemade jam as a treat for her brood. Irene worked hard and loved harder, and managed well through every hardship except losing her children; she had ten children in all, but three of them died as infants or toddlers.

The first one, Thelma, was a curly-headed three-year-old angel and Irene's only girl when she died of pneumonia in 1929. For the rest of her life, Irene would pass girls on the street and say, "Jack, look, she's about the age Thelma would be if she had lived." Thelma's picture occupied a permanent place of reverence on the mantelpiece. "I know that when my mama died," Daddy said, "and she met God, she didn't say, 'Tell me about the Trinity, I've always wondered how God could be three in one.' What she said was, 'Have you taken good care of my Thelma? And when can I see her?' " A second girl, Velma, died of diphtheria in 1938, when she was ten months old.

Soon after Velma died, Irene entered her eleventh pregnancy. The family doctor thought that having another baby would be a threat to her health, and her husband sided with the physician. After much persuasion, Irene checked into the little country hospital in Wilson to undergo a hysterectomy, which would abort this pregnancy and prevent any more. When Jack left the house to see her, he sternly instructed the seven older children to take good care of little Eugene, who was three, and to scrub out the entire house. The boys boiled water on the stove and dumped each full pot into the galvanized tin tub set on the wide boards of the kitchen floor. But before they had filled the washtub, little Eugene teetered backward, plopped down into the scalding hot water, and screamed.

Lying on her bed in the tiny hospital, Irene heard the crying infant being hustled into the emergency room. "That's *my* baby," she yelled, and the nurses had to restrain her to keep her from running to see him. Badly burned from the waist down, little Eugene died during the night. His father carefully dressed the boy, combing his hair and carefully cleaning his fingernails with a pocketknife, before they went to the cemetery to sing "Safe in the Arms of Jesus" and lower Irene's precious boy into the sandy loam of Greene County. Irene felt terribly guilty about the abortion and blamed herself for the tragedy. My great-aunt Pauline, about sixteen at the time, came to live with Jack and Irene's family for several months afterward to help out with the housework. "Rene-rene was just devastated," Pauline recalled. "As far as she was concerned, this was God's way of saying, 'I decide who lives and who dies, not you.' She just sort of broke down after that."

Robert G. Teel, Gerald's father, grew up in this same brutal world of tenant farming and hardscrabble survival. He was born in Pitt County the year after my father, in 1930, the son of Lucy Barrow and Moses Teel, only a few miles down the same lonesome stretch of blacktop where the Tysons lived. Young Robert's mother and father separated early in their marriage; there were rumors that a drunken father had physically abused Robert. Lucy took her son and went home to her parents' farm near La Grange. "We was staying with my grandparents until Ma and my stepdaddy married," Teel told me later. "We were farmers, worked hard, got along pretty good." The Teel family could not have had much more money than the Tysons and, like my father, Gerald's daddy had sometimes worn underwear stitched from flour sacks. Collard greens, fried fatback, field peas, and fried cornbread were standard table fare. Young Teel did not always get that much. "I came from a real poor family," Teel explained. "Real, real poor."

After a time, apparently against the will of her parents, Lucy remarried to a man named Jesse Smith. Robert Teel kept his first father's last name but idolized his new stepfather. Years later, Teel still called him "one of the greatest men I have ever known." The Barrows, however, never accepted Jesse Smith. "They told me you're not supposed to listen to your stepdaddy," Teel said. Teel and Smith shared an aversion to formal schooling. "I was kind of hardheaded, didn't much want to go to school," Teel recounted, "and I thought I shouldn't have minded listening to my stepdaddy." Teel dropped out of high school at sixteen, lied about his age, and joined the army.

I have often contemplated the differences between my father and Gerald's father, and how they shaped our lives. Daddy and Teel were within a year of each other in school and grew up only a few miles apart. Neither of them liked school worth a damn. They wore overalls, ate cornbread and beans, drank their iced tea heavily sweetened, and knew what it was to work hard in the tobacco fields from sunup to sundown. Each of them left eastern North Carolina wanting something better, something more. The difference between them couldn't be boiled down to socioeconomic class; neither of their families had a pot to piss in or a window to throw it out of, as the saying went. In fact, while Teel had his G.I. Bill educational benefits to pay his way through any school, my father had to borrow and scrounge. But Daddy went to a liberal arts college founded by the Quakers, where he met pacifists, liberals, radicals of various descriptions, and black people far more educated than himself. More important, he had Reverend Jack Tyson for a father. At the heart of our differences, I think, stand the many-sided visions of Jesus that haunt the South. Although eastern North Carolina was awash in Baptist fundamentalism, the Teel clan did not seem to have had the softening influence of the gospel in their lives, at least not the same gospel that Jack Tyson preached.

During World War II, for example, my grandfather resigned one of his pastorates rather than permit the church to buy war bonds. When the radio played the popular song "Praise the Lord and Pass the Ammunition," Jack said to turn that mess off; he was not going to have it in his house. One night, driving from Pikeville to Stantonsburg, according to my father, Jack let them listen to the whole song. "I want you to know why I object to it so much," Vernon remembered him explaining. He understood people passing the ammunition, but didn't hold with them praising God while they were doing it. Jack was not a pacifist, certainly not in the face of Adolf Hitler, but in his mind it was not the place of the church to make war, nor was it appropriate for Christians to celebrate slaughter. Not surprisingly, since race stood at the center of Southern life, race was the issue where Jack clashed with his fellow Christians most sharply.

The racial views of the Almighty were well known to the white citizens of eastern North Carolina. Most white Christians believed that white supremacy was the will of God; the Lord Himself had placed them above the "sons of Ham," whose appointed purpose was to be hewers of white people's wood and drawers of white people's water. The segregationists' favorite biblical citation was Genesis 9:18–26. In the ninth chapter of Genesis, Noah got drunk, and his own son, Ham, saw him naked. This embarrassed Noah, evidently, and he cursed Ham's son, Canaan, his own grandson, who had nothing to do with it. "Cursed be Canaan," Noah declared, "and let him be a bondman of bondmen to his brethren."

Right-wing fundamentalists invoked Noah's little domestic incident as God's blessing upon slavery, segregation, and white supremacy; children's literature from the White Citizens Councils in the 1950s confidently assured white youngsters that heaven, too, would be segregated. Jack himself accepted these distortions of Scripture early in his life, back in the 1920s. Once he began to read and ponder the Book for himself in the 1930s, however, it became clear to Jack that the Bible said no such thing. For one thing, the author of Genesis did not utter one damn word about the pigmentation of Ham or his sons. In fact, it stands to reason that Ham looked right much like Noah's other sons. And Jack observed that it was not God who had cursed Ham, but Noah when he was drunk as a busted bicycle, not to mention butt naked. In this undignified condition, Noah hardly seemed to Jack the most likely vehicle for eternal proclamations about the social order.

White Southerners, with their abiding sense of place, also saw God's blessing for the social order in the natural world around them. "Segregation is a fundamental law of nature," one of Jack's contemporaries wrote to the editor of his hometown paper, "and the mockingbirds and robins lead separate and peaceful lives." Any challenge to white supremacy would represent "a violation of God's eternal laws as fixed as the stars," the North Carolina superintendent of schools told an auditorium filled with African American college students when my father was a boy. If God had intended black and white people to mix as equals, most white folks figured, He would not have made them different colors. Of course, looking around the barnyards and fields where he lived, Jack could see that the segregationists drew their examples from the natural world as selectively as they read the Bible. They never argued that black horses wouldn't mate with white horses, since they clearly did. Mockingbirds and robins were not just different colors, like people, but separate species. And the ubiquitous mules that plowed the tobacco fields and hauled the cured leaf to market brayed every day in witness to the failure of donkeys and horses to discern the Divine plan.

Like the mule, Jack enjoyed the sound of his own voice, and I think it is important to concede that his contrarian views about race partook in some measure of his arrogance and cussedness. On race, and on several other topics, Jack's brilliant mind and his powerful ego sometimes set him at odds with other folks. His ministry was important to him, and he did not offend the folks in the pew lightly. But at some point, he simply stopped obeying many of the racial folkways that both reflected and created the architecture of social power in the South. Black Southerners worked alongside white people, for example, "but they didn't drink out of your dipper," my father recalled. "And when they cooked for white people, they didn't eat at the main table. But in the 1940s, the blacks who helped us on the farm began to eat at our table." It was not easy for blacks to cross the line, Vernon remembered. "They weren't really sure they were welcome. But my daddy taught us to just say, 'Oh, yeah, come on in here and eat with us.' It was not something we talked about so much but just something we did."

For all of his iconoclastic radicalism on race, even my grandfather never entirely shook the presumptions of his white supremacist culture. Nor were his white supremacy and his racial egalitarianism always easily separated. When Jack's friend "Uncle Rudy" Clegg, the black janitor of the local high school, asked Jack to officiate at the wedding of his granddaughter, Jack did not hesitate to agree. He came home and told the family that Rudy had assured him that these nuptials would be "the biggest thing that Biscoe ever pulled off," and they all got a laugh out of what seemed a poor black man's presumption. The Tysons quoted Rudy laughingly as sort of a playful "coon" story, as if Rudy were the blustery "Kingfish" in *Amos 'n' Andy*. But Mr. Clegg was a man of substance on the other side of the color line, and he knew what he was talking about. The crowd at Big Bethel was so large that Jack literally had to crawl in the rear window of the church. He loved every minute of the service and attended the reception afterward. When the congregations at his white churches heard the outlandish news—that Preacher Tyson had married a black couple—there were angry words and cold stares, but he won them back. Jack generally kept his white congregations for the same reason that he welcomed black folks at his front door and sat them down at his dinner table; he was openhanded and warmhearted, a deeply religious man who earnestly believed in what he would have called "the fatherhood of God and the brotherhood of man." If he sometimes offended his congregations, they always knew where he stood. Of course, it did not hurt any, a friend of his assured me, that when Jack Tyson "stood like a ramrod up there in the pulpit, he was the damnedest preacher I ever heard. I mean the best, and by a long shot, too."

Jack's heyday in the pulpit came during the 1930s and 1940s, when the challenge to segregation and white supremacy was beyond the vision of most Americans. And Jack didn't preach about race very often. Like my daddy always said, if you asked him about his sermon ahead of time, Jack preached "about God, and about twenty minutes." But when the Spirit spoke to him about race, he heeded the call. One Sunday afternoon in 1945 while Jack was serving the Biscoe-Star-Candor circuit in Montgomery County, C. V. Richardson, the big textile mill owner up at Star, came by the parsonage in a huff and told him to stay away from the subject of race.

By the 1930s, the Carolinas had surpassed New England as the world's leading producer of yarn and cloth. Despite the long hours at low pay, hard-pressed farm families poured into cotton mills like the one Richardson owned. These jobs "furnished almost the only refuge for the white laboring people of the South from the strong competition of cheap negro labor," as the *Southern Textile Bulletin*, the mouthpiece of the mill owners, warned. It would be wrong, the *Bulletin* argued, "to work negroes in association with white women and children." Except for a handful of janitorial jobs, the cotton mills stayed lily-white. For the first two-thirds of the twentieth century, the mill owners constantly warned that "communist" labor unions had targeted the mills with their radical agenda of "race mixing" and social overthrow. "The Communists may harangue until judgement day," the *Southern Textile Bulletin* vowed, "but they can never convince the cotton mill operators of the South that negroes are their equals." Mill owners like Richardson took care to hold preachers under their thumbs; the money men depended on the ministers to help keep black and white working people at each other's throats, labor unions at bay, and wages in the cellar. Richardson, who donated a large portion of the church budget, warned Jack that he'd already "heard just about enough of those 'nigger sermons.'"

Soon after Richardson issued the warning, Jack mounted his pulpit and told the congregation about a dream. It wasn't like the dream Martin Luther King Jr. would lift up for the ages at the March on Washington almost twenty years later—in fact, it was a white man's strange nightmare—but it worked toward the same ends. Jack told the people that in his dream, he woke up one morning and his skin had turned black. He was the very same person inside, he said, with all the same hopes, needs, and aspirations, but no one knew him anymore. His wife would not let him in the house, and his children turned away from their daddy. In his dream, Jack told the congregation, he walked the streets alone and could not find a job or a place to sit down and have a cold drink. He was a man without a country and a wanderer in a world that walled him away. At the end of his sermon, Jack broke the spell of his tale and confessed to his parishioners that it hadn't been a dream at all, just something he'd been thinking about one day—that God Almighty was not a respecter of persons, and He did not care about the color line. "And I think all of you ought to think about it, too," he added, motioning the piano player to start the last hymn.

On the way down the aisle, Jack saw the textile mill owner glowering at him and knew fully the price he might pay. Although it was only his third year in Biscoe and the standard hitch for Methodist preachers in those days was four years, the church's administrative board voted not to renew his contract, and the bishop moved Jack to Carrboro, North Carolina, on the edge of Chapel Hill. He died there in 1953; but his family always remembered his defiance with unmasked pride. Jack's children grew up knowing that you stood your ground on some things.

And they began to have to stand that ground with him, in part because it was safer for the townspeople to assail his sons than to take on Jack face-to-face. "I became his defender," my father recalled. "Down at Lonnie Hurley's taxicab and fuel oil station, I had to defend my papa. I said, I was there, I heard what he said, and this is what he meant by what he said. I explained it, but I didn't apologize for him. I was proud of him." Terms like "nigger lover" were intended to hurt, but they became a badge of honor for the Tyson boys. "That was about the worse epithet you could get in those days, if you were white," he remembered. "If people really wanted to smear you, if they really wanted to hurt you, that is what they would say, and sometimes they would say it about my daddy. But I would have rather been a poor boy at his table," my father told me, "than to have been eating at the table of the rich, with somebody that compromised over something important."

That spirit of rebellion was not merely a matter of ethics, religion, or kindness, though it might partake of all those things. My second cousin Elias Tyson, whom the family called "the Gator," was not so much the wellspring of that rebel spirit as its most dramatic expression. The Gator was a two-bit drunkard, a shiftless Casanova, and a charming gambler who was cruel to everyone who cared about him. He was Jack Tyson's sister's youngest son. But where Jack, who had his own demons, nevertheless pursued the things of God, the Gator was a sensual, passionate, faithless man whose insatiable appetites for whiskey and sex ruled him and whose violent capacities brought his whole family to heartbreak.

Anywhere from ten to twenty years older than my uncles, the Gator came across as a striking example of untamed manhood. "Gator was an extremely handsome man when he was young," said my uncle Dewey. "Movie-star handsome. About six foot four, weighed two twenty-five, black wavy hair and pretty brown eyes, good skin. The girls just hung around him in droves." The strapping young rounder "was a sharp dresser, too," Dewey observed. "He wore fine clothes, brown suits, and he looked good in them." He may not have had a lot of clothes, my uncle Tommy added: "None of us had much money, but he had rather have two or three really nice shirts instead of a closet full of cheap stuff. He had good taste." Decades later, when one of my uncles would swagger in front of the mirror, combing his hair a little too carefully, one of the others might playfully announce, "I believe that must be the Gator in there, don't y'all?" Or when a beloved nephew came in drunk or got somebody pregnant, his uncles might say, "I believe that boy has got a little more than his share of the Gator in him."

The Gator was funny and full of himself, always ready with a smile and a song or a lewd joke, a pint of whiskey stashed somewhere in the car. "He was smooth," said Dewey, who knew something about smooth himself. "Yes, hell, he was smooth, naturally smooth. He was not a sophisticated, Dean Martin kind of fellow, but he would have been if he'd had any education. And when he wasn't too drunk he was pleasant to be around." The Gator would get a little liquor in him and ladle his charm over whoever was around to provide an audience. He'd entertain his younger cousins with snatches of lowdown blues that he picked up in the roadhouses of eastern North Carolina:

It takes a long, tall, dark-skinned gal,
To make a preacher lay that Bible down.

They would all laugh, and I heard bits of the songs and jokes years later, sitting at my uncles' feet while they played spades and told stories, but none of them failed to note that Elias's angels and his demons resided much too close for comfort. "When the Gator would get to drinking and carousing," Dewey continued, "he was liable to do anything in this world. And hurt anybody who got in his way. He didn't care how much he loved them or didn't love them—that was beside the point. When he got to drinking and got mad, he was going to tear somebody up—he would flat out hurt you, and hurt you right quick."

His rawboned style of masculinity made a mark on his cousins for good and ill. One day when the Gator was full of whiskey he went into a cafe in Snow Hill with my uncle Dewey, who was only a boy. The chief of police came in and exchanged words with the Gator, Dewey said, "and come over there to where Elias was to arrest him, and Elias hit him hard, knocked him cold as a cucumber. Just knocked him out flat on his back on the floor in the cafe. I think he plead guilty to assault or something like that, but he got off pretty light." Young Robert Teel, growing up nearby, may even have been encouraged by the Gator's example. In any case, our illustrious kinsman spent most of his time running up and down the roads, bouncing back and forth between his wife, a string of girlfriends, and the hookers down at Sugar Hill. Along the way, if anyone crossed him, the Gator responded with his fists. "He loved a good fight," Dewey recalled, "because he had a talent for it and was equipped to handle the situation. In fact, in all the fights he had, I never knew anybody to whip him."

"He was a little sadistic with women, too," Tommy added. Elias Tyson liked to go on fishing trips to the beach, his cousins all agreed, because they would always drive past Sugar Hill, the infamous brothel district in Kinston. Dewey recalled a "fishing trip" on which Elias carried him and DuLoyd Gay, another cousin, both of them teenaged boys. "We went down toward the beach," recounted Dewey, "and long about Kinston we stopped up on the highway, and there was a motel, some little old cabin or something, and the Gator was drinking, and he picked him up a whore at Sugar Hill and took her to bed. Stayed with her most of the night, and in the same room where me and DuLoyd was sleeping, or trying to sleep, anyway." His marriage to Margaret Fields, a passionate and well-intentioned young woman from Snow Hill, was predictably stormy because her plans to reform him did not put an end to these escapades. "I wouldn't be surprised if he cheated on her on the honeymoon," speculated Dewey.

Whatever happened on their honeymoon, the Gator did behave himself for a short period of time after the wedding. In a few weeks, though, he was back to drinking and gambling and carrying on, and his young wife decided to confront him about it. "The first time he come in drunk, after the wedding," Daddy told me, "she let him get in the bed, and then she slipped out of bed and got his belt out of his trousers, and ripped back the covers and lit into him." Lashing the belt across his backside, she told him not to come home with whiskey on his breath and expect to sleep in her bed. "And he tolerated the whipping for a little while," Daddy continued, "and then after a while he just reached up and grabbed her, slung her across his knee, and spanked her with the flat of his hand." Their bitter passion could not sustain a family life, and their marriage never went long without unhappy incidents that packed Margaret and the children back home to her mother, and sent Elias careening off into the roadhouses and brothels, whiskey-bent and hell-bound.

"When the Gator's mother was sick and nigh unto death," Daddy recounted, "laying up in her deathbed, Elias went off and got drunk." Somehow, in his maudlin alcoholic fog, the Gator figured he was going to make up for all the pain he had caused his mother. "He went down to the bakery and bought six pies," Daddy told me. "And he came lurching in the room with that armload of pies, all kinds of pies, and put them all up on the bed beside his mama, who was laying up there dying, and he announced, 'Ain't nothing too good for my damn mama—if she wants pie she'll have pie, damn it.' Up there white with her last dying breath, and he was laying out pies, like that was going to make everything all right."

The farce turned to tragedy on a hot summer evening when the Gator and his twenty-two-year-old nephew, Mack Gay, his sister's boy, were sitting on a woodpile playing poker and drinking corn liquor. They were alone at the house; the women had all gone to town, and the other men were working down at a tobacco barn. While it is hard to know exactly what happened, family lore has it that the two men got drunk and began to argue. The younger man came at the Gator. "Elias said he had a knife, but nobody ever found the knife," my uncle Dewey related, "and anyway, Elias hit him with the axe. I don't think he hit him in the head. He hit him somewhere on his body, though, and the blood just gushed out everywhere, and Mack died right there by the porch." It began to drizzle. The Gator couldn't stand to leave the boy in the rain, so he dragged him up under the porch a little. "And Elias ran off," Dewey said, "but not far, just ran off down in the woods and that's where the sheriff found him, on the edge of the woods, huddled up like a dog, crying in the rain."

Just after the murder, my father went to see the Gator, much deflated in spirit, as he awaited trial in the county jail. They talked through the bars for quite some time, the Gator pouring out his anguish. "And I said, 'Elias, I know that's awful, what you done is terrible, but God's got a mercy,' I told him, 'and if you ask for mercy, I believe God would give you mercy. I believe He would forgive you.' And the Gator said, 'Hell, Vernon, I don't want no mercy, all I want is justice and a fair trial.' And he got exactly what he wanted, because they sentenced him to thirty years." Daddy would tell that as a funny story— not light comedy, of course, but a story of dark humor and absurd pride that is deeply connected to what is best and what is worst in our blood.

The humor in the Gator stories is collectively self-deprecating and, like many stories that human beings tell, it both defines the boundaries of our community and connects us to a larger humanity. It says to the family member: you are one of us forever, in your blood and bone. The fulcrum of this folk humor is a profound sense of the absurdity of our gall and arrogance. Its theological function is nothing more than a restatement of the concept of original sin, reminding us through our hilarity that the distance between our highest and our lowest capacities is not as far as we might like to think. But even as the story of the Gator admonishes us to yield to the good within us, it reflects a perverse pride: we might be saved by grace, but that doesn't make us "little tailor-made Jesus boys," as my daddy might say. Redeemed sinners, yes, but there are things that can make a preacher lay that Bible down. Our laughter is communal and cathartic, binding us to one another while it expresses, and hence (we hope) disarms, the darker impulses we all share.

It is hard to say whether it was the Holy Spirit or the Gator, exactly, or maybe a little bit of both, that whispered into my uncle Earl's ear in 1957 and inspired his fateful collision with white supremacy. In the years after the United States Supreme Court had struck down segregation in the *Brown v. Board of Education* decision, pressure on Southern racial dissidents grew far more intense. "The echo of shots and dynamite blasts," the editors of the *Southern Patriot* wrote, "has been almost continuous throughout the South." On September 25, 1957, mob violence in Little Rock, Arkansas, forced President Eisenhower to send the 101st Airborne to protect nine African American students as they entered Central High School. This smacked of Reconstruction-era federal intervention and fanned the segregationists to white-hot fury. The Arkansas legislature charged that the unrest in Little Rock had been "planned, schemed and calculated" in Moscow as part of "the international communist conspiracy of world domination," despite President Eisenhower's rather dubious communist credentials. Thomas R. Waring Jr., the editor of the leading newspaper in South Carolina, called for a new secession movement. As one of the leading segregationist intellectuals, Waring envisioned that soon white Southerners would find themselves "fashioning homemade bombs to hurl at federal troops."

Several months before what Waring denounced as "the invasion of Little Rock," the bishop had appointed my uncle Earl to the Louisburg circuit, six rural Methodist churches fifteen miles outside Raleigh. In early October, about a week after the federal troops marched into Central High, Earl got a ticket for driving with an expired license. Earl arrived at the courthouse in Louisburg early and sat on the front row in the empty courtroom reading his Bible, oblivious to the shuffling of shoes and the scraping of chairs as people filed in behind him. But then came a hand on his shoulder, and Earl turned to meet the kind gaze of an elderly black man, who said, "Son, what are you doing here this morning?"

"Well," Earl replied with a grin, "I believe I came to give the judge forty dollars." Earl explained that he was planning to plead guilty, pay up, and get out as fast as he could. Unbeknownst to Earl, the small, dark-skinned man who had spoken to him was Judson King, director of the Franklinton Center at Bricks, North Carolina, a black educational institution with roots in the Reconstruction era that most people simply called "Bricks." Though the school taught vocational training along the lines advocated by Booker T. Washington, Bricks also bred a kind of homegrown black nationalism, teaching young African Americans race pride, community uplift, and quiet defiance. Judson King, short and slight, almost bald, and "black as the ace of spades," as my grandfather described him, spent much of his time teaching black sharecroppers to read and do arithmetic, and the rest of it encouraging them to find the courage to confront their landlords. "One of your boys pulled a pencil on me!" a white banker in Roanoke Rapids had once roared at King, a story that he retold with great pride, and an inflection that suggested that a pencil *was* a kind of weapon in this war. Though Judson King was a race man of the first order, one of the foundation stones of the freedom movement in eastern North Carolina, he was also a man of deep Christian conviction, and in Earl's soft eyes that morning he saw a brother in the faith.

"Don't you worry," King assured him in his warm, resonant voice, "you give the man that forty dollars and the Lord will give it back to you. The Lord will take care of you if you'll let Him." Earl looked into Judson King's eyes and he, too, recognized a brother in Christ, and they introduced themselves and began to share their Christian witness with each other. This had absolutely nothing to do with politics. Meanwhile, the courtroom had filled up behind them. When the bailiff told everybody to stand, Earl saw that he was the only white man on that side of the aisle. He instantly knew, too, that he could not repudiate his bond with Judson King by moving over to the side designated for whites. "As I was sitting back down," Earl recounted, "I made up my mind that I was not going to move." But then Earl felt another hand on his shoulder, and this time it was a burly sheriff's deputy.

"Buddy, you have to move," the officer told him. "This is the colored section."

"No, thank you," Earl replied. "I choose to sit here." The deputy squinted at him angrily.

"I told you, you have to move," the deputy insisted.

"And I told you I choose to sit here," Earl shot back.

Earl watched as the deputy walked up to the judge and whispered in his ear. And then he saw the judge cup his hand and hiss back, "Are you sure he's not one of those New York niggers?" The trouble could be averted, perhaps, if Earl was just a light-skinned black man who was unfamiliar with local laws and customs. But the deputy shook his head and informed the judge that Earl was not only a white man but the local Methodist preacher.

"Reverend Tyson, would you step up here?" the judge asked, and when Earl did, he quietly ordered Earl to get on the right side of the courtroom so that they could proceed to hold court.

"If you can tell me where to sit," Earl responded, looking the judge right in the eye, "you can tell me what to think, and what to say, and I don't believe you have that authority. I just don't think the Lord has conferred that authority upon you. All I want to do is plead guilty, pay my fine, and be on my way. But while I am here, I am going to be sitting right there."

The week after federal troops landed in Little Rock, the white South was about as likely to forgive dissenters as they had been in 1864, when General Pickett hanged all those boys at Kinston. The judge looked him in the eye and uttered, "You do that and you'll be sorry." In October 1957 that was the not-so-gospel truth. Earl didn't move his seat, just paid up and went home.

Sorry came quick. Earl scarcely had time to get to his house before five men from his Louisburg church were standing outside the parsonage. He knew them all, and counted every one of them as a friend. "Those men loved me," Earl recalled. "And I had been there long enough for them to know that I was a fine preacher, and I had prayed with some of their relatives in the hospital, and visited in their homes and eaten at their tables. But their faces were set hard against me, and they looked at me like I was a rank stranger." The men refused to go inside, but said that they had heard what he had done at the courthouse, and wanted to know why. Had the NAACP put him up to this? Was he aware that it was the communists who were stirring up this stuff? Was *he* a communist? Why had he gotten mixed up in this mess?

"Mostly because I was sitting with a black brother in Christ," Earl said, "and the Lord told me not to move. I could not turn away from him without doing injury, and I believe that I was guided by the Holy Spirit in that." He'd seen all of them working alongside blacks down at the tobacco packinghouse, Earl reminded them, sitting closer to black men than he had been sitting in the courthouse. The men insisted that that was different. "Maybe it is," Earl told them. "And I am not insisting that you do it, but I do insist that you set me free to do it." They had no such intention, in fact, and informed him that he was no longer welcome in the pulpits of any of the churches on the Louisburg circuit. Earl didn't stand in those pulpits at their invitation, he reminded them, but by the calling of the Lord and the appointment of the bishop of the Eastern North Carolina Conference. If they wanted the bishop's telephone number, Earl said, turning to go inside, he would be happy to give it to them.

Earl's wife, Betty Jo, was eight months pregnant with their third child as he turned his back on those men. He had recently been rejected for admission to Duke Divinity School because, as Dean Cannon had told him, "I am not going to have any more Tysons up here making trouble." At that point, the dean was fully conversant with Dewey, Tommy, George, and Vernon, and claimed that Dewey was "the only sane one" in the bunch, and that he didn't like him much, either. Earl was serving a minimum-salary circuit with six churches, and there was nowhere else for him to work. He went and spoke to all of his churches about what had happened and tried to smooth things over while still standing his ground. Most people sat there in stony-faced silence, and Earl got no public support from any-one at any of the churches. Some people crossed the street to avoid him and others muttered curses. When the threatening phone calls started, Earl moved Betty Jo and the kids to stay with her mother.

Lying in bed alone at the parsonage a few nights later, Earl heard a knock at his back door. He thought it might be the Klan coming to make good on their threats, but saw what appeared to be a white woman standing near the back porch. It was too dark to tell who it was, and the figure had moved back away from the house after knock-ing. Earl opened the door and reached for the light switch. "Please don't turn on the light," a female voice stammered. "I just wanted you to know how proud I am that you are my preacher. I just wanted you to know that." And then she hurried away into the darkness.

The bishop, who was somewhat less proud of Earl, called to tell him that the local churches had stopped his salary, and that the Eastern North Carolina Conference had no funds to pay him. He was sympathetic to Earl's situation, though, and there was a three-point circuit up in Virginia that he knew about. He'd make some calls and get back to Earl right away. "But don't do anything like this again," the bishop told him. "If you do, it will mark you." Less than a month after he had refused to move out of the "colored" section, Earl and his fam-ily were unpacking boxes in a ratty old farmhouse in the Virginia tide-water at a tiny place called Surry Courthouse. "I didn't know a soul in Virginia," he recalled years later, "and I had only been out of North Carolina a couple of times in my life." Earl had been banished.

On his first day in Surry Courthouse, Earl recalled, one of his new members dropped by the house in an old pickup truck and offered to take Earl into town and introduce him to some people. Earl was glad to go with the quiet, warm, and unassuming farmer. On their way into town, however, they stopped behind a yellow school bus. This must have jarred something in the farmer's mind, because he said very softly, without looking at Earl, "Preacher, I don't know what you think about this integration business. But the less you say about it, the better."

Exile hurt Uncle Earl deeply, and it also furnished a double-edged lesson to his brothers, who had seen their father forced from a pulpit for advocating racial equality. My own father's diary from those days reads, "Earl has had a difficult time. He moved from the Louisburg Circuit because of a racial incident. I glory in his spunk and I appreciate his being a faithful witness to the truth of God." But the incident at Louisburg earned him some support, too, and not just from his family. When Earl applied to Union Theological Seminary in nearby Richmond later that year, the dean looked over his application and asked him two questions. First, he asked Earl what he thought about the race issue. Earl swallowed hard. "I am called to treat every person as my brother or sister in Christ," he replied, "regardless of color."

The dean's second question cut straight to the heart of the matter. "Earl, you're a North Carolina boy," the dean said. "Your whole family lives down there, and all your folks are preachers down there. What on earth are you doing up here in Virginia?" Earl swallowed hard again, and then told him the whole story of what had happened in the courtroom in Louisburg, and how the churches had responded to him. The dean listened to the whole story, then smiled warmly at Earl.

"Your academic record is a little spotty," the dean said, "but that whole courtroom episode alone qualifies you to enter this seminary, even if you weren't obviously a fine preacher already." Within a couple of days, Earl learned that Union Theological Seminary had granted him a full scholarship. And his thoughts could not help but go back to his brother in Christ, whom he had met in the courtroom that morning in Louisburg. "Don't you worry," Judson King had told him, "you give the man that forty dollars and the Lord will give it back to you. The Lord will take care of you if you'll let Him."

CHAPTER 9

THE CASH REGISTER AT THE POOL HALL

WHILE MY CRAZY uncle Earl believed that the Lord would take care of you if you'd let Him, the Black Power generation took the more conventional view that the Lord helps those who help themselves. Even though the new movement in Oxford had been launched from the steps of the First Baptist Church, the Black Power crowd attended services, you might say, at the Soul Kitchen, the old Ridley Drive-In on the Chavis homeplace, which Ben Chavis had reopened when he'd moved back to town in 1969. "It was a nice little spot that everyone would go to," Carolyn Thorpe, a young black activist, recalled. "Because of course there were no activities for young black people in Oxford—it was a nightspot where everyone gathered." The Soul Kitchen was a simple setup with booths, a bar, a meeting room, and a dance floor. Its kitchen poured forth steaming platters of fried chicken that remain legendary. The jukebox pounded out "Otis, Marvin, the Temptations, a lot of James Brown," according to Thorpe. Another regular, Linda Ball, bragged, "Honey, we could *dance!*" Junior Walker's "Shotgun" and James Brown's "Say It Loud (I'm Black and I'm Proud)" and "Payback, Part 1" were favorite hymns.

The tone of the Black Power crowd disturbed some of the older, more traditionally minded African Americans in Oxford. A lot of the uneasiness was nothing more than the shopworn worries of an older generation. More thoughtful observers, however, fretted that the young people hadn't experienced enough to understand the battle before them, and that their rhetoric sometimes served psychological needs rather than political goals. Some thought the militants were not rooted enough in the gospel vision that had helped black folk survive for four centuries. Even those uneasy with Black Power, though, knew something decisively important was afoot.

When Aretha Franklin demanded "R-E-S-P-E-C-T," the dance floor at the Soul Kitchen pounded out the rhythms of a new black sense of self. Like the Soul Kitchen itself, which had been a black-owned business in earlier incarnations, and had always been owned by a political family bent on black uplift, Black Power was not entirely new. Its communal and defiant ethos drew on African American traditions and echoed the spirit of the sanctified church, even if it expressed itself in an angry new voice. But nonviolent direct action held little promise for these young people. They had little appreciation for mere "civil rights" if it meant that black people could buy an Orangeade at the drugstore but were still regarded as a class of untouchables by whites and apparently could be shot down with impunity.

The assassination of Dr. King sealed the death of nonviolence, even as a tactical approach. In short, virtually nobody believed anymore, as Dr. King had, that "unarmed truth and unconditional love will have the final word in reality." And in Oxford, the murder of Henry Marrow "made us look again at every aspect of our situation here," Ben Chavis explained. "The fact that there were no blacks working downtown. Not one in City Hall, not even a secretary. The highest-ranking black officer in the police department was a patrol officer. None in the fire department. And lots of Oxford still segregated. I mean, we just decided enough is enough."

"Them young folks was mad as hell," Golden Frinks said, "but they was on a high. They had drank the intoxication of that desired freedom and it was really the best kind. They had breathed that aroma of the seeking, the seeking of that freedom wine." At the Soul

Kitchen, a movement culture emerged that was cool and defiant, seething and analytical. If the "civil rights" generation found their vision in the uplifting strains of gospel music, the Black Power generation leaned more toward the improvisational genius of jazz and the blues-inflected rhythms of soul. Though the jukebox at the Soul Kitchen pounded out soul music day and night, the young insurgents around the tables pieced together their revolution like jazz musicians, improvising on their traditions in order to imagine a new world. Black militants from across the state and sometimes from across the country gathered in the booths to brainstorm and banter. "That's where I met Frank Ballance, at the Soul Kitchen," Eddie McCoy recalled, referring to a prominent civil rights attorney who was later elected to the U.S. House of Representatives after many years in the state legislature. "G. K. Butterfield, Henry Morris, Milton Fitch and his dad, all those guys," he said, naming only a few of the statewide organizers. "That's where we met, at the Soul Kitchen. What we was doing was strategy—how to work it."

Part of both the style and the strategy of Black Power was scaring local white people and keeping white authorities off balance. In a Southern town as small as Oxford, any outsider became the object of suspicion, and a steady stream of movement visitors offered the perfect opportunity to terrify white folks. "Every time a new fellow would come to town," Eddie McCoy recounted, "Ben would send him downtown. And what we would do is get 'em to walk through downtown like they was casing the town out. You had some of them with bald heads, some of them with bushy beards, lots of them with big old Afros on their heads, and they were *strangers*. That was worrying them white people all day long." This may have been more political theater than physical threat, but it cannot be denied that the Black Power style scared whites half to death. There was some satisfaction in that, even if the results were not always politically productive.

Richard Wright once observed that a black man in the Jim Crow South had three options with respect to white people, none of them politically promising. He could adopt a docile and religious posture, accepting his racial subordination. He could play the part of the "respectable Negro," superior to the poor blacks beneath him, and thereby become complicit in the racial caste system. Or the final—and frequently suicidal—option was to adopt the "criminal attitude" of the black desperado, the "bad nigger" who haunted the fearful imagination of the white South. This almost nihilistic figure affirmed white terrors that what lay behind black masks of servility was a boiling black rage that had few other outlets.

In the first half of the twentieth century, these desperadoes, or those who acted the part, often ended up twitching at the end of a rope or wrapped in a logging chain at the bottom of a river, where their tragic fate warned other blacks that resistance was suicide. In the Black Power era, when it became possible to terrify white people without necessarily dying, this "bad nigger" posture became a kind of irresistible pose. When the scary-looking strangers walked through Oxford, Eddie McCoy explained, "We'd go through town and say to white people, 'Man, did you see the *Black Panthers* is in town? Ain't those some *baaaad* dudes?' All through town the word would get out. The white folks would say, 'Lord have mercy, we got them *Black Panthers* in town.' We kept them all upset."

Though white people tended to see the black community as monolithic, the movement that emerged in Oxford after the murder of Henry Marrow was fragmented from the very beginning. Ironically, the movement reached its crescendo of energy and effectiveness at the same moment that it began to fracture from within. The younger radicals had a magnificent ferocity that fueled the movement, but they did not always remember that they had inherited as well as energized the struggle. With greater patience, they might have been able to keep things together more. But as the movement grew, the divisions grew, too, many of them along generational lines.

The issue of violent protest was perhaps the best litmus test for the political, social, generational, and philosophical fissures. Older, middle-class blacks like Sam Cox, who frequently negotiated with city officials, definitely supported the movement and recognized that the moment to push forward had arrived. Cox and his peers were not necessarily prepared to countenance violence. "He was the ideal person to be the spokesperson for 'em," Mayor Currin said. "Sam was trying to get everything quiet just like I was. I am satisfied that Sam never had anything to do with any rioting or burning or any suggestion of anything like that."

The incongruous result, of course, was that white city officials tried to negotiate an end to the rioting and the arson with people who could not have done anything to stop it. "The top people couldn't negotiate," Eddie McCoy jeered, "because if they did negotiate it was just bullshit, because they couldn't control nobody because they didn't even associate with 'em. The white people didn't want to negotiate with nobody but the middle-class blacks, but the street people was the ones that was organizing and doing everything and keeping [the violence] going." The "street people," too, included people who were so angry at the racial caste system that the idea of "negotiations" meant little. "We just wanted to burn the motherfucker down," one of them told me years afterward. "It didn't make no difference who said what, they would have changed all this shit after the fucking Civil War if they gave a damn about us. It was straight-up payback time."

Ben Chavis, though hardly among the "street people," stood at the center of the organizing but was not a wholehearted party to the violence that angry young blacks committed in the name of freedom. "I have an objection, in principle, to violence," he explained. But if he did not endorse or organize violence, Chavis was more than willing to use the violence committed by others as negotiating leverage. The heart of Chavis's political strategy was economic pressure against the most wealthy and powerful whites. Though he did not counsel firebombing, he rationalized black violence against white property by placing it in the context from which it had emerged. "What we were protesting against was racial violence," he explained later. "What Teel did was an act of racial violence. And what the police and the courts did was to sustain this racial violence. What the white business community did, excluding blacks from employment and stigmatizing them with segregation, was a different kind of racial violence. And violence begat violence."

Whites would blame Ben Chavis for nearly all the destruction that occurred in Oxford after the murder, but the African Americans who committed much of it actually held Ben Chavis in a curious mixture of respect and disdain. "He could talk and make them speeches," one of them reported. "But he wasn't down with no violence." By all reports, Chavis sought to diminish acts of arson and vandalism, even though his conversations with city officials occasionally contained what amounted to veiled threats. His ability to control the chaos in the streets was never clear. "Shit, he wouldn't let us do a lot of things that we just did anyway," Boo Chavis recalled. "If Ben knew that we had did something in a violent manner, he would say, 'Well, we're not going to gain anything by this,' but we didn't care, you know, because we wasn't gaining nothing noway."

While Ben Chavis sought with mixed success to curb the angrier impulses of a movement he had organized in large measure from high school students, he may have been unaware of a small, separate movement within the movement. On the other hand, he may have known a fair amount about this cabal; it is not a subject that lends itself to easy candor, even decades later. In the weeks after the murder, and for the rest of that summer, about a dozen men, most of them black veterans who had recently returned from Vietnam, met after hours to make their own plans—and to make firebombs. Nearly all of them were veterans in their mid-twenties or older. They had learned well the lessons of their years in the Mekong Delta, the Dominican Republic, and in various military training camps. They were not the only blacks in Oxford who were angry enough to burn it down. But they laughed at the high school students who sometimes hurled Coca-Cola bottles full of gasoline at buildings and who were occasionally caught by the police. "That way they kept thinking it was some prank or some shit," one of the vets recalled, "and that way we knowed we wasn't going to get caught. Because this was a military operation."

The arson and vandalism perpetrated against white-owned property was a curious mixture of carefully planned, politically calibrated
"military operations" and spontaneous, uncontrollable expressions of
rage and vengeance. "We said, the onliest way this is going to work is
that we gonna have to burn somebody's buildings down and break
somebody's windows out," one of the men explained to me years afterward. "And we would sit around and discuss it, have a meeting." But
nobody wanted to propose in a roomful of people, even these close
friends, exactly what should go up in flames, and so the operations were
never explicitly planned at these so-called meetings. "Somebody would
say something," the man continued, "and something might get burned
up, and we knew it had to come out of our group but didn't nobody say
nothing in the group." The street violence remained decentralized "in
territories" another veteran explained. "You know, it won't no use trying to tell 'em, tell somebody what they was gon' do or not do." At the
same time, Mayor Currin pointed out, "we had some forty-odd firebombs thrown or lit," and the black veterans who ignited most of those
bombs knew one another and frequently cooperated on planning in private. "I had a lot of common sense or brains, you know," one of them
recalled, "and I used to draw the maps, when we would set around talking, and say, well, about the time the cops come around, we gon' do this
here and we gon' hit that place over there, we gon' do it like that."

The way whites often viewed the black community as an undif-
ferentiated mass made it harder for white authorities to get a fix on
the violence. The sophisticated efforts of the black Vietnam veterans
were one thing; the spontaneous street violence, most of it perpetrated by black teenagers, was quite another. And both kinds of
attacks were hard to stop. "When we'd walk home," Boo Chavis
recounted, "we would take the furniture off white people's porches,
put it in the middle of the street, and burn it up." Plate-glass windows furnished irresistible targets. "We knew the paths and shortcuts
all through Grab-all," another one of the young vandals explained.
"Once we got up in there, that was it, you could go anywhere. I used
to get up in a tree and look at [the police] and laugh at 'em. It was
dark up in there."

Both the unplanned outbursts of the young street toughs and the "military operations" of the black veterans generally took place without prior knowledge by Ben Chavis or the more mainstream movement leadership. "Ben Chavis didn't know shit," one of the black veterans spat. "We didn't give a damn about his Martin Luther King bullshit." Eddie McCoy agreed that Chavis didn't advocate violence. "When Ben found out about the shit it was already done," McCoy recalled, "and he never advised anybody to do anything that wasn't within the law. He was very careful about what he said." Carolyn Thorpe, one of the Soul Kitchen insurgents, complained that Ben Chavis would not let the young people dynamite the Confederate monument—and they *had* dynamite. "You know, I have never wanted to blow up anything in my life," she said, "but I begged him, pleaded with all of them to just take the dynamite and blow it up. He would not let us do it. A lot of stuff we just did anyway. But he was not for the violence. He really wasn't."

The young people raising hell in the streets were confident, however, that the force of fear was their most powerful weapon. The liberal Raleigh *News and Observer* condemned "the tossing of rocks and bottles and firebombs" in Oxford as "the most fruitless form of protest imaginable," arguing that "discussion is a more promising way to racial accommodation than destruction." But the indisputable fact was that whites in Oxford did not even consider altering the racial caste system until rocks began to fly and buildings began to burn. Chavis may not have approved of the firebombers but, apart from the gasoline and the matches, their logic was not distant from his own strategy of economic pressure. "It was like we had a cash register up there at the pool hall," one of the arsonists recalled years later, "just ringing up how much money we done cost these white people. We knew if we cost 'em enough goddamn money they was gon' start doing something."

Of course, firebombs are not "democratic" in any meaningful sense; no organization representing the people decided to burn buildings and smash windows. No vote was taken, and those too young or too old to participate, those who did not approve of the violence or those who were terrified by it had no voice. Violence that did not represent a broad community consensus could hardly be ended at the negotiating table, especially when no one who approved of the violence had a seat at that table. The negotiators did not speak for the rioters, so they could not promise to stop the riots in exchange for concessions. Not everyone cared. "They just killing us off like it was nothing," one street fighter insisted, "and the judge just as well have on his Ku Klux Klan suit." One young black woman made the point that property destruction forced the white power structure to abandon its intransigent posture: "They had to give us some respect," she insisted. "They might not like it but they damn sure had to do that. We was getting ready to tear this motherfucker all to hell, and all of a sudden [white people] decided to listen."

Of course, one might argue that they *did* "tear this motherfucker all to hell," given the level of destruction, but clearly some young African Americans considered burning only white business property—warehouses, for example—a moderate half measure. After all, the white folks had killed a man and then barely even gotten around to arresting the murderers. The whites "were lucky we didn't do what we could have done, what we had every right to do," one of the young Black Power folks told me. In her view, the Black Power generation in Oxford had been very moderate.

In politics, *everyone* regards themselves as a moderate, because they know some other sumbitch who's twice as crazy as they are. The man who blockades abortion clinics considers himself a model of restraint because he does not bomb them; the fellow who bombs them after hours thinks he's a moderate because he didn't bomb them at rush hour like his cousin Elmer wanted to do; the White Citizens Council member who assassinated Medgar Evers in Mississippi undoubtedly regarded himself as a moderate, since he didn't kill the whole family. Nixon felt that a lesser man might have used atomic weapons on North Vietnam, but he displayed the statesmanlike restraint to use only conventional ordnance—albeit by the time Nixon signed a ceasefire agreement in 1973, America had dropped three times the tonnage unleashed on Europe, Africa, and

Asia during World War II—all of it on a country the size of Texas.
And in the fire of the black freedom struggle, there were always people on both sides who were willing to crank it up another notch,
claiming moral authority over the cowards who wouldn't go that
far, and thinking of themselves as "moderate" for not taking it still
further.

Even though the black community was not of one mind on questions of tactics and strategy, violence or nonviolence, "civil rights" or
"Black Power," nearly all African Americans agreed that the murder
of Henry Marrow indicated a need for unified action. On Sunday,
May 17, the day after Marrow's funeral, Golden Frinks, Ben Chavis,
Sam Cox, Eddie McCoy, and the black churchwomen who had traditionally supported the movement organized the first in a series of
Sunday afternoon marches. Announced from black church pulpits,
through black businesses, and by word of mouth, the first mass meeting convened that Sunday afternoon at four o'clock in the large sanctuary at First Baptist. Ben Chavis spoke briefly, and there were some
songs to get the Spirit moving. The large crowd, led by Chavis and
Frinks, then retraced the path of the previous day's funeral march
downtown. Along the way, three white men armed with knives and
pistols menaced the marchers but did not attack. "We had our shit
with us, too," Eddie McCoy explained. "They just couldn't see it. If
they had hurt somebody, they would have flat gone down." Golden
Frinks estimated the crowd at roughly two thousand; the Oxford
Police Department claimed that only 250 people marched. The
Oxford Public Ledger echoed the police figure, but printed the number beneath a photograph in which nearly twice that many persons
were visible, and the camera had not captured the entire line of
marchers.

At the Confederate monument, Frinks addressed the crowd in his
customary golden dashiki, raising roars of applause as he called for
action and announced a march from Oxford to the state capital in
Raleigh that would begin five days later, on Friday. Acknowledging
that the marchers might face Klan violence or police crackdown,
Frinks lightened the moment by joking that "last time I went jail I

took three hundred and fourteen peoples with me and the only ones that got hurt was white people having heart attacks." As they lifted up the anthems of the movement, some of the young people singing with the raised fist of the Black Power revolt, it was clear that the "freedom wine" remained in good supply.

In the months ahead, the "Sunday march" would furnish one much-needed expression of black unity. Granville County's black community had long been divided, not merely by class, religion, generation, and political orientation, but by geography; blacks lived in a few small communities and tended to stay within those boundaries. After the murder of Henry Marrow, Ben Chavis said, "it was like everybody lived on the same street." These Sunday marches continued to be the best glue of the local movement, which tended to move in a variety of different directions the rest of the week. "The onliest time everybody got together was on Sunday for the Sunday march," Eddie McCoy recalled. "Every Sunday, everybody after church would meet up at First Baptist Church, and we would march downtown about four o'clock and have a speaker, come back and let 'em know we won't gon' take it." And every Sunday afternoon, that "same street" to which Chavis referred led from First Baptist Church to the Confederate monument downtown.

Eleven o'clock on Sunday morning continued to be, as Dr. King liked to point out, the most segregated hour in American life, and the only whites visible after church at the Sunday marches were newspaper reporters and camera crews. The single white person visible in news photographs of the marches may as well have worn a sign saying MARXIST GRADUATE STUDENT FROM CHAPEL HILL. Apart from Henry Marrow's funeral, neither my father nor any other local white people marched with the movement in Oxford. By 1970, the level of white involvement in the freedom movement anywhere was small; the Student Nonviolent Coordinating Committee, probably the most integrated organization in the movement in the early 1960s, had expelled its handful of remaining white members in 1965. With the shift toward racial separatism that came afterward, many whites felt alienated, as my father had, and many African Americans were no longer willing to be seen with whites. "My black minister friends just disappeared," my father said mournfully. "One or two of them explained that we just couldn't be friends anymore, but I never quite accepted it, though I kept leading my folks as best I could. It hurt my feelings." Whites dedicated to racial justice worked the white side of the color line, where they knew the terrain; they wrote small checks and pushed people as far as they felt they could, winning few battles and little applause. The mistakes that brought about this state of affairs had been made long before, and Oxford's handful of white believers in racial equality literally had nowhere to go politically.

I have often pondered whether or not my father and his handful of allies could have done more to preserve the ties between blacks and whites. By 1970, it was clearly too late. But even a decade earlier, when the sit-ins began, my father and his middle-aged white liberal friends had left the demonstrations to black Southerners and the handful of young white idealists who had nothing to lose. Signing a petition here, writing a letter to the editor there—it did not amount to much. Those whom Martin Luther King Jr. termed "people of goodwill" were rarely willing to consider more than piecemeal measures that were insufficient to the evils of the day. And the rank-and-file white churchfolks did even less than that, though the moral distance between Dr. King and George Wallace could not have been clearer. Daddy tried hard to live his convictions; he acted on his faith and risked his safety and his livelihood trying to persuade his white congregations to do the right thing. But the fear that he'd expressed in his diary in 1962—"I hope it is not too late"—turned out to be prophetic. And in the late 1960s, when Black Power hit them from one side and the white backlash hit them from the other, white liberals like my father were left with few options. "It was obviously a very racially divided community," Daddy explained. "There was only so much we could do." The American racial problem has never yielded much ground to moderate solutions.

It was a little frightening that Graham Wright, a white banker, thought he was a moderate, too. "I haven't reached the point *myself* where I think some kind of retaliatory action is necessary," he said, "but I hear an increasing amount of talk about it from my friends." Mayor Currin told reporters, "Oxford's no different from most any town. Things were going along real well until the shooting," he said, "and that could have happened anywhere. There is an element anywhere that will take advantage of something like that to become violent and destructive." In an assessment that managed to be both factual and meaningless, the mayor called the troubles in Oxford "part of a general trend toward lawlessness spreading across the country." The Raleigh *News and Observer* wondered. "The view that things in Oxford were going along fine until the Marrow killing and its 'exploitation' by a few 'outside agitators' prevails," a reporter noted. "But it is not unanimous." Black businessman James Gregory told the reporter that "even some black folks want to believe we've made a lot of 'progress' in race relations, but deep down they know that things are bad."

White citizens, Mayor Currin told me later, "did not think the killing was sufficient to excuse the violence we had." John K. Nelms, the head of the city planning commission, acknowledged white reluctance to accept change but stated publicly that "blacks have been trivial, unreasonable, and uncompromising in their demands." Black residents, however, felt that it was hardly trivial to ask for equality before the law and acceptance in the public sphere. According to the *News and Observer*, however, city officials willingly talked off the record about striking back violently against the black community. "Many whites feel as though they've been betrayed," Nelms explained. "Either that, or they're afraid they might be burned out next."

The upheavals in Oxford were the best thing that had ever happened to the local Ku Klux Klan, which quickly held a series of rallies in Granville County, seeking to exploit the polarized racial climate. "They had rallies," Ben Chavis recalled, "major rallies. There were Ku Klux Klan rallies all over Granville County after the murder. Some of them were held out at Stem, and one in Wilton. They were advertised in the *Oxford Ledger*. We couldn't get them to take our advertising for mass meetings, but they advertised Klan ral lies." Robert Teel most likely had been a member of the Ku Klux Klan. And as my sister Boo and I had observed, the men in what my uncle Bobby always called "those reversible choir robes" had arrived quickly to protect the Teel family in the hours and days after the murder. "There were people stayed at my house there for weeks," Robert Teel told me later, "twenty-four hours a day, guarding the place."

Teel recalled hearing that the Klan had rallied at crossroads communities in Providence, Stem, Wilton, and Bell Town. Their headquarters was on the Hazel Averett farm near Providence, about five miles from Oxford. These rallies attracted hundreds of white people, who stood around the huge flaming crosses and heard the angry racial diatribes. Mayor Currin, in keeping with long-standing Southern traditions, always insisted that "people from outside the county" were responsible for the Klan rallies and downplayed their importance. "That was just the way some people got their jollies," he explained to me later. "These people parading with the flag and the uniforms, if it had really gotten down to it and somebody had wanted to fight—if a 'jig' had jumped out in front of them with a switchblade—you'd see a whole lot of running. For a certain type of people, it was just a way to get together."

The increasingly large crowds at local Klan rallies and the support for the murderers of Henry Marrow among an even larger segment of white people in Granville County spurred black activists to take their protests to a higher level. As the murder trial loomed, Teel had little trouble raising an enormous defense fund. Some of the wealthiest people in the county contributed to his war chest. In a quiet way, the defense of Robert Teel and his family became a symbolic cause, a way local whites could express their resentment of the changes that were being forced upon them, especially school integration, which was scheduled for that fall. Although few people were willing to stand up for Teel in the newspapers, plenty of them were happy to give money. The court proceedings did not look promising. "After it became clear, in the preliminary hearing stage, that all of white Oxford was backing Teel," Ben Chavis recalled, "we decided that we needed to raise this issue statewide and nationwide. That's when we decided to march to Raleigh."

An ad hoc committee to plan the proposed fifty-mile march to the state capitol began meeting in the basement of First Baptist Church, led by Ben Chavis. Golden Frinks, who helped plan the march, obtained funding from the Southern Christian Leadership Conference. "I had the money, see," Frinks recalled, "and I would say, 'Well, what we gon' do is, we gon' march from here to Raleigh, and we gonna get a mule cart'—I had all this in mind." Frinks negotiated with the highway patrol, letting them know that he was willing either to cooperate with them or to defy them. Two students from Shaw University in Raleigh, John Mendez and Janet McCoy, obtained a city permit for the march, which said that the marchers would assemble on the capitol grounds on Sunday, May 24, at noon. Frinks sent Governor Robert Scott a telegram asking to meet with him at two o'clock. "We got that mule hitched up, we put that lady and a makeshift coffin up there and took off."

There were both official and unofficial efforts by local whites to stop the march. Mayor Currin drove out to the Chavis homeplace to persuade Ben not to hold the trek to Raleigh. "He said, 'Please don't march. Can't we work this thing out? Don't you know the highway is dangerous? Some of y'all might get hurt out there on the highway,' " Chavis recalled.

"I did warn them that I didn't think they ought to march," Mayor Currin confirmed. "The only thing I was concerned about was that it be a peaceful thing. I didn't want folks to get hurt, anybody to get hurt." The Ku Klux Klan had announced that they would not allow the march to leave Granville County, so the mayor's fears were not groundless. The town's Human Relations Council called an emergency meeting. The black leaders they talked to, however, were in no position to call off the protest even in the unlikely event that they wanted to do so. In a concession that suggests their impoverished understanding of what the black insurgents wanted, Mayor Currin and City Manager Tom Ragland announced on the day of the march that six basketball goals would be built on city property. That's just how clueless local white authorities were—they thought that black people might stop complaining if the town simply built enough basketball courts.

Other whites in Oxford tried to deter the march in their own ways. "My daddy was living down on Charles Adcock's farm," Carolyn Thorpe, an activist and a sharecropper's daughter, remembered. "Adcock told him that if he did not stop [his daughters] from marching, he was going to fire him." On the morning of the march, Carolyn Thorpe and her sister saw their father's landlord at a local service station. "I went up and told him, 'Fire my father if you want to, but I am going to march and my sisters are going to march, and if you get in my way or mess with my family, you will have to deal with me.' He could not stop us from marching." Thorpe's father kept his job.

About seventy marchers left Oxford on Friday, May 22, walking down the Jefferson Davis Highway behind a mule-drawn wagon. Atop the wagon sat Willie Mae Marrow, the bereaved widow, visibly pregnant with the dead man's third child, wearing a dark veil and holding one young daughter on her lap while comforting another. "That was the symbolic part," Frinks explained. The mule cart echoed the one that had hauled Dr. King's coffin through the streets of Atlanta two years earlier. The mule was a Southern-inflected symbol of the fact that the humble Jesus had ridden into Jerusalem on a donkey, and also of the menial labor that white supremacy had imposed upon black people; the black woman was "de mule uh de world," as Zora Neale Hurston once wrote. The protestors draped the coffin in black to mourn not only Henry Marrow but the deaths of many others across the country that month. Signs noted the four students killed and eleven wounded at Kent State on May 4; the six killed and dozens wounded in Augusta, Georgia, on May 12; and the two students killed and twelve wounded at Jackson State on May 16. A placard around the neck of the mule listed black uprisings that sounded the threat of retaliation: REMEMBER WATTS, DETROIT, NEWARK, OXFORD.

Despite the sweltering heat that afternoon, hundreds of young blacks joined the march as it made its way down the Jefferson Davis Highway toward Creedmoor, where the marchers planned to sleep at a black church that night. Eddie McCoy had raised money and rented two trucks to carry supplies from Oxford. Buck Peace, a black man who had recently run unsuccessfully for sheriff in Granville County, used his own truck to ferry cold drinks out to the thirsty marchers. "We would go back to the pool room and take up money for all the sodas," McCoy said, "and people would give you like five, ten, fifteen, or twenty dollars, and we'd buy 'em by the case, ice 'em down good, and Buck Peace or I would bring them back on a truck." Though it was a serious occasion, people enjoyed themselves. "We bought hot dogs, sandwiches, people carried food like going on a picnic," chuckled McCoy. "They would cook up chicken, make up boxes of food. There was no problem about food and things to drink."

The march was no picnic, though. The Ku Klux Klan had sworn to stop it, and they showed up at various points along the route. The highway patrol had no choice but to protect the marchers. "Our first interruption," Frinks remembered, "was when we got on the Creedmoor Road, and Captain Jenkins got out of the car and told us that the Ku Klux Klan was gathering up by this store up ahead on our right hand." The state troopers lined their cars up in the right lane, forming a protective line between the openly armed Klansmen and the less visibly armed marchers. "There were quite a few of them," Frinks said, but no one fired their weapons.

Despite the traditional songs and chants of the movement, which balanced the new Black Power anthems, the marchers were well armed. No one carried a weapon in plain view, but people like Herman Cozart, selected to serve as a marshal, kept their guns close at hand and out of sight. Eddie McCoy literally stuck to his guns, too. "Ben and them said it had to be nonviolent," McCoy recounted, "but we all had our shit with us. That wagon with the mule had more guns on it than a damn army tank. A lot of 'em like me had been in the army, combat veterans, and we told Ben and them, 'All nonviolent ever got Martin Luther King was dead, or else he'd be out here with us.' We wasn't gonna start nothing but we was ready. We wasn't going out there without our guns, no way." That night in Creedmoor, hundreds of local blacks brought food and joined the marchers for supper and singing. Armed sentries protected those who slept at the church. Carloads of whites fired two or three shots at blacks standing around outside, but screeched off into the night when the guards returned the fire.

Golden Frinks arranged for a busload of young blacks from Hyde County, way down in the state's eastern swamps, where the movement was still boiling hard, to join the march in Creedmoor Saturday morning "to get the numbers right," he said. Other activists trickled in from all over the state. The mule-drawn wagon creaked out of Creedmoor full of guns and grape soda at about ten o'clock that morning, with Willie Mae Marrow and the coffin once again perched on top. "She stood up very bravely," Ben Chavis said later. "She was getting death threats all the time at home, and there she was up there on the wagon where everybody could see her."

The atmosphere on the highway heated up on the second day. Carloads of whites would drive by and shout obscenities. "We got a lot of threats, especially after we left Creedmoor," Herman Cozart recalled. "You got some of everything throwed at you—'Hey, nigger, what you doing? Get off the road!' People blow at you, stick their finger up and holler," Cozart continued. Some of the cars carried well-known Klansmen, and one of the Teels, a brother and son of the men charged with killing Henry Marrow, rode in one of the cars that circled back again and again. "They would go so far and then come back around, trying to see who was marching and all," Cozart said. One carload of hostile whites fired pistols into the air. Another group of marauders lit a string of firecrackers and threw them under the wagon to try to spook the mule.

But the most tense moment occurred after lunch on the second day as several hundred marchers made their way past two mobile homes on the right side of the road, near a little store just over the Wake County line. A Confederate flag flew from one of the trailers and, as the march approached, several white men with rifles came outside and took firing positions. "Niggers! Hey, niggers!" the cry went up from the trailers. "They had done gone outdoors with their rifles setting out there," said Herman Cozart. Some of the marchers tried to inconspicuously make ready to return fire. "I said, 'Y'all keep walking, long as they don't shoot,'" Cozart said. "'Don't even say nothing to 'em or even try to look at 'em.' But some of us was ready to jump. They was hollering, 'Hey, nigger! Where y'all going, niggers?' But we just kept walking." Several of the marchers remembered that the hecklers had fired several shots, though perhaps only in the air. "There were at least three shots fired," Linda Ball said years later. The highway patrol sent officers over to talk to the armed white men, "but I never did see a police car taking anybody away or anything like that," she added. Nobody shot back at the trailers, according to Ball, who carried a .32-caliber pearl-handled revolver, "but it was quite a panic there for a while." That night, the marchers slept at a church on the outskirts of Raleigh.

"The march just swelled," Ben Chavis reported, "to almost a thousand people by the time it got to Raleigh." Entering the city, the marchers paraded past the First Baptist Church, whose most illustrious member, Jesse Helms, was an increasingly popular commentator on WRAL-TV. Helms, who had begun his career as a public relations official for the North Carolina Banking Association, was making a statewide reputation by opposing the civil rights movement. He liked to outline what he called "the purely scientific statistical evidence of natural racial distinctions in group intellect," and he defended the Ku Klux Klan as being no different from the NAACP, even though the former was a terrorist group and the latter operated primarily through the courts. The grist for the cranky commentator's mill—"forced integration" and alleged "communists" and "sex perverts" in the black freedom movement—fed his growing popularity. Coming into Raleigh on Sunday morning, the marchers delighted in making a stir as they filed past the church where Helms taught Sunday school every week—and which he would eventually abandon, allegedly after the congregation took in a black member. "Yes, sirree, we went right by Jesse Helms's church," Golden Frinks recalled, "and we let 'em know we were out there."

The procession led by Frinks, Chavis, Willie Mae Marrow, and Reginald Hawkins, a black dentist from Charlotte who had recently run for governor as a protest candidate, arrived at the state capitol at about one-thirty. Students from Shaw University, St. Augustine's College, and North Carolina Central University swelled their ranks. "Every time you do one of these things," Chavis said, "you learn a lot about how to keep people together, how to keep their spirits high, and how to keep them on target, even if you have a setback." Chavis addressed the throng on the capitol steps, as did Frinks and Hawkins. "Granville County has some of the meanest white folks I have ever seen," Frinks told the crowd, "and they are lucky the black people have not taken the law into their own hands."

It was a well-attended rally, and the press had given the march heavy coverage. "We couldn't believe how many people had showed up," Eddie McCoy remembered. "There was people from all over the place, thousands of people." The organizers had contacted Governor Robert Scott's office several days ahead of time and informed him that they would like to discuss the troubles in Oxford and the larger problems of black citizens in dealing with the judicial system. But the governor's aides had finally told them that Governor Scott would not meet with them. Ben Chavis and Willie Mae Marrow knocked at the statehouse door for a long time, but nobody came. "I remember going to the door, the state capitol door," Chavis said, "and knocking on the door, and couldn't get an answer. A lot of people in Oxford who had marched all the way," Chavis continued, "was hoping and praying the governor would give us an audience, that the governor would step up and call for justice in Oxford. It did not happen."

Chavis, Hawkins, and Frinks returned to the rally and reported that neither the governor nor any of his staff would receive them. "The day for begging for black people in North Carolina is over," Hawkins declared, vowing to register enough black voters to end this disrespectful treatment. "What killed Henry Marrow," Golden

Frinks preached to the crowd, "was symbolic of racism in North Carolina. And what the governor just told us by his absence is that to the white power structure, it's just another nigger dead." These sentiments at the podium echoed those among the rank and file of the marchers. "We got all the way to Raleigh," Carolyn Thorpe recalled bitterly, "and [the governor] was not even there. We could not talk to him. All that walking and marching and they said he wasn't even in there. That told me everything I needed to know."

While the other marchers worried about getting the governor's attention, Eddie McCoy had what he considered a far more serious problem: he and two of his friends had borrowed the mule for the march from Lonnie Fields, a black farmer in Granville County, and now they had to get it back to him—two days late. "Lonnie Fields was the meanest man in Granville County, and he would kill you," McCoy laughed. "I don't mean he might kill you, I mean he *would* kill you." On top of that, to borrow the mule they had found it necessary to tell Fields a deliberate lie. "We told him we was just gon' take the mule out to the edge of town," McCoy recalled, "and be back that afternoon. And that evening we still won't back with the mule, and Lonnie Fields went in the house, turned on the news, and saw his mule on television, and he sent some people to tell us he was gon' kill us, and he won't kidding. He said to tell us he was gon' kill every damn one of us." Two days later, they were in Raleigh with Lonnie Fields's mule, and trying to figure out how to get the mule back without walking him the whole fifty miles.

The young men got the U-Haul truck they had used to carry provisions for the marchers and decided to load up the mule to return it to the furious farmer. But when they tried to walk the animal up the gangplank into the back of the truck, the mule planted his front feet, brayed and snorted, and refused to move. They tugged on the lead rope and even tried beating the mule with a stick, but the stubborn beast would not budge. "I told them we ought to just leave the mule in Raleigh," McCoy chuckled, "because if we didn't take the mule back Lonnie Fields was gon' kill us, and if we took the mule back Lonnie Fields was gon' kill us anyway, so I told 'em, said to hell with the damn mule." But they struggled on. Their fathers and grandfathers had loved mules, studied mules, sat around the store and bragged about mules, but the Black Power generation didn't know much about mules beyond their political symbolism. Finally one of them went to a pay telephone and called his grandfather, who advised them to blindfold the beast. "We took a sack and covered that mule's head," McCoy said, "and walked him around until he didn't know where he was, and then just led him right on up into the truck. But when we got back to Oxford, didn't nobody want to return the mule. Finally we found one of Lonnie Fields's children and got him to take the mule back. And Lonnie Fields said he was gonna kill *him* for helping us."

The leaders of the march had even worse luck with the governor than McCoy and his friends had with the mule. Governor Scott was not blindfolded, and his decision not to meet with the black protestors made crystal clear electoral sense. A "law and order" Democrat, Scott was resisting a Republican tide strengthened by the cresting waves of white backlash against civil rights gains. Two years earlier, during the presidential election of 1968, the Democratic tally in the state had dropped 42 percent; George Wallace, the slick-haired race-baiter from Alabama running on the American Independent Party ticket, had outpolled the Democrats in North Carolina. Jim Gardner, the Republican Party candidate for governor in 1968, actually endorsed Wallace for president of the United States, though he nonetheless narrowly lost to Scott, whose father had been one of the state's most notable governors. "I've never heard Wallace say anything that I disagreed with," Gardner explained. Presumably this included Wallace's most famous declaration: "Segregation now, segregation tomorrow, segregation forever!"

As the 1960s ended, both Democrats and Republicans knew full well that the whole electoral process was cascading into a one-issue waterwheel, with race at the hub. In 1972, North Carolina would elect James Holshouser, its first Republican governor since Reconstruction. White voters would also elevate the state's most prominent opponent of racial equality, Jesse Helms, to a seat in the

U.S. Senate, which he would never lose. So in 1970 the incumbent Democrat, Governor Scott, ignored black concerns, apparently having forgotten that the majority of whites backed Gardner, and that only black voters had saved him from defeat in 1968. Black voters were hardly likely to swing over to the party of Jesse Helms, but white voters were pouring out of the Democratic Party in a racially driven realignment of political loyalties. Maybe Scott was right, at least in electoral terms, to keep his distance. But it made the demonstrators who had walked fifty miles from Oxford bitterly angry.

The governor's refusal to acknowledge the protest reignited the anger of black incendiaries in Oxford who felt that his political posture showed that he and the white-dominated state apparatus stood with the murderers of Henry Marrow. "Everything was going fine," Mayor Currin told a reporter. "Then, wham, Sunday it started happening again. We thought the black community was satisfied." Around midnight, after most of the marchers got home from Raleigh, someone threw firebombs into a small antique store in a downtown alley called Bank Street. James Currin Antiques was an easy target, white-owned property hidden from view and readily accessible, through back streets and alleyways, to the black neighborhood around Granville Street. This was only the diversionary attack, however; a few minutes later, flames roared through the Chapman Lumber Company on McClanahan Street, within sight of my father's church. The vast, two-story lumber company building held large quantities of paint and turpentine, as well as sizable stores of lumber. In a matter of minutes, the blaze completely engulfed the building. This was the first truly serious calculated blow to white economic power in Oxford, and the most costly fire in Oxford during the twentieth century—until the following night.

CHAPTER 10

PERRY MASON IN THE SHOESHINE PARLOR

O**N MONDAY, MAY 25,** a week after the murder, half a dozen black veterans huddled in the back room at McCoy's Pool Hall, mixed several gallons of gasoline with half a box of Tide washing powder, and made firebombs. The soap "thickens it up good," one of them observed. "Makes it stick to things long enough so it doesn't just flame out but catches everything on fire. The military taught us how to make 'em." Downing several quarts of Miller High Life beer while they worked, the men used a homemade funnel to pour the mixture into the empty bottles, which they stoppered with rags. Big enough to ignite a good-sized blaze, the Miller quarts flew like small footballs and were made of thin glass that would always break. "Shit, man," one of them said, "a Coke bottle is so thick the damn thing won't even break. The big quart was the thing."

They devised a careful plan for their fiery announcement to the white-controlled legal system. "They could get an all-white jury and let 'em off, they could sure enough do that if they wanted to," one of the black men said years later, "but we were going to sure enough let 'em know that we won't gonna take that shit." The black veterans synchronized their watches, took careful note of police patterns of surveillance, and rarely attacked without a coordinated diversionary operation. "We'd light up some tool shed or something easy like that on the other side of town," one explained, "and then Andy and Barney would haul ass over there and then, bam, we'd burn the damn warehouse. It was a military operation."

Two of the younger black men agreed to torch a white-owned house on New College Street that had been standing empty for months. "We burned that one house, trying to get a diversion up," one of them recalled. "See, once you hit the railroad tracks," another arsonist explained, "we could split up—they couldn't catch you. All we had to do was make it to the railroad tracks. If you couldn't run that fast, you didn't have no business doing it." The older black veterans would then take out the real targets. That night, they set their sights high, planning to torch two large tobacco warehouses, Planter's Warehouse and the Owen Warehouse Number Two. Inside these warehouses were eight hundred thousand pounds of golden cured tobacco, a known flammable substance, with a total value of more than a million dollars.

Just before midnight, as police and firefighters rushed to the flaming house on New College Street, two squads of veterans crept through darkened alleyways to the enormous warehouses downtown. Lookouts posted earlier gave the all-clear sign. Quickly stretching duct tape across the large windowpanes—"that shit muffles the sound"—the men shattered the windows with bricks, lit the rag stoppers on the bottle bombs, and "just threw our shit in there and ran down to the corner where we could just watch it go," according to their leader.

The magnitude of the fires surprised even the arsonists. At first they stared wide-eyed at the huge blazes, and then they hurried to a row of homes behind the warehouses to help the families hustle their furniture out. They used garden hoses to soak the rooftops with water to prevent fiery debris from igniting the whole neighborhood. Soon more than a hundred firefighters were battling the blaze, six fire departments from nearby towns having sent men and trucks. The old pine-and-brick structures stacked high with the cured leaf roared like piles of tinder. By the time the first fire truck reached Planter's

Warehouse, it was already engulfed in flames. Moments later, the front wall of the enormous building blew out in a great explosion, scattering bricks and flaming debris into the street, pulling down telephone and power lines as the side of the building fell. Glowing debris landed on residential lawns miles away.

The screaming sirens woke up my family, and we children followed Daddy and Mama onto the brick walkway in front of the house on Hancock Street, huddling together in our pajamas. Like a hundred-foot torch held skyward, the flames from the warehouses licked into the night sky. Farmers twenty miles away smelled the smoke and saw the horizon lit up with a bright red glow, as though the sun were setting in the middle of the night. From four blocks away it looked to me like the whole world was on fire. I wasn't quite eleven years old, of course, and I had clean sheets waiting inside and nothing could harm me, as the old song says, with my mama and daddy standing by. What would come of all of this destruction and anger and fear? I did not know enough history to understand what was happening, and it would be many years before I did, but Oxford would burn in my memory for the rest of my life.

The pool hall conspirators had wanted their attack to hit the white community where it mattered most, in the economic engines of the town. To that end, several African American men employed at Burlington Mills on the third shift ran through the plant at the prearranged hour shouting that Oxford was burning. These in-plant co-conspirators, who had synchronized their watches with those of the arsonists, urged their coworkers to rush home and make sure their families were all right and their houses did not burn. When the employees ran outside and saw the raging red skyline and the town shrouded in smoke, most of them left their jobs and hurried home. Although the *Oxford Public Ledger* stressed that this only caused workers to lose wages, the black insurgents working the "cash register at the pool hall" calculated that the biggest losers would be mill management. The *Ledger*'s lead editorial on the day after the fires, "Lessons To Be Learned from Memorial Day," highlighted the Confederate origins of this "day for decorating the graves of the men who fell in the War Between the States" and did little to suggest that the editors understood what was happening in their hometown.

Whatever the *Oxford Public Ledger* might report, Oxford's all-white economic elite had been hit and hit hard. The next day, Mayor Currin estimated the damages at "well over a million dollars, though it is hard to say at this point." (In 2003 dollars, the total damage would amount to something approaching $5 million.) Not only the warehouses and the empty house on New College Street had gone up, but also three smaller buildings downtown. Coordinated attacks had occurred all over town, although further investigation revealed that not all the squads of arsonists had been successful. Law enforcement officers found failed firebombing attempts at six other buildings: the Southern Railway Station, the clubhouse of the all-white Veterans of Foreign Wars, the Fleming Warehouse Number One, and three smaller structures. The charred landscape in the business district awed the teams of journalists and officials who came to survey the damages. A large section of downtown Oxford, the Raleigh *News and Observer* reported, "look[ed] like Berlin following the Allied bombing raids of World War II."

On the night of the bombings, the Oxford Police Department arrested six young black males, ranging in age from fourteen to seventeen, who were running the streets in defiance of the curfew. One or two of them carried Coke bottles full of gasoline. White Oxford breathed a deep sigh of relief, reassuring itself that the culprits responsible for the devastation had been swiftly apprehended. Unfortunately for those who relied on this line of reassurance, the police had taken the young men into custody in the hours *before* the fires. It is possible, though not likely, that the boys may have been responsible for one or two of the failed arson attempts around town that night or the previous night. But the arrests and investigations never threatened to disrupt the "military operation" raging in the shadows of Granville County. No one could have been more pleased at the arrests than the pool hall enclave of black veterans. The police were happy to pat themselves on the back without actually catching any of the conspirators. The youngest three teenagers, all of them fourteen or fifteen years old, were released on bond and confined by the court to their homes pending trial. Authorities held the three older boys, all seventeen-year-olds, for ten days and then released them under large bonds. None of the boys could be linked to any of the firebombings, and the court eventually dropped all of the charges to misdemeanor curfew violations. "[City officials] probably knew better, but they let people believe it was just a bunch of shirttail boys burning up stuff," one of the older veterans recounted.

The black veterans who actually burned down the warehouses in Oxford and the activists who applauded their efforts had no illusions about the prospect of colorblind justice in Granville County. "We knew damn well they won't gonna convict Teel and them," one of their ringleaders commented. This makes the arson smack of pre-emptive vigilantism but, given the experiences of these men in Vietnam and in Oxford, they could hardly place their faith in the white-dominated legal system. In their minds, the courts were owned and operated by their enemies, who considered them unfit for full citizenship. "There wasn't no need to wait around and see what might happen," the bomb thrower continued. "They won't gonna convict 'em noway."

The white prosecutor, W. H. S. Burgwyn, a gray-haired, steely-eyed veteran of the courts and the scion of North Carolina political aristocracy, felt more hopeful. Burgwyn's father had been a judge, planter, and politician, and the direct ancestor of illustrious heroes of the American Revolution and the Civil War. Something of a court-room legend himself, Burgwyn knew that the murder case confronting him posed the most serious challenge he had ever faced as a prosecutor. "The whole community was in an uproar," Burgwyn recalled. Support for the murderers had taken on the air of a cause célèbre among some whites, he acknowledged. "The Klan was kicking up a fuss," he said, "and some of the country club crowd had raised a big defense fund," but he still thought he had a strong case. "We felt that this boy had been cold-bloodedly murdered, in a helpless state, shot on the ground," he said.

He conceded some confusion, however, about exactly what had

happened in the shadows beyond Teel's store. "We had a dead man," Burgwyn explained, "with three or four white men standing over him with a gun. We knew which gun had killed him, but we couldn't place the gun in the hands of any one individual at the time of the shooting." It was getting dark, he explained, and most of the witnesses had run away from the scene. Boo Chavis had had the best view, but he may have seemed an unreliable witness because of his criminal record. Still, the prosecutor insisted, he had a strong case. Neither the black veterans, who had no faith in the legal system, nor prosecutor Burgwyn, who had spent his life in it, could have predicted what would actually happen in the Granville County courthouse that summer. Years later, referring to the popular television attorney of the time, whose cases always ended with a dramatic courtroom twist, Burgwyn said, "It was just a Perry Mason kind of thing."

In a sense, the legal proceedings had begun shortly after the murder. "Go call the ambulance," Robert Teel told me he had snapped at twenty-one-year-old Roger just after Marrow was shot. Teel walked quickly down the front of the cement-block building with his large ring of keys, shooing out a handful of customers, gathering up all the money, and locking the grocery store, the barbershop, the laundry, and the motorcycle shop, and stacking the guns in the trunk of his car. After he closed down all the businesses, the Teel family drove to their home on Main Street, only a few hundred yards from the courthouse and the police station.

At the house, as unattestable rumor echoed it down the years, the family had a discussion in which Robert Teel decided that Roger, who certainly had helped kill Henry Marrow, would have no part in whatever consequences were to follow. Roger's wife, Betsey Woodlief Oakley, was six months pregnant. She had already suffered two miscarriages. Roger was to stay home with her, no matter what. At around ten o'clock, an hour after the murder, Teel called his attorney, William T. Watkins, who reportedly told him to gather up as much cash money as he could and put it in a pillowcase, then wait for him at the house. Teel was not to talk to anyone, the lawyer insisted.

Whether Billy Watkins, a ruthless lawyer and cagey politician with a dry, cottonmouth smile, advised Teel on how to confuse the police we may never know. The local courthouse legend in Oxford says that Watkins suggested that Roger Oakley and Larry Teel exchange clothing and that Larry wear Roger's eyeglasses to the police station. Roger and Larry were both slender young men of medium height. The smearing of their appearances might have bewildered witnesses and investigators and thereby permitted Roger to avoid prosecution, at least for the moment. The reputation of Billy Watkins as a wily and unscrupulous attorney may explain the persistence of this rumor. Or the story may simply be a fiction that local people used to explain the inexplicable. Teel himself credited Watkins but did not mention the alleged subterfuge. "Billy told me not to say a word to anybody," recounted Teel, "and let them accuse whoever they wanted. And we did not tell them who or whatever," he continued, "but just let them build their own case. We listened to Billy Watkins."

"The name Watkins," said a member of one of Granville County's leading families, "just stood for and stands for a lot in Oxford." Billy Watkins was already Oxford's leading attorney in 1970, the fifty-one-year-old scion of political power and the avatar of ruthless ambition. The year before, he had been elected to the state legislature. The son of a local planter who had been "one of the most reputable politicians this area ever had," Watkins was fast becoming a leading figure in the Democratic Party. He was on his way to the chair of the legislature's powerful appropriations committee, from which he and his chief political ally, Speaker Liston B. Ramsey, would come to exercise almost invincible sway in the General Assembly. Watkins would never face serious political challenge in his district and would become one of the two or three most powerful men in the state. As soon as he arrived at the Teel house on Main Street, Watkins took complete control of the case. "I was aiming to tell what I had shot, and what Roger had done," Teel recalled, "but Billy listened to the whole story, and we told him, and so he handled it from there on and we went by his advice."

While it remains a matter of speculation, I am almost certain that

Billy Watkins telephoned the Oxford Police Department that night and told them that he would bring the Teels in for questioning later. Otherwise, it becomes difficult to explain why the police did not take the thirty seconds necessary to get to the Teel house in a squad car and make an arrest. They had known about the killing, including the identity of most of those involved, since about nine o'clock. Such a telephone call reflects the day-to-day workings of power in the small-town South, which relied on personal authority and informal relationships among a certain class of white men. It is possible, as many local black folks believed, that the white police considered the killing justified and were slow to arrest a man whom they saw as having protected his family and property against the spirit of black insurrection that was sweeping the nation. But it seems more likely that Billy Watkins called and told them not to worry about it right away, that he would see to it that the Teels turned themselves in directly. Watkins was one of the few people whose authority was sufficient to ensure that the police would sit back and let Teel come in at his own convenience. Just when Robert and Larry Teel actually went to the police station remains a matter of dispute.

The *Oxford Public Ledger* claimed a few days later that Billy Watkins accompanied the Teels to the police station around ten o'clock Monday night. Mayor Currin and Chief of Police Nathan White both later claimed that the Teels surrendered sometime shortly after the shooting, that the magistrate draw up a warrant immediately, and that the two suspects went to jail at about six o'clock Tuesday morning. None of the black witnesses who went to the police station that night saw them there, however. Other reports indicated that the two men went to the police station sometime Tuesday morning. But the most reliable document—the official arrest warrant—indicates that Robert and Larry Teel were arrested at eight-thirty on Wednesday morning—almost thirty-six hours after the killing. "There was a hell of a mix-up in the Oxford police station," W. H. S. Burgwyn acknowledged. "It was very confusing." The young black people running through the streets did not feel confused.

If blacks interpreted this delay as a display of whites' determination to protect one of their own and preserve white power, Robert
Teel certainly did not believe that he was the beneficiary of the white
power structure. "My lawyer told me he'd have me out in twenty-
four hours," Teel said later. "He told me to go on over to Raleigh and
let them book me and fingerprint me, and go through the regular
processing, and he'd be over there with people to go my bond, and
have me out in twenty-four hours. It took four months."

After arresting Teel and Larry, state troopers took them to Central
Prison in Raleigh. At first, they were in a large holding cell. In a few
days, however, "it got to be common knowledge between the blacks
who we were and what we were there for and the pressure was
building up," Teel remembered. "The sheriff had to put us in a private cell because they had the two of us whites locked up in a cell
with thirteen blacks and this boy that was a trustee running up and
down the hall telling everybody who we were." Soon the police
transferred the father and son to the jail in nearby Henderson for the
duration of the trial; they were kept together at all times. "They tried
to make me believe that [the incarceration] was for my own safety
and my own protection," Teel complained. "And I cannot say
whether it was good or bad for my protection or somebody else's
protection, but they seemed to be saying that I would have shot
another black or else I would have been shot. Which very well could
have been true, but my understanding of bond is that it is not what's
good for the man but only whether you will appear in court or not."
In any case, the father and son remained in custody after their arrest
in mid-May.

On July 27, the first day of jury selection, sheriff's deputies led
Robert and Larry Teel into the old red brick courthouse, accompa-
nied by a team of five attorneys. Billy Watkins and his law partners,
Gene Edmundson and Charles W. Wilkinson, employed Frank
Banzet, a lawyer from a prominent family in Warrenton, to join the
defense team after it became clear that the pool of jurors would be
drawn from Warren and Wake Counties. Warren, northeast of
Oxford, was an old plantation county, with a heavy black majority and

a firmly entrenched white aristocracy built on cotton, tobacco, and black slave labor; Banzet would handle the jury pool. Edmundson, a junior partner in Watkins's firm, didn't much like defending the Teels, but he was philosophical about his duties. "I had to look at it not as an individual but as an attorney," he recalled. "We were there to do a job."

At the prosecution's table, William Burgwyn was flanked by Charles White, an attorney from his office, and James E. Ferguson, a black attorney from Charlotte and one of the leading civil rights lawyers in the state. Burgwyn, though clearly an "establishment" figure in North Carolina, was regarded as extremely able and completely honest. And Ferguson was a very gifted attorney with a strong track record. "Ferguson had already played a pivotal role in the civil rights movement in North Carolina," historian David Cecelski writes. "He had led or been involved in most of the civil rights lawsuits arising in eastern North Carolina; he had been successful enough to have the Ku Klux Klan target him for assassination." His new partner, Julius Chambers, narrowly escaped death in 1965 when his car was bombed in New Bern."

The attorneys for both sides prepared to fight the case in front of Judge Robert Martin. Martin, who would preside over a series of racially charged trials in North Carolina in the 1970s, had campaigned for hard-core segregationist I. Beverly Lake a decade earlier. Judge Martin "hardbored no prejudice" against African Americans, he told one reporter. "I was raised in a mainly black county," he was quoted as saying. "I ate with them and played with them. We had an instinctive love for the Negro race. Why, my secretary is black. That should show you how I feel about them."

Whatever the judge may have felt in his heart, the atmosphere in the ancient courthouse grew exceedingly tense as jury selection began. Though the courtroom was no longer formally segregated, 250 local black folks crowded the left side of the aisle, while 150 white observers sat on the other side. "There was a lot of people there," Carolyn Thorpe said later. "It was packed. There was a black side and a white side. There was a lot more blacks than whites—that place was full of black people." State troopers searched everyone who entered the room. "Rumor had it that there were some Black Panthers that were recognized that were in the courtroom," court reporter Rebecca Dickerson explained.

The prosecution initially moved to have the trial relocated outside Granville County, where white support for the murderers and white fears of black revolt ran high. Though Robert Teel had not been accepted among the leading white families of the county prior to the murder, many of them now rallied around him. "Teel was the white champion," said a white woman born of an old and prestigious local family. "It was the fear of integration—it was not so much that you identified with Teel but that his skin was white. It was like you had to band together." Anywhere would be an easier place to get a conviction, Burgwyn reasoned, and it certainly was not hard to establish that the local community was too turbulent for a trial. The charred wreckage of the warehouses still scarred downtown, carloads of armed men continued to cruise the streets, and headlines like "Oxford—A Quiet Town Becomes a Battleground" were a regular feature in the state's leading newspapers. Judge Martin ruled that the trial would stay in Granville County, but that a pool of jurors would be brought in from outside the community.

Lawyers for both sides questioned seventy prospective jurors from Wake County and thirty from Warren County. Frank Banzet, playing exactly the role for which Watkins had hired him, quickly moved to have all the jurors from Wake County rejected on the grounds that the juror selection cards had been stored in the basement of a hospital. They should have been kept in the office of the register of deeds, he argued. Only nine of the one hundred jurors chosen for examination were African Americans, despite the fact that Warren County was over two-thirds black and Wake County was more than one-third black. When James Ferguson of the prosecution complained that blacks had been systematically excluded from the pool of jurors, Banzet ridiculed the black attorney. Yes, there had indeed been discrimination, Banzet chuckled. The names listed all began with letters from *L* through *W*, he charged satirically, "thus obviously 'systematically excluding' persons whose names begin with the letters A through K." Moreover, all jurors from Wake County should be excluded, he persisted, because Wake's juror selection cards "are punched with numerous holes which are incomprehensible to a person of ordinary learning and understanding." Wake County used then-novel and now-obsolete computer punch cards for its jury lists. These computing machines had made "more than 27 mistakes in the past three weeks," he claimed, coming up with a remarkable statistic on the spot.

What truly bothered Banzet about Wake County was that it was home to several universities and the state capitol in Raleigh and therefore relatively liberal compared to Granville. Warren County, on the other hand, had always been tobacco country, much like Granville, with a black majority dominated by an agricultural and political elite descended from slaveholding planters. Even though the county was mostly black, the courthouse crowd in Warrenton had a long history of making sure that jury lists would be mostly white. Frank Banzet knew how things worked up there. The attorneys for Robert and Larry Teel wanted an all-white jury, and preferably an all-white jury drawn from a conservative, rural county.

The questions the Teel defense team posed to the prospective jurors clearly revealed their legal strategy. "Do you believe that a citizen has the right to self-defense?" they asked over and over again. "Do you believe that a man has the right to take the life of another man to protect himself or members of his family from harm?" The defense struck all nine of the black jurors and got their all-white jury, seven men and five women, half of them from Warren County. Every member of the jury had conceded that he or she did, in fact, support the right of citizens to defend themselves and their families by force. The prosecution was crestfallen, and the black people attending the trial were incensed, if not surprised. At the end of the day, Judge Martin ordered the jurors sequestered at a local motel for the duration of the trial.

The confusion among the police and the prosecutors—and the Oxford Police Department's failure to arrest Roger—became Billy

Watkins's secret weapon. At the outset of the trial, Watkins made a successful motion to Judge Martin that all of the state's witnesses be sequestered. Therefore, the witnesses would be unable to hear one another's testimony or the testimony of the defense witnesses. This approach took maximum advantage of the confusion created because the prosecution had failed to indict everyone who had participated in the murder, which Watkins knew. Prosecutor Burgwyn countered by asking the judge to sequester all of the defense witnesses as well. "When we went to court," Boo Chavis recounted, "they put us in different rooms."

It is not clear how the defense attorneys managed to have most of their witnesses elude the judge's sequestration order. Roger Oakley was not listed as a witness and did not even come to the trial until the last day. In the end, Colleen Teel did not testify, and the court managed to compel only one of the five eventual witnesses for the defense to obey the sequestration order. This was true despite the fact that the defense team knew they would be calling those witnesses. Watkins even knew he would be calling Roger Oakley to the stand, but he kept silent. "We knew right after the arrest what had happened," defense attorney Edmundson recalled. "[Roger Oakley] came in and we talked with him, took tapes, and put them in the safe, and no one else knew."

At about three in the afternoon on Wednesday, July 29, the bailiff picked up the big courtroom Bible and Willie T. Harris, the seventeen-year-old African American who had driven the dying Henry Marrow to the hospital, swore to tell the truth, the whole truth, and nothing but the truth. Harris, the first witness to take the stand, told the court that he had been sitting in his automobile under the shed at the Tidewater Seafood Market with three other young men on the evening of the murder. He heard Marrow and someone else—a white man, he thought—arguing loudly. Harris got out of his car to see what was going on and observed Larry Teel standing in front of the motorcycle shop with a big stick, swinging it at Henry Marrow. Almost immediately, Robert Teel dashed out of the barbershop with a shotgun, Harris said, "and I ran." As his feet carried him down Highway 158 and up into Grab-all, he had heard two or three shots. Returning a few minutes later, Harris told the court, he saw Marrow lying on his back behind the Tidewater Seafood Market with Larry Teel standing over him.

The second witness for the prosecution was Boo Chavis. After all the violence in Oxford in May and June, the Chavis family had sent Boo to New Jersey to keep him safe and out of trouble, although the authorities had already apprehended him in several cases involving theft. Just as he got off a bus in Newark, sheriff's deputies handed the young man a subpoena and told him he had to testify at a trial in North Carolina. The diminutive young Chavis, who wore small spectacles, opened his testimony by recounting how he had been walking to the store after a game of bid whist at a friend's house down the street. His testimony was familiar to both sides because of the earlier hearings and the newspaper coverage. Chavis was probably the most damning witness for the prosecution, and the defense attorneys were determined to rattle him.

Chavis continued to testify that he had been on his way to the drink machine when four boys flew by him, running as fast as they could. The last one yelled, "Come on, Dickie," recounted Chavis. He heard a shotgun blast and saw Dickie Marrow skidding onto his face in the gravel behind the Tidewater. Moments later, shotgun pellets burned his face, arms, neck, and hands, and the pain and blood blinded him for a second. Robert Teel accosted him in the doorway of the Tidewater Seafood Market and "put a shotgun barrel in my face and pulled the trigger," Chavis said that he testified. When the shotgun clicked on an empty chamber, Teel and his sons ran over to the fallen Marrow and began kicking and beating him. "Okay, you got me," Chavis reported that Marrow begged his attackers. "Let's forget it." According to Chavis, Robert Teel then barked at his son, "Shoot the son of a bitch!" Another shot rang out "that sounded about like a cap pistol," said Chavis—the .22-caliber rifle shot that ended Henry Marrow's life.

In a move that must have been calculated to inflame the racial feelings of the all-white jury, Banzet "asked me did I seen the man [who had fired the shot that killed Henry Marrow] in here, and I told him yes." Recalling the scene years later, Chavis said, "He said, 'Will you get up and go touch him.' And I said, 'Yeah, sure.' " Chavis walked across the courtroom and stepped up to Larry Teel. "I went over there and touched him, like that," Chavis recounted, extending his index finger. For a defiant young black man to put his hands on a white man in court could not help but make white jurors uneasy, but the judge did not intervene.

Billy Watkins, who sat impassively chewing Life Savers during the entire weeklong trial, calmly cross-examined Chavis in an effort to discredit his powerful testimony. "Watkins, when I was on the stand, he asked me had I ever been in any trouble." Trouble was one big reason why the Chavis family had sent Boo to New Jersey, and his local police record indicated that he had had plenty of clashes with the law. "I told him, yeah, but I ain't on trial." Watkins forced Chavis to recount more or less his entire rap sheet in front of the jury. "What was I on probation for, what had I been in, all that," Chavis said, "and I told him aiding and abetting, receiving stolen goods, breaking and entering, but I said I still wasn't on trial and I didn't kill nobody, either." Watkins had made his point.

"This other lady that saw it, Mrs. Downey," Chavis explained to me, "she was standing behind a bush, but she didn't want to cooperate." In fact, the next witness, a fearful black woman named Evelyn Downey, had kept silent until she was subpoenaed and had refused to admit except under oath that she had seen any of the events behind the Teel place on the night of the murder. It was rumored that the Ku Klux Klan had threatened to burn her family's house and store if she testified. "Mrs. Downey testified she had not disclosed her knowledge of the shooting until last week when an agent of the State Bureau of Investigation, Ray Freeman, told her she would be subpoenaed as a witness," the *News and Observer* reported. "Mrs. Downey said she had kept silent because she feared for her elderly in-laws who own and operate Downey's Grocery, located near the scene of the shooting." The tiny store, only a few yards from the Teel place, was really little more than a shack that sold snacks and soft drinks. Mrs. Downey told the court that she had been inside at about eight forty-five on the night of the murder when she heard shouting and the sound of several people running past the store. She stepped outside under a tree and looked over toward the Tidewater Seafood Market and Teel's place.

"There were three white men standing over a boy, kicking him back and forth on the ground," Downey testified in a quavering voice. "And I yelled, 'You better stop before you kill him.'" Robert Teel replied, "You better get back into the store," according to Downey. She did not really recognize the other two men, she said, nor did she go back inside. "They kept kicking him back and forth and hitting him with the guns," Mrs. Downey testified, "and then Mr. Teel said 'Shoot the son of a bitch.' Then he said it again, 'Shoot the son of a bitch nigger.' And I heard the shot and ran back into the store." It was Larry Teel, she indicated, who'd held the rifle. Mrs. Downey collapsed in tears after testifying, and the bailiff helped her out of the courtroom. At that, the state rested its case against the Teels.

Judy Teel, Larry's eighteen-year-old wife, was the first witness for the defense the next day. She had seen a bunch of "them," she said, referring to the young black men, coming over from the fish market before the trouble started. She testified that Henry Marrow, whom she said she had never seen before, had called out to her, "Hey, white girl. Hey, white girl." Larry had stepped out of the shop and told the black man not to speak to her like that, in her account, and Marrow had advanced on her husband with a knife and used foul language, she told the court. Larry did not kick Henry Marrow, like some people said, she asserted, but when Marrow attacked him she ran to the front of the barbershop to get Teel and Roger to "help Larry. I just yelled for them to help Larry." She knew that there were guns in the barbershop, she admitted, but she never saw anyone with a gun at any time. In a massive irregularity that I cannot explain, Judy was the only witness for the defense who followed Judge Martin's sequestration order and thus did not hear the testimony of the other witnesses.

Neither Larry Teel nor his father had been expected to testify at the trial. But Billy Watkins called him to the stand. "In a surprise move here Thursday," the *News and Observer* reported, "Larry Teel, 18-year-old son of a local barber, Robert Teel, took the witness stand in Granville County Superior Court and denied that he shot and killed a local Negro man." According to Larry, whom one seasoned courtroom observer described as "obviously terrified," he and his wife had been rolling motorcycles into the shop when Marrow walked toward them. "Hey, white girl. Hey, you son of a bitch," Larry quoted the young black man as having said. When Larry objected to Marrow's talking to his wife disrespectfully, he told the court, the black man replied, "Come on, I am a soul brother," and brandished a knife at him. When Marrow rushed at him, "I kicked him in the chest," Larry Teel said, contradicting his wife's testimony. "He staggered back and grabbed a handful of gravel and threw it at me. About that time I heard a shotgun."

When he found the young black man on the ground, Larry claimed, he straddled Marrow, hit him several times with his fists, took the knife away from him, and jumped to his feet. As he stood over Marrow, the younger Teel claimed, he saw a gun pointed at the fallen man's head. "I was looking down at a rifle barrel," said Teel, "and it jerked and went off." His father and another man were standing with him at the time, Larry swore, but he didn't see who the other man was. He had not fired a gun, nor even held a gun at any point that night, Larry maintained. Though he admitted to having had one foot on either side of Marrow's body when he heard the gunshot, he did not know who was holding the weapon. He said he had absolutely no clue who might have fired the gun that killed Henry Marrow, though he admitted that his father was present. Larry recognized his father's voice, he conceded, "when he told me 'I'm going to go call an ambulance and the police.' "

As hard as it must have been for anyone in the room to believe Larry Teel's shaky and sullen account of the killing, what happened the next day was even more far-fetched. In fact, the last day of testimony fully justified prosecutor Burgwyn's comparison to the Perry Mason show, which my father and I often watched together. In those days, Perry Mason was television's most popular detective, a dark, brooding defense attorney who unraveled mysterious murders in an hour, not counting commercials. By the third or fourth commercial break, the handsome TV lawyer knew who the killer was—but he wasn't telling. In the climactic courtroom scene of each episode—the accused was always innocent—the real murderer would stand up and blurt out a startling confession and the blameless person before the bar of justice would go free. The plots on Perry Mason were predictable even to an eleven-year-old, but no one except Billy Watkins seemed to anticipate what was about to happen in the Granville County courthouse on August 31, 1970.

That morning, Watkins called Roger Oakley to the stand. Roger had not been named as either a witness or a suspect; the prosecution witnesses had all identified his brother Larry as the one who had fired the lethal bullet. Roger had not even attended the trial, despite the fact that his brother and his father sat charged with first-degree murder. "The trial of an Oxford man and his son on charges of murdering a 23-year-old black man took a startling turn on Friday," a reporter for the *News and Observer* wrote, "when another member of the defendants' family testified in Granville County Superior Court that he was holding the gun that fired the fatal shot." He was working on the boat parked in front of the barbershop with his father, Roger Oakley testified, when he heard his brother's wife "holler for me to help Larry."

He ran around the corner of the motorcycle shop and saw a black man coming at his younger brother with a knife, he told the court. When he saw his father run out of the barbershop with a shotgun, he went inside and got the combined .410 shotgun and .22 rifle over-and-under and ran after his father, who fired the 12-gauge shotgun at a man who was running. Oakley testified that when he got to the other side of the seafood market, he saw his father and Larry standing above the fallen Henry Marrow, and he joined them, aiming the gun down at Marrow's head. At no time, he said, did Larry have a gun in his hand that night. "Someone bumped my shoulder and the gun went off," Roger said quietly, tears streaming down his face. "I didn't mean to kill nobody."

Prosecutor Burgwyn, red-faced and nearly sputtering, roared into his cross-examination. "Why haven't you told the truth before?" he demanded. "If this was an accident, why did you let your father and brother stand trial for first-degree murder?"

"Because my lawyer told me not to," Roger Oakley whispered. "My lawyer told me not to say nothing."

"Do you mean to tell this jury that you let your father and your brother stay in jail without privilege of bond since May 12, and didn't tell anybody you shot the man, and that the shooting was an accident?" Burgwyn asked. Roger replied that he had only decided to testify the week before. "Your father and your brother were on trial for their lives in this courthouse," the gray-haired prosecutor said softly to the young man. "On trial for their *lives*," he repeated, "charged with capital murder. And you have not set foot in this courtroom. Why haven't you come here before?"

Roger Oakley stared at the floor. "My attorney told me not to come," he whispered.

"So your brother Larry never touched that gun? Did I hear you correctly on that point?" the prosecutor asked.

"Yes, sir," Oakley replied. "I never saw him touch a gun the whole time."

"Both barrels of that gun had been fired," Burgwyn said. "The rifle barrel that killed Henry Marrow, and the .410-shotgun underneath had been fired, too. Did you fire the shotgun and the rifle?"

"I refuse to answer on the grounds that it may incriminate me," Roger chanted quietly, as if he were talking to himself.

"The boy who lay on the ground, begging for his life, helpless, Roger—did you kick him?"

"I was kicking him," Oakley replied quietly. "We was all kicking him."

"Did you beat him with the stock of that rifle?" Burgwyn asked. "His skull was fractured, Roger," the prosecutor added. "You say you were standing above him with a rifle. Did you hit him with it?"

"I refuse to answer on the grounds that it may incriminate me," Oakley said once more in the same distant monotone.

"Who told you to say that, Roger?" the prosecutor demanded. "Who told you to plead the Fifth Amendment?"

"My lawyers," Oakley whispered. "Frank Banzet and Mr. Watkins." At this point, the court reporter remembered, the young man began to cry softly.

"You know, of course, that neither your wife nor your attorney can testify against you, don't you? They told you that, too, didn't they? And they told you that all the witnesses had testified that Larry was holding the gun, didn't they?" Burgwyn continued. "And they told you that if you said you'd shot the rifle, but that it was an accident, your brother and father might not have to go to prison, didn't they? And they told you that it would be hard to convict you of something you didn't do, when all the witnesses had already testified that your brother had done it, didn't they? Isn't that more or less what they told you, Roger?"

"I refuse to answer on the grounds that it may incriminate me," the young man said weakly.

"Your brother shot that boy, didn't he?" Burgwyn said. "And you and your daddy helped kill him, didn't you? They let you stay home with your wife and the baby, isn't that right? And now you're supposed to help them get out of jail by saying that you had the gun the whole time, when you know there isn't a witness anywhere that can testify to that effect, aren't you? Nobody but your wife and your attorney, and neither one of them can testify against you. Tell the truth."

"No, sir," Roger Oakley sobbed softly. "I'm sorry."

"No further questions," Burgwyn told the judge. The defense rested its case before lunch. The attorneys for both sides would begin offering summations that afternoon at three.

During the recess, Lieutenant J. C. Williams of the Oxford Police Department and Bill Burgwyn fielded questions from reporters who wanted to know why Roger Oakley had not been charged in the case. "There was a third party mentioned from time to time during the investigation as a participant in the slaying," Lieutenant Williams stammered. "But none of my five witnesses could make a positive identification of the third person. And none of the five witnesses told investigating officers that the third party was the one who pulled the trigger. Frankly, I don't know what to make of it, either." Burgwyn told the reporters that Roger Oakley would have been charged in the original indictment with first-degree murder, since he had clearly helped Larry and Robert Teel kill Henry Marrow, but that the prosecution "could never positively identify the other man" who had been standing with the pair over the body. The prosecutor denied any implication that the investigators had charged the wrong man: all of them had participated in the killing, he said, which was true, and it made little difference who had pulled the last trigger. Every witness for the defense was a member of the Teel family, and he did not see any reason to take Roger's confession, which could not be verified, over the testimony of five witnesses for the state, all of whom agreed that Larry Teel had fired the fatal shot.

The trial resumed at three, at which time attorneys for both sides prepared to make their final addresses to the jury. James Ferguson gave a striking and memorable summation for the prosecution that Friday afternoon. "From the first day of this trial," Ferguson told the jury, "we have heard 'self-defense, self-defense, self-defense.' When every one of you and the other prospective jurors was questioned from this side of the table," the seasoned civil rights lawyer said, gesturing toward Billy Watkins and Frank Banzet, "you were asked again and again whether you believed in the right of a man to defend himself. This was the central issue, the defense told us. It was a question of 'self-defense.' " His eyes swept up and down the row of five white women and seven white men who sat impassively in the jury box before him. "Henry Marrow was running away just as fast as his legs would carry him when they shot him the first time," Ferguson said. "They had to shoot him to stop him from leaving. And then he was flat on his back, bleeding, begging for his life, and then unconscious, after they beat him half to death, more than a hundred feet off the Teel property, when they shot him in the head. And yet Mr. Watkins and his colleagues tried their best to persuade you that it was a question of 'self-defense.'

"And now, after the state has proven beyond any doubt that this killing was by no stretch of the imagination an act of self-defense," continued James Ferguson, "they have come up with this story of an 'accidental shooting.' It was an accident, they tell you now." He looked up and down the jury once more, and then delivered the hook. "I guess we might say this is what you'd call *accidental self-defense*. I don't know about y'all, but I have never heard of 'accidental self-defense,' myself. This may be the first instance of 'accidental self-defense' in recorded history."

Of course, Ferguson told the jurors, most of whom stared at the floor, there was no such category as "accidental self-defense," and nothing remotely like that had happened. They all knew what had happened, and five witnesses for the state had made it clear what had happened. All of the witnesses for the defense, Ferguson reminded them, were members of the Teel family. No one could blame them for trying to keep their family together, but a man had been killed and justice must be done. "If you turn these men loose," Ferguson told the jury, "you may as well hang a wreath on the courthouse door on your way out, because justice is dead in Granville County." At that, Judge Martin ended court for the day, and announced that court would continue to meet through the weekend.

Saturday morning, Watkins and Burgwyn presented a dramatic clashing of styles. Watkins made a professional presentation that all the observers agreed was long and dry. "Watkins spoke to the jury for an hour and 30 minutes," the Raleigh *News and Observer* noted. He explained that the prosecution had decided to charge Larry Teel with firing the fatal shot but actually had not known whether or not that was true; the prosecution's case was "a shot in the dark," he said.

The other point that Watkins made again and again was that the jury could not rely upon the word of the prosecution's witnesses, especially Boo Chavis, who not only had a significant criminal record but had practically grown up in the same house with the deceased. "Most of [Watkins's] time was spent in an attempt to discredit the testimony of the state's witnesses," the newspaper reported, "particularly William Augustus Chavis, [the] young Oxford Negro who testified he had seen Larry Teel place a rifle muzzle against Marrow's forehead and pull the trigger."

"This is one of the most serious cases ever to be tried in this state," Burgwyn noted, opening his brief summation. "The outcome will affect events in this community, the entire state of North Carolina, and across the nation." The murder of Henry Marrow was "a useless, senseless death," he said, but it occurred "at a moment of great upheaval on the subject of race. We cannot tell the world that we have one system of justice for Negroes and another for whites," Burgwyn advised the jury. The grizzled prosecutor, weary from lack of sleep, rubbed his eyes and squinted as he reminded jurors of the brief testimony of Page Hudson, the state's chief medical examiner, on the first day of the trial. "As Dr. Hudson told you, Henry Marrow had two serious fractures of the skull, one on the top of his head and another on the back of his head," Burgwyn stated. "He might well have died even if that last bullet had never blasted through his brain, but it did." Who fired the shot really didn't matter, he said, since they had all intended to kill him. Burgwyn asked the jury to recall the bruises and abrasions all over Marrow's body, including the shotgun wounds on his buttocks and the back of his legs, "wounds that immobilized him," said Burgwyn.

"After they shot him down, and while he was laying there, flat on his back, unable to get up," the prosecutor continued, "they kicked him and stomped him and hit him in the head with a shotgun butt over and over again. They beat him while he begged for his life, beat him until he was probably unconscious. And then they shot him in the head like you or I would kill a snake." Burgwyn turned and walked slowly toward the prosecution table, apparently overcome with emotion.

"Right at that moment," recalled the court reporter who had been taking notes during the trial, "when it was quiet, we all heard a baby crying outside the courtroom. The window was open, and you could hear it all through the room. We could all hear it. And I just started crying." Two decades after the trial, as I interviewed her, her eyes filled with tears again. "I was thinking about that little baby, the one whose father had been killed, and the little baby that had just been born in the Teel family, Roger's little girl. And how none of this was their fault, none of it. All of this was our fault, not theirs. It was all our fault."

Seizing the moment, Burgwyn turned around to face the jury once more. "When I hear that little baby cry," he said, "I think about a little girl that is going to grow up without knowing her father. And I can't help but hear that cry as a cry from the deceased from his grave, saying, 'Vindicate my death. Vindicate my death. Don't let them kill me and just tell the world, "It was an accident." Don't let them do that to me. Please don't let them do that to me.'" And then he went back to the table.

After Burgwyn sat down, Judge Martin gave instructions to the jury. They could bring in one of five verdicts, he explained. They could find the defendants guilty of murder in the first degree. They could rule the defendants guilty of murder in the first degree with a recommendation of life. They were also free to decide that the defendants were guilty of second-degree murder or manslaughter. If they believed that the defendants were not guilty of anything, Martin told the jurors, they could find the defendants not guilty. In North Carolina, he added, a verdict of first-degree murder without a recommendation of life imprisonment meant an automatic death sentence. If they found the defendants guilty of first-degree murder, they would need to decide whether they felt the death penalty was appropriate. With that, he sent them out to determine the fate of Robert and Larry Teel and left the court in session but "at ease" until six-thirty that evening.

All afternoon the town waited on the jury. "We were scared to death," Gene Edmundson, one of the defense lawyers, remembered. "You just don't know." Forty or fifty young black men and women stood around outside the courthouse, doing their best to look militant and disdainful of it all, as if they knew that the white men would be acquitted. Many of them, however, still managed to hope for a conviction. Klansmen stood around brooding. Two dozen armed white men, the "auxiliary police," some of whom reportedly belonged to the Klan, too, stood at ten-foot intervals up and down the sidewalk outside the courthouse, helmets on and riot clubs at the ready.

Highway patrol units with tear gas and shotguns were on full alert nearby. When the judge called the trial back into session at six-thirty, hundreds of people filed quietly back into the courthouse, state troopers patting everyone down for weapons at the door. Judge Martin brought the twelve white jurors back in after six long hours of deliberation and asked the foreman if a verdict had been reached. Charles M. Shaw, an elevator inspector from Raleigh and the foreman of the jury, said that they had not come to a verdict yet. The judge then ordered the jury sequestered for the night, and the spectators filed out again.

The next morning, many people went to the courthouse instead of church. A courtroom packed with more than four hundred people, about three hundred of them African Americans, waited for the verdict. Deliberations had begun in a locked chamber adjacent to the courtroom at nine-thirty, and it was just an hour and a half later when foreman Shaw notified the judge that they were ready to report. As it happened, churches all over town were starting their eleven o'clock services. "The jury came out at eleven o'clock in the morning," defense attorney Edmundson recalled, "and when they knocked on the door to the courtroom, the church bells all over town started ringing." The twelve jurors filed out and took their seats. Judge Martin asked the foreman, Shaw, to stand. "Have you reached a unanimous verdict?" he entoned.

"We have, Your Honor," Shaw replied, handing the signed verdict to the bailiff, who passed it to the judge. After Judge Martin silently scanned the verdict, he handed it to the clerk to announce: "We, the members of the jury, unanimously find Robert Larry Teel not guilty of murder in the first degree." The room erupted into wailing and yelling. "Everybody jumped up yelling and crying," recalled Carolyn Thorpe, one of the young black women in the courtroom that morning. "Everybody was totally shocked, furious. It was something like reading a fiction book. I just couldn't believe it was happening like this. It was like a cartoon."

"Order in this court! There will be order in this courtroom!" Judge Martin exclaimed, pounding his gavel. "This court will toler-

ate no further outbursts." The judge ordered the bailiff to arrest anyone else who said anything out of order on charges of contempt of
court. The second and third verdicts found Robert Teel not guilty of
first-degree murder and not guilty of aiding and abetting first-degree
murder, and the announcements were greeted with silence and tears.
Larry Teel threw his head into his hands and wept. Prosecutor
Burgwyn insisted on polling the jury, forcing each juror, one by one,
to pronounce the words "not guilty." After the jury left the room,
Judge Martin ordered the spectators to depart one row at a time, in
orderly fashion, alternating between the black and white sides of the
courtroom. Deputies enforced the edict. As the young blacks filed
out, most of them crying or fuming, they spread the word that everyone should go to a mass meeting at the First Baptist Church to decide
what would happen next.

The Raleigh *News and Observer*'s lead editorial the next morning
was entitled "Sham and Mockery." The jury was "doubly conned," the
editors wrote, if it believed "the incredible testimony of a surprise
witness who surfaced on the last day of the trial and said *he* had fired
the fatal shot into Marrow's brain *accidentally.*" The newspaper's
editors noted all the irregularities in the case and pointed out the
obvious: that even the testimony of the defense witnesses themselves
would have supported a conviction of manslaughter. It was as though
the jurors had decided to give Robert and Larry Teel a medal. The
whole affair, the *News and Observer* said, "has been a sham and a
mockery of justice."

Decades later, prosecutor Burgwyn remained philosophical about
losing the case, but shook his head in disgust. "I thought it was
absolutely the worst miscarriage of justice I had ever seen," he said,
"and I still do. They should have convicted, but they didn't." Billy
Watkins and Gene Edmundson of the defense team both denied that
politics outside the courtroom had affected the trial's outcome. They
simply thought they had done a better job than the prosecution,
although Edmundson was not sure that the verdict would have been
the same with what he called "modern methods of investigation."
Teel himself agreed that Billy Watkins's legal representation was

decisive. "I'm pretty sure if he hadn't been a smart attorney they would have gotten me," Teel told me. "I think he was a very, very smart man by keeping our mouths shut and letting the prosecution go on and hang themselves." But the most eloquent analysis came from one of the young black men who had been sitting under the shed at the Tidewater Seafood Market that night. Jimmy Chavis had held Henry Marrow's head in his lap on the way to the hospital. "That court," Chavis told me years later, "that court won't nothing but a shoeshine parlor."

CHAPTER 11

WE ALL HAVE OUR OWN
STORIES

I N THE ONLY published local history of Granville County, sponsored by the chamber of commerce, the authors offer the story
that my hometown of Oxford undertook a "voluntary desegregation"
program in 1964. That is one *big* white lie, and anybody who actually
believes that mess, my grandmama Rene-Rene might say, don't even
have a bucket to carry it in, bless their heart. Even if Oxford had
abandoned racial segregation that year, which it certainly did not, a
decision to *obey federal law* stretches the meaning of the word "voluntary."

But truth and falsehood keep house on both sides of the color line,
and we all have our own stories to tell. In the 1980s, when Eddie
McCoy would talk about how murder, marches, and mayhem had—
and had not—changed everything back in 1970, local black folks
would sometimes dismiss the movement with a wave of the hand.
"Y'all didn't do nothing," they would say. "Y'all didn't even have to do
that stuff. President Kennedy and them done all that. They had all that
stuff planned out up in Washington. Y'all didn't do nothing." The people who dismissed local organizing, of course, had not participated in
the movement. The majority of African Americans in Oxford and elsewhere had stayed on the sidelines, paralyzed by fear, indifference, or

their inability to imagine a better world. The black middle class—hardly a middle class at all, since many of them were only a few paychecks away from poverty—was especially reluctant. Having missed the freedom train in the 1960s and 1970s, the bystanders now told the story that the train had never come, that freedom had been an easy walk, or that the tracks had been laid by a federal grant.

That last narrative had a grain of truth in it—the role of the federal government in the black freedom struggle *was* considerable—and yet added up to less than a half truth, offered at least in part to defend the storytellers against the fact that many of them were freed by a movement they had been afraid to support. Years later, McCoy would try to tell his stories to young black men who'd grown up on hip-hop and Ronald Reagan, taking both the gains of the movement and the contempt of their fellow Americans for granted, and they would scowl and mutter, "Ain't nothing changed." Sometimes McCoy was tempted to agree with the young bloods of the hip-hop nation, who disdained what they had been told about the civil rights movement; their stories resonated with some bitter realities about black America in the late twentieth century. But their dismissal of the movement was not the whole story, either.

Those who tell us that nothing has changed have simply forgotten, if they ever knew, how bad things were for black people in this country only a few decades ago. From the day the first Africans accompanied European explorers into the Carolinas in the mid-1500s until sometime after the passage of the Civil Rights Act of 1964—for the first four hundred years of the African American experience—almost every white vision of the commonwealth excluded African Americans, even though they were inseparable from its destiny.

Black Southerners forcibly altered that narrative in the 1950s and 1960s by stepping outside their assigned roles—and compelling a reluctant federal government to intercede on their behalf. As often as not, they had to be prepared to defend themselves physically from terrorism by white reactionaries. White liberals, with their hesitancy and quibbling, were sometimes very little help. In North Carolina, white liberal paternalists did not stand in the schoolhouse door as

George Wallace had in Alabama. Instead, journalist Osha Gray Davidson observes, they "would quietly appoint a committee to deliberate for eternity over exactly which door, and of what dimensions, would best facilitate the ingress and egress of all students. The style of a Wallace was different, but the result was the same." And so sometimes it was necessary to escape from an endless and pointless conversation with white paternalism by striking hard and sometimes violently against the architecture of their oppression—Oxford's tobacco warehouses being only the local example.

The struggle was far more violent, perilous, and critical than America is willing to remember. Those who tell themselves that white people of goodwill voluntarily handed over first-class citizenship to their fellow citizens of color find comfort in selective memory and wishful thinking. And those who believe that the federal government rode over the hill like the cavalry and rescued the poor black folks from white "rednecks" have forgotten or never knew what happened in the civil rights–era South. On the way to learning some truths, if not *the* truth, about these histories of all our hometowns, I managed to reexamine some of my own precious but partial narratives about race, politics, freedom, and morality.

The freedom movement in Oxford did not end with the trial of Robert and Larry Teel. The acquittals shocked most black people in Oxford—even those who said they'd expected nothing different— and shamed many white people; the street battles and warehouse fires terrified even the shameless. But though it may have taken violence or the credible threat of violence to budge the racial caste system, it also required a coordinated, economically targeted, community-wide effort from the black community. Before the embers of arson had cooled, the newly founded Granville County Steering Committee for Black Progress met at the First Baptist Church and planned an economic boycott. "The economy of Oxford depended on black consumerism," Ben Chavis said later, "and we decided we were not going to spend our money with businesses that were supporting injustice." With African Americans making up more than 40 percent of the population, Oxford's white-owned businesses could not afford to have the black community unified against them. The acquittal of Henry Marrow's accused killers, terrible as it was, brought a new degree of unity to the black community, and Oxford business leaders were forced to take note.

Presenting himself as the voice of that consensus, Chavis went before the all-white chamber of commerce and explained the threatened boycott: the problem went beyond just the killing, beyond even the lack of justice in court, he said. Whites still excluded blacks from jobs at the stores downtown. Banks refused to hire blacks except as janitors and were reluctant to give them loans for anything except automobiles. The movie theater remained segregated. Blacks were welcome downtown only as retail customers or night-shift janitors. Some of the people in this very room had donated money to defend Robert Teel, Chavis reminded the white men, even though their establishments depended upon black patrons. A black boycott, he warned, could bring the town's economy to its knees. Though Chavis apparently was not himself a man of violence, he was not above using the fear of violence as a negotiating tool, and he hinted to the white businessmen that he could not be responsible for what might happen if they failed to respond. "They said they thought something could be worked out," Chavis recalled, "but nothing was worked out, so we boycotted. The next week, Oxford looked literally like a ghost town."

As whites had rallied along caste lines after the murder, some wearing sheets, some writing checks, now blacks, too, seized the moment for solidarity. "Black people stuck together here," recalled Linda Ball, one of the energetic organizers. "At least for that particular time. The murder and them letting the murderers go brought us together." Black women were at the center of the boycott, partly because they did most of the shopping. "The women always be the first to come out anyway," Ball explained. "The First Baptist Church would be filled with women." The Steering Committee organized picketing at the department stores and the grocery stores. Women handed out flyers explaining the boycott to prospective shoppers. The committee arranged for a small fleet of private automobiles and volunteer drivers to take black shoppers to nearby towns. "How we had it networked," said Eddie McCoy, "is we were carrying people to Henderson. People would call us and we'd take you to Henderson to buy your food, to buy your clothes."

In the early days, right after the murder and the acquittals, the anger in the black community made it easy to sustain the boycott. But when outrage began to fade toward apathy, the black women running the boycott were not above intimidation, either. Along with their signs and leaflets, they carried cameras. "We would take your picture when you'd come out the store," one of them told me. "That way we would check and see who was going into the stores." Someone might contact these people by telephone and explain the purposes of the boycott or make veiled threats; more often, the cameras furnished coercion enough. At the grocery stores, young black men and women would occasionally knock groceries out of black customers' hands in the parking lots. This may seem appalling to those who grew up with the story of Rosa Parks and her tired feet, but the same story could be told from Montgomery to Memphis, from the earliest years of the movement; there were always black people too fearful, too attached to "their" white folks, too pessimistic or too beaten down by white supremacy to stand up for themselves. And black activists dealt with their dissenters emphatically, because freedom itself was on the line. "We'd bust a bag of sugar, break a couple of jars of jelly," McCoy recounted. "Didn't nobody try to hurt nobody. They just needed to know we weren't playing that shit. Black people had to work together."

The picketing persisted into autumn. When virtually no blacks attended the county fair that fall, the white men of the chamber of commerce decided it was time to negotiate. The merchants agreed to hire blacks in retail positions. The movie theater quietly desegregated. The town's one black police officer got a promotion, and the police department moved toward hiring others. The public schools underwent full-blown integration that autumn, though many white parents pulled their children out of the public schools and enrolled them at Vance-Granville Academy, a "Christian" school that did not admit black children. And in an act that revealed the immensity of the shift in relative political power, the city of Oxford eventually moved the Confederate monument out of the main intersection in front of the courthouse and tucked it away among the cedars and magnolias behind the public library.

In a real sense, the local black freedom movement had won. But it had taken the physical threat of "Black Power" to make the moral argument of civil rights mean anything on a local level. It had taken widespread violence to bring about an uneasy racial truce, let alone "voluntary" acceptance of the Supreme Court's *Brown v. Board of Education* decision of 1954 and the Civil Rights Act of 1964. Under the terms of that truce, the courts in Granville County became much less a mechanism of white domination, though thirty years later African Americans still regard the judicial system with great suspicion. Nevertheless, most who remember the past with any clarity concede that in some respects it is truly a new day. Eddie McCoy, once a dedicated Black Power revolutionary, eventually became the first African American elected to the Granville County commission, in small part because of a significant number of white allies; this was not the usual legacy of Black Power, of course, but owed much to McCoy's remarkable combination of street credibility among blacks and easygoing business reputation among whites. As in many other towns, in Oxford it took a murderous and avoidable tragedy, and some luck, to summon the political will to change things a little.

The social changes wrought by the black freedom movement came about by a complex mixture of violence and nonviolence, economic coercion and moral appeal. "A lot of what we did was wrong," McCoy told a class of college students thirty years later, "but it worked. What one of those fellows that burned the warehouses might say to you if he was here is 'I know it was not my property, but you wouldn't hear me, and it did make a difference.'" That those hard-won and morally ambiguous victories generated a great deal of fear and resentment should surprise no one. "The black man has functioned in the white man's world as a fixed star, as an immovable pillar," James Baldwin explains, "and as he moves out of his place, heaven and earth are shaken to their foundations." And so one of the major by-products of the freedom struggle, in Oxford and across the country, was a white political backlash of sustained ferocity.

In the end, that white backlash pushed my family to leave Oxford. The summer I turned eleven, that perilous summer of blood and fire, my father accepted a position at Wesley Memorial United Methodist Church in Wilmington, North Carolina, and we moved away. I hated to leave, and I had no idea of the logic behind my father's decision to take a job far away. And so I clung to my old hometown. For several weeks that summer, and many weeks in a dozen summers to come, I worked and played on a farm in Granville County owned by Ben and Joy Averett, members of our church and the parents of my friend Ed.

Ben was a brawny, forthright man whom I liked to call "Pharoah," because he kept me and Ed busy picking up rocks, weeding the garden, and carrying wood for the fires. Ben worked us hard, but he also showed us how to ride horses, shoot guns, catch fish, and think for ourselves. Though he had a gruff manner and a quick temper, he was also gentle and kind, quick to forgive, and defied all stereotypes. Ben kept rifles, shotguns, and pistols of all descriptions, drove a pickup truck, and liked country music. He made the best barbecued chicken the South has ever seen. Possibility was his playground. "Anything that you ever want to do, there is a book about it at the library," Ben liked to say. And his life bore testimony to his philosophy: he could build houses, do plumbing and electrical work, grow peaches, lay tile, and dance like nobody's business. Growing up, I considered Ben a model for what a man ought to be and do, and I was not far wrong. One day Ben decided that writing a sonnet couldn't be any harder than building a house, checked out a bunch of books about sonnets, and wrote a masterful sonnet—about building a house.

Ben's wife, Joy Burwell Averett, was a lovely and gracious woman with fair skin and beautiful red hair who taught English at Webb High School. I loved her from the moment I met her, when I was seven. Her language sashayed with a musical lilt, and she was one of the kindest people I have ever known. When Ed and I were mere tots, she would assign us to write poems and then tell us how good they were; the purpose of literature, it became clear to me, was to please Joy Averett. And I will always remember a moment when I was eleven or twelve and she walked into the kitchen, singing a playful little song and laughing. Suddenly I realized that she was the most beautiful thing I had ever laid eyes on, an angel walking the earth. She asked me what was wrong, and I could only stammer with the little air available to me. Though puberty came and went, Joy would always be my sweetheart and my first real teacher. I am sorry that she did not live to see me write books, since that would have delighted her so much.

The farm where the Averetts lived was less than a mile from the spot where Henry Marrow died. My friendship with them has endured for the rest of our lives. But what also stayed with me is the story of Henry Marrow's murder. When the adults would send us boys to the store for cold drinks, I would carry the sweating bottles of Coca-Cola through the dust where Marrow died. Every time I went to that store, which the Teel family no longer owned, I waded through Henry Marrow's blood. And once again I would hear Gerald Teel's words in my head: "Daddy and Roger and 'em shot 'em a *nigger.*"

During those summers I also began to learn more about why my family had left town. At first, it was just the occasional passing remark from other children. "Your daddy got run out of town," a seventh grader taunted me at the swimming pool. "Why'd y'all have to move?" a little girl asked me from her family's backyard trampoline, and it was clear from her tone that her parents must have already told her the answer and that she expected me to be ashamed. As I became a teenager, grown-ups in Oxford assumed that I knew that my daddy had been "run off" by church members alienated by the memorial service for Dr. King, the black preachers invited to share his pulpit, and the "race mixing" among the young people at Wesley House.

Ben Averett, whom I regarded as an unwavering rock and something of an oracle, served on the pastor-parish relations committee at Oxford United Methodist Church during my father's tenure there. When I was in my late teens, Ben informed me that several committee members had made it plain that they were tired of Daddy's liberal politics. "They started getting ready to vote to not ask your daddy to come back the next year," Ben told me. "And I told them they could go ahead and do it if they wanted to, but if they did I was never going to set foot in that church again." More than twenty years passed before Ben set foot in Oxford United Methodist Church again, and then it was only for Joy's funeral, at her request.

Years later, when I returned to Oxford to research this book, Mary Catherine Chavis squeezed my hand warmly and said, "Your father was too good for this town." Plainly out of respect for his sacrifices, though she is a generous soul anyway, Mrs. Chavis got on the telephone right away and lined up several interviews for me. I could overhear what she would tell her listeners: "He's the son of Reverend Tyson," she would say. "You remember, the white preacher that they run off after Teel killed Dickie."

This was not exactly how Daddy told the story. When I came home from talking to Ben, I asked him to tell me what had happened at the church. Daddy just shrugged and said it had been time to leave Oxford, and Wesley Memorial was a stronger church anyway. By his lights, Daddy told me, he had done all he could in Granville County, and it was time to move on. If he'd wanted to stay, Daddy said, he could have stayed. My father had no taste for losing, and in his story he had not lost. "Maybe some of those old boys were glad I left," he said. "You know they were. And maybe some of them were trying to make me leave, and maybe they did some crowing after I was gone. You know, the rooster crows and the sun comes up, and the old rooster thinks he has done it. But the Lord sees it a little bit differently."

Over the years I came to see his account as a cheerful, bighearted liberal story that he clearly believed was true. That was just Daddy's way. But I never shared his equanimity, nor did I feel much Christian forgiveness toward those who had scorned his expansive vision of God and humanity, and pushed our family into a harder history. That summer, as my hometown burned and my family moved away under a cloud, a curtain fell between that eleven-year-old boy and the adult world, a world that began to seem incorrigibly dishonest and cruel. As I grew into my late teens, I learned more about the circumstances of our departure, and my heart began to harden against the stupidity and hatred that had sent us away.

When our family moved from Oxford to Wilmington, I had just turned eleven. We piled into my mother's wood-paneled station wagon and drove through tobacco fields to Benson, a farming community in Johnston County where Mule Day every fall rivals Christmas. From Benson we rolled through more tobacco land to Spivey's Corner and stopped at the Green Top Grill for a barbecue sandwich and a bowl of banana pudding. In the booth, Daddy amused us with tales of the annual Spivey's Corner Hollering Contest, which celebrated the dying art of hailing neighbors from half a mile away. From there, we turned down through the long, lonesome stretches of piney woods to Wilmington. The last fifty miles of low-lying coastal plain were almost desolate in those days, and my mother cried quietly in the front seat. "I felt like I was going to Siberia," she said in later years.

For us children, it was exciting to cross the bridge over the river and drive into Wilmington, a coastal city near the mouth of Cape Fear, whose river district of cobblestoned streets and rotting mansions evoked the Old South. Almost tropical, Wilmington seemed unimaginably distant from the tobacco-farming country where we had always lived. It had been the most important Southern port during the Civil War, and statues of Confederate generals loomed on street corners along the riverbank. From the old hulk of the battleship *North Carolina*, permanently anchored as a museum in the Cape Fear River, we saw *alligators* in the dirty water. The scrub-oak woods where we played were quick with red-winged blackbirds. In the pines we peered at trumpet plants and Venus flytraps. The streets in our new neighborhood seemed all but paved with dead frogs, squashed by passing cars. Ruby-throated lizards darted all over our patio. Dangling Spanish moss, flowering oleanders and azaleas, and gracious antebellum architecture hinted at an unspoken history that still exerted a controlling influence on both sides of the color line.

Distant and exotic though Wilmington was, the troubles in Oxford seemed to follow us all the way there. Ben Chavis, who had articulated the anger and aspirations of young black people in Granville County, became a field organizer for the United Church of Christ's Commission for Racial Justice, which promptly dispatched him to Wilmington. Chavis, having become a leader in his early twenties, confronted a predicament for which no one his age could have been prepared. Controversy over school integration plans and the bloody legacy of an unacknowledged local history made Wilmington a racial tinderbox. Reverend Leon White, director of the Franklinton Center at Bricks—where Judson King had worked back in the 1950s, when he'd met my uncle Earl in the courtroom—took young Chavis as a protégé and soon ordained the talented young firebrand as a minister. But, as my father remarked years later, "Ben really put on that collar before he knew what to do with it."

In Wilmington, the newly minted Reverend Chavis opened a storefront Black Power church called the Church of the Black Madonna. There and at nearby Gregory Congregational Church, Chavis stoked the fires of black revolt among the young, leading protest efforts against the closing of Williston Senior High School. Founded by local blacks as Williston Industrial High School in 1919, this revered and vital black institution had once drawn students from across the South whose parents could scrape up enough money to send them. One of the four college students who launched the sit-ins in Greensboro in 1960 was a Williston graduate and, according to local legend, at least, Dr. King had been scheduled to speak in its auditorium the day after he was assassinated. In 1970, white authorities transformed proud Williston into a junior high school, its school colors, teachers, coaches, and history seemingly cast aside by integration plans that had no regard for black educational traditions. The white-dominated plan for integration in Wilmington involved building new suburban schools in white communities and shipping black students from inner-city neighborhoods out to suburbs where they were not welcome. Discrimination against black students, the closing of cherished black institutions, and the demotions and dismissals of black principals and black teachers stirred deep resentments into this recipe for disaster.

By the time we had been in town for six months, Wilmington hovered on the edge of racial cataclysm. As in Oxford, buildings burned almost every night. The chief of police reported more than thirty cases of arson during the first week of February 1971, with property damage that week at more than half a million dollars. A white terrorist group called the Rights of White People (ROWP) roared through the city, spraying bullets; with their own armada of trucks armed with CB radios and military weapons, the ROWP could put hundreds of men on the street at any given time. One city official noted that by comparison the Ku Klux Klan was, "believe it or not, a moderating force in the community." In fact, a 1965 U.S. Senate investigation had revealed that the New Hanover County sheriff and most of his deputies belonged to the Klan. At the height of the conflict in early 1971, black snipers fired at police officers from rooftops downtown. Six hundred frightened National Guard troops patrolled the streets. Someone bombed a restaurant three blocks from our suburban home in the middle of the night, shaking our windows. The New Hanover County schools reported thirty-two bomb threats during a single month the first year I was enrolled there. Police officers frequented the hallways of my junior high school because of the incessant violence.

I was attending Roland-Grise Junior High when the first busloads of black students arrived for full-blown integration, fifteen years after the *Brown v. Board of Education* decision. Roland-Grise had been named in honor of H. M. Roland, the recently retired former superintendent of schools, a rabid segregationist who spent his spare time writing "scientific" tracts that purported to prove that African Americans were, as he put it, "genetically inferior to the Anglo-Saxon race." After I left Roland-Grise, in 1972, I was among the first white students to attend Williston Ninth Grade Center. ROWP terrorists smashed up the venerable old school just before I started classes. Someone shot and killed two security guards at the school one night soon afterward. Fistfights at school were common. To go to the bathroom, especially alone, was to risk being beaten up, or worse. One boy cut another with a straight razor. Several others bashed another boy's head with a brick. Someone shot and wounded two boys in a racial clash after a basketball game. Many students carried knives and brass knuckles. Full-scale riots erupted several times a year; we would be sitting in the cafeteria, hear a loud crash of silverware and plastic trays clattering to the floor, and the bloodhounds of race would come flying off their leashes. We grimly referred to early spring as "riot season," as though it were a varsity sport.

I played basketball every day on the outdoor asphalt courts behind the school. Sometimes we played shirts versus skins, with whoever had called "next up" putting together five players to take on the winners of the previous game. Other times, we played "salt and pepper," meaning that five black players faced five white ones. Would-be militants of both races, with their Black Power Afro picks and their Confederate flag patches, respectively, loitered elsewhere, smoking cigarettes and sometimes looking for trouble. Even in "riot season," the basketball court generally remained congenial. But a hard foul or a hard word could start a scuffle, which would quickly become racial and sometimes turn into a big brawl. These outbreaks placed me in a difficult position. In a riot, it was always "salt and pepper," and you either ran or fought; nobody stopped to check your political credentials.

Neither running nor fighting were special talents of mine, however, and sometimes I tried to talk to the black boys who proposed to beat me up. This worked a great deal better if it occurred to them that they might not be able to beat me up without getting hurt. False bravado and "talking trash" as if the whole thing were a joke sometimes worked. One day at the close of sixth-period physical education class, a muscular black boy named Franklin Steele backed me up against the fence in a distant corner of the athletic field and began patting my pants pockets for loose change. He heard my dimes and quarters. "Gimme the money, boy, else I'm gon' have to kick your ass," Steele said. I pushed him away hard. "You know I can kick your ass," he said, cocking his fist. "Give it up."

He may have had a good solid point. I was still a pasty little boy, stocky but short for my age, and Franklin seemed more like a grown man who unloaded trucks all day. I had seen him bloody another boy's face in a fistfight, and even *that* boy could have clobbered me. I felt as outmatched as the Polish cavalry during the Nazi blitzkrieg. But I did not want to back down. "That's right, Franklin," I replied, "you can kick my ass. But I am going to hurt you more than fifty cents' worth. I am going to hurt you bad."

Franklin looked at me with disbelief and delivered a speech about the full range and vast extent to which he would kick my ass, including a variety of gesticulations and false starts. But I had seen the doubt flicker in his eyes, and I pressed my hopes. "Come on, then, Franklin," I told him. "Let's just get it over with. You come over here and kick my ass. But remember one thing: I am going to hurt you." I was even starting to believe it myself. And then I looked down and saw a Coca-Cola bottle against the fence behind my foot. And suddenly it occurred to me what Franklin wanted. He wanted to slip off campus through the trees behind the fence and buy a cold drink.

What occurred to Franklin, however, was that I was about to pick up that drink bottle and bash him upside the head with it. Realizing that, I ran with the concept. I picked up the bottle quickly and held it by the neck like a hammer. For all I know, Franklin figured he could take it from me and kill me with it if he wanted, but his face read as clearly as a billboard: "This white boy is crazy." My dimes and quarters were getting too expensive. And when I sensed that, I saw my way to rescuing both my neck and my would-be manhood.

"Let's just forget about it, Franklin," I said, lowering the bottle. "We got nothing to fight about." I saw his edge fading and his fists falling. He still had not quite figured out how to leave. I said, "Hey, Franklin, let's just forget about this shit and go get a drink." We both knew the way. We slipped off campus as though we were old friends and went to the vending machine, where I emptied my pockets and bought both of us a Nehi grape soda. On my way back to classes, just after Franklin and I slapped five and parted company, the gym teacher and the principal suspended me from school for three days for leaving campus without permission. I considered the whole episode a complete triumph, and spent three days reading on the couch, too. Daddy came home each day and took me out to lunch at the Neptune, our favorite spot at Wrightsville Beach, for clam chowder and cheeseburgers. I never even told him that I had left campus in order to defuse a bloody fracas.

Having a friendly acquaintance with a number of black kids, a good jump shot, and a reputation as a decent white guy provided me some protection at school. But often it was just a matter of luck. One morning between classes, I was getting something out of my locker, my head inside the metal door, paying no attention, when the floor began to rumble. Dozens of African American boys had massed at one end of the hallway and charged up the corridor, striking out at every white face that they saw. Before I collected my wits, someone ran into the locker door full tilt, slamming the door on my head. When I pulled myself out of the locker, a black boy swung a padlock on a string and hit me in the back of the head, splitting the flesh. The lights went out, and when I came to and touched my hand to the swelling knot on the back of my head, my fingers were bloody. I walked home and did not even mention it to my parents; I threw away the shirt I had been wearing to avoid having to explain the bloodstains.

My experiences of race, at that point, were so complicated that my early-teenaged self found the subject hard to discuss, even with my father. Liberal pieties offered little help. In the 1970s, my father had little direct connection to the black struggle but, to his children, at least, he continued to talk about race problems in a "civil rights" paradigm, as though all that we had to do was pretend that black people were white and accept everyone as God's children. In retrospect, I am sure that he did not believe it was that simple; he just didn't want us to become haters. But Daddy's approach of meeting anger with love did not help much at school.

Though awkward friendships did sometimes occur, most of the African American kids I knew at school wanted no political solidarity from a white boy. My white friends and I lived in a kind of prison-movie terror in the hallways. Few days passed without some black boy who seemed much tougher than me trying to separate me from my lunch money or my dignity. It appeared to me that the black boys instigated most of the violence at school. It seemed equally clear that school authorities punished them more severely than they did white boys. Of course, even then I realized that we were in the middle of a social revolution gone sour. And I also knew that the ROWP and the Klan had their youthful counterparts throughout the student body. The ordinary conflicts that occur in every schoolyard in the world would suddenly explode into dangerous brawls when some idiot muttered a racial epithet. Black kids perceived the suburban Roland-Grise Junior High as white turf where they were unwelcome guests and Williston Ninth Grade Center as black territory now occupied by invading white power. "We're in *their* school," a black student at a suburban high school explained to a newspaper reporter in 1971. "They don't like it because it's their school and we had to join it. But our school was taken away from us."

With respect to the racial crisis, the mostly white teachers and administrators were a mixed bag. Many of them were dedicated, noble, tired human beings confronting tough problems the best way they knew how. Others revealed plainly enough their nostalgia for the segregated all-white schools where they had worked until recently and that now seemed paradise lost. And still other adults in my life defended their outraged sense of white privilege. One of my junior high school football coaches showed me the sawed-off, weighted baseball bat he kept in his car. "This is my nigger knocker," he bragged. Some grown-ups encouraged white boys to antagonize their African American classmates. My shop teacher took me aside and urged me to beat up Robert Hardy, a troublesome, loudmouthed black boy about half my size who was giving him headaches. "You're not afraid of Robert Hardy, are you, boy?" he taunted me. Small wonder that racial tension and open violence in the hallways nearly brought public education to a halt in Wilmington the year after we moved there.

This local inferno was only a microcosm of the racial crisis at the height of the Black Power movement. In North Carolina and across the country, it was an agonizing time for white liberals, but my father tried hard to ease the violence and nurture interracial community. In matters of race and many other questions, he always taught us to walk a mile in the other fellow's shoes before we passed judgment. Like many white liberals, of course, Daddy was still mired up to his ankles in racial paternalism. But unlike some white liberals, my father had guts enough to speak and brains enough to listen. And that is why he went to see Ben Chavis at the Church of the Black Madonna.

Daddy regarded Chavis's mother highly, knew the twenty-three-year-old reverend reasonably well, and often had recommended Chavis to white officials as someone they could trust. But the news coverage of the racial situation in Wilmington made Daddy wonder if Chavis had learned the wrong lessons in Oxford. As it had so often across the nation in the civil rights era, the question boiled down to the role of violence. In Oxford, Chavis may have used the black violence against white property to gain political leverage, but he had not been a man of violence himself. In Wilmington, however, many suspected that Chavis was encouraging a campaign of street violence to strengthen his political hand or, as young radicals used to say, to heighten the contradictions.

Daddy was not willing to rely on hearsay. He went to the Church of the Black Madonna to see for himself whether it was possible to build a bridge across the color line, even at this violent and chaotic moment. He had to walk through a war zone; both the Rights of White People militia and the Church of the Black Madonna had their headquarters downtown on Castle Street. Sniper fire had recently killed a white man who'd tried to approach one of the movement's churches. We knew at least a dozen white people whose windshields had been shattered by a brick or a bottle as they'd driven through downtown Wilmington. Although Daddy almost never wore his clerical collar, he put in on that day—he wanted everybody to know he was a preacher, not a combatant—and headed downtown. Parking about two hundred yards from the storefront church, Daddy walked down the middle line of the deserted street with his hands in plain view.

When he got to the Church of the Black Madonna, about a dozen young black men blocked his pathway. No white people were allowed inside, they told him. Daddy slowly reached into his shirt pocket with two fingers and slid out his business card. "Just tell Reverend Chavis that Vernon Tyson wants to see him," he told the guards, handing one of them the card. And there he stood, a middle-aged white preacher among young black revolutionaries in their berets and dashikis, wondering what kind of damn fool would even be here.

Ben Chavis, wearing a black shirt and clerical collar with his stylish Afro, appeared in a few minutes, shook Daddy's hand warmly, and led him inside, past the tables piled with Maoist and black nationalist literature, into the sanctuary where sixty or seventy people were sitting. The walls were bedecked with children's artwork and political posters. He served Daddy grape Kool-Aid and a sugar cookie and apologized for the guards. "How are you doing, Reverend Tyson?" he asked. "What can I do for you?"

"Well, I hadn't seen you since Oxford," Daddy replied, "and I just wanted to have a little talk." Chavis indicated that he did not have much time but would be happy to hear anything my father had to say. "If all I believed about you was what I read in the newspapers," Daddy told him, "I would think you were crazy. But I know you, and I know you are made of good stuff. I know you are a person of good judgment and leadership ability, and I am certain you have good reasons for doing what you're doing." They looked at each other uneasily, sipping their Kool-Aid from Dixie cups. "I have come so that if you'll tell me what you're doing and why you are doing it," Daddy continued, "I will help interpret you to the white community. We have got to make it possible for white people, at least the ones who will listen, to hear what you have to say. All they're hearing now is the language of war, coming from both sides. I don't see that any good can come of it."

He'd gone to talk to Chavis, Daddy explained to me later, because there was hardly anyone else except the two of them who could build a bridge—and even their success was uncertain. "Most of the white people in Wilmington couldn't cross the color line and get anything done," he said. "The Uncle Toms couldn't do it, because even if the white people heard what they had to say, the black community was not going to follow them. If peacemakers and community builders were going to emerge, it would have to be people like us. It might not have helped much, but we had to try." My father had feared back in 1962 that it was too late for those whom Dr. King called "people of goodwill" to come together for racial justice; unfortunately, most of those people took almost another decade to begin to grasp the problem.

The delay was not because of a shortage of goodwill, exactly, but rather a gross imbalance of power. What needed to happen was for millions of Americans to find the political will and the material resources to help address slavery's lasting legacy. What my father may not have understood at the time was that this could not happen without some measure of coercion. Unless the people who believed in racial justice could summon the resources to force change, the hour would remain too late. If we had insisted on waiting for popular consensus, it would have been too late ever since the first slave ship arrived at Jamestown in 1619. And if we could not remember how to form the interracial political coalitions necessary to the process, then it had been too late in North Carolina for at least the seventy years that had passed since the Wilmington Race Riot of 1898, of which Daddy knew nothing at the time.

We are all the captives of our origins, especially when we do not fully know and understand them. The conversation between my father and Ben Chavis at the Church of the Black Madonna drew its paradoxes and predicaments from deep in the American story. That American story does not begin with the blood of patriots at Lexington and Concord, though unlike my father, Chavis was descended from Revolutionary War soldiers. The American story did not start when Thomas Jefferson wrote that all men have certain inalienable rights, among them life, liberty, and the pursuit of happiness, words perhaps penned by the light of a lamp fetched by his slave mistress or one of his slave children, human beings to whom he held a deed of ownership. The origins of the American story are much deeper, as deep as the dark Atlantic, where the bones of somewhere around ten million Africans settled into the sand, thrown overboard by the slave ships that plied those waters in the early days of the republic.

The slave trade and its consequences carved a chasm between my father and Ben Chavis as deep as the Atlantic and, paradoxically, bound them inseparably to one another. If it had been sufficient merely to ease the material predicaments of black Americans and ensure equal access to the resources of this society, perhaps the young black preacher and the older white one could have joined forces and moved forward together. But the slave trade was a crime so enormous that the men who profited from it had been compelled to concoct a justification for it. At first, they rationalized this profitable death machine by pointing out that the Africans were not Christians. But the conversion of the enslaved Africans to Christianity threatened to undermine that story of "heathens" from Africa, lifted up to Christ by their kidnappers. And so the slave traders and the larger society that depended on them conjured up the poisonous lie of white supremacy; that is, the notion that God conferred moral, intellectual, and cultural worth upon humanity on the basis of pigmentation, with lighter-skinned people inherently more worthy and darker-skinned people intrinsically less worthy. Both Ben Chavis and my father carried this poisonous lie deep in their minds, but there it operated in divergent ways that made it hard for them to work together.

As a white liberal, my father's unconscious white supremacy tempted him to feel that he knew what was best for the black freedom struggle. Never mind that he had rarely even been directly involved in that struggle. Of course, even if he had not examined all of his racial assumptions, he really did have a damned good political mind, and he knew what his congregation was thinking. To him, it was plain that most white people either opposed the movement or found it terrifying. Daddy thought the important thing was to persuade those who feared racial equality to examine the question calmly, so that they could join together and oppose those who insisted upon white domination.

You could call it naiveté, but Daddy practiced a wonderful kind of unjustified hope whose power derived from its gentle audacity. In the end, he believed, we were all God's children and we were all in this together. He believed that progress depended on dialogue, which depended on civility and communication. Lasting change required entire institutions to open their doors and rethink their traditions, and this would not happen overnight. He understood that black radicals like Chavis needed to press those institutions, but he also thought that they needed to be patient and avoid alienating potential white sympathizers. Because of his Tyson family history of dissent and service, Daddy was able to imagine himself as a "swinging door" across the color line, he told me later. He hoped to become a peacemaker and help explain blacks and whites to one another. For that reason, Daddy wanted the black freedom struggle to behave itself in a way that would help him reassure white people.

But the young black preacher sitting across from my father that morning in the Church of the Black Madonna had his own story, and it didn't cater to my daddy's desires. Chavis was a direct descendant of Reverend John Chavis, a black man who had fought in the American Revolution, become one of the leading preachers of his day, taught Latin and Greek to North Carolina's prominent white families, and was said to have died at the hands of white terrorists because he'd refused to stop teaching slave children. Ben Chavis had grown up with that story the same way that Daddy had grown up on stories of William Tyson's dissent from the Confederacy. Chavis was a radical because the race problem was literally radical; that is, white supremacy went to the very root of the social order. White men could never lead black Southerners into some peaceable kingdom beyond color.

Chavis knew that white supremacy was not just a matter of an all-white chamber of commerce, a Ku Klux Klan rally, or an all-white jury. Those things harmed black people, to be sure, but the white supremacy that was even more insidious and deadly was the internalized white supremacy that made African Americans believe, deep down, that they could not stand up for themselves. Black people needed to oppose white supremacy in the fiercest possible terms and to confront it not only in the streets but in their own souls. The challenge was not just to create a new social order but to create a new black sense of self. White paternalism, from this perspective, was nearly as toxic as white backlash. Chavis also knew that, in practical terms, gradualism nearly always rested on empty promises; "later" always meant never. He believed, with Frederick Douglass, that power concedes nothing without a demand, and that black people could have what they had the power to take and could keep what they had the power to hold. To Chavis, all that my father could offer was the chance to blur the tough issues, ease the inherent contradictions, forestall the necessary conflict, and smear salve on a wound that needed surgery. The problem was that the world that had to be destroyed had a lot of people like my father and Thad Stem in it. But his personal regard for Daddy could not alter the situation.

Chavis was polite, even warm, but it would have been a shocking departure if he had not rejected my father's liberal logic. Instead of candor, he offered decorous evasion. "I am down here with a group of people from Raleigh, Vernon," he said, gesturing toward the roomful of people around them. "I really don't have time to talk today. We have to get back to Raleigh late this afternoon. But the next time I am in town I will call you, and we'll have some time together and see if we can figure something out." That conversation never happened. The next time my father visited Chavis, the most notorious of the world-famous "Wilmington Ten" was wearing a prison uniform instead of a clerical collar, and guards of a different sort monitored their conversation.

Chavis went to prison because he led a militant movement in Wilmington that fanned the fires of white reaction into a small race war. On February 6, 1971, finding themselves under sporadic gunfire from passing carloads of white men, Chavis and his followers barricaded themselves in the basement of Gregory Congregational

Church. The New Hanover County Sheriff's Department, which was heavily infiltrated by the Ku Klux Klan, blocked off all the streets that led to the church. Even so, truckloads of heavily armed white terrorists from the Rights of White People paramilitary forces roared past the church, firing their weapons; ROWP terrorists shot down a respected local black minister who walked into the area that afternoon to appeal for peace. Soon state highway patrol units and then National Guard troops joined the blockade around Gregory. A police officer shot and killed Steven M. Corbett, a black student leader who was carrying a shotgun, in the shadows near the church. It seemed to many inside the church that they might not survive the night. Some of the young men may have slipped out and set fire to a nearby grocery store; arson reports flared all over the city. When firefighters and police officers arrived to battle the blaze, snipers fired at them. But bottles of gasoline and ragtag weaponry could hardly stand against National Guard troops, and many of the people in the church were soon arrested. That was not enough for Wilmington's Superior Court Judge Johnny Walker, who declared to reporters, "Maybe we should have brought in Lieutenant Calley"—the army officer charged with murdering hundreds of Vietnamese civilians at My Lai—"to go in there and clear the place up."

The Wilmington Ten cases, which were based largely on the accusations of arson at the grocery store, dragged on for much of the 1970s, prompting protests around the world and imposing a burden on U.S. foreign relations during the Carter administration. It became clear, whatever the facts of the case, that the prosecution had flung down and danced upon the U.S. Constitution. In 1972, Chavis, the most well known of the ten defendants, received a thirty-five-year prison sentence, and others tallied terms nearly as long. Rallies all over the world called for authorities to free the Wilmington Ten. James Baldwin appealed to President Carter to intervene. The *New York Times*, the *Washington Post*, *Newsweek*, and many other publications provided editorial support. In 1977, Amnesty International launched a campaign to free the Wilmington Ten, calling them "political prisoners." James Weschler of the *New York Post* compared the case to the Scottsboro trials of the 1930s. The controversy, featured on *60 Minutes* and investigated by the U.S. Congress, eventually persuaded Governor Jim Hunt to reduce their sentences. In 1980, a federal court reversed the verdicts. The prosecution's tactics had worked hand in glove with the FBI's COINTELPRO operation to shut down the black freedom movement. It is clear that several of the defendants were entirely innocent; in other cases, it seems more likely that the authorities "framed a guilty man," as one local black man said of Chavis.

Chavis, a talented and passionate organizer, admitted when my father visited him in prison a couple of years later that he had made many mistakes in Wilmington. He had since fasted and prayed, he told Daddy, and repented of his errors. After his release, he attended Divinity School at Duke University and later used his Wilmington Ten notoriety to forge a remarkable career as a national activist. In the 1990s, Chavis rose to the post of executive director of the NAACP. Forced to resign because of a sex scandal, Chavis then turned to the Nation of Islam under Louis Farrakhan and orchestrated the 1996 Million Man March. He later assumed Malcolm X's old job as minister at the Nation of Islam's Temple Number 7 in Harlem. Like his illustrious ancestor Reverend John Chavis, Ben Chavis made some history, though probably much less history than his talents would have permitted had his opportunities been different ones.

The power of history hung palpably over Wilmington, my father learned quickly. That history served as a terrible obstacle to progress, even though many people did not know the events that exerted such a power over their lives. "Sometimes murder does its best work in memory, after the fact," historian Glenda Gilmore has written of events in Wilmington more than seventy years earlier. "Terror lives on, continuing to serve its purpose long after the violence that gave rise to it ends." This point became clear to my father in the midst of the upheavals, when he called a series of meetings of black and white parents to see whether something could be done to find a pathway toward racial reconciliation.

At the first meeting, which he convened at our church, Daddy heard African American parents make bitter references to "what happened" and "what caused all this"—as if the causes of Wilmington's racial turmoil were self-evident. Yet the quizzical expressions and vacant nods of white parents made Daddy suspect that the white parents were oblivious to something that every black person in the room understood. "When you say, 'What caused all this,' what are you talking about?" he finally asked the black parents. At first, the black parents refused to believe that he did not know what they meant. Finally, one black mother paused to point in the direction of the Cape Fear River. Flashing her mind's eye seventy years into the past to November 10, 1898, she told him, "They say that river was full of black bodies."

In fact, though none of the white people in the room knew what had happened along the banks of the Cape Fear in 1898, the Wilmington Race Riot was probably the most important political event in the history of the state. Its omission from North Carolina history may have been the biggest of the lies that marked my boyhood. This "riot"—better described by H. Leon Prather Sr. as a massacre and coup d'état—signaled a turning point in American history, a period when African Americans lost their civil rights and the new social order of segregation was born. White people, of course, and many blacks believed that Jim Crow segregation simply had replaced slavery—still oppressive, but better—and had accepted it as a kind of natural stage of progression toward equality rather than the bloody and undemocratic counterrevolution that it really was. Even my father, though he'd grown up in North Carolina, had never heard about the white supremacy revolution that had voided interracial democracy until the civil rights era.

At the turn of the century, Wilmington was the largest city in North Carolina. It had electric lights and streetcars in the 1890s, when most of the state remained a remote backwater. With a large black majority, the port city was the center of African American economic and political power. Wilmington boasted large numbers of African American artisans and businessmen: ten of the city's eleven eating houses were owned by blacks, as were twenty of its twenty-two barbershops. Black financiers and real estate agents helped make Wilmington prosper. The *Daily Record*, edited by Alexander Manly, was the only black daily newspaper in the United States.

In the 1890s, hard times and clear-eyed politics brought a kind of interracial democracy revolution in North Carolina—one conducted in the shadow of slavery by mutually suspicious allies, but a revolution nonetheless. This interracial Fusion alliance between mostly black Republicans and mostly white Populists swept every election and captured the governorship, the General Assembly, every single statewide office, and countless local positions. Black and white together appeared to have ushered in a new era of free and equal citizenship, though the racial politics of the coalition were far from perfect and anything but simple. White men controlled most of the important offices. In Wilmington, despite its black voting majority, only three of the ten aldermen were black; the rest were white Populists. Even so, white Democrats, who also called themselves the Conservatives, could not abide the democratic process. Before the next election, the self-proclaimed "party of white supremacy" launched a campaign of racist appeals and political violence aimed to shatter this reprehensible cooperation between blacks and whites. "We will not live under these intolerable conditions," Colonel Alfred Waddell, soon to become mayor of Wilmington, told a crowd of cheering Democrats. "We will never surrender to a ragged raffle of negroes, even if we have to choke the current of the Cape Fear with carcasses."

Waddell, a former U.S. congressman and Confederate veteran, revealed the Democratic Party's electoral strategy the night before the 1898 elections. "Go to the polls tomorrow," he declared, "and if you find the negro out voting, tell him to leave the polls, and if he refuses, kill him, shoot him down in his tracks." This strategy led to victory at the polls, but the white Democrats were not satisfied. On a chilly autumn day two days after the election, armed columns of white business leaders and working men seized the city by force. Led by Colonel Waddell and Hugh McCrae, an MIT-trained textile mill owner, hundreds of white vigilantes burned the *Daily Record*'s print-ing press. Next they marched into the neighborhood called Brooklyn, where they left a trail of dead and dying African Americans. Armed with the latest repeating rifles and rapid-fire guns, they outgunned black men who sought to defend their homes with antique revolvers and shotguns.

Nobody really knows how many African Americans died in Wilmington in the bloody counterrevolution that overthrew one of early-twentieth-century America's few chances for meaningful democracy. The most readily confirmed estimate is fourteen; the leader of the white mob said "about twenty." Hugh McCrae boasted later of ninety dead. Echoing the stories of their grandparents, many African Americans in Wilmington say they believe that the death toll exceeded three hundred. That night and the next day, hundreds of black women and children huddled in the swamps on the outskirts of the city while white men with guns built a new social order. The white insurgents forced the remaining city officials, whether they were black or merely had made alliance with blacks, to resign at gun-point, and took power for themselves, issuing a fiery "Declaration of White Independence." Colonel Waddell assumed the mayor's office. Conservatives drove their political opponents, black and white, into exile and forcibly banished the city's most prominent African American professionals, confiscating their property. One reason the death toll remains so difficult to determine with any accuracy is that fourteen hundred black citizens fled the city during the next thirty days.

Approval, not condemnation, thundered down on the vigilantes from white pulpits, editorial pages, and political podiums across the United States. White dissent in North Carolina had been rendered almost impossible, and black dissent suicidal. The Wilmington Race Riot was the centerpiece of a white supremacy revolution that swept the state in 1898, and the first thing the new regime did was to take the vote away from African Americans. This created what one of the nation's leading Democrats, Raleigh *News and Observer* editor Josephus Daniels, hailed as "permanent good government by the

party of the white man." Without their black political allies, the
dissenting whites of that day had nowhere to go. Most signed on with
the new order, encouraged by their ministers and elected officials.
"We have taken a city," the Reverend Peyton H. Hoge declared from
the pulpit of the First Presbyterian Church in Wilmington. "To God
be the praise." Governor Charles B. Aycock, one of the architects of
the white supremacy campaign that robbed blacks of their civil and
political rights, assessed the role of the Democratic Party this way:
"We have ruled by force, we have ruled by fraud, but we want to rule
by law."

The events of 1898 were a source of great pride to the Democratic
Party in North Carolina, and the next five governors of the state were
all selected from among the authors of the white supremacy crusade.
During the New Deal, however, its luster began to fade and the self-
proclaimed "party of white supremacy" dropped all references to
their glorious counterrevolution. North Carolina history textbooks
never mentioned anything about either the massacre in Wilmington
or the white supremacy campaigns of which the killings were the cap-
stone. What black schools taught about this white-supremacy revolution I do not know. Governor Aycock, who'd helped organize the
campaigns, became known as "the education governor," the founding
icon of North Carolina's "progressive" self-image, and the leading
political figure in the history of the state. For twenty years or so, the
white supremacy campaigns became a springboard to political success," Glenda Gilmore writes. "And those who had failed to participate found it difficult to win any office." And then the white power
revolt faded from popular memory. The architects of white supremacy
became heroes, and the bloody and undemocratic means by which
they came to power were largely forgotten among white people.

The ghosts of 1898 walked among us in the 1970s, and the fact
that so few of us knew the past did not loosen its compelling hold on
the present. Late one afternoon my junior high school friends and I
were playing baseball in Hugh McCrae Park, named for one of the
leaders of the massacre. As the day dimmed toward evening, my
comrades and I huddled in a dugout to smoke cigarettes and discuss

the mysteries of sex. As we chattered in the dark, we began to hear car engines racing and car doors slamming. At first we thought that it was just the first stirrings of a Little League baseball game. But when we looked out, hundreds of white men and a few women had gathered on the baseball diamond, many brandishing rifles and shotguns and waving American and Confederate flags. Several held up a banner that proclaimed the name of the organization: THE RIGHTS OF WHITE PEOPLE. Suddenly I realized that these were the people who had fired their guns in the air near my junior high school. These must be the people who'd threatened to lynch the school superintendent, Heyward Bellamy, whom my mother considered a hero. For the ROWP, the memory of 1898 was not chilling but bracing. Their paramilitary leader, Leroy Gibson, walked up to a makeshift microphone and began bellowing about how the "niggers" and "nigger lovers" had all the rights and white working people had none. "The niggers keep talking about how Waddell said in 1898 they were gonna clog up the river with carcasses," he jeered. "I don't know if they did or not. But if this integration and rioting business doesn't stop, we're going to clog that river with dead niggers this time, and I mean it."

The lies that instantly seemed so transparent to me in that dugout were part of the craziness that sent me into a long tailspin as those Wilmington years wore on. Everywhere I turned, a new falsehood seemed to stare me in the face. I loved to read and write, but I hated school, and started skipping classes frequently. The authorities at school carried no meaningful authority for me. From the news reports on television, it became clear that President Nixon was a crook, despite his assurances to the contrary; the men who spoke for him on television spewed phrases that would have fit into the mouth of a Mafia lawyer. Racism stained the nation. Hypocrisy infested the church. Anyone who set out to challenge the corruption of the system seemed to get assassinated. And it appeared clear to me—partly because of the lies that filled my history textbooks—that the intent of formal education was to inculcate obedience to a social order that did not deserve my loyalty. Defiance seemed the only dignified response to the adult world.

At fourteen, I began partying heavily on weekends, trying to numb my misfit's agonies. The inevitable adolescent distance between my father and me became a yawning chasm. From a distance, he blurred into the backdrop of the world that had caused all this mess. In those years, fathers and sons across the country fought bitterly about the war in Vietnam, the chaos in the streets, the length of people's hair, and the icons of music, religion, and popular culture. Daddy and I never hated each other. But we did lose touch. By the time I was sixteen, I had abandoned school and soon left home, careening into a counterculture that promised a gentler world but failed to deliver it.

One snapshot from the period helps explain what happened between my father and me. When I was about sixteen, I began wearing bib overalls every single day, no matter where I was going, including church. I'd latched onto bib overalls by way of the sixties counterculture, but I knew the etymology of the uniform; that is, I knew that I was wearing bib overalls in imitation of Abbie Hoffman, the jester of the New Left, who was wearing them in homage to Bob Moses and the organizers of the Student Nonviolent Coordinating Committee, pronounced "Snick," who had adopted bib overalls from the black sharecroppers they were trying to organize in Mississippi. It never occurred to me that my father, himself a sharecropper's son, had worn these every day of his early life.

One day Daddy walked into our suburban house and saw his son wearing those overalls again. He shook his head in bemused contempt, muttering, "I worked for twenty-five years so I would never have to wear those damn things again." I tried to explain, but of course in my boundless sixteen-year-old understanding of the world, I was far too enlightened to communicate with someone who probably didn't know about Bob Moses or Abbie Hoffman or SNCC. I can't remember what I said to him, but it must have been insufferable. I liked my father immensely but regarded him as another benighted member of a hopeless generation, those ineffectual and naive people whose liberal optimism blinded them to the perniciousness of "the System." Hadn't "the System" killed both the Kennedys and Dr.

King? Hadn't "the System" lied about Vietnam and slaughtered a couple of million Vietnamese rice farmers and sixty thousand American boys for nothing? Hadn't Watergate demonstrated that "the System" was hopelessly corrupt? Somehow my father managed to retain not only some of his patience but all of his sense of humor, and eventually we developed a running joke about the difference between "Snick" overalls and "hick" overalls.

My hippie friends and I tried to escape the South and ended up finding it. Rob Shaffer and Stacy Weaver, fledgling radicals and aspiring writers whom I met in high school, shared my belief that America's promise had foundered on the rocks of race and Vietnam. Though they were two years older than me, we all shared books, music, basketball, and a utopian vision of eluding this terrible history and making a brand-new world. Together we braved suburban conformity and suffered the persistent efforts of our high school's principal to censor our school newspaper and, even worse, force us to attend classes like everyone else. Though we were children of the suburbs, we cast ourselves as lonely dissenters who defied a hardhearted world, easing our anguish by founding a happy tribe. This worked fairly well for me until Rob and Stacy left for college.

A year later, though, when I was almost seventeen, the three of us made a pact to drop out of our respective schools and move to a remote corner of northeastern North Carolina, where we lived in an old two-story tenant farmhouse not unlike the ones where my father had grown up. Rob and Stacy packed up their dorm rooms at Duke and UNC and rolled down the road feeling good, arriving some months before me. I crawled out the window of my parents' suburban home in the dead of night with what I liked to think of as all of my worldly possessions—Tom Sawyer pretending to be Huck Finn—in a duffel bag and lit out for Flat Branch, North Carolina, where they had rented this broke-down palace surrounded on three sides by enormous cornfields and backed up by the Great Dismal Swamp. I left my parents a note explaining that school and suburbia were driving me crazy (a short trip, I might have noted) and that I loved them very much but there is a tide in the affairs of men, which, taken at the flood, it becomes necessary to dissolve the political bands, which—I have a dream! Remember the Alamo! Don't trust anyone over thirty! And so on.

Daddy found me near the bus stop in Ahoskie, where I was just starting to walk the remaining twenty-seven miles to Flat Branch. In the front seat beside him was Roscoe Wainwright, an elderly homeless man who was his closest companion in those days. My grandfather Jack Tyson had performed Roscoe's wedding some decades earlier. Roscoe had left eastern North Carolina to serve in the army in France during World War I. When he returned from France, Mr. Wainwright developed quite an enthusiasm for some of our less expensive American wines. When the weather was good, Roscoe slept in the bushes at our church; on cold nights, he frequented a crawl space near the boiler room. Roscoe lived on a monthly check from the Veterans Administration. After Daddy discovered that the other street people would often rob Mr. Wainwright after he cashed his check, he arranged to have the check sent to the church office, and Daddy would give him five dollars a day. "It was the perfect example of a well-intended liberal social program gone awry," my father chuckled years later. "He used to get drunk once a month, and then get robbed and have a hard time finding a drink the rest of the month. After I saved him from the muggers with my five-dollars-a-day program, he got drunk every single day the rest of his life." Sometimes, in those days, I would come home and find Mr. Wainwright in the other twin bed in my room, sleeping off one of his benders after Daddy had brought him home, fed him, and given him a bath.

My parents, of course, were mortified when they discovered that I had run away from home. But something told them that things would only get worse if they tried to make me stay home. And they also thought that a couple of years of paying my bills by the sweat of my brow would not hurt me too much. Mama and Daddy talked it over and decided to let me follow my own lights, once they knew that I was safe, so Daddy and Roscoe set out that morning to find me. Roscoe perched in the front seat of my father's car, the Bible between them, and he'd pull out the pint of Wild Irish Rose and take a drink every few miles. When night had fallen and still no one knew my whereabouts, Daddy became truly worried and began to wonder out loud where on earth his idiot son could be at this hour of the night. "Carload of niggers probably picked him up and dragged him up in the woods and knocked him in the head," Roscoe speculated as they sat near the roadside bus stop in Ahoskie.

"Shut up, Roscoe," Daddy said. "Just shut up."

My father's deep voice startled me as I plodded down the darkened roadside. But when I saw his face in the car window, he was beaming at me. "Hey, Little Buck," he said. "Let's go to Flat Branch." I climbed into the back seat, scarcely able to comprehend what he had just said. But it became faintly imaginable when I saw that he had brought a gallon bucket of peanut butter, several dozen pairs of outlet socks, an ancient black-and-white television set someone had given him, and an old black leather Bible. We rolled down the two-lane blacktop through the swamp, turned onto unpaved Flat Branch Road, and then rumbled up the long driveway to the falling-down farmhouse where my long-haired friends waited excitedly, having already talked to Daddy and Roscoe earlier in the day. Standing between the cornfields, my father and I wrapped our arms around each other and held on tight for a long time. He laid his thick hand on my head and thanked God for giving him this fine son—one is not under oath when delivering such prayers—and asked Him to stand by me in the days and years to come. Then he pressed into my hands the Bible that Jack Tyson had given him on the day he'd left home, and drove away.

Like many people in the mid-1970s, my young friends and I were trying to escape from history. We loved Dr. King and the black-and-white film footage we'd seen of the movement in the streets of the civil rights–era South. We loved the idealism of the young people who'd gone to Mississippi and died, some of them, to change America. But that was not our generation. The dreams of the civil rights movement and the New Left that inspired us, even though we'd been too young to go to Selma or Chicago, had soured into agonies of assassination, defeat, and delusion. Taught to believe in leaders, we came to believe that anybody with a fighting chance to alter the reactionary trajectory of American political history ended up assassinated. Trained to revere democracy, we saw the American presidency disintegrate on television in an electronic haze of lies.

With our vast teenaged overview of world history, we children of the middle class saw that American society was insane and, in fact, doomed, and we became profoundly "alienated," as people used to say. The answer was simply to quit, let the world go by, and make our contribution through moral example (translate: growing tomatoes with manure instead of chemical fertilizer) and artistic statement (translate: scribbling in my journals for two or three hours a day, singing folk songs, and composing love letters to a revolving array of angels of the female persuasion). One day, I thought, the world would find my box of scribbling and regret that it had failed to heed my blistering social critiques or relish my poetic meanderings. The fact that all this seemed gravely political to me at the time reflects both the charmed innocence of the young and the confused legacy of the 1960s and 1970s.

Ralph Waldo Emerson wrote in "Self-Reliance" that "to be great is to be misunderstood," and I suppose that we were tempted back then to take the inverse to be equally true. We called ourselves a "commune," though that seems a little pretentious now, given that there were only three of us and we could not have been less deliberate. Our hairy tribe founded a new world that demanded a great deal from us in some ways and virtually nothing from us in others. We planted a large garden and grew much of our own food. The crumbling tin woodstoves that heated the house consumed enormous quantities of wood, which we cut and hauled without chain saws or even a wheelbarrow. To take a shower, we pumped water from the well by hand, heated it on the stove, and poured it over each other's heads from the front porch with a five-gallon watering can. Even in the South, this gets rather bracing in February. In my journal that spring, I copied from the *Dhammapada:* "Let us live happily then, though we call nothing our own. We shall be like the bright gods, feeding on happiness." And, though I made no note of it at the time, feeding also on the chocolate-chip cookies and fresh-baked bread my mother shipped to us. Thoreau would have understood.

If our material circumstances demanded great exertion, our countercultural lifestyle was morally less strenuous. Entirely persuaded of our own rectitude, we reveled in our superiority to "the South" all around us. In our minds, "the South" was white, and therefore hypocritical, uptight, and censorious. Black people, by contrast, were noble, soulful, and fun. It never occurred to us that black people could be Southerners or respectable or that Jerry Lee Lewis and Little Richard were only working different sides of the same street. And it was years later before any of us knew much of anything about our political ancestors—dissenting white Southerners from whose mistakes and achievements we could have learned. Instead, we drew our haphazard, well-meaning politics from thin air and the anger of betrayed children. We wore bib overalls in the style of the SNCC organizers who had lived in the rural South fifteen years earlier, but we knew little of their politics except to assume that they were, like ourselves, firmly on the side of the angels. Up and down Flat Branch Road, the black, rural poor lived in squalor; I remember the falling-down tenant houses, all but unheated, and the outhouses slumped behind them. The house where we sometimes bought moonshine liquor from a woman with ten children had fallen open to the weather at one corner and had collapsed at another. None of the black families on Flat Branch Road enjoyed running water or indoor plumbing; for the runaway children of the suburbs, poverty could seem romantic. But we did little to alleviate the abject deprivation all around us and rarely even contemplated it. It was enough that we were good, to say nothing of hip.

One source of self-congratulation was our racial politics. Here we actually achieved some things that still make me proud of that boy in overalls and his bleary-eyed band of brothers and sisters. To a degree that was almost unknown in that time and place, we managed to create meaningfully interracial lives. In a remote rural county, our farmhouse became a place where black and white young people gathered to laugh out loud without fear of the world. On the edge of the Great Dismal Swamp, we built a basketball court where salt met pepper and forgot to keep score. The intelligent daughters of the leading white families in the county, the kind of young women who soon would be off for UNC or Duke, gathered at our house. We would sing and talk into the wee hours. Though there were only a few white boys in the community who wanted to get to know us, the young black men who partied at Flat Branch were charming rogues like ourselves. Friendships and romances developed across the color line, providing an education that was sometimes bountiful and occasionally cruel. All the girls knew about a local girl who'd ended up getting shipped away to boarding school the year before I got there because she had dated a black boy. Some white parents banned their daughters from our company. Young black men and women feared reprisals for hanging around with us. Occasionally, white boys with their trucks and guns threatened us for allowing "their" girls to meet black men at our house. In retrospect, I am astounded that our flouting of the color line caused as little trouble as it did.

One of the guiding angels of our secession was Perri Anne Morgan, the feisty and sumptuous daughter of one of the county's leading farm families. The year she turned fourteen, Perri helped cause a furor in Parker's Fork United Methodist Church, which her family had attended since antebellum days. It was Memorial Day, and the minister at Parker's Fork announced the formation of a whites-only softball league for the county's white children. The men of the community had decided to announce it through the churches only, he said, to avoid including "the other segment of the population." After he had made his plug for segregated softball, the minister preached a sermon entitled "The Land of the Free and the Home of the Brave." Most people probably didn't even think about the contradiction, but Perri and a few others grew more and more enraged. After his allegedly patriotic drivel was over, Beth Polson, who had grown up in Parker's Fork but had moved to California to work as a television producer some years earlier, stood up in the back row. "I have spoken in this church many times," she said, "and I am afraid that what I have to say this morning won't be as welcome. But I have never heard such hypocrisy here before, and I am really disappointed."

The misguided minister was clueless. "I don't know what you are talking about," he replied.

Perri's mother, Doris Morgan, had been watching her daughter's face in the choir loft. In a brilliant stroke of motherhood, she piped up from the front row. "I think Perri Anne could tell you," she said, loudly enough for everyone in the church to hear.

Fourteen-year-old Perri stood up right there in front of God the Father Almighty, maker of heaven and earth, and declared, "I don't understand how you can stand up there and announce a softball league for white kids only, and then preach a sermon 'America, the Land of the Free and the Home of the Brave.' It doesn't make any sense." Perri sat down, and it was her mother's turn to speak.

Getting to her feet, Mrs. Morgan told the congregation that she had seen the faces of the young people in the choir during the announcement and the sermon. They were the future of the church, if it had one, she said, and their views needed to be expressed, which was why she had called on Perri Anne. And she wanted people to know that she agreed with her daughter. "I think this sets a terrible example for the young people," she added. Some people started crying and others stomped out of the sanctuary. Maybe the minister never did figure out why the black freedom movement in the South had forced so many Christians to reexamine their white supremacist beliefs. But whatever it had accomplished, Perri became one of the leading lights of our merry band at Flat Branch. If her parents weren't entirely happy about the company she kept—and who can blame them for that?—well, it does sometimes appear that our subsequent marriage and two lovely children have helped them recover.

Though we bravely confronted some of the lies that the world had whispered into our ears even before we were born, the Flat Branch tribe rested upon our own fundamental falsehood: that we could find a hiding place outside of history. We could not secede from the South and build Utopia in the woods, safely beyond the hard history that had brought us there. What one friend laughingly called "the church of dissipation" offered no authentic moral center to sustain us. Though the liberal vision of my father had not proven adequate to the political collisions of the late 1960s, my dropout vision in the 1970s offered nothing more workable. There was no place to run from history; history was not just the past but also the present and the future. I was lost. I was utterly lost. When the Flat Branch gang fell apart, as inevitably we did after a couple of years, I wandered to Chapel Hill, apprenticed myself to a local culinary genius, and learned the craft of a restaurant cook.

After I had drained the fryers, cleaned the grills, and mopped the concrete floors, I staggered around the college town in the best tradition of the Gator, doing my best to lose myself still more deeply. Not only had I failed to find a hiding place from history; I could not even find a place to hide from the rage that seethed inside me. I tried to rinse away that rage in gin to no avail. I lived in a rooming house full of drunks and misfits. My nights were passed among the stoned out, the lonesome, and the forlorn. I knew every tribe of junkies and every barroom rowdy in town, and took comfort where I could. My idea of a perfect night was to get off work, swill some beers at the Cave, toss back a couple of shots at Tijuana Fats, go dancing at the Cat's Cradle, and persuade a carload of waitresses to go skinny-dipping at Clearwater Lake. My favorite song was Tom Waits's "Bad Liver and a Broken Heart," in which he avows, "I don't have a drinking problem, except when I can't get a drink."

Local organizers from the Communist Workers Party, seeing a lost young man drawn by experience and temperament to a left-leaning politics of rage, invited me to attend some meetings in the fall of 1979. Led by a group of idealistic young medical professionals, the CWP worked among the poorest of the poor, offering free medical care and leftist agitprop to impoverished white working people and their underemployed black counterparts. If they had only been more fun, I probably would have joined, but I remained a reluctant recruit.

Still, I promised to ride with a carload of CWP loyalists to a rally in a Greensboro housing project on Saturday morning, November 3,

1979. I was supposed to meet them at eight that morning, but I had poured down my last beer of the evening at about five A.M. By the time I'd finished my coffee early that afternoon, I heard on the radio that Ku Klux Klansmen and Nazis had come to the rally, calmly retrieved their rifles from the trunks of their cars, and killed five of the CWP organizers I had met only a few days earlier. An undercover agent from the Bureau of Alcohol, Tobacco, and Firearms had ridden with the killers; the vigilantes had carried a police department map of the march in the car. Even though the five killings had occurred while television cameras were running, an all-white jury acquitted the murderers. Watching the videotape of the Greensboro massacre and reading news accounts of the acquittals, needless to say, did little to still my anger and ease my alienation. Meanwhile, the country lurched further and further to the right, Ronald Reagan rode into the White House on a campaign that made blacks and the poor his scapegoats, and America seemed less and less interested in the visions of racial justice that had nurtured my early political consciousness. My favorite political slogan from those years was something spraypainted onto the ice plant next to my apartment by a housing-project poet: "Who need ice when you got Nancy Reagan."

One day soon after the Greensboro killings, I drove up to Oxford to see Thad Stem. At that point, he was beset with kidney failure and seemed pretty frail, and I was about twenty. He asked about my writing, and I told him I had scribbled some notes about what had happened in Oxford. I couldn't answer any of his questions about the writing project, though, and finally he reached over, squeezed my hand with a strange and lovely tenderness, and said, "You're too close to it, now, Tim, but you'll write about it someday."

Leaving his house on Front Street, I walked to the graveyard, retracing the steps Thad and Daddy had made in 1970 on the day of Henry Marrow's funeral, when they'd left the Black Power chants and gone home for lunch. It was almost summer, just as it had been back then, and the smells of fresh-cut grass and honeysuckle made the air thick and sweet by the cemetery. I didn't know where he was buried. But I walked along the fence and straight to a small gravestone in the back corner, as if I were family and knew the path by heart. The stone read, HENRY D. MARROW, JAN. 8, 1947–MAY 12, 1970. VIETNAM.

As I knelt beside his grave, I did not even try to pray. But some things came clear to me. My own scrawled indictment against the world had begun, though it did not end, with the words "Daddy and Roger and 'em shot 'em a *nigger.*" Some people's worlds are organized around a wartime trauma, a lucky break, a crucial mentor, or a lost love affair. As the years pass, they come to see the whole world through that particular lens of loss or luck. In my case, what was lost was a kind of faith that I wondered if I would ever find again. I had not seen my family killed in front of my eyes. My village had not been obliterated from the earth. My people had not been categorically barred from acknowledgment as human beings. These cruelties occurred all over the world, but what held their place in my mind was the killing of a man I had not even known. The black veterans who'd buried Henry Marrow, having only a small stone on which to explain all that was wrong, had inscribed one word for a fellow soldier who had never left North Carolina: VIETNAM. In the graveyard of my own hopes, on the stone that marked where I had buried my past and my future, I wrote his name. And I drove back to Chapel Hill one step closer to finding my way home, though I did not know it at the time.

Soon after my trip to Henry Marrow's grave, my life of disengagement ended when I almost killed myself in a moment of inspired stupidity. The night I was named head chef at a local restaurant, I came home plastered after a long procession of tequila shots and salty margaritas at Tijuana Fats. A woman at the bar had given me a couple of Seconals—powerful barbiturate tablets—to take home "for later." Never one to procrastinate when it came to pleasure, I grabbed a bottle of white wine from the fridge, polished off the pills, and sat down happily at my typewriter, flush with chemical inspiration. Tonight, I thought, I might write the thing that illuminated it all somehow. In the morning, when I woke up facedown on the floor beside my desk, there was a pool of dried vomit beside my face. In the middle of the pool sat half an undigested pill. If I had fallen backward instead of forward, I instantly understood, I would have drowned in my own vomit and never awakened. That day, I realized that I had to take control of my life. If I did not turn to confront the demons that drove me, they would eventually catch me from behind. I began to study and to contemplate the reasons why I was lost, and that process led me to examine what had happened to the movement that had once promised to redeem the soul of America from its original sin.

Though I no longer lived in the woods, I still scribbled in my journals and read hundreds of books. I thought I had fled school for good, and I never once aspired to go to college. Julia Stockton, a dark-eyed beauty and gifted poet who endured my boozy chaos for a couple of years, held diplomas from Exeter and Yale and had nearly finished her postgraduate work in English. She glanced up from her writing one day and said, "You're completely wrong about college, you know. You will love college." Something about her inflection was persuasive. A few weeks after that, Daddy drove me to enroll at the University of North Carolina at Greensboro, mostly because they would admit anyone over twenty-two as a probationary "special student"; my D average and my indecipherable transcripts did not matter. And the first thing I did as a twenty-three-year-old freshman was to drive to Oxford, North Carolina, to ask Robert Teel why he'd killed Henry Marrow.

CHAPTER 12

"Go Back to the Last Place Where You Knew Who You Were"

I F, IN MOVING through your life, you find yourself lost," said Bernice Johnson Reagon, the guiding spirit of the SNCC Freedom Singers and now Sweet Honey in the Rock, "go back to the last place where you knew who you were, and what you were doing, and start from there." Soon after I took her advice, I found myself with a straight razor at my neck—held by none other than Robert Teel. The first thing I had done as a college student was to arrange an independent study with one of my history professors. In the course of that study, I went back to Oxford and interviewed as many people as I could persuade to talk to me about what had happened back in 1970—starting with Teel.

Though he had been the champion of white resistance in the summer of 1970, aided and applauded by the country club and courthouse crowd, those same people had dropped Teel like a dirty tissue after the trial ended. When they discovered that the changes the black freedom movement brought did not land a black man in every white woman's bed or have Granville County declared a Soviet republic, the white upper classes did not wish to be reminded that they had sanctioned public murder and had turned a violent tragedy into a late-model lynching. Teel had lost his big white house on Main Street with the columns and the magnolias. At sixty, he lived in a small brick bungalow beside a barbershop he'd opened on the outskirts of Granville County, in a remote crossroads community called Stovall. As the tires of the old gray-blue Falcon I'd borrowed from Julia crunched the gravel of his driveway, I wondered who else would drive this far to get their hair cut. And I wondered if I should have come that far myself.

Frankly, I was scared. At the courthouse earlier that morning, I had read Teel's arrest record. Over the years, he had been charged with virtually every violent crime I'd ever heard of, more than a dozen different charges. Getting on the fighting side of Robert Teel was not hard, and it had landed several people, including two cops, in the emergency room. Pulled over for drunken driving on two occasions, each time he had pounded the arresting officer unconscious with his fists. Reading over the long list of charges, I had learned that Robert Teel had an enduring habit of attacking anyone who crossed him, with whatever weapon lay at hand. The fine legal distinctions between "assault with a deadly weapon" and "assault with a deadly weapon *with intent to kill*" suddenly seemed very interesting, even compelling. How hard did you have to hit someone with the hammer to demonstrate "intent to kill"?

Before I went to see him, I took an ice pick, impaled a marble-sized wad of duct tape on its tip to keep it from poking through my jacket, and slipped it into the pocket of my old gray suit. As I pulled into the driveway, my hand instinctively moved down to make sure that the ice pick was still there. I hadn't come to fight with him, and I wasn't even planning to argue with him. But if the sumbitch tried to hurt me, it was going to be blood for blood—or so I told myself.

When I walked into the barbershop, Teel was sitting in his own chair, reading the newspaper as if he were waiting for a haircut. He was red-faced, short, and husky, a fireplug of a man, but hardly an imposing figure. Except for a certain hardness around his eyes, he did not look like a killer or the kind of fellow who coldcocks the same police officer twice. When I offered him my hand, he took one finger, very gingerly, as if he had never shaken hands before. My heart sank at his reluctant reception, but I lowered myself onto the red leatherette couch across from him. We had been neighbors years before, I explained, and I had been good friends with Gerald, his youngest boy. Teel plainly did not remember me or my family, which was some comfort, although I kept worrying that he was lying about that part. I lit a Marlboro to calm my nerves, but the glowing cigarette, waving visibly, only called attention to my sudden palsy. Teel saw my quaking hands at the same time I did, and I winced until I caught the unmistakable pleasure in his expression. I think he liked people to be afraid of him. "You're shaking like a leaf, boy," he said, with evident satisfaction.

"I think I had too much coffee this morning. I'm not used to drinking coffee," I lied. I was a restaurant cook, a college student, and a would-be writer at the time, and two pots a day was the minimum daily requirement. I explained to Teel that I was writing a history paper for school on all the stuff that had happened back in 1970—the death, the burning, the trial, and so on. That was true, as far as it went. I mean, that is how this all got started. It seemed an unlikely homework assignment to him, I could tell. At the same time, the murder had been his moment, and I could see that he wanted to talk about it. When I asked if I could tape an interview with him, he said, "Sure, I will talk to you. What do you want to know?"

I started with some questions about his early life. Teel quickly began to narrate the history of his rise to success as a businessman in Oxford in the 1960s. The killing of Henry Marrow, it became clear, was the crucial point at which his life had fallen apart, and Teel saw himself as the principal victim in the matter. "People still ask me, 'Why'd you have to kill him?' " Teel said, "and I say, 'Yeah, if you'da told me he was coming I woulda been in Florida, why didn't you tell me?' " But Robert Teel steered away from the particulars of the killing itself. "I could see my way clear to being a millionaire," he told me, "before what happened happened."

I saw my opportunity. "So, what happened?" I asked him.

Teel fell silent. I felt the blood rush to my face. He looked at me with a blank, strangely animal expression, his eyes darting back and forth. He thought hard, then let out a long sigh, reached over, and turned off my tape recorder. "I can't talk to you about that," he said. "I am sorry, but I just don't remember you. I am sure you are who you say you are, but I just don't remember you. It's been a long time. No offense, I like you just fine, but for all I know you are working for the N-double-C-A-P." N-double-C-A-P. I did not laugh. "Feller came out here some years back," he said, "and he seemed like a nice enough feller to me, and I talked to him about it, and it turned out he was writing for some communist magazine up in New York City. I just can't talk to you." Teel walked over to the red metal icebox and fished out a seven-ounce Coca-Cola, thrusting it toward me. "You want a drink?"

Making a note to check communist magazines for articles about Oxford, I decided to stick around and talk to him about sports, the weather, anything he wanted, until he asked me to leave. When he wanted me to leave, though, I didn't plan on sticking around one minute longer. I was still scared half to death that he was going to suddenly remember that race-traitor preacher who'd lived around the corner on Hancock Street. Thank God the Teels had not been members of our church. A customer came in for a haircut, and I watched Teel work, taking careful mental note of his mannerisms and his rhythms of speech, hoping that it would help me describe him someday. I wanted to hold on to his every word and gesture, to forget nothing. The intensity of this hunger to understand surprised me; now that I was there, I had an almost physical craving to hear what Teel had to say, and I wasn't going to leave until I had.

Teel seemed to have a similar urge to tell the story. Once in a while, as he was working, he would be unable to restrain himself and would unleash an outburst about racial politics or the Marrow murder case. "I'll tell you one goddamn thing," he would say, then voice his festering resentment about how everyone had forgotten him or how much easier life would be if he had been a black man. Even the Klan came in for a scornful attack; the bedsheet boys, too, had abandoned him in his hour of need. "Oh, yeah, if you wanna drink a bunch of liquor and sit around talking about the niggers, they're behind you all the way. They're all behind you," Teel snarled. "But if you wanna talk about shooting somebody or burning somebody out," he continued despairingly, "the Klan is behind you, all right—waaaaaay behind you."

This was when I decided to have Teel cut my hair. Another barber had shorn most of my bushy curls the week before, so I wouldn't look like a hippie, but there was still plenty left for Teel. I remembered as I was settling into the barber's chair that he had given me several of the only crew cuts I had ever had, back on Saturday mornings in the 1960s. I smiled to myself as Robert Teel chattered on about race, politics, and local gossip and once more skinned me damn near bald with his electric clippers. Finishing my buzz cut and brushing the hair off the back of my neck, he turned to another task and I pondered the past.

My amusement, nostalgia, and the buzz of the clippers were sharply interrupted by the rhythmic popping of the strop as Teel whisked the blade of a straight razor across it. His cadence slapped out a familiar barbershop sound from the old days, one that I associated with the clean aroma of lather whipped up in a cup with a wooden-handled brush and the cloying smell of hair tonic. But now it took on a perilous aspect as I pondered the prospect of Robert Teel shaving my neck with a straight razor. I wished I hadn't seen his criminal record that morning at the courthouse. If his voice hardened and his razor hand curled inward, pressing that blade across my throat, would it be first-degree murder? Manslaughter? Accidental self-defense? If somehow I managed to escape, would that make it assault with a deadly weapon with intent to kill, inflicting serious bodily injury? Underneath the smock he had tied around me, my hand slipped to the ice pick in my jacket pocket. Somehow I managed to hold myself together as the razor slowly scraped my neck, then was replaced with a hot towel. Teel tenderly cleaned the leftover lather from my ears and my temples, which were pounding with unspilled blood.

Just as he brushed the hair off my shoulders and pulled the tissue paper from around my neck, an orange four-by-four pickup with headlights mounted across the top of the cab pulled up in front of the barbershop. Even before I saw him, I somehow knew that it was my old friend Gerald stepping out of the truck. He walked into the shop wearing brogan boots like the ones we used to wear as boys, jeans, a flannel shirt, and a baseball cap. We had not seen each other in years, but he did not even pause. *"Tim Tyson!"* he said, grinning at me happily and extending a warm handshake. He hadn't laid eyes on me, he said, since the old days when he and Jeff Daniels and I used to smoke Jeff's mama's cigarettes in the woods. Seeing Gerald again was like seeing a ghost; a dozen years earlier, this young man had said something that had changed my whole life, and then we'd both moved away. Now somehow it appeared to have been no big deal.

We chatted for a few minutes about our days as juvenile delinquents. Gerald was working at a local factory. I talked about working construction, cooking in restaurants, and how my girlfriend had persuaded me to try going to college. He wanted to get together and have a beer one of these nights, and I got directions to where he was living. While we were laughing and talking, his father wordlessly picked up my tape recorder off the Formica-topped coffee table and plopped into an armchair with the device on his lap, studying the buttons. He pushed "Record" with both thumbs and said, "I'll talk to you. Is this thing on?" As I stepped toward him to make sure it was, Teel issued what he considered the summary assessment of what had happened back on May 11, 1970: "That nigger committed suicide, wanting to come in my store and four-letter-word my daughter-in-law." That was the moment I became a historian.

During my research trips to Granville County, which continued for years after Robert Teel uttered those fateful words, I always stayed with Ben and Joy Averett on their farm, which was on the outskirts of town in more ways than one. Though I had no way of knowing it when I'd met them as a little boy, I now came to understand that Ben and Joy operated their own little bohemian arts colony of a sort. Their annual Brunswick stew, made outdoors over a fire in a huge cast-iron cauldron, brought musicians and writers and friendly folks from across the country. Thad Stem was the only person allowed to smoke in their house, and he relished their company and their cooking. Their lovely cottage in the woods was filled with books of all kinds. Ben built Joy an elevated dance floor in the woods behind the house. When they had enjoyed that for a while, he turned it into the floor of a little cottage where she could pursue her weaving, painting, writing, and pottery. Though they had both grown up in Oxford and hardly seemed foreign to its folkways, Joy and Ben provided a well-rooted example of how to live an independent and artful life without "getting above your raising," as the old saying goes. I was not only lucky to know them while I was growing up but lucky to have a place to stay while I searched for the story of what had happened to Henry Marrow, and to me, that summer in Oxford.

Journalists have an old saying: "R.F.P.," which means "Read the blankety-blank paper," and that is where I began. After I had exhausted the coverage in the Raleigh *News and Observer*, which was available in the college library, I drove up to Oxford to see if I could find the *Oxford Public Ledger*. The local newspaper had been owned for decades by the Critcher family; their contributions to local political culture, as I have said earlier, included responding to the worst moment in Oxford's racial crisis with an editorial calling for more attention to "the graves of the men who fell in the War Between the States." The Critchers printed ads for Ku Klux Klan rallies but blamed blacks for all their troubles. Even so, the *Ledger* would provide an important gauge of local opinion. But when I went to the public library to look it up, the librarian came back to the desk with a puzzled look on his face. "It's gone," he said. "I know we had it once upon a time, but the microfilms of the *Oxford Public Ledger* from that entire period have just disappeared."

When I walked across the street to the *Ledger* office, I found an ancient Mrs. Critcher at the counter. When I asked about back issues of the *Ledger*, she seemed agreeable enough, but then said, "What are you researching?" I explained in a sentence or two. "Those papers are gone," she said. "We must have thrown them away when we moved the newspaper office." As I dithered in front of her, trying one way and another, her story changed a couple of times. There had been a fire, or perhaps it was a flood or hungry locusts, but in any case the *Oxford Public Ledger* for the entire post–World War II era was missing. That would not explain why it was missing from the library, of course. Nor would it enlighten us as to why the papers were also missing from the state archive in Raleigh when I checked there. Someone had gone to considerable lengths to destroy the paper trail. "I will tell you one goddamn thing," Ben said at the farm later, proving that he had the instincts to write history as well as build houses. "They didn't just walk off by themselves."

At the courthouse, I collided with a similar stonewall. The records for the Teel murder trial had disappeared, they told me. They did not really save court records. On my way toward the front door, however, I saw a staircase to the basement, where I would have expected to find the records. No one was watching, so I slipped down the stairs and found rows and rows of file cabinets. Since I had the case numbers, it was easy enough to look up the files. There was only a tiny partial transcript of the trial, but the arrest records were intact. In the bottom of the big folder, I found the yellow-handled knife that Henry Marrow allegedly carried when he was killed. I held it in my sweaty palm for a moment and wondered what he had been thinking when he'd realized that it was a pocketknife against two shotguns and that he was about to die. I stared into the angry eyes of Robert Teel and the bewildered face of Larry Teel in two police snapshots; the pictures themselves were period pieces, the thick Polaroid prints that roll out of a slot and develop before your eyes. I even found a few yellowed copies of the *Oxford Public Ledger*, presented as evidence by prosecutor Burgwyn in a plea for a change of venue. Nervous as a teenaged shoplifter, I stuffed the whole folder into my briefcase and headed for the public library, where I photocopied all the documents. Then I slipped back into the courthouse and replaced the folder. I was not going to steal the records, the way my adversaries had done. Two weeks later, when I came back to look at the photographs again, the folders were empty. It baffles me that people think that obliterating the past will save them from its consequences, as if throwing away the empty cake plate would help you lose weight.

Given the trouble getting newspapers and documents from white sources, I decided to interview white people in Oxford first; if the whites heard that somebody was talking to the black folks, I reasoned, they would be likely to clam up. Local blacks would not be terribly concerned whether or not I was talking to white people; they would assume that a white boy was talking to white people. And when I got to them, I hoped, I would probably get more cooperation. For a white boy, it seemed, it was easier to cross the color line than to penetrate the white veil of silence.

The day after my unsettling interview with Teel, I called Representative Billy Watkins in Oxford, attorney for the Teel family in 1970, and I nearly dropped the telephone when he agreed to talk to me. Watkins was probably the second-most-powerful man in the state of North Carolina the day I called him. He was usually described as the "hatchet man" to Liston Ramsey, Speaker of the House, and was said to handle money matters for their powerful political machine. Some years earlier, Watkins had been considered a strong candidate for governor. My historian's intuition, though I don't have one bit of evidence to sustain it, says that Watkins's supporters probably stole the *Oxford Public Ledger* from the library and the state archives. Though Watkins had come of age in a Democratic Party in which African Americans were irrelevant, by the mid-1970s, black voters exercised a near veto over the Democratic nomination. If opposition researchers or investigative reporters had been able to produce one well-timed news story of Watkins's role in the Teel murder trial, Watkins's larger ambitions could have been destroyed. Even though that did not happen, he remained chief bagman for the Ramsey machine. By the time I arrived at his office, he had changed his mind. "I am sorry," the gray-haired, craggy-faced legislator said, squinting at me curiously. "The attorney-client privilege really keeps me from being able to talk to you the way I would like to do."

Regardless of why he had changed his mind and decided not to talk to me about the murder, Watkins could not stop himself from talking about race. Nobody these days understood the ways white and black people had gotten along in the South where he had grown up, Watkins insisted. It wasn't as bad as I probably thought it was, he told me. Black people and white people had always gotten along in Granville County. "A black man was my hunting partner," he said. "He kept the dogs and fed them, and I bought the feed. Relations were always good here. A black man keeps my horses now. I've got horses, and was raised on a farm, and we had some blacks out there who stayed on our farm for fifty years and more."

Watkins was an immensely powerful man whose sole study was the accumulation and exercise of political and economic leverage. No dreamer or scholar, he was instead a student of appropriations bills, paving contracts, and campaign contributions. Even his acute understanding of power, however, could not penetrate the wishful thinking and guilty apologetics that kept him from understanding the power dynamics behind the paternalistic relationships he described. Like many white people, most of what he thought he knew about race he'd learned from African Americans who had worked for his family, and most of it was ludicrous. Sensing that he had failed to persuade me somehow, he seemed reluctant to part company, offering one example and another of his beneficence to black people in a strange plea for an irrelevant absolution that it was not my place to offer. "You know," he said as I turned to leave, "a black girl worked in my office during that whole trial."

When I walked into the police department across the street from his law office, I knew immediately that Watkins had warned someone there. Nathan White, who had been chief of police back in 1970, and Doug White, his brother and former assistant chief of police, met me at the door. They were both part-time detectives now, on their way toward retirement. "Your father was a good man," Doug White said, inquiring about my daddy's health. "Everyone in Oxford remembers him very warmly. A lovely man." Picking up two strapping police officers as they walked me down the stairs, the two elderly gumshoes escorted me into a windowless concrete-block room in the basement of the police station and seated me at a Formica table. Doug White did all the talking. "Tell us about this paper you're writing," he said. I told him I was interested in the murder of Henry Marrow in 1970 and the riots and all of that. He nodded warmly, waiting impatiently for his chance to speak.

"Your father was a good man," he repeated unctuously. "We all just thought the world of him, didn't we?" Four heads nodded. "And we're so proud and pleased that you're in school—that is just wonderful, isn't it?" Nods all around. Then he lowered the boom. "But the thing is, you *can't* write about this. All it will do is stir up bad feelings and cause trouble. Before all that trouble, things were good around here. And things have been good around here for a long time now." He cleared his throat, and the three other men all nodded as if their throats, too, had been cleared. "You can't write about this. No good can come of it." It was clear that White had been working on his speech. "We are glad you're back in Oxford, Tim, we really are. There are a lot of *good* things to write about around here, and we would be glad to help you with anything else. But the thing is, you can't write about *that*. All it is going to do is stir up trouble."

I was only twenty-three, and so green that it did not even occur to me at first that they had brought me down into the basement to intimidate me. Despite my bumbling, cherubic appearance, I played a tough hand of poker. "Well, this is what I came to research and write about," I said. "And this is what I am going to research and write about." For good or ill, I aimed to finish my project, I insisted. "Some of the stuff people are telling me makes the police department look pretty bad," I added. "I would hate to have to write my account without the department getting the chance to present its own point of view. I really don't think it would be fair." This is the hard-boiled, veteran journalist's response—fine, don't tell me your side, and let's just see what you look like in the newspaper after your enemies tell it. How I came up with it is a mystery to me, since I was anything but hard-boiled, and until the day before I had not been a veteran of anything more harrowing than late-night skinny-dipping with waitresses. The policemen did not like my answer one damn bit, either. The men stood up, and White said in a menacing tone, glowering at me, "Tim, I said you *can't* write about this. And I mean that thing." Suddenly I was truly frightened, but I also knew that I was a middle-class white boy, with all the privileges that implied. My daddy was a preacher and my mama was a teacher, as Mrs. Roseanna Allen used to say, and they weren't going to beat me up in the basement of the police station. I picked up my daddy's old briefcase and walked right out the door without saying a word.

Rattled, I went to Julia's old gray-blue Falcon with the mismatched orange fender and scribbled furiously, hands trembling, on a legal pad. I wrote down every word that had been uttered in that basement that I could remember. And then I pulled into the street and began heading for Ben and Joy's farm.

Quickly an imposing blue police van appeared in my rearview mirror. A short-haired, blank-faced white man in an institutional blue shirt hunched over the steering wheel. He roared up to within a couple of inches of my back bumper. I checked my speed, thinking he might pull me over for speeding. I was going twenty-five miles an hour on a side street. Passing the liquor store and the doctor's office, heading into a residential area, I accelerated a little, and he stayed literally almost right on my bumper, glaring at me. It began to occur to me that he had been sent to frighten me, but I brushed the thought aside as paranoia. Just to prove to myself that this was my lurid imagination, I turned directly into a residential neighborhood and took a right, then a loft, then a right, thinking that he would disappear. But the van stayed inches from my bumper. He was playing some kind of game, and if it was supposed to scare me, it was damn sure working.

I took the next left onto College Street, the boulevard of old homes where many of the wealthiest white families lived in Victorian splendor. He wouldn't do anything to me here, I reasoned. But suddenly it looked as if this police van had been welded to my bumper. When I slowed down, the van actually bumped the Falcon hard. I floored it. Heading down College Street, I went faster and faster: forty, fifty, sixty, seventy miles an hour in a thirty-five-mile-an-hour zone. I thought he would probably flash the blue lights and sound the siren, but instead the blue van stayed right against my back bumper.

Racing past the orphanage, I wanted to turn left on Highway 158 at the Three-Way Diner, heading for the farm. But a continuous line of oncoming cars was approaching the intersection, and I was not going to slow down. At the last possible second, an opening in the traffic let me take a hard left turn on two wheels, gas pedal pressed to the floor. Surely I had shaken him, I thought. But when I looked into the rearview mirror, I saw the van careening across traffic and racing up 158. In seconds he was on my tail again.

When we got to Four Corners, up at the old Tidewater Seafood Market, where Henry Marrow had lost his life, I cut the wheel to the right and gunned the Falcon's pathetic little engine as hard as I could. On the one hand, it frightened me that we were heading out of town. On the other hand, I knew Ben Averett was working in his shop, and that he had plenty of firepower to handle one crazed police officer if it came to that. Ben's driveway was less than a mile away, and if this maniac followed me up there, he was likely to be sorry. The van stayed literally inches from my back bumper, and I was going about eighty; the Falcon wouldn't go any faster. I kept wondering—and I still wonder—what I might have discovered about this case that would make this police officer willing to risk his life to scare me away.

The driveway to Ben's farm empties into the paved road in a kind of wide, funnel-shaped gravel turnaround. It was coming up soon on my right, which I knew and the policeman, presumably, did not know. For all he knew I was headed for the Virginia state line, which was not far away, either. He was still welded to my bumper when I suddenly peeled off to the right, running the Falcon headlong into the driveway and pulling the wheel sharply to the right and then back. The car skidded sideways across the gravel, spraying up a cloud of rocks and dust and making a hideous noise, then finally slowing enough that I could gun it across the wooden bridge and up the driveway at axle-cracking speed. Relieved to have made the sliding turn in one piece, I glanced into the rearview mirror. The van was gone. I had lost him. When I drove into the yard, Ben was splitting sweet-gum stumps with a maul axe. I told him what had happened. "You'd better watch your ass," he said quietly.

SEVERAL YEARS LATER, I enrolled in the doctoral program in American history at Duke University, forty miles down the Jefferson Davis Highway from Ben Averett's farm in Oxford. One of the first friends I made was Herman Bennett, a big, dark-skinned fellow, charming and warm, if somewhat stormy and brooding at times, too. Our friendship really blossomed in the summer of 1992, when I was writing my master's thesis and Herman was finishing his dissertation. Several nights a week, after the day's writing was done, we would drink beer, listen to Muddy Waters or Sonny Boy Williamson, and talk mostly about race until daylight chased me home. His father's family was from Wadesboro, North Carolina, but Herman had grown up mostly at army bases in Germany, and this rich, complicated experience of race had given Herman many stories to tell me. I told him many of the stories in this book, and some other ones, too. It was an intimate friendship marked by brutal honesty—though, as we will see, less than I thought—and always wild hilarity. Sometimes it was all I could do to keep from wetting myself during his satiric imitations of the ponderous academics and rigid ideologues that beset us. Our laughter kept us strong, and we both plowed on through our graduate work and celebrated when Herman got a job at the University of North Carolina at Chapel Hill.

When we got to drinking, sometimes we'd sing "When a Man Loves a Woman," made famous by Percy Sledge. So when I heard that the great soul singer was playing at a bar not too distant, of course I called Herman. He said, "I'm there. Pick me up on your way through town."

As I pulled up at his house, Herman walked out with Rhonda Lee, who had just arrived from Canada to start graduate school. Rhonda was a striking woman, over six feet tall with lovely fair skin, long brown hair, and legs that seemed to begin somewhere above my head. As usual in those days, she was not dressed to deflect male attention. We were quite a sight: Rhonda looking like the beauty queen from Planet Amazon, me resembling a tree stump in bib overalls, Herman tall and handsome with his dreadlocks and broad shoulders. Herman and I regaled our new Canadian friend with Southern stories, one or two of which may have had some basis in fact, as we rolled up the highway to Allen's Country Nightlife, a roadhouse on the highway just north of Greensboro, some seventy miles due west of Oxford.

At the door of the club, I asked the cashier if we could pay for our tickets with my credit card. As a blood relative of the Gator, I was concerned, naturally, that we'd have plenty of cash for whiskey and beer. When a Southern feller says "whiskey," of course, he means bourbon, but a Canadian generally means Scotch. And Herman usually drank beer in those days. So we were waiting for our tickets and chuckling about the fact that a round of drinks for the three of us was the name of a famous blues song: "One Bourbon, One Scotch, and One Beer." But our laughter was interrupted when a short, red-faced man with a cigarette hanging out of his mouth walked briskly from inside the bar and stood in the doorway. "We don't allow blacks in the club," he said. His name, I learned later, was Allen Willetts.

The words would not fit into my brain. "What?"

Willetts said it again. "We don't allow blacks in the club. You and your lady friend can come in if you want to, but we don't allow blacks in the club."

Herman was standing right behind me, but the club owner would not look at him. Instead, Willetts kept his eyes fixed squarely on me. "We don't allow blacks in the club," he repeated. I could see several large white men moving around in the shadows behind him, watching what was happening. The blood rushed to my face and I could feel my fists clinching at my sides. "Have you met Mr. Sledge?" I asked him.

"We make an exception for the entertainers," the man said. "But we don't allow black customers in the club."

"That is illegal," I told Willetts. "That is a violation of federal law." Apparently our distinguished colleague had not yet heard about the Civil Rights Act of 1964.

"This is a private club," Willetts snarled, taking a last deep drag on his cigarette butt and throwing it past me. "You join at the door. And since it is a private club, we have the right to determine the membership."

"You can't do that," I replied. "That is definitely illegal. And it ain't right, either." All the anger that had accumulated in my heart since I was a little boy in Oxford pulsed through my body all at once. The blood pounded in my temples, my chest swelled with rage, and all I could think about was knocking a hole in this man's head. I wanted to kill him for talking that way in front of Herman. I realized, too, that Herman was one of the few people I knew who might have a worse temper than I did. I had a bad feeling that this seedy nightclub owner was about to get double-Gatored. I did not want that to happen, but I damn sure did not see how we were going to stop it. This could be bad. I was too angry to back off, and I knew that behind my rage was the absolute determination not to fail Herman somehow.

"We *can* remove you," the club owner said, glaring at me. "We have the right to remove you from the premises if you refuse to leave." I glared right back.

I turned around to check with Herman, and sure enough his face looked like a stone wall, but somewhere in his eyes I saw murder. "I want to kill these motherfuckers," I muttered. "What are we going to do?"

"What about Rhonda?" he asked. We both noticed that she was wearing heels, not exactly running shoes, and we both thought about the fact that she had been in the United States for only a few days, and probably had no idea where we were. If we got into a brawl here, she was going to have quite a bad night, at the very least. As Herman and I looked into each other's eyes in hopeless ferocity, he lifted his chin, signaling behind me. When I turned to look, I saw three or four big white guys coming around from behind the bar, and the first one had a baseball bat. This was not the World Series, and nobody had a glove or a ball. And sure enough, Rhonda couldn't run in those shoes worth a damn.

I pulled the rusty old Toyota out of the parking lot and gunned it down the highway, sputtering profanity and pondering revenge. As I veered off the road at the first rest stop, Herman and I had both already decided, independently of each other, to burn the place down. Anything that happened to that sorry bastard at the nightclub now, he had bought and paid for, I figured. We could buy a couple of gallons of milk, pour it out, and fill the jugs with gasoline. Then again, four out of the five arsonists I had interviewed in recent years had recommended empty quarts of Miller High Life. Herman was the first to point out that the club was full of people who had nothing to do with what had happened. Some of them could be hurt if we fire-bombed the place. "After hours," I said. "We could wait until late, after everybody's gone."

"What if the owner's brother-in-law passed out drunk and they left him to sleep it off in the office?" Herman said. "We could end up killing somebody we don't even know." We were not going to burn the joint. I realize now that Herman might have saved me from going to the penitentiary or the graveyard; thank God he didn't say we had to go back and kill the sumbitch, or somebody—probably me— would have ended up dead. But I had to do *something*. I walked over to the pay phone and dialed quickly. "Who did you call?" Herman asked when I got back.

"The police," I said.

"Did you tell them they kicked us out?" Herman asked.

"No, I told them that some crazy man had planted a bomb under Allen's Country Nightlife and that it would go off in twenty minutes." We jumped back in the car and got out of there in a hurry, just in case they were tracing the call and dispatching a squad car to the phone booth.

I was reeling with rage and adrenaline, and Herman was angry and hurt. Rhonda was furious, too, and we all spewed venom steadily for several miles. "I'm sorry," I said.

"It's not your fault," he replied.

"I know, but I am just sorry you had to go through that."

"Hey, I'm sorry any of us had to go through it," said Herman.

And then we went back at it again, cursing the club owner's extended family tree and pondering elaborate modes of revenge. But soon it became clear that what all three of us needed was love and comfort from one another. I pulled over at a little rural convenience store, not unlike the one where Henry Marrow had died. We bought a six-pack of tall ones, and Herman and I stopped by the men's room. There were two urinals side by side on the plywood wall, and carved right between them were the letters KKK and a racist joke that does not bear repeating. When we got back to the car, we passed around one of the beers as if it were communion wine, downed it in seconds, and had a little group hug in the parking lot. Herman and I didn't tell Rhonda about the men's room.

At that point, Herman and I had been talking about race, violence, politics, sexuality, and all sorts of personal things nearly nonstop for almost a year. Our friendship was intimate and easygoing, and I thought we knew each other very well. We were capable of analyzing and then laughing about matters that most people would not even dare to bring up, especially in an interracial context. In those days, we were blood on blood, mafia, and there was nothing I would not have told Herman. I already knew that Herman's father had been a sergeant in the U.S. Army, stationed in Germany, when he'd met Herman's mother. And I was aware that his mother was white. Herman had sketched their family history for me. When the young family had moved back to the United States in the early 1960s, it had not been safe for his parents to even visit Wadesboro as a mixed-race couple. When they had gone to see Herman's father's family, his mother had had to crouch in the back seat of the car, covered with a blanket. They had decided to move to a city "up North," where presumably things would be different. Milwaukee, however, had not treated them any better, so they had moved back to Germany. But nothing could have prepared me for what Herman said next: "They killed my sister."

"What?" I stammered.

"They killed my sister." His voice quavered, and when I glanced over at him from behind the wheel of the car, tears were streaming down Herman's face. "In Milwaukee," he sobbed. "That's why we left the country. I had a little sister."

Herman was six years old and his sister was only an infant. But the racial struggle in the North in the early 1960s was nearly as bitter as the struggles across the South—and the central issue was housing. Soon after they moved into what someone obviously considered the wrong neighborhood in Milwaukee, people who objected to their family's racial makeup threw a firebomb into the window of their home, where the Bennett children were sleeping. His baby sister perished in the flames, but Herman escaped.

No one was ever charged in the crime, and the trauma and loss resonated at depths of agony that lingered in bitter memories and in deep family silences that cannot be explored here. Suffice it to say that this act of murderous terrorism was why Herman did not grow up in America. Exiled from the country whose uniform he continued to wear, Herman's brokenhearted father moved the family back to Germany. The land that had produced Hitler seemed safer for a mixed-race American family than the nation that had lifted up Martin Luther King Jr. Herman grew up there on the army base, an American but not an American, haunted by the unspoken memory of this ghastly racial nightmare. And until we'd had this bizarre 1990s Jim Crow experience, Herman had never said one word to me about the murder that had driven his family from their homeland.

I don't quite remember what we said after Herman dropped his bombshell of memory and grief. But I drove us straight to my house, pulled down a bottle of bourbon, fried a chicken, made sweet-potato biscuits and sweet iced tea. We huddled around the kitchen table and listened to blues, gospel, and old soul music. After a while, we even played Percy Sledge's "When a Man Loves a Woman," and sang it with improvised new lyrics: "When a Man Loves a Negro," "When the Klan Loves a Nightclub," stuff like that. At some point, when the camaraderie and the whiskey began to take full effect, Herman looked at me and said, "You ain't nothing but a damn redneck. You know that, don't you?"

"Don't make me cut you," I replied. And we hugged each other tight and cried a little bit. What occurred to me then and still strikes me now is how much of the painful past we have yet to confront, even when we love one another and think that we know one another. So much of what agonizes and divides us remains unacknowledged. Even more of it simply fades into oblivion.

There it should stay, many people seem to think—why dredge this stuff up? Why linger on the past, which we cannot change? We must move toward a brighter future and leave all that horror behind. It's true that we must make a new world. But we can't make it out of whole cloth. We have to weave the future from the fabric of the past, from the patterns of aspiration and belonging—and broken dreams and anguished rejections—that have made us. What the advocates of our dangerous and deepening social amnesia don't understand is how deeply the past holds the future in its grip—even, and perhaps especially, when it remains unacknowledged. We are runaway slaves from our own past, and only by turning to face the hounds can we find our freedom beyond them.

And that was why I had to go back to Oxford and write this history. When I came back to do more interviews in order to complete my master's thesis, the ice pick in my pocket had been replaced by what Colonel Stone Johnson in Birmingham had taught me to call a "nonviolent .38 police special." But nobody bothered me, and people seemed a little more willing to talk, too. Maybe the passing years had seen the old guard disappear. Watkins, for example, had been the victim of a legislative political coup that toppled the Ramsey machine and took away most of his power. In any case, I never felt threatened again, except by the remarkable and sometimes uncomfortable history that Eddie McCoy taught me.

I thumbed to James Edward McCoy's name in the telephone book because he was the head of the Granville County chapter of the organization Robert Teel knew as the "N-double-C-A-P." Like Billy Watkins, he readily agreed over the telephone to talk to me. But I had no idea who I had actually called. I knew that McCoy was a prominent local black businessman. He had been the first African American elected to office in Granville County in the mid-1970s. In 1988, I knew, McCoy had been the county campaign manager for Jesse Jackson's bid for the Democratic presidential nomination, and Jackson had taken the county, winning almost the entire black vote and a surprising number of white ballots. I had originally gotten McCoy's name from the state NAACP office, whose secretary had said he was president of the Oxford chapter. But the man I called on the telephone was a much more impressive and complicated figure than the average local NAACP official.

At first, Eddie was exactly what I would have expected, a well-dressed and friendly African American businessman, a little more easygoing and funny than the average fellow, but with a very serious side that would appear suddenly. We had some laughs and he shared some local political history, and I told him something about our family's story. He remembered my father only vaguely. "I wasn't much interested in white liberals in those days," he laughed. "Especially a damn preacher."

After a couple of visits, one day he called and asked me to drop by his office. When I walked in the door, McCoy said he had some things to tell me, and that I needed to talk to some other people, too. "I was in the movement and all," he said, "but I had just got back from the Dominican Republic. I was in the army, and we invaded the Dominican Republic back in 1965. When I came out, I didn't want to take any shit off white people anymore. And all these brothers on the block out here, they was just back from Vietnam, a lot of them, and we weren't into that Martin Luther King shit."

"So *you* burned the warehouses?" I asked him.

"No, but I did a lot of other stuff," he laughed. "I was in the movement, and not with the nice little boys and girls. I don't know how much of it I want to talk about. But I know you're good people, and I can take you to some people you need to talk to. You can't get this history out of a book. You can't be telling shit that people don't want you to tell, though." I nodded. "We have to be clear on that," McCoy said flatly. "But you can't write about this shit without talking to the people who did it. You have to understand, in them days I was a street guy, and these guys are mostly Vietnam veterans, mostly still on the street, and we got to take care of them. But they'll talk to you if I go with you. Bring your tape recorder."

And then we rode from house to house, from McDonald's to the Three-Way Diner, from dilapidated rural farmhouses to housing-project apartments, from automotive repair shops to drug dealers' houses, meeting the black men he called "my boys." Everywhere we went, Eddie used more or less the same rap, which I paraphrase here: "Hey, brotherman, how you doin'? Look, man, I want you to meet my man Tim here. He's working with me on this book thing, man, you know, about all that stuff we did back in 1970 on the Teel thing. I want you to help us out, blood, just tell Tim about that night out at Peanut's place and how y'all did up the warehouse and shit." Then, the ice broken for me, we would go in and sit and I would get a seminar in black history that went beyond anything I could ever have learned at the university. And thus Eddie McCoy became one of my most important teachers. Since the late 1970s, he had been a very active historian and was collecting oral histories in Granville County himself, focusing on the emergence of black educational institutions after the fall of slavery. I gave him some books to read. But he gave me back my hometown. With his help, I could keep the promise that I had once made to Thad Stem—that someday I would write that story from my own little postage stamp of soil.

MONTHS LATER, MY father drove me up the Jefferson Davis Highway to Oxford, the two-hundred-page manuscript on my lap. Bernice Johnson Reagon's advice to "go back to the last place where you knew who you were, and what you were doing, and start from there" had helped work a kind of transformation in my heart. But before I went any further, I had to finish that master's thesis—which would later provide the research for this book—and leave it for the people of Oxford. Now, at least, there was an honest accounting alongside the official story about "voluntary desegregation." Going back and collecting my own version of events had been a milestone in the process of my own healing. Turning to face the past meant that perhaps I could set the record straight, be free of it, and move forward. Placing the manuscript in the public library meant that other people in town could at least start to undertake that same process. Daddy pulled his blue Volkswagen Jetta around behind the public library, in the shadow of the relocated Confederate monument and a large magnolia tree. "I think I will just stay here with the old soldier and smell the magnolia blossoms," he laughed.

When I got inside the library, I walked past a huge oil painting of Thad Stem, who had died a few years earlier; he was now officially commemorated by a number of people who had refused to even speak to him in life. Behind the counter, I recognized the older white woman who'd long ago tried to prevent my mother from reading a novel by a black woman. But things had changed. The library now welcomed and even employed African Americans. And so I also saw the gracious face of Helen Amis, a lovely and kindly black woman who had been active in the freedom movement. I had called to let her know I was coming, and she smiled as I held out the manuscript. "Do give my best regards to your father," she said quietly, taking the stack of paper from my hand.

BLOOD DONE SIGN MY NAME

LIKE BLACK SOUTHERNERS in the segregated South where he had grown up, Daddy rode through Dixie in the back of the bus, but the mark of subordination had become a place of honor. In 2001, we took forty college students on a two-week bus trip through the South, visiting battlefields of the African American freedom struggle and meeting the local people who had overthrown old Jim Crow. Though I was supposed to be a teacher, the most eloquent thing I was able to share with the students was my daddy, whose massive frame filled the rear bench of the bus from Highlander Folk School in Tennessee to the Sixteenth Street Baptist Church in Birmingham.

At seventy-one, Daddy exuded wisdom, grace, and an openness to the things of the Spirit. In Hattiesburg, Mississippi, Daddy went to the grave of Vernon Dahmer, murdered by Klan terrorists in 1966, with Dahmer's widow and son and prayed with them. In Birmingham, he seemed to have hugged every single member of Body of Christ Deliverance Ministry, where we met Autherine Lucy, Colonel Stone Johnson, and many of the foot soldiers of the Alabama Christian Movement for Human Rights. From Beale Street in Memphis to Bourbon Street in New Orleans, he deeply touched the lives of those students. They laughingly took to calling his perch "the confessional," because one by one most of them slipped to the back of the bus to talk to him about their aspirations and fears. I would hear the soft, rich timbre of his deep voice from time to time, and glance back to see him laying a gentle hand across the shoulder of a student weeping or laughing.

Black and white together, we rolled through Dixie, singing the songs of the movement and challenging ourselves to confront the deeper truths of American history. We held classes on the bus, on city sidewalks, in hotel lobbies, and at crowded soul food restaurants. Day after day, we met local movement organizers, toured slave markets and sugar plantations, heard great gospel singers, and talked with people whose memories of the movement made history walk and talk. Night after night, we huddled in hotel rooms and explored our deepest feelings about the meaning of race in America. Although age tends to narrow some people's focus, I could not help but notice my father's broadened outlook and ease of manner. Daddy instructed all of us by the quiet grace with which he approached the people we met and the unblinking courage with which he confronted the painful history that we uncovered along the way.

My mother, of course, had been the teacher in the family, and I liked to think of myself as following in her footsteps. She was the truth teller, too. Unlike my father, my mother was not a romantic liberal, looking for some kind of redemptive interpretation of a tragic past. With her, you knew you were getting the straight stuff; the blind didn't see and the lame didn't walk and what was dead stayed that way, to paraphrase Flannery O'Connor. In some respects, my work as a historian drew upon the strengths I inherited straight from my mother—her ability to confront uncomfortable truths and her eye for the telling contradiction, for example. I ain't no damn preacher, I had told myself, I am a historian. But as I'd learned my new trade at a deeper level, I'd discovered that I had not escaped the call to ministry as cleanly as I might have thought. I had not only followed my mother into the classroom but my father into the pulpit, never mind that I preached on weekdays instead of Sundays. There I was, pacing the lecture hall with chalk dust on my pants, day after day. Even if I'd had to move to a foreign country—and Wisconsin *is* a foreign country—I felt at peace with the heritage that had been both a blessing and a burden.

This mixed blessing was never so clear as on that morning in New Orleans when our bus took us up the River Road to Destrehan Plantation in a driving rain. Those of us who had helped plan the trip knew this would be a hard visit. We had selected this place on purpose, knowing that our students would learn things here that were impossible to convey any other way.

Thousands of Africans and their descendants had poured out their lifeblood at Destrehan to make the cane planters some of the wealthiest men of their day. In 1811, slaves from Destrehan and other nearby plantations rose up by the hundreds and marched down the River Road toward New Orleans, battle flags snapping in the breeze. Improvised drums banged out what one historian called their "suicidal quest for freedom that belied many white planters' basic assumptions that their slaves were passive, docile laborers who would never challenge white authority." United States Army troops confronted the slave army on the second day of their trek and slaughtered sixty-six of them. The clash was more butchery than battle; the white soldiers would turn captured black men loose one by one and shoot them for sport as they fled. The slaveholders tried the rest at Destrehan Plantation, where a handpicked jury of planters sentenced most of them to death. Roughly 150 were either killed on the River Road or hanged in front of their fellow slaves. "The heads of the executed shall be cut off and placed atop a pole," the judge ruled. Months later, the levee along the River Road remained "ornamented with poles," said one newspaper, "on which are placed numbers of the heads of these unfortunate wretches."

Though my students and I had studied the grisly history of this place, nothing could have prepared us for what we found as we stepped off the bus beneath the spreading live oaks with their canopy of Spanish moss. Private investors had turned the plantation house, with its enormous columns and three-foot-thick brick foundations, into a monument to what one tour company's brochure called "the good old days" of the antebellum South. Young women in swirling skirts and sun bonnets greeted us at the door. The presence of a mixed-race group made them visibly uneasy. The tour included virtually no mention of slaves or slavery, let alone the 1811 revolt. A black handyman working outside told some of the students that the management had recently fired a young tour guide who'd insisted on talking about slavery. "Our guide's presentation was about prayer schools, parlors, ladies' portraits on the wall, tall ceilings, hand-carved banisters," one of the students wrote in his journal. "It was surreal."

After a few minutes, I looked out a window and saw one of the black students on her knees in front of the levee, her forehead pressed against the ground, pounding the grass with her outstretched palms. Many of us, especially the African American students, could not hold back tears of frustration and sorrow. It was hard for me, too, but I had seen this kind of thing before. I made a couple of polite attempts to get our guide to talk about the lives of the people who had worked on the plantation, but she seemed to panic at the questions. Part of me wanted to protest. But as a Southerner myself, I knew that a busload of college students from Wisconsin would have a hard time saying anything without being dismissed as ignorant, meddlesome Yankees. Before the tour ended, about half of the students were sitting in groups of two or three under the trees, many of them crying. I tried to stop Rhea Lathan, an African American student, as she headed down the walkway toward the bus. She waved me off and stomped past me, muttering, "There are bodies hanging all over these trees."

By the time we filed slowly back onto the bus, the whole group was emotionally devastated. I saw Daddy in the back of the bus talking with a teary-eyed Rhea. And then the broad-shouldered preacher stood up in the aisle and said to the silent busload of students, "Let us pray." Every head on the bus, atheist, agnostic, Christian, Jew, and Muslim bowed in unison. "Oh, Lord," he intoned, "we pray your blessing upon all those who lived and loved and labored in this place; for those who poured out their gifts on land that could never be their own; for women who birthed babies unattended; for children whose genius went unacknowledged; for all your children who cut cane and sweated in the hot sun, and knew in their bones there was a better place." I could feel the balm of his words spreading through the rows of angry and emotional people. "And we ask your peace and your healing for those on this bus whose cheeks burn with tears and whose eyes have been seared by sights that hurt them deeply," he continued. "We ask that these pains of love might bring a harder wisdom."

But Daddy was not going to leave us on the high horse of moral superiority. Before the tears could dry, he challenged us to find that harder wisdom. "And we ask your help, Lord," Daddy continued, lifting his thick hands, "that we not become prejudiced against those who are prejudiced, or whose prejudices may not be our own." Here it came. "For we acknowledge and confess to you that we, too, like the men who once owned Destrehan Plantation, have been tempted to love things and use people, when you have called us to love people and use things. We ask your forgiveness for our complicity in these evils, and in the evils of our own time, and pray your healing for our hearts. Thank you for the love that binds us one to another, and to our homes and families, and to you." I could tell that the students on that bus, who rarely find such clarity in their college classes or campus coalitions, were astonished and grateful. But this harder wisdom was less surprising to me, having once read a letter of protest signed "A fellow sinner, Vernon Tyson."

Those words were not false humility; as my father well knew, Tyson blood was anything but a straight ticket to sainthood. After all, our family had literally grown up in the same soil that had produced Robert Teel, and the self-willed spirit of violence and the deeply ingrained white supremacy that drove Teel was not foreign to our family. The passionate intensity that the Tyson brothers carried into the pulpit on Sunday mornings was not entirely separate from the violent carnality that some of their kinfolks displayed on Saturday nights. My father, the most gentle and loving man I have ever known, could roar into a room like a grizzly bear and make his children wonder, at least for a moment, whether they would survive. All of his brothers were tenderhearted, comical, and expansive, and devoted to the love of Jesus. But one of the reasons I liked Muhammad Ali so much as a boy was probably because he reminded me of my uncles, bragging and strutting in a sweet way that was also faintly dangerous.

More than one of the Tyson boys had been a high-style sinner in his day; a sexual history of the family would not be the stuff of Sunday school literature, though it might well involve Sunday school teachers. But the faith was there, even when they stumbled, and they worked hard to do better, even when they fell. The Tysons had broken some of the shackles of fundamentalism and white supremacy and they had all had gotten some education. More importantly, the family nurtured a tender and redemptive vision that would never quite let them forget that everyone, including Robert Teel, is a child of God. It cannot be denied, however, that the Tysons harbored a spirit that rebelled not only against an unjust social order but sometimes against their own best lights, too. Any one of the Tysons—not just the Gator—was capable of the kind of murderous rage that killed Henry Marrow.

In that sense, like the story of the Gator, this book is really a story of the blues and a story of the gospel. Both the blues and the gospel started as Southern things but speak to the whole human dilemma. The blues are about looking a painful history straight in the eye; the gospel is about coming together as a community of faith in order to rise beyond that anguish. If anyone wonders why a white boy from eastern North Carolina teaches black history in Wisconsin, the timeless wisdom of the blues has one answer. Ralph Ellison expressed the central meaning of the blues better than anyone. "The blues is an impulse to keep the painful details and episodes of a brutal experience alive in one's aching consciousness," Ellison wrote, "to finger its jagged grain, and to transcend it, not by the consolation of philosophy but by squeezing from it a near-tragic, near-comic lyricism. As a form, the blues is an autobiographical chronicle of personal catastrophe expressed lyrically." In that sense, this book is a kind of blues expression that urges us to confront our rage, contradictions, and failures and the painful history of race in America. As in that history, there is no clean place in this story where anyone can sit down and congratulate themselves. My family has sometimes tried, for reasons mixed and sometimes unclear, to help those who wanted a new world to be born. But beyond the bitter legacies of slavery and white supremacy, when we look into the mirror, no matter our color, none of us can forget that the Gator lurks in there somewhere, staring back at us. Like Thad Stem used to say, we not only *have* problems, we *are* problems.

As a nation and as individual human beings, we would rather hear the gospel stories of Mrs. Roseanna Allen and Miss Amy Womble's witness than the blues stories of murder, retribution, and injustice that mark our actual history. The story of how my daddy and Miss Amy and Dr. Proctor transformed our church is true, of course, and I consider myself fortunate to know it firsthand. All that the triumph of goodness required was a combination of the leading African American educator and preacher of his generation, a local white minister with deep roots in a place he knew in his bones, and the timely intervention of a prophetic hometown saint who happened to have been a first-grade teacher to most of the other people in the story. This makes for good narrative, but it is not a reliable recipe for social transformation. Unjust social orders do not fall merely by appeals to the consciences of the oppressor, though such appeals may be an important element; history teaches us that they fall because a large enough number of people organize a movement powerful enough to push them down. Rarely do such revolutions emerge in a neat and morally pristine process. Unfortunately, Miss Amy's witness is a far less normal American story than that of Henry Marrow's murder and the conflagration it caused in Oxford the summer I turned eleven.

Even so, Miss Amy's witness is a perfect match for the only history of the civil rights movement that most Americans willingly remember. In this story and in popular memory, a respectable and eloquent black preacher came to the pulpit to confront white America. A handful of us welcomed him, most of us feared him, and some of us hated him. But when this elegant man of the cloth arrived, he was not so threatening after all. Instead, his sonorous voice evoked our best selves and reminded us just how *good* we really were. Prodded by the simple sense of decency we learned as children, we listened nervously as the black minister promised to make the rough places smooth and the crooked places straight, and asked only our tolerance.

Like Dr. Proctor, the black preacher then went away and bothered us no more, leaving us congratulating ourselves for a change of heart that need not change our ways or our world. And we cherish the conventional story of Dr. King and nonviolence, in fact, precisely *because* that narrative demands so little of us. The problem is not *that* we cherish the story, exactly, nor is the story itself entirely false. Miss Amy's witness is true, and many of the things we admire about Dr. King are factual. The problem is *why* we cherish that kind of story: because we want to transcend our history without actually confronting it.

We cannot address the place we find ourselves because we will not acknowledge the road that brought us here. Our failure to confront the historical truth about how African Americans finally won their freedom presents a major obstacle to genuine racial reconciliation. In some instances, white people rose to the call of conscience, though only a handful followed their convictions into the streets. More often, what grabbed white America's attention was the chaos in those streets and the threat of race war. The federal government intervened in domestic racial politics, in the end, because segregation had become a threat to American foreign policy and domestic stability. Most whites—and many middle-class blacks—recoiled in fear of these changes and huddled in the suburbs of their own indifference. The civil rights movement knocked down the formal and legal barriers to equal citizenship, but failed to give most African Americans real power in this society.

In the intervening years, the nation has comforted itself by sanitizing the civil rights movement, commemorating it as a civic celebration that no one ever opposed. The enemies of the struggle ascended to national power and sought to diminish its memory, often by grinding off its rough edges and blunting its enduring critique of a dehumanizing economic and political system. The self-congratulatory popular account insists that Dr. King called on the nation to fully accept its own creed, and the walls came a-tumbling down. This conventional narrative is soothing, moving, and politically acceptable, and has only the disadvantage of bearing no resemblance to what actually happened.

The work we face is to transcend our history and move toward higher ground. To find that higher ground, we must recognize, as Dr. King tried to teach us, that we are "caught up in an inescapable network of mutuality, tied in a single garment of destiny." Dr. King's vision, like the gospel and the blues, came from the South but belongs to the ages. The chorus of the song that gave this book its name traces that connection of blues realism to gospel transcendence: *Ain't you glad, ain't you glad, that the blood done sign my name?*

"The Blood Done Sign My Name," which I first heard sung as a blues song, started out as a slave spiritual. After the fall of the Confederacy, it emerged as a paradoxical blues lament, sung by Huddie Ledbetter (Leadbelly) from a Mississippi prison cell and by his counterparts across the black South. In the 1930s, as black hopes for a new America began to rise, "The Blood Done Sign My Name" evolved into a gospel song. My favorite version of it, recorded in the late 1940s by the Radio Four, echoes the sorrowful roots of the blues and elevates the transcendent spirit of gospel, but listen closely and you can hear Chuck Berry rocking down the line. My own hopes for this country have taken a similar trajectory, moving from deep blues through gospel reconciliation and on into the full-throttle ebullience of rock and roll. And yet my ascendant spirits, like the future of our country, depend upon an honest confrontation with our own history.

That history reveals the blood that has signed every one of our names. The sacrifice has already been made, in the bottoms of slave ships, in the portals of Ellis Island, in the tobacco fields of North Carolina and the sweatshops of New York City. The question remains whether or not we can transfigure our broken pasts into a future filled with common possibility.

And so we turn to history not to wallow in a fruitless nostalgia of pain but to redeem a democratic promise that is rooted in the living ingredients of our own lives. America owes a debt that no one can pay, and yet it probably remains what Lincoln called "the last, best hope" of human freedom. As the spirit of empire stalks the land, the bitter irony of that possibility should not be lost on anyone. While it remains possible that our unacknowledged pasts will rise up and put an end to us, I believe that we can lay these ghosts to rest someday, provided that we turn and face them. I continue to believe, with James Baldwin, that if we do not falter, we "may be able, handful that we are, to end the racial nightmare, and achieve our country, and change the history of the world."

I believe in this possibility because as I have continued to sift the evidence and search for the meaning of a senseless death in my hometown, I found something much larger. It may not be an easy, add-water-and-stir redemption, but it opens a history in which we can all recognize the faces of flawed, well-meaning people like ourselves. Black Southerners, rooted in long-standing traditions that spoke to the best and confronted the worst in our common humanity, toppled the American racial caste system. The struggle in the South, like the struggles in Milwaukee, Chicago, Newark, Philadelphia, New York, and your own hometown, did not take place in some ethereal realm, removed from the sins of the past, but in the fallen world, among the imperfect people who had inherited a deeply flawed history. Everyone in this struggle, adversaries and advocates alike, grew up steeped in a poisonous white supremacy that distorted their understandings of history and one another. That history is not distant. Many of those who marched with Dr. King in Alabama and started the movement in Oxford were the grandchildren of slaves. The boy who told me "Daddy and Roger and 'em shot 'em a *nigger*" is barely middle-aged. And the enduring chasm of race is still with us, in some ways wider than ever.

"The past is never dead," William Faulkner reminds us; "it isn't even past." White supremacy remains lethal, though most of its victims die more quietly than Henry Marrow. It shoots down black youngsters who learn from the images of themselves on BET, CBS, and FOX that their lives are worthless enough to be poured out in the crack wars. Almost half of all African American children grow up in poverty in a deindustrialized urban wasteland. Blacks fall behind whites, sociologist Glenn Loury observes, in almost every observable measure of well-being: "wages, unemployment rates, income and wealth levels, ability test scores, prison enrollment and crime victimization rates, health and mortality statistics." The majority of Americans reject social programs that could help close the enduring chasm of race, believing *it is not our history, but their genes.* The ancient lie of white supremacy lurks in the unconscious assumptions of most whites and many blacks, who believe, deep down, that *something is wrong with black people.* Many people who care are mired in guilt, as if the agonies of history could be undone by angst. The kinds of employment, education, and infrastructure initiatives that it would take to heal the enduring scars of slavery's legacy are off today's political chart. It remains easier for our leaders to apologize for the past than to address its lingering impact in our society. We can wring our hands over the horrors of slavery but cannot imagine an employment program for our cities.

And yet the freedom struggle persists, even though it has not prevailed, in its battle against what Dr. King called the "thingification" of human beings. The traditions that gave us the movement will always be there for us to call upon, but we cannot wait until the saints come marching in; they never have, and they never will, at least not on this side of the river Jordan. But we must not forget, and I cannot forget. "The struggle of humanity against power," Milan Kundera once wrote, "is the struggle of memory against forgetting." The tragic murder of Henry Marrow—and the assassination of Dr. King and the loss of all those whom the slave poets called "the many thousands gone"—cannot be erased. But that blood, too, has the power to redeem our history. We only have to name it, and heed the call of justice that still waits for an answer. Like the nameless slave poets who wrote the spirituals, we must look our brutal history in the eye and still find a way to transcend that history together. I am standing here until the Lord takes me somewhere else, because the blood done sign my name.

Author's Note

STORIES CAN HAVE SHARP EDGES. If you don't believe it, read the Bible. Cain's people wish someone had told *his* side of the story: Abel had it coming. The Chamber of Commerce in the Sodom-Gomorrah Greater Metropolitan Area would like to point out that much has changed since the old days, when a handful of misfits and outsiders marred the reputation of their fine community. Several persons in the Scriptural list of who-begat-whom still don't see why the New Testament historian found it necessary to use their real names.

Though tempted to change a few names to protect the guilty, principally, the wholly innocent in this story being hard to find, I have used real names in this book. The sole exception is one childhood friend, whom I no longer know but remember fondly, and do not wish to embarrass here without cause. I also have altered the identity of one distant relative, whose daughter pleaded that his grandchildren needn't know the historically unimportant details of his misdeeds, which are sufficiently distinctive that most of the family will recognize him anyway. Several informants wished to remain anonymous, an understandable preference, given the various felonies involved, and I have respected their requests.

This book is both memoir and history. I have hewn to the rules of evidence and argument that I learned in the doctoral program in the Department of History at Duke University. I first told the story in a master's thesis submitted at Duke in 1990, *Burning for Freedom: White Terror and Black Power in Oxford, North Carolina*, and available at the Richard H. Thornton Library in Oxford, North Carolina. Historians may wish to consult the thesis for an exhaustive, if not exhausting, degree of documentation.

There are at least two crucial things missing from that novice's work of scholarship, however. First, someone in Oxford went to the library and tore out the pages where I narrate the killing of Henry Marrow, presumably to prevent other people from reading them. I could have replaced them, of course, but I have chosen not to do so. Those missing pages make my central point more clearly, in some respects, than their contents ever could have. Our hidden history of race has yet to be fully told, and we persist in hiding from much of what we know.

The second critical gap in the master's thesis reflects my own limitations; in the entire thesis, all two hundred pages and more, the reader never learns that I lived in Oxford, that I knew many of the people in the story when I was a boy, or that my family was marginally, though intensely, involved in these events. I was trying to write an objective history, grounded in scholarly research, and did not wish to undermine my empirical plodding in favor of anything more personally revealing. That approach has its place. In the years since then, I have published a number of scholarly works of history, and read many others. As I have pondered the past more deeply, however, I have come to see that my master's thesis, despite its research and documentation, constitutes a species of lie; that is, I failed to share my heart and my experiences with the reader, and hid behind my footnotes.

This account bares not only my labors as a scholar but also my life as a human being. It explores what happened in Oxford, North Carolina, and what happened in my own soul. I am under no impression that my memories reflect the indisputable facts of the matter, though I believe them to be true; still, I have treated them with the same scrutiny as other historical sources, and perhaps more. I have attempted to verify them carefully, as I do with other sources, by checking against other documentary accounts and other people's recollections.

Generally speaking, I have used quotation marks only when I could verify a quote, in the manner of historians. But I have sometimes accepted a trusted source's account of a conversation to which I have no other source. This has two or three times led me to use a quote that I would have considered hearsay in my role as an academic historian.

I have done my best to write a book that honors both my historical training and the Southern storytelling tradition of wayward preachers and saintly teachers from whom I have sprung and to whom I remain accountable. In my heart, I believe that these things work together, each strengthening the other, and that in the end I have come much closer to the truth than I did when I was merely piling up scholarly citations. Historians who wish to follow my trail will find it easy to trace my sources in the bibliographical notes at the end of the book. I have also used these appendices as a way of acknowledging my extensive debts to other scholars.

Love and work have taught me that Eudora Welty was right that "people are mostly layers of violence and tenderness wrapped like bulbs, and it is difficult to say what makes them onions or hyacinths." If some of the people in these pages have left a bitter taste in my mouth, others have brought fragrant blossoms season after season. And who wants to live without onions? Anyone intent on moral clarity might want to find another book and, in fact, might not want to go anywhere near the enduring chasm of race in the United States. Indeed, they might wish to find another planet. But if, as Robert Frost said, earth's the right place for love, those of us who believe in love and freedom cannot look away.

The bloody, tangled history that taints and confounds all of us could have been much better if human beings had acted differently, and it could have been far worse, too. It may yet be unspeakably worse; no one should underestimate the venom of ancient wrongs. But I remain stitched to the labors of redemption and to what Charles Chesnutt, another storyteller from North Carolina, called "the shining thread of hope" that permitted him, over a century ago, to close his own story of white supremacy, racial murder, and unresolved injustice: "There's time enough, but none to spare."

Timothy B. Tyson
Madison, Wisconsin

Notes on Sources

My most important sources, aside from our family's memories and diaries, are the criminal court records from the Granville County courthouse and the Francis B. Hays Collection at the Richard H. Thornton Library, both in Oxford, North Carolina; the National Association for the Advancement of Colored People Papers at the Library of Congress in Washington; the Governor J. Melville Broughton Papers, the Governor R. Gregg Cherry Papers, the Governor Kerr Scott Papers, the Governor Terry Sanford Papers, and the Governor Robert Scott Papers, all at the North Carolina Division of Archives and History in Raleigh; the James Edward McCoy Papers and the Jonathan Daniels Papers at the Southern Historical Collection in Wilson Library at the University of North Carolina at Chapel Hill; the James William Cole Papers at the East Carolina Manuscript Collection at the J. Y. Joyner Library at East Carolina University in Greenville; the Raleigh *News and Observer* and the *Oxford Public Ledger,* although I also used a number of other newspapers as listed below; and my own interviews with participants and observers of the events in this book. As noted in chapter 12, the *Oxford Public Ledger* is missing for this entire historical period, but I was able to retrieve several key issues from criminal records 70-CR-1847 and 70-CR-1849 at the Granville County courthouse. Below, scholars and readers can trace specific sources by chapter. Eventually, all of my research materials, including transcripts of the interviews, will be housed in the James Edward McCoy Papers.

Chapter One: Baptism

My sources for the riot in Oxford the night I heard about Henry Marrow's death are State Highway Patrol Civil Intelligence Bulletin, May 13, 1970; North Carolina Good Neighbor Council report, May 12, 1970; State Bureau of Investigation Civil Intelligence Bulletin, May 13, 1970; and Western Union telegram from Mayor Hugh Currin to Governor Robert Scott, May 13, 1970, 11:41 A.M., all in Governor Robert Scott Papers. See also Raleigh *News and Observer,* May 14, 1970, and *Oxford Public Ledger,* May 15, 1970. I also relied heavily on my interviews with former assistant chief of police Doug White, Mayor Hugh Currin, Carolyn Thorpe, Linda Ball, Eddie McCoy, Herman Cozart, and several others who prefer to remain anonymous. Sources for the nationwide violence in May 1970 are cited below in my notes for chapter 6. The quote about the threat to "the whole economic and social structure of the nation" comes from *Business Week*, May 16, 1970.

CHAPTER TWO: ORIGINAL SINS

Population figures for Granville County are drawn from the United States Census of 1970. For the economic development of Granville County after World War II, see *Statistical Profile of the Henderson-Oxford, North Carolina Redevelopment Area* (Washington: United States Department of Commerce, 1962). See also *Oxford, North Carolina Population and Economy* (Oxford: Granville County–Oxford Planning Commission, 1965) and *North Carolina Profile on Granville County*, n.d. Another very useful source is Dennis McAuliffe, "The Transformation of Rural and Industrial Workers in Granville County" (Ph.D. dissertation, New School for Social Research, 1984), especially the tables on pages 71–72. All of these studies are available in the North Carolina Collection, Wilson Library, University of North Carolina at Chapel Hill. For information on tobacco production in Granville County, see *Heritage and Homesteads: The History and Architecture of Granville County, North Carolina* (Oxford: Granville County Historical Society, 1988), 27, 34, and 61. For the 1887 fire, see Laura Edwards, *Gendered Strife and Confusion: The Political Culture of Reconstruction* (Urbana: University of Illinois Press, 1997), 218, 244–46.

Much of the narrative here relies on my father's diary, which he was gracious enough to let me use, and on my interviews with him and my mother. I have verified the reaction inside the Oxford United Methodist Church in my conversations with Ben and Joy Averett. The descriptions of race relations in Oxford rest on interviews with Mayor Hugh Currin, William A. Chavis, James Edward McCoy, James Chavis, and Mary Catherine Chavis. For the evolution of the U.S. Supreme Court's rulings with respect to racial covenants, see Donald Nieman, *Promises to Keep: African-Americans and the Constitutional Order, 1776 to the Present* (New York: Oxford University Press, 1991), 122, 129, and 144. For interracial contacts in Greensboro in the late 1940s and early 1950s, see William H. Chafe, *Civilities and Civil Rights: Greensboro, North Carolina and the Black Struggle for Equality* (New York: Oxford University Press, 1979), 29–34.

In fact, all scholars of racial politics in North Carolina and in the United States owe a great debt to the insights in Chafe's landmark work on Greensboro. For racial paternalism in North Carolina, see Chafe, *Civilities and Civil Rights*, 7–10, 38–41, 48, 67–70, 204, 236. See also Stephen Kantrowitz, "The Two Faces of Domination," in David S. Cecelski and Timothy B. Tyson, *Democracy Betrayed: The Wilmington Race Riot of 1898 and Its Legacy* (Chapel Hill: University of North Carolina Press, 1998), 95–111. For race relations in

Granville County before and shortly after World War II, see F. E. Hunt Jr.,
"Oxford, N.C.," 1947, and untitled paper by Francis B. Hays, July 5, 1948, in the
Francis B. Hays Collection, vol. 22, 254–61. Dr. King's reference to the "thingification" of human beings comes from Martin Luther King Jr., *Where Do We Go
from Here? Chaos or Community* (Boston: Beacon Press, 1968), 123.

The colonial origins of the race and sex taboo that has marked racial politics
in the United States, particularly in North Carolina, are explored in Kirsten
Fischer's brilliant *Suspect Relations: Sex, Race and Resistance in Colonial North
Carolina* (Ithaca: Cornell University Press, 2002). My early thoughts about the
subject responded to insights found in Winthrop Jordan, *White over Black:
American Attitudes Toward the Negro, 1550–1812* (Chapel Hill: University of
North Carolina Press, 1968); Peter Wood, *Black Majority: Negroes in Colonial
South Carolina from 1670 Through the Stono Rebellion* (New York: Oxford
University Press, 1975); James Merrell, *The Indians' New World: The Catawbas
and Their Neighbors from European Contact Through the Era of Removal*
(Chapel Hill: University of North Carolina Press, 1989), and "The Racial
Education of the Catawba Indians," *Journal of Southern History*, vol. 50, no. 3
(August 1984): 363–84; and Leon Higginbotham Jr., "The Ancestry of Inferiority,
1619–1662," in Edward Countryman, ed., *How Did American Slavery Begin?*
(New York: Bedford–St. Martin's, 1999), 85–98. See also Timothy B. Tyson,
"Radio Free Dixie: Robert F. Williams and the Roots of Black Power," Ph.D. dis-
sertation, Duke University, 1994, 1–12. For the insight that our ideas about "race"
are not simply handed down but constantly retranslated, see Barbara Fields,
"Slavery, Race, and Ideology in the United States of America," *New Left Review*
181 (May-June 1990): 95–118. For a contrasting view, see Alden Vaughan, *The
Roots of American Racism: Slavery and Racism in Seventeenth Century Virginia*
(New York: Oxford University Press, 1995), 136–74. I am also grateful to colonial
historians Peter Wood, Elizabeth Fenn, Kirsten Fischer, and Jennifer Lyle
Morgan for their advice on conceptions of race, freedom, and sexuality and the
relationship of those concepts to the social structure of colonial America.

All of the material about slavery in Granville County, North Carolina, comes
from interviews housed in the James Edward McCoy Papers in the Southern
Oral History Project in the Southern Historical Collection, Wilson Library,
University of North Carolina at Chapel Hill. These include McCoy's tran-
scribed interviews with Lonie Allen, Helen Currin Amis, Novella Allen,
William Baskerville, Rachel Blackwell, Lucille Peace Blalock, Lois Braswell,
Judge Chavis, Mary Catherine Chavis, Thomas Chavis, Annie Bell Cheatham,
Ethel Carrington Clark, Frank Clark, Johnny Crews, R. F. Cousin, and Mary
Thomas Hobgood. The sources of specific quotations are indicated in the text.
My views of the distinctive Afro-Christianity in the South have been shaped
most strongly by Albert Raboteau, *Slave Religion: The "Invisible Institution" in
the Antebellum South* (New York: Oxford University Press, 1978), Charles
Joyner, *Down by the Riverside: A South Carolina Slave Community* (Urbana:
University of Illinois Press, 1984), 141–71, and Howard Thurman, *Jesus and the*

Disinherited (1949; Boston: Beacon Press, 1996). The quote from W. E. B. Du Bois is from his timeless work *Black Reconstruction in America, 1860–1880* (1935; New York: Touchstone, 1995), 124.

The material here on sex and race in the Jim Crow and civil rights-era South derives from work by a number of scholars, principally John Dollard, *Sex and Caste in a Southern Town* (New Haven: Yale University Press, 1937), 134–72; Jacquelyn Dowd Hall, "The Mind That Burns in Each Body," *Southern Exposure* (November-December 1984): 64–69; and *Revolt Against Chivalry: Jessie Daniel Ames and the Women's Campaign Against Lynching* (1979; New York: Columbia University Press, 1993). One of the most lucid explorations of the racial politics of sex, the sexual politics of race, and what W. J. Cash called "the rape complex," is Glenda Gilmore's brilliant essay "Murder, Memory and the Flight of the Incubus," in Cecelski and Tyson, eds., *Democracy Betrayed*, 73–93. See also Gilmore's classic work of Southern history, *Gender and Jim Crow: Women and the Politics of White Supremacy in North Carolina, 1896–1920*, especially pages 91–118. See also Danielle McGuire's pioneering essay " 'It Was Like All of Us Had Been Raped': Black Womanhood, White Violence, and the Civil Rights Movement," Rutgers University, forthcoming.

The quote about "the destruction of the purity of his race" by the North Carolina editor is from Bignall Jones, "Only One Way to Maintain Schools," *Warren Record*, April 2, 1955. For William F. Buckley's opposition to voting rights for Southern blacks, see *National Review* 4 (August 24, 1957): 149. For James J. Kilpatrick's advocacy of white electoral supremacy, see "Down the Memory Hole," *New Republic* 193 (July 1, 1985): 9. The exchange between Kilpatrick and James Baldwin about blacks and whites marrying each other's daughters is quoted in Paul Spickard, *Mixed Blood: Intermarriage and Ethnic Identity in Twentieth-Century America* (Madison: University of Wisconsin Press, 1989), 268. The story about racial clashes over the "girlie show" at the county fair in Yanceyville comes from Good Neighbor Council report, September 21, 1970, Governor Robert Scott Papers. Reactions to these dynamics of race and sex with regard to the integration of the Granville County schools come from interviews with Mayor Hugh Currin, Reverend Don Price, and several others who preferred not to be cited.

CHAPTER THREE: "TOO CLOSE NOT TO TOUCH"

My description of Grab-all rests upon my own memories and observations, but also on McAuliffe, "Transformation," 122, and my interviews with Mayor Hugh Currin, James Edward McCoy, Mary Catherine Chavis, William A. Chavis, James Chavis, Roberta Chavis, Fannie Chavis, and Benjamin Chavis. For relations between the Teels and the African American community, I relied on my interviews with Robert G. Teel, William A. Chavis, James Chavis, Herman Cozart, Billy Watkins, Richard Shepard, and Goldie Averett. On economic development in Granville County during the decades after World War II, see my sources for chapter 2.

For an excellent account of the material and cultural life of tenant farm families in eastern North Carolina during this period, see Lu Ann Jones, *Mama Learned Us to Work: Farm Women in the New South* (Chapel Hill: University of North Carolina Press, 2002). Roy G. Taylor, *Sharecroppers: The Way We Really Were* (Wilson, N.C.: J-Mark Press, 1984) is also useful. For a scholarly examination of the economic realities beneath the crop lien system, see Roger Ransom and Richard Sutch, *One Kind of Freedom: The Economic Consequences of Emancipation* (Cambridge: Cambridge University Press, 1977). For readers who seek an engaging tour of the rapidly changing American South from the 1930s through the 1950s, I recommend three excellent recent books that have shaped my thinking in different ways: John Egerton, *Speak Now Against the Day: The Generation Before the Civil Rights Movement in the South* (New York: Knopf, 1994); Patricia Sullivan, *Days of Hope: Race and Democracy in the New Deal Era* (Chapel Hill: University of North Carolina Press, 1996); and Pete Daniel, *Lost Revolutions: The South in the 1950s* (Chapel Hill: University of North Carolina Press, 2000). Numan Bartley, *The Rise of Massive Resistance: Race Relations in the South During the 1950s* (Baton Rouge: Louisiana State University Press, 1969), sets a standard for all other scholars of that subject.

For the mid-1960s Ku Klux Klan revivals in North Carolina, see especially David S. Cecelski, "Ordinary Sin," *Independent Weekly*, March 19, 1997. See also David S. Cecelski, *Along Freedom Road: Hyde County, North Carolina, and the Fate of Black Schools in the South* (Chapel Hill: University of North Carolina Press, 1994), 36–39, 183. Almost all of the specific information in my account of the Klan revivals comes from coverage in the Raleigh *News and Observer* in 1965: the U.S. congressional investigation that named North Carolina the number one Klan state was covered on October 20, October 23, and October 24; for the Methodist church in Smithfield that invited the local Klan leader to speak, see November 13; for the Fayetteville KKK rally with fifteen thousand in attendance, see November 10; Jim Gardner's comments are from the October 24 issue; the story of the bombing of the black migrant labor camp is from October 1; the New Bern funeral home bombing, the arson attack on Mayor Royce Jordan's barns, and the attack on the college students were covered on October 3; the torture of the interracial drinking buddies can be found in the October 9 issue; the arson of the black schools in Mars Hill and Johnston County can be located on October 12 and 26, respectively; the statewide KKK campaign of burning crosses on courthouse lawns is from October 22; and the story of Judge Pretlow Winborne and the wiener roast was reported on November 3. The *New York Times*, October 30, 1966, reported the story of the Ku Klux Klan booth at the North Carolina State Fair.

For the Klan revival of the late 1940s and the quotes from Thomas Hamilton, see John Powell, "The Klan Un-Klandestine," *Nation*, September 29,

1951, 254–56; *Time*, February 25, 1952, 28, and August 11, 1952, 21; Wyn Craig Wade, *The Fiery Cross: The Ku Klux Klan in America* (New York: Simon and Schuster, 1987), 290–91.

The 1950s Klan career of Reverend James Catfish Cole is a fascinating and largely unexplored topic. I rely mainly on the James William Cole Papers. For the fabled clash between the Klan and the Lumbee Indians in Maxton, North Carolina, see Timothy B. Tyson, *Radio Free Dixie: Robert F. Williams and the Roots of Black Power* (Chapel Hill: University of North Carolina Press, 1999), 61–62 and 137–41. See also "Klobbered Klan," *Raleigh News and Observer,* April 19, 1964; Harry Golden, *Carolina Israelite*, January–February 1958; "Editorially Speaking," *New Mexican*, January 21, 1958; *Chapel Hill News Leader*, reprinted in *News and Observer,* January 30, 1958. The Lumbees repelled the Klan with a long-standing tradition of armed resistance to white oppression, extending back to the Henry Berry Lowery gang in the nineteenth century. See William McKee Evans, *To Die Game: The Story of the Lowery Band, Guerrillas of Reconstruction* (Baton Rouge: Louisiana State University Press, 1971).

For the route of Catfish Cole's Klan by the Monroe NAACP, see Norfolk *Journal and Guide*, October 12, 1957; B. J. Winfield and Woodrow Wilson interviews with Marcellus Barksdale, Duke Oral History Project, Perkins Library, Duke University; Robert F. Williams, *Negroes with Guns* (New York: Marzani and Munsell, 1962), 57; Andrew Myers, "When Violence Met Violence: Facts and Images of Robert F. Williams," M.A. thesis, University of Virginia, 1993. The story of the murders of Mr. and Mrs. Frank Clay comes from Henry Lee Moon to Roy Wilkins, November 29, 1957, Box A92, NAACP Papers. My descriptions of the Klan in Granville County and Teel's relationship with the Klan rely on three independent interviews.

For the ubiquitous nature of armed self-defense among black Southerners of the civil rights era, see Timothy B. Tyson, "Robert F. Williams, 'Black Power,' and the Origins of the African American Freedom Struggle," *Journal of American History*, vol. 85, no. 2 (September 1998): 540–70. See also Tyson, *Radio Free Dixie;* Akinyele K. Umoja, "Eye for an Eye: Armed Resistance in the Mississippi Freedom Movement," Ph.D. dissertation, Emory University, 1996, and "Ballots and Bullets: A Comparative Analysis of Armed Resistance in the Civil Rights Movement," *Journal of Black Studies*, vol. 29, no. 4 (March 1999): 558–78; Lance Hill, *The Deacons: Armed Self-Defense and the Civil Rights Movement* (Chapel Hill: University of North Carolina Press, 2004); Simon Wendt, "The Spirit and the Shotgun: Armed Resistance and the Radicalization of the African American Freedom Movement," Ph.D. dissertation, Free University of Berlin, 2004; and Gail Williams O'Brien, *The Color of the Law: Race, Violence, and Justice in the Post–World War Two South* (Chapel Hill: University of North Carolina Press, 1999). For armed self-defense by Martin Luther King Jr. see Stewart Burns, *Daybreak of Freedom: The Montgomery Bus Boycott* (Chapel Hill: University of North Carolina Press, 1997), 22. For armed self-defense by Medgar Evers, see Charles Payne, *I've Got the Light of Freedom: The Organizing Tradition and the Mississippi Freedom Struggle* (Berkeley: University of California Press, 1995), 49–50. The quote from the Jackson, Mississippi, *Eagle Eye* is from the August 20, 1955 issue, which I located in the Governor Paul Johnson Papers at the University of Southern Mississippi. For armed self-defense by Daisy Bates, see Daisy Bates to Thurgood Marshall, August 3, 1959, Box 2, Daisy Bates Papers, Wisconsin State Historical Society, Madison, Wisconsin. See also Daisy Bates, *The Long Shadow of Little Rock* (New York: David McKay, 1962), 162; and *Arkansas State Press,* May 23, 1959.

For Robert G. Teel's police record of violence, see Granville County criminal court records 69-CR-1239, driving while under the influence of intoxicants; 69-CR-1238, assault on an officer; 70-CR-425, assault on an officer; 70-CR-1532, assault by pointing a gun and assault and battery; 70-CR-1847, murder by aiding and abetting Robert Larry Teel; 70-CR-1848, assault with a deadly weapon with intent to kill, inflicting serious bodily injury; 70-CR-3232 murder by aiding and abetting Roger Oakley; 72-CR-1812, assault and battery; 72-CR-1813, assault and battery; 75-CRS-1907, assault on a female; and 77-CRS-3708, assault with a deadly weapon. My accounts of Teel's violent confrontations with members of the Oxford Police Department and with school teacher Clyde Harding rely on Granville County criminal court records 69-CR-1238, 70-CR-425, and 70-CR-1532 and on my interviews with Robert G. Teel, William A. Chavis, Gene Edmundson, James Chavis, and Billy Watkins. For a description of Billy Watkins's political career, see his obituary in the Raleigh *News and Observer,* August 28, 1989.

CHAPTER FOUR: MISS AMY'S WITNESS

The story of Dr. Samuel Proctor's visit to our church in Sanford relies largely on my interviews with Vernon Tyson, Martha Tyson, Samuel Proctor, and Sarah Godfrey. I have also used materials from my parents' diaries from the period, for which I am grateful to them.

For the national and international dynamics of the Cold War and the African American freedom struggles in the South, see Mary Dudziak, "Desegregation as a Cold War Imperative," *Stanford Law Review* 41 (November 1988): 61–120. See also Mary Dudziak, *Cold War Civil Rights: Race and the Image of American Democracy* (Princeton: Princeton University Press, 2000); Tyson, *Radio Free Dixie,* 51–53, 59–60, 103–104; 90–136; and Thomas Borstelmann, *The Cold War and the Color Line: American Race Relations in the Global Arena* (Cambridge: Harvard University Press, 2001). The quote from Dr. King about the Cold War comes from Taylor Branch's classic work *Parting the Waters: America in the King Years, 1955–1963* (New York: Simon and Schuster, 1988), 791.

Regarding the Greensboro sit-ins, I rely here on Chafe, *Civilities and Civil Rights*. My account of the Birmingham campaign relies on Branch, *Parting the*

Waters, 673–802; David Garrow's irreplaceable standard *Bearing the Cross: Martin Luther King, Jr. and the Southern Christian Leadership Conference* (New York: William Morrow, 1986), 231–86; Adam Fairclough's important organizational history *To Redeem the Soul of America: The Southern Christian Leadership Conference and Martin Luther King, Jr.* (Athens: University of Georgia Press, 1987), 111–61; Andrew Manis's lovely biography *A Fire You Can't Put Out: The Civil Rights Life of Birmingham's Reverend Fred Shuttlesworth* (Tuscaloosa: University of Alabama Press, 1999); Diane McWhorter's deft combination of memoir and history *Carry Me Home: Birmingham, Alabama—the Climactic Battle of the Civil Rights Revolution* (New York: Simon and Schuster, 2001); and especially Glenn T. Eskew's trail-blazing and thorough history *But for Birmingham: The Local and National Movements in the Civil Rights Struggle* (Chapel Hill: University of North Carolina Press, 1997). The quote from Colonel Stone Johnson came from my notes taken at Body of Christ Deliverance Ministry in Birmingham on June 3, 2001. I am grateful to Andrew Manis for fact checking the chapter.

CHAPTER FIVE: KING JESUS AND DR. KING

For our family's move to Oxford, I rely on my interviews with my parents and my father's diary. My stories about Thad Stem draw on my interviews with my father, on Stem's written work, especially *Entries from Oxford* (Durham, N.C.: Moore Publishing, 1971), and on Stem's glittering correspondence with Jonathan Daniels, which can be found in the Jonathan Daniels Papers. For the history of the Confederate monument in Oxford, see *Heritage and Homesteads*, 86; *Oxford Public Ledger*, January 3, January 7, and May 2, 1947; see also Hays Collection, vol. 22, 196.

For the decisive role of World War II on African American freedom struggles, see Timothy B. Tyson, "Wars for Democracy," in Cecelski and Tyson, eds., *Democracy Betrayed*, 253–75. See also Richard Dalfiume, "The 'Forgotten Years' of the Negro Revolution," *Journal of American History*, vol. 55, no. 1 (June 1968): 90–106; Harvard Sitkoff, "Racial Militancy and Interracial Violence During the Second World War," *Journal of American History*, vol. 58, no. 3 (June 1971): 663–83; and Harvard Sitkoff, "African American Militancy in the World War II South," in Neil McMillen, ed., *Remaking Dixie: The Impact of World War II on the American South* (Jackson: University of Mississippi Press, 1997), 70–92. See also Neil Wynn, *The Afro-American and the Second World War* (New York: Holmes and Meirer, 1976), and Herbert Garfinkel, *When Negroes March* (New York: Atheneum, 1973).

The first quote from A. Philip Randolph comes from the *Philadelphia Tribune*, July 10, 1943. The second is from Randolph, "A Reply to My Critics: Randolph Blasts Courier as 'Bitter Voices of Defeatism,'" *Chicago Defender*, June 12, 1943. See also Randolph, "Call to Negro Americans," July 1, 1941, Office File 93, Franklin Delano Roosevelt Papers, Hyde Park, New York. For

NAACP membership-growth figures and the expansion of African American newspaper circulation, see Sitkoff, "Racial Militancy and Interracial Violence," 663, and Sitkoff, "African American Militancy in the World War II South," 77. For the wartime sit-in campaigns by the Congress of Racial Equality, see Pauli Murray, "A Blueprint for Full Citizenship," *Crisis* 51 (November 1944): 358–59. There were also widespread reports during the war that young black men in North Carolina sat down at drugstore lunch counters, demanded service, and were arrested by the police. See Howard Odum, *Race and Rumors of Race* (Chapel Hill: University of North Carolina Press, 1943), 93.

For wartime clashes in Oxford and the story about the women at the sewing room, see the Raleigh *News and Observer*, May 3, 1944, and *Oxford Public Ledger*, May 2 and May 5, 1944, in Hays Collection, vol. 22, 139. See also *Heritage and Homesteads*, 121.

Information about early civil rights stirrings in Granville County, the Good Neighbor Council, and other efforts at racial amelioration in Granville County come from my interviews with Richard C. Shepard, James Edward McCoy, Mayor Hugh Currin, and Golden Frinks, and also from Capus M. Waynick, et al., eds., *North Carolina and the Negro* (Raleigh: North Carolina Mayors' Cooperating Committee, 1964), 135–38. The quote from Tom Ragland comes from the Raleigh *News and Observer*, May 15, 1970, 3. Thad Stem's story about Major Stem, Mrs. Shaw, and the bootlegger comes from Stem, *Entries from Oxford*, 32–33. The quote from Richard Baxter about preaching comes from "Love Breathing Thanks and Praise," *Poetical Fragments* (1681; New York: McGraw Hill, 1971).

While this is not a broad history of "*the* civil rights movement," a project I would consider somewhat misguided in any case, historians of the African American freedom movements in the twentieth-century South are making their way toward an understanding of these struggles as essentially local but also inescapably national and international in their dynamics and implications. The pathbreaking works in the unfolding of these movement histories include John Dittmer, *Local People: The Struggle for Civil Rights in Mississippi* (Urbana: University of Illinois Press, 1994); Payne, *I've Got the Light of Freedom*; Robin D. G. Kelley, *Hammer and Hoe: Communism in Alabama During the Great Depression* (Chapel Hill: University of North Carolina Press, 1990); Eskew, *But for Birmingham*; David S. Cecelski, *Along Freedom Road: Hyde County, North Carolina and the Fate of Black Schools in the South* (Chapel Hill: University of North Carolina Press, 1994); and Chana Kai Lee, *For Freedom's Sake: The Life of Fannie Lou Hamer* (Urbana: University of Illinois Press, 1999).

My account of the white backlash is based on Dan T. Carter, *The Politics of Rage: George Wallace, the New Conservatism, and the Transformation of American Politics* (New York: Simon and Schuster, 1995) and *From George Wallace to Newt Gingrich: Race in the Conservative Counterrevolution, 1963–1994* (Baton Rouge: Louisiana State University Press, 1996); Rick Perlstein, *Before the Storm* (New York: Hill and Wang, 2001); Kari

Frederickson, *The Dixiecrat Revolt and the End of the Solid South* (Chapel Hill: University of North Carolina Press, 2001); and Earl Black and Merle Black, *The Rise of Southern Republicans* (Cambridge; Belknap-Harvard, 2002). The quote from Senator Josiah Bailey of North Carolina comes from the latter work, 32. Lyndon Johnson's prediction comes from Perlstein, *Before the Storm*, 365.

Most of the best books on Martin Luther King Jr. have been cited above for the Birmingham campaign. King has been fortunate, however, in his biographers, especially the early but still important David Levering Lewis, *King: A Critical Biography* (New York: Praeger, 1970), which brims with insight even though it was written before the papers of Dr. King and the SCLC were available to researchers. For a recent and useful revision to the more traditional view, see Michael Eric Dyson, *I May Not Get There with You: The True Martin Luther King Jr.* (New York: Free Press, 2000). Adam Fairclough's *Martin Luther King, Jr.* (Athens: University of Georgia Press, 1995) provides a concise and considered biography. Marshall Frady's *Martin Luther King, Jr.* (New York: Viking Penguin, 2002) is both brief and eloquent. For Dr. King's views on affirmative action, see his book *Why We Can't Wait* (New York: Signet, 1964), 134–41. The quote from Dr. King's "Advice for Living" column comes from Garrow, *Bearing the Cross*, 99. Documentation of the FBI's effort to push Dr. King into committing suicide may be examined in Michael Friedly and David Gallen, eds., *Martin Luther King, Jr.: The FBI File* (New York: Carroll & Graf, 1993), 48–49. See also Kenneth O'Reilly, *"Racial Matters": The FBI's File on Black America* (New York: Free Press, 1989), 144–45.

My account of the aftermath of Martin Luther King's assassination comes from William H. Chafe, *Unfinished Journey: America Since World War II*, 4th ed (New York: Oxford University Press, 1999), 367–68. Ronald Reagan's comment on the assassination comes from the *New York Times*, April 10, 1968. The quote from Richard Wright is from *Twelve Million Black Voices* (1940; New York: Thunder's Mouth Press, 1988), 10.

CHAPTER SIX: THE DEATH OF HENRY MARROW

My account of Henry Marrow's life and death has been cobbled together from transcripts of testimony by Edward Webb, Donnie Eaton, and William A. Chavis in the June 2, 1970, habeas corpus hearing for cases 70-CR-1847 and 70-CR-1849; the transcript of Roger Oakley's testimony in both the cases above on June 2, 1970; and the coroner's report signed by Dr. William B. Tarry and Dr. Harold L. Taylor, May 11, 1970, all of which I obtained in the Granville County court records. I also relied upon newspaper coverage of the trial, principally in the Raleigh *News and Observer*, and upon my interviews with Robert G. Teel, Mary Catherine Chavis, Beatrice Chavis, Benjamin Chavis, James Chavis, Roberta Chavis, William A. Chavis, Herman Cozart, Hugh Currin, Carolyn Thorpe, William H. S. Burgwyn, and several sources who preferred to remain anonymous.

The story of John Chavis's life here is drawn from Marvin Hunt, "The Life and Legacy of John Chavis," Raleigh *Spectator,* May 25, 1989, 5–6, and John Hope Franklin, *The Free Negro in North Carolina, 1790–1860* (New York: Knopf, 1943), 12. The quotes from Helen Chavis Othow are from her book *John Chavis: African American Patriot, Preacher, Teacher and Mentor* (Jefferson, N.C.: McFarland, 2001), 9, and from an Associated Press story in the *Augusta Chronicle,* May 5, 1998. See also Larry Reni Thomas, "A Study of Racial Violence in Wilmington, North Carolina, Prior to February 1, 1971," M.A. thesis, University of North Carolina, Chapel Hill, 1980, 42–45; Benjamin Chavis interview with Sam Bridges, October 30, 1984, transcript in possession of the author; Sam Bridges, "Radicalism in Black Religion," unpublished paper, Wesleyan University, 1984, copy in possession of the author.

For the violence in Augusta, Georgia, see the Raleigh *News and Observer,* May 12, May 13, May 16, and May 17, 1970. See also the *Pittsburgh Courier,* May 23, June 4, and June 27, 1970, and the *Atlanta Daily World,* May 17, 1970. My account of the shootings at Jackson State University rests upon the Durham *Carolina Times,* June 6, 1970, and the Raleigh *News and Observer,* May 18, 1970, which ran a national wire service story that is the source for the quote from the Mississippi state trooper. *The Militant,* May 26, 1970, published telling photographs of the windows of the women's dormitory. The quote from Dr. Aaron Shirley is from the *Pittsburgh Courier,* August 8, 1970. See also George Katsiaficas, "Remembering Kent and Jackson State," *Zeta* (May 1990): 33–37.

The quote about the North Carolina State Highway Patrol is from the Durham *Carolina Times,* May 30, 1970. See also Good Neighbor Council report, May 12, 1970, Scott Papers, in which the GNC explains that blacks in North Carolina "see the police as the establishment's militia whose job is to control and suppress the people." My account of the curfew draws on Mayor Hugh Currin, Western Union telegrams to Governor Robert Scott, 11:41 A.M., May 13, 1970, and 12:56 P.M., May 14, 1970, Governor Robert Scott Papers; Oxford city ordinance 1697-11-1; State Bureau of Investigation Civil Intelligence Bulletin, May 13, 1970, Governor Robert Scott Papers; *Oxford Public Ledger,* June 1, 1970; Raleigh *News and Observer,* May 14, 1970; and my interviews with Mayor Hugh Currin, James Edward McCoy, and Herman Cozart. Information regarding the arrests came from the *Durham Morning Herald,* May 15, 1970; the Raleigh *News and Observer,* May 16, 1970; and the *Oxford Public Ledger,* May 19, 1970; and also the Granville County court records.

My account of the hearings and the Human Relations Council meeting are drawn from the Raleigh *News and Observer,* May 23, 1970; the *Pittsburgh Courier,* May 23, 1970; the *Oxford Public Ledger,* May 15 and June 1, 1970; McAuliffe, "Transformation," 125–26; State Bureau of Investigation Civil Intelligence Bulletin, May 23, 1970, Scott Papers; and my interviews with Benjamin Chavis, Linda Ball, Sam Cox, Mayor Hugh Currin, Vernon Tyson, and several others who prefer to remain anonymous.

For the first march to the courthouse on Black Solidarity Day, I drew on Elizabeth Finn, "North Carolina, Ben Chavis, and the Wilmington Ten," chapter 3; the *Oxford Public Ledger*, May 15, 1970; and my interviews with James Edward McCoy, Golden Frinks, and Benjamin Chavis.

CHAPTER SEVEN: DRINKIN' THAT FREEDOM WINE

The story about the African American men who drove into the roadblock with a carload of dynamite and weapons comes from the *Durham Morning Herald*, May 16, 1970; the Raleigh *News and Observer*, May 16 and May 19, 1970; the *Oxford Public Ledger*, June 1, 1970; Wayne King, "The Case Against the Wilmington Ten," *New York Times Magazine*, December 3, 1978; Thomas, "A Study of Racial Violence in Wilmington Prior to February 1, 1971," 44; and my interviews with Hugh Currin, James Edward McCoy, and Benjamin Chavis.

My account of the first round of firebombings in Oxford draws on the *Durham Morning Herald*, May 16, 1970; the Raleigh *News and Observer*, May 16, 1970; the *Oxford Public Ledger*, May 19, 1970; and my interviews with Mayor Hugh Currin and three anonymous sources.

My account of the funeral of Henry Marrow draws on the *Durham Morning Herald*, May 17, 1970; the Raleigh *News and Observer*, May 17, 1970; my interviews with Vernon Tyson, Golden Frinks, Benjamin Chavis, and James Edward McCoy, and my conversations with Thad Stem.

There is a blossoming historical literature on the Black Power movement. Ephemeral early works echoed the vacuous mainstream media, portraying Black Power as a "new black mood" or a "radical response to white America"— a black backlash to the betrayals of white liberals and the assaults of white reactionaries. The first real breakthrough in the scholarship came with Clayborne Carson, *In Struggle: SNCC and the Black Awakening of the 1960s* (Cambridge: Harvard University Press, 1981), especially pages 191–228, which recognize that Black Power "affirmed the legitimacy of a long-standing tradition of armed self-defense in the rural deep South" and that it reflected "dormant traditions of black radicalism" in Dixie. William L. Van Deburg's landmark *New Day in Babylon: The Black Power Movement and American Culture, 1965–1975* (Chicago: University of Chicago Press, 1992) points beyond disillusionment and despair toward Black Power's important cultural self-affirmations. Komozi Woodard, *A Nation Within a Nation* (Chapel Hill: University of North Carolina Press, 1999) documents the national and international implications of the Black Power movement in one city through the life of Amiri Baraka, one of the movement's critical figures. See also Tyson, *Radio Free Dixie*, William W. Sales Jr., *From Civil Rights to Black Liberation: Malcolm X and the Organization of Afro-American Unity* (Boston: South End Press, 1994), and Charles Jones, *The Black Panther Party Reconsidered* (Baltimore: Black Classic Press, 1998). Valuable memoirs of the Black Power generation in the South include James Forman, *The Making of Black Revolutionaries* (1972; University of Washington

Press, 1997) and Cleveland Sellers, *The River of No Return: The Autobiography of a Black Militant and the Life and Death of SNCC* (1973; Jackson: University of Mississippi Press, 1990). A thoughtful and refreshing contemplation of the rise of Black Power in Mississippi can be found in Payne, *I've Got the Light of Freedom*, 338–90. For an excellent overview of the literature on Black Power, see Peniel E. Joseph, "Black Liberation Without Apology: Reconceptualizing the Black Power Movement," *Black Scholar*, vol. 31, no. 3-4 (fall-winter 2001): 2–19.

All discussion of the Fusion movement in North Carolina must begin with Helen G. Edmonds, *The Negro and Fusion Politics in North Carolina, 1894–1901* (Chapel Hill: University of North Carolina Press, 1951), and H. Leon Prather Sr., *"We Have Taken a City": The Wilmington Racial Massacre and Coup of 1898* (Cranbury, N.J.: Associated University Presses, 1984). See also Gilmore, *Gender and Jim Crow*, and Eric Anderson, *Race and Politics in North Carolina, 1872–1901* (Chapel Hill: University of North Carolina Press, 1981). The quote about the Fusion movement in Granville County comes from *Heritage and Homesteads*, 77–78.

CHAPTER EIGHT: OUR "OTHER SOUTH"

The phrase "Other South" comes from Carl Degler, *The Other South: Southern Dissidents in the Nineteenth Century* (New York: Harper and Row, 1974). The assertion of Ulrich B. Phillips that "the South" is "a people with a common resolve, indomitably maintained—that it shall be and remain a white man's country" is quoted in C. Vann Woodward, *The Strange Career of Jim Crow* (1955; 3rd rev. ed, New York: Oxford University Press, 1974), 8.

Much of the family history collected here comes from my father's research and his own stories. See Vernon Tyson, "The History of Our Family Reunion," unpublished pamphlet, 2001, in the author's possession. I have also relied upon my interviews with Dewey Tyson, Tommy Tyson, and Pauline Pearce. The information about Robert G. Teel's boyhood comes from my interview with him.

The best sources for Southern white dissidents during the Jim Crow era and the post–World War II decades include Frank Adams's excellent *Unearthing Seeds of Fire: The Idea of Highlander* (Winston-Salem: John F. Blair, 1975) and especially *James A. Dombrowski: An American Heretic, 1897–1983* (Knoxville: University of Tennessee Press, 1992); Anthony Dunbar, *Against the Grain: Southern Radicals and Prophets, 1929–1959* (Charlottesville: University Press of Virginia, 1981); John T. Kneebone, *Southern Liberal Journalists and the Issue of Race* (Chapel Hill: University of North Carolina Press, 1985); Morton Sosna, *In Search of the Silent South: Southern Liberals and the Race Issue* (New York: Columbia University Press, 1977); David Chappell, *Inside Agitators: White Southerners in the Civil Rights Movement* (Baltimore: Johns Hopkins University Press, 1994); and Catherine Fosl, *Subversive Southerner: Anne*

Braden and the Struggle for Racial Justice in the Cold War South (New York: Palgrave McMillen, 2002). See also Timothy B. Tyson, "Dynamite and the 'Silent South': A Story from the Second Reconstruction in South Carolina," in Jane Daily et al., eds., *Jumpin' Jim Crow: Southern History from Civil War to Civil Rights* (Princeton: Princeton University Press, 2000), 275–93. John Egerton's *Speak Now Against the Day* is also an excellent source on white Southern dissenters of various stripes. For one remarkable story, see Kathryn Nasstrom, *Everybody's Grandmother and Nobody's Fool: Frances Freeborn Pauley and the Struggle for Social Justice* (Ithaca: Cornell University Press, 2000). A thoughtful commentary on generations of similar stories is Fred Hobson, *But Now I See: The White Southern Conversion Narrative* (Baton Rouge: Louisiana State University Press 1999).

Useful memoirs of white Southern dissenters include Anne Braden, *The Wall Between* (New York: Monthly Review Press, 1958); Lillian Smith, *Killers of the Dream* (New York: W. W. Norton & Co., 1949); Stetson Kennedy, *I Rode With the Klan* (London: Arco, 1954); and Virginia Durr, *Outside the Magic Circle: The Autobiography of Virginia Durr* (New York: Simon and Schuster, 1987). For a memoir more akin to this one—that is, not the story of a civil rights activist but the story of a young white Southerner who cared about racial injustice and grew up to be a historian—see Melton McLaurin's lovely *Separate Pasts: Growing Up White in the Segregated South* (Athens: University of Georgia Press, 1987).

For the history of eastern North Carolina during the Civil War, including both runaway slaves and dissident whites, see David S. Cecelski's lyrical and scholarly masterpiece *The Waterman's Song: Slavery and Freedom in Maritime North Carolina* (Chapel Hill: University of North Carolina Press, 2002), 121–201. The quote from General Ambrose Burnside is from page 187. For the story of the twenty-two local men who were hanged in Kinston by the Confederates under General George E. Pickett, see Gerard A. Patterson, *Justice or Atrocity: General George E. Pickett and the Kinston, North Carolina Hangings* (Gettysburg: Thomas Publications, 1998).

My understanding of the growth of the textile industry in the Carolinas and its racial politics draws on Jacqueline Dowd Hall et al., *Like a Family: The Making of a Southern Cotton Mill World* (Chapel Hill: University of North Carolina Press, 1987), 183–236. The *Southern Textile Bulletin* is quoted in John A. Salmond, *Gastonia 1929: The Story of the Loray Mill Strike* (Chapel Hill: University of North Carolina Press, 1995), 113. See also Liston Pope, *Millhands and Preachers* (New Haven: Yale University Press, 1965).

For the *Brown v. Board of Education* decision, see Richard Kluger's definitive work *Simple Justice* (New York: Knopf, 1976). A brief but thoughtful exploration of the case is provided by James Patterson, *Brown v. Board of Education: A Civil Rights Milestone and Its Troubled Legacy* (New York: Oxford University Press, 2001). For the white reaction against the decision, see Michael Klarman, "How Brown Changed Race Relations: The Backlash Thesis," *Journal of*

American History 81 (June 1994): 81–118. My story of the Gator draws on my interviews with Dewey Tyson, Tommy Tyson, and Vernon Tyson.

For the campaign of segregationist terrorism in the late 1950s, see, for example, Tyson, "Dynamite and the 'Silent South.'" See also "Intimidation, Reprisal, and Violence in the South's Racial Crisis" (American Friends Service Committee, 1959); Barbara Patterson, "Defiance and Dynamite," *New South* 18 (May 1963): 8–11. The quote referring to "shots and dynamite blasts" comes from *Southern Patriot,* vol. 15, no. 1 (January 1957): 1. The Arkansas legislature called the integration crisis in Little Rock part of "the international communist conspiracy" in a December 1958 report by the Special Education Committee of the Arkansas Legislative Council, reprinted in Wilson Record and Jane Cassells Record, eds., *Little Rock U.S.A.* (San Francisco: Chandler Publishing, 1960), 196–99. South Carolina editor Thomas Waring called for secession and sanctioned a terrorist bombing campaign in the pages of the Charleston *News and Courier* and is quoted to that effect in A. M. Secrest's "In Black and White: Press Opinion and Race Relations in South Carolina, 1954–1964," Ph.D. dissertation, Duke University, 1971), 217–18. Waring was even more explicit in conversations with Reverend John B. Morris, who made notes of the exchange that are housed in the Reverend John B. Morris Papers in the South Carolinia Library, University of South Carolina.

My account of my Uncle Earl's collision with Jim Crow comes from my interviews with him and with my father, and from my father's diary.

CHAPTER NINE: THE CASH REGISTER AT THE POOL HALL

My account of the march to Raleigh relies on the Raleigh *News and Observer,* May 23, May 24, May 25, and May 28, 1970; the *Oxford Public Ledger,* May 26, 1970; "Application to Use Public Buildings and Grounds," May 21, 1970, Golden Frinks to Office of the Lieutenant Governor, May 21, 1970; and "Black Grievances and Demands," all in Governor Robert Scott Papers; McAuliffe, "Transformation," 126–27. My interviews with Benjamin Chavis, Mayor Hugh Currin, James Edward McCoy, Golden Frinks, Herman Cozart, Carolyn Thorpe, William A. Chavis, and Linda Ball provided information for my account of the march and also for my description of the Soul Kitchen. For more on the freedom movement in Hyde County, see Cecelski, *Along Freedom Road.*

Richard Wright's observations about the options available to an African American man in the South come from "How Bigger Was Born," an introduction to *Native Son* (1940; New York: Perennial, 1987), vii.

For the history of racial separatism in the Student Nonviolent Coordinating Committee, see Carson, *In Struggle,* 191–228. See also Wesley Hogan, *Many Minds, One Heart* (Chapel Hill: University of North Carolina Press, forthcoming).

For the politics of racial backlash in North Carolina, including the figures quoted in the text, see Jack Bass and William DeVries, *The Transformation of Southern Politics* (New York: Basic Books, 1976), 444 and 476–77. See also William Billingsley, *Communists on Campus: Race, Politics and the Public University in Sixties North Carolina* (Athens: University of Georgia Press, 1999). Jim Gardner's endorsement of George Wallace is from Earl Black, *Southern Governors and Civil Rights* (Cambridge: Cambridge University Press, 1976), 111. The early ascension of Jesse Helms is covered in Billingsley's fine book and in Julian M. Pleasants and Augustus M. Burns, *Frank Porter Graham and the 1950 Senate Race in North Carolina* (Chapel Hill: University of North Carolina Press, 1990). Ernest Furguson, *Hard Right: The Rise of Jesse Helms* (New York: Norton, 1986), explores his later rise to national prominence. See also Juan Williams, "Carolina Gothic," *Washington Post*, October 28, 1990, and also Black and Black, *The Rise of Southern Republicans*, 102–111. The quotes from white banker Graham Wright, black businessman James Gregory, and city official John K. Nelms are all from the Raleigh *News and Observer*, May 29, 1970.

CHAPTER TEN: PERRY MASON IN THE SHOESHINE PARLOR

My sources for the big fires in Oxford on Monday, May 25, 1970, include several interview sources who wish to remain anonymous. I cross-checked their accounts with news stories in the Raleigh *News and Observer*, May 26, May 27, May 28, and May 29, 1970; the *Oxford Public Ledger*, May 29 and June 1, 1970; McAuliffe, "Transformation," 126–27, as well as my interview with Mayor Hugh Currin. The quote comparing downtown Oxford to Berlin after the bombing raids of World War II is from the Raleigh *News and Observer*, May 29, 1970. The account of the young boys' arrests for firebombings relies on the *Oxford Public Ledger*, June 1 and June 5, 1970. It was also very helpful to look at the scores of photographs taken in Oxford in the summer of 1970 that are housed in the *News and Observer* collection at the North Carolina Division of Archives and History.

My account of the trial of Robert G. Teel and Larry Teel relies foremost on Granville County court records Robert G. Teel, 70-CR-1847, murder by aiding and abetting Robert Larry Teel; Robert G. Teel, 70-CR-1848, assault with a deadly weapon with intent to kill, inflicting serious bodily injury; Robert Larry Teel, 70-CR-1849, murder. I obtained a partial transcript from one of the folders. My characterization of Judge Robert Martin comes from Michael Myerson's *Nothing Could Be Finer* (New York: International Publishers, 1977), 180. For the quote about James Ferguson, see Cecelski, *Along Freedom Road*, 74. I also relied on my interviews with Robert G. Teel, Billy Watkins, William H. S. Burgwyn, Carolyn Thorpe, William A. Chavis, Benjamin Chavis, Linda Ball, Gene Edmundson, James Ferguson, and James Chavis, along with three others who asked not to be identified, and on coverage of the trial in the Raleigh *News and Observer*, July 24, July 28, July 29, July 30, July 31, August 1, and August 3, 1970.

CHAPTER ELEVEN: WE ALL HAVE OUR OWN STORIES

The quote about Oxford's "voluntary desegregation" program comes from *Heritage and Homesteads*, 64. The quip about white liberals in North Carolina comes from Osha Gray Davidson, *The Best of Enemies: Race and Redemption in the New South* (New York: Scribner's, 1996), 83–84, and refers specifically to Governor Luther Hodges, something of an archetypal Tarheel liberal. The best source for this political tradition is Chafe, *Civilities and Civil Rights*.

My account of the post-trial boycott in Oxford relies upon Raleigh *News and Observer*, August 4, 1970; McAuliffe, "Transformation," 128–29; and my interviews with Benjamin Chavis, Mayor Hugh Currin, James Edward McCoy, Linda Ball, and several who preferred to remain anonymous. For the coercive aspects of other civil rights–era boycotts, see, for example, Adam Fairclough, *Race and Democracy: The Civil Rights Struggle in Louisiana, 1915–1972* (Athens: University of Georgia Press, 1995). The quote from James Baldwin comes from *The Fire Next Time* (London: Michael Joseph, 1963), 20.

There is not yet a strong account of the Wilmington Ten convulsions of the early 1970s; these were complex and controversial events, and it is not surprising that their full history has yet to emerge. Larry Reni Thomas, *The True Story Behind the Wilmington Ten* (Hampton, Va.: U.B. & U.S. Communications, 1982), is an invaluable account in that the author had unique access to African American sources at the base of the movement in Wilmington. John Godwin, *Black Wilmington and the North Carolina Way: Portrait of a Community in the Era of Civil Rights Protest* (Lanham, Md.: University Press of America, 2000), contains much helpful information but is an ideologically driven liberal interpretation, grounded in a defense of Wilmington. Michael Myerson, *Nothing Could Be Finer* (New York: International, 1978), offers useful research but remains an unreliable work of advocacy journalism on behalf of the Wilmington Ten defendants. My brief account of the troubles in Wilmington owes something to all three of these accounts. But my most important sources for the struggles in Wilmington are in the two years of research I did there in the late 1980s. These sources include the *Wilmington Morning Star*, the *Hanover Sun*, the *New York Times*, the *Washington Post*, *Newsweek*, and my own interviews with about fifty local residents, including members of the Rights of White People organization.

Sheriff Marion Millis's admission that he and many of his deputies were members of the Ku Klux Klan was reported in the Raleigh *New and Observer*, October 27, 1965. Wayne King, "The Case Against the Wilmington Ten," *New York Times Magazine*, December 3, 1978, 160–76, was especially helpful and is the source for the "framed a guilty man" quote. Dr. Heyward Bellamy, former New Hanover County Superintendent of Schools, shared with me white supremacist propaganda by his predecessor, H. M. Roland. The quote from ROWP leader Leroy Gibson, which refers to the white supremacy campaign of 1898, is from "Transcript of Speech by Leroy Gibson," Hugh McRae Park,

November 11, 1971, Rights of White People (ROWP) File, Wilmington Police Department, courtesy of Dr. Heyward Bellamy. Dr. King's scheduled appearance at Williston the day after his assassination is reported in the *Wilmington Morning Star*, April 5, 1968.

My account of the Wilmington Race Riot of 1898, which Dr. H. Leon Prather Sr. more properly terms a "massacre and coup d'état," rests upon Prather, "*We Have Taken a City*"; Gilmore, *Gender and Jim Crow*; Herbert Shapiro, *White Violence and Black Response: From Reconstruction to Montgomery* (Amherst: University of Massachusetts Press, 1987), 64–75; and Cecelski and Tyson, eds., *Democracy Betrayed*, especially Dr. Prather's masterfully concise summary of events, "We Have Taken a City: A Centennial Essay," 15–41.

The story of my sojourn in the Flat Branch "commune" relies heavily on my diary from those years and on conversations with Rob Shaffer and Perri Morgan. The account of the racial controversy at Parker's Fork United Methodist Church comes from my conversations with the Morgan family and Beth Polson.

Those who wish to further explore the 1979 murders of the Communist Workers Party leadership by Ku Klux Klan and American Nazi Party terrorists in Greensboro should consult Elizabeth Wheaton, *Codename Greenkil: The 1979 Greensboro Killings* (Athens: University of Georgia Press, 1987), Signe Waller, *Love and Revolution: A Political Memoir* (Lanham, Md.: Rowman and Littlefield, 2002), and Sally Bermanzohn, *Through Survivor's Eyes* (Nashville: Vanderbilt University Press, 2003).

CHAPTER TWELVE: "GO BACK TO THE LAST PLACE WHERE YOU KNEW WHO YOU WERE"

The quote from Bernice Johnson Reagon comes from Lucy Massie Phenix and Veronica Selver, *You Got to Move* (1986), a film about the Highlander Folk School. My account of my interview with Robert Teel rests on my own memories and on the taped and transcribed interview itself. My account of my conversations with Doug White and other members of the Oxford Police Department and also with attorney Billy Watkins relies upon my notes. To tell the story of my trip to Allen's Country Nightlife with Herman Bennett, I consulted the newspaper accounts in the Greensboro *News and Record*, the *Atlanta Constitution*, the Raleigh *News and Observer*, and the *North Carolina Independent Weekly*, and talked with Rhonda Lee and Herman Bennett.

EPILOGUE: BLOOD DONE SIGN MY NAME

The bus trip I took with my students from the University of Wisconsin at Madison has been documented, including the wording of my father's prayer at Destrehan Plantation, at an excellent website: *www.news.wisc.edu/freedom*. I am also grateful to my students for permitting me to read and quote from their journals. The statistical assessment of the life chances of African Americans is from Glenn C. Loury, *The Anatomy of Racial Inequality* (Cambridge: Harvard University Press, 2002), 4. "The past is never dead—it isn't even past" is from William Faulkner, *Requiem for a Nun* (New York: Vintage, 1975). Dr. King's reference to the "thingification" of human beings is from King, *Where Do We Go from Here?* 123. Milan Kundera is quoted in Griffin Fariella, *Red Scare: Memories of the American Inquisition* (New York: Norton, 1995), 23.

Acknowledgments

WHEN MY DAUGHTER, Martha Hope Tyson, was eleven, she accompanied her brother and me to the Harmony Bar in Madison, Wisconsin, to watch the Atlantic Coast Conference basketball tournament. Royally indifferent to the clash between good and evil, Hope came only for the french fries. While Sam and I watched the (good) Blue Devils battle the (evil) Tar Heels, she read the first draft of this manuscript, devoured every word without even looking up. The memory of her happy absorption sustained me for the two years of labor that came afterward, and I am grateful to her. I hope she likes the final product nearly as well.

No fundamentalist zealot of any of the world's religions is more devoted to his or her faith than I am to the rituals of the Harmony Bar Writers Collective. (Hat's off to Keith and Alison, et al.) Our resident shaman, Craig Werner, combines genius and generosity in equal measure, and has been a brilliant head coach. He sat through my endless stories, and then gave them back to me configured as an outline, which I followed dutifully, seventeen different times. (Hat's off to Keith and Alison, et al.) Our "editorial meetings" were the spark plugs and map of this book's long road home. Steve Kantrowitz has leavened every page of the manuscript with his matchless analytical and aesthetic sense, and thankfully not his hideous puns, which history will never forgive. He always set aside whatever he was doing to help me with literary chores frequently more ridiculous than sublime. And then there was the whiskey to finish. David S. Cecelski remains my brother until the last shred of real pork barbecue has been flushed from eastern North Carolina by fast-food conglomerates and health inspectors. He sometimes labored over this manuscript for fourteen or fifteen hours at a sitting with nothing but steaks, ribs, chopped barbecue, crab cakes, smoked chicken, mashed potatoes, collard greens, butterbeans, sweet potato biscuits, bourbon, and seven-dollar cigars to sustain him. Any lingering flaws in this book are entirely his fault, every single one of them.

I wish to thank the people of Granville County, North Carolina, some of whom will find fault with this book, and rightly so, since we have not only a flawed history but a flawed historian. Many granted me interviews or otherwise helped with this book, including the late Goldie Averett, Linda Ball, Helen Canady, Rev. Benjamin Chavis Muhammad, Dr. Francine Chavis, James Chavis, Mary Catherine Chavis, William A. Chavis, Sam Cox, Herman Cozart, Hugh Currin, Rebecca Dickerson, Roberta Gabbard, Lettie McCoy, Robert G. Teel, Carolyn Thorpe, the late Billy Watkins, Nelda Webb, Doug White, Dr. Doris Terry Williams, and many others, some of whom preferred to remain nameless. A special thanks to Tom and Grey Currin, for singing so beautifully and for catching some important spelling and factual errors. All of these folks taught me something and some of them taught me everything.

James Edward McCoy, a brilliant historian of Granville County, taught me at least as much history as I learned down the road at Duke University. I am obligated to him literally more than I can say. And the people of Granville County owe him even more. Thanks to his diligent efforts to document the past, their struggles over the legacy of slavery will illuminate the pathway for those who come afterward. I hope that folks black and white in Oxford, especially the young people, will go up to the Southern Historical Collection at Chapel Hill and read through his dozens of interviews with their elders, many of whom are no longer with us. If this book offers McCoy some token of appreciation and respect, that will please me, but I can never really repay what I owe him.

The day my family came to Oxford United Methodist Church, I met Ben and Joy Averett, who over the years taught me to work hard, love words, and live free. I wrote much of the master's thesis that became this book (twenty years later) in Joy's tree house in a dark time. Joy, my first real teacher and my first real sweetheart, too, did not live to read any of my books. Without the unearned grace of her love, I never would have written a book and might not even have survived my own stupidity. As I sat by her bedside in the oncology ward at Johns Hopkins, she gave me love's last lessons. And when Ben scattered her ashes in the orchard, he showed me how to accept those lessons. Thanks also to Amy Averett, Ed Averett, and the Burwell and Averett families for their many kindnesses.

To paraphrase Professor Kantrowitz, some of my best teachers have actually been, well, teachers. As noted in the text, this book began as a freshman history paper in 1982. In high school, Helen Mask and Betty Grady taught me to write essays and gave me dozens of good books, and many hours of detention hall in which to read them. My undergraduate mentors—John Bellios, Dan T. Carter, Fred Chappell, James Clotfelter, Janet Varner Gunn, Fraser Harbutt, James Thompson, and Allen Tullos—recognized talents that I did not quite see and pressed me to cultivate them. The seeds they planted at night school in Chapel Hill and at the University of North Carolina at Greensboro and at Emory University sprouted in due season. That same freshman year, William H. Chafe spoke at UNC-G and inspired a shy undergraduate in the crowd to pursue oral history on his own.

Five years later, I joined Chafe's graduate students in the Department of History at Duke University, where his scholarly energy, personal integrity, and irrepressible spirit taught us not only how to write and teach history but how to live. Bill continues to guide me with his friendship and counsel, and he read every page of this book more than once. I also owe much to Lawrence Goodwyn, whose devotion to clarity and democracy sustained me, and to John Herd Thompson, who mentored me as a writer and sustained me as a friend, sharing a cold brown one from time to time and just the wee sidecar, too. James Applewhite gave me *All the King's Men* and, Thomas Wolfe's admonitions aside, showed me the way to go home again. Julius Scott, Syd Nathans, and Raymond Gavins drilled me in African American history. John Hope Franklin was an inspiration. And Vivian Jackson kept me from losing my mind as I gained my doctorate.

After I left graduate school, I found other strong mentors among historians. Dan T. Carter, who helped me with the research for this book when I was an undergraduate, has continued to be my teacher and friend for twenty years. John Dittmer has been a constant fountain of encouragement and assistance, and remains a hero of mine. Charles Payne and Kalamu ya Salaam taught me some hard things. Robin D. G. Kelley read part of the manuscript and urged me onward, not to mention inspired me by his example.

The first historian I ever met was Frank Adams, who taught me about people like Myles Horton and Septima Clark, introducing me to the best Southern dreams of freedom when I was only a teenager and no doubt tiresome. And more recently, he read a draft of the manuscript and gave me both his blessing and his thoughts. Like the old song says about Jesus, Frank, Margaret, Sam, and Mary Thom gave me water, and not only from their well.

In more recent years, I have been fortunate to pursue my labors as a historian alongside people such as Curtis Austin, Anthony Badger, Marcellus Barksdale, Beth Bates, Charles Bolton, Julian Bond, Tim Borstelmann, Taylor Branch, Dorothy Burlage, Clayborne Carson, David Carter, Jeffrey Crow, Connie Curry, Jane Dailey, Pete Daniel, Mary Dudziak, John Egerton, Glenn T. Eskew, William McKee Evans, Adam Fairclough, Elizabeth Fenn, Kari Frederickson, David Garrow, Thavolia Glymph, Van Gosse, Vincent Harding, Nancy Hewitt, Lance Hill, Darlene Clark Hine, Wesley Hogan, Gerald Horne, Kenneth Janken, Will Jones, Peniel Joseph, Sudershan Kapur, Tracy K'Meyer, Steven Lawson, Chana Kai Lee, Andrew Manis, Neil McMillen, Mark Naison, Sydney Nathans, Kenneth O'Reilly, Nell Painter, Jonathan Prude, Barbara Ransby, James Roark, Bryant Simon, Harvard Sitkoff, Patricia Sullivan, Jean Theoharis, Brian Ward, Rhonda Williams, Peter Wood, Komozi Woodard, Howard Zinn, and a full crew of other able and generous scholars, many of whom are busily redefining "*the* civil rights movement," pointing out that the familiar saga from Montgomery to Memphis was only the most visible culmination of a much larger and more complex story. We are far from done.

The place where I try to do my small part, the Department of Afro-American Studies at the University of Wisconsin–Madison, is one of those rare institutions that almost works. On the fourth floor of Helen C. White Hall, I have found a warm place on the frozen prairies. Among my fine colleagues, Henry Drewal, Stanlie James, Nellie McKay, Richard Ralston, and William Van Deburg have been especially helpful to me. Jeannie Comstock and Trina Messer remain my guardian angels. I can't even talk about Christina Greene.

Years before I was exiled to the tundra, I found a warm quilt of love and friendship without which I cannot complete a sentence, let alone a book. Glenda Gilmore, in addition to being the Queen, gave me love and wisdom, always straight up. Blood brothers Nick Biddle and Herman Bennett and I may have acted like kindergarteners, but even our critics must concede that we played well with others. And I am also grateful to Herman for letting me tell his family's story, even though it was a painful one. Danielle McGuire, sturdy as a tree, worked hard to help me and helped me to work hard, and I will always be proud of her. Rob Shaffer's reading of the first drafts was invaluable, and made up for those toxic waste socks. Katherine Charron, Kirsten Fischer, Christina Greene, Rhonda Lee, Jennifer Morgan, and Adriane Smith have constantly reminded me of the purpose of literature, and they all read the manuscript for me, too, and offered helpful insights and loving friendship. Lane Windham always knew why I did this in the first place. So did Dave Marsh, and he told half the world, too. Robert and Mabel Williams taught me more than words can say and, though Robert has passed on, Mabel continues to warm my heart. Nan Enstad edited an early draft and her confidence inoculated me against writer's block. Don Baylor remains the king of gumbo, his skill at the grill surpassed only by his bountiful spirit. Paula McLain sang like nobody's business and gave me matchless editing help, too. David LaCroix read this entire manuscript in the early stages and gave me useful criticism and warm encouragement. Buddies like Deborah Baldwin, John Ferrick, Melody Ivins, Marie Kohler, Tom Loeser, Kathy Nasstrom, and Kim Vergeront read this work early on and gave me timely advice. David Ikard, a brilliant writer and scholar, read this whole book and saved me from at least part of my own ignorance. Peggy Vergeront gave me a crucial critique, to say nothing of her good company. James Danky, a sparkling soul and a smart reader, keeps me laughing all the way to the gallows. Judy Kantrowitz gave the manuscript a thoughtful polish, practically overnight. And I can't overlook the kindness of Leslie Brown, Shirley S. Portwood, and Annie Vaulk, the infamous "Strawberry Ice Cream Gang," in reading the manuscript for me.

Though I confess to being a mind-numbing geek, it is not necessary to edit my work to earn my gratitude. Barbara Forrest, the Beauty Queen of the east side, and Suzanne Desan, a one-woman Tour de France, lavished me with chicken enchiladas and many other comforts of home. Nina Hasen remains a peach. Lorrie Moore provided sage advice and sang with me. Jerry Noack is working on a building for the Lord. Cynthia Dubin was rooting for me all along. Linda Gordon did me the matchless favor of introducing me to Charlotte Sheedy, for which I will always be grateful. Bethany Moreton brought me meatloaf and greens. Mary Ellen Curtin, Jess and Kathy Gilbert, Ben Kiernan, Patty Kohlman, Beth Loveland, George Loveland, Lynn Loveland, Bill and Bobbie Malone, Kim Miller and Bryan Trabold and now little Gabriel gave me great good cheer. My neighbor Win Eide has kept my spirits up with her good company and my weight up with her cakes and sandwiches. Thanks to Ian Lekus, cheerful comrade, for the author photograph. I know that Howard Wolfson and Hugo Lindgren have no game, but the world seems to think so, and I am proud of them anyway. Col. David Johnson and his bride, the keen and lovely Wendy Frieman, gave me heart and hospitality. Colonel Johnson is a great American, a fine scholar, and a dear friend—thanks for the ride, Dave. Charles Gaddy, who sang to me when I was a boy and told me great stories, has been a constant source of support.

My compadres in Bookclub Number 6—Dick Cates, Andy Cohn, John Frey, Steve Kantrowitz, Tom Leiterman, Stewart Prager, Tim

Size, and Michael Weiden—endured my endless blathering on about this book, and then read the manuscript for me. I cherish their company and counsel, and I thank them from the bottom of my heart, which Dr. Frey assures us remains in fine condition, thanks to my consumption of smoked pork, dark beer, red wine, and other health and beauty aids.

My students at Duke University and at the University of Wisconsin–Madison have provided a bottomless fountain of purpose and meaning for my work. Alison Stocking signed on as a sister. Charles Hughes is a dangerous man and must be stopped. Joe Fronczak has a job to do, and he does it well. Katie Givens, the budding spiritual leadership of Idaho and Manhattan, will lead us in prayer. (I am grateful to her mama, too.) And Rhea Lathan is a one-woman gospel choir. I missed Thaddeus Bower when he moved to New York, where he told his boss at Crown to ask me to write a book, for which I am indebted to him. As for my other debts, I cannot list fully here even the students who have helped me with this project, let alone those who have given me joy and purpose. But to permit a small constellation of names to stand for a vast, starlit sky, I am grateful to John Adams, Shanna Benjamin, Elise Bittrich, Vanessa Bliss, Britt Bjornson, Joe Cavise, Marjorie Cook, Matt Danky, Katie De Bruin, Jerome Dotson, Ben Doherty, Jay Driskell, Gwen Drury, Jon Effron, Jessica Engel, Steve Furrer, Amanda Gengler, David Gilbert, Dan Ginger, Benedikt Glatz, Heather Goodwin, Michelle Gordon, Brenna Greer, Molly Grosse, Heather Guenther, Phyllis Hill, Helen Hoguet, Jo Hunt, Patrick Jones, Kate Jorgenson, Lexie Kasdan, Elizabeth Keeney, Princess Kent, Matt Levin, Jennifer Olsen Mandel, Story Matkin-Rawn (and her mama and daddy), Holly McGee, Trina Mikonowitz, Leah Mirakor, Josh Moise, Jim Neighbors, Zoe Van Orsdol, Heather Peto, Julie Posselt, Mia Reddy, Jacob Schultz, Vanessa Solis, Tyina Steptoe, Jake Strand, Eduardo C. Sundaram, Megan Vail, Neelum Wadhwani, Simon Wendt, Stephanie Westcott, Lisa Woolfork, Melvina Johnson Young, and the students of Afro-American Studies 231, 272, 302, and 671 who endured my stories and sharpened my sensibilities.

I am also grateful to students in the Afro-American Studies

Department at Yale University, the Folklore and History departments at the University of North Carolina at Chapel Hill, and the Center for Documentary Studies at Duke University for reading parts of this book and engaging me in helpful discussions. Martha Bouyer at Body of Christ Deliverance Ministry in Birmingham and Joanne Bland at the National Voting Rights Museum in Selma were generous hosts who became fast friends. I also want to thank Leslee Gilbert and the students at St. Mary's College of Southern Minnesota, Ed Pavlic and the folks at Union College in Schenectady, New York, and the students at Welcome Middle School in Greenville, North Carolina, and the North Carolina School of Science and Mathematics in Durham for receiving these stories so warmly. I am also grateful to Emily Auerbach and Norman Gilliland of Wisconsin Public Radio's "University of the Air" for letting me yammer on to their listeners.

A special word of appreciation is necessary for my former colleagues at Manuel's Tavern and the Euclid Avenue Yacht Club, two world-class watering holes in Atlanta, Georgia. Wisely or unwisely, they believed in me at a time when more sober and less discerning judges sometimes did not. When I was getting ready to drop out of graduate school, they got on their motorcycles and drove all the way to North Carolina to see that I did not. They threatened to kick my ass but I am pretty sure they would not have done it. A hearty shout goes out to Don Sweet, whatever star the Lord has let him ride into glory, and to Hippy, Michelle, Fay Lynn, Shawn, Big Jeff, ol' Pete, Curtis, and all the gang. Part of me will always stand behind the bar, right beneath William James: "Sobriety divides, discriminates, and says no; drunkenness unites, affirms, and says yes. Not through mere perversity do men run after it."

I began telling this story in the spring of 2001, when I was supposed to be doing something else, naturally. In this context, I should thank the Institute for Research in Humanities at the University of Wisconsin–Madison, which gave me that spring semester off, even though (actually, *because*) I promised to write something quite different. Tom Rankin at the Center for Documentary Studies at Duke sheltered me for a crucial week of writing and editing. I am also grateful to the staffs of Perkins Library at Duke, the Wisconsin State Historical Society, the North Carolina Division of Archives and History in Raleigh, and the Richard H. Thornton Library in Oxford, North Carolina.

Many people in the book publishing business have been a great help to me. David Perry and Kate Torrey at the University of North Carolina Press have been steadfast friends and trusted advisers. Tom Campbell at the Regulator Bookshop in Durham, North Carolina, my home-court bookseller, gave me solid guidance. Allen Ruff at Rainbow Bookstore Cooperative in Madison, Wisconsin, is a mensch. At Crown Publishers, Steve Ross and Chris Jackson placed their chips on the book, and made it happen. Emily Loose, with her strong narrative sense, worked wonders as editor before she moved on. And Doug Pepper, the final editor, won the heavyweight title with his deft advocacy and dazzling literary judgment. Thanks also to Genoveva Llosa, Amy Boorstein, Alison Forner, copyeditor Bonnie Thompson, Lauren Dong, and Laura Duffy for their fine work.

Above all, I want to thank my agent, the wise and beautiful Charlotte Sheedy, who defended the author against all enemies, foreign and domestic, even when the enemy was the author himself. I can never repay her many kindnesses and her sage counsel. And I would not play poker with her if I were you—don't say I didn't warn you.

As ever, I drew my deepest strength from family. My grandmother, Jessie Buie, died before any of my books were published, and she is probably too busy managing her proper portion of the Hereafter to read them now, but I will always love her. My uncle, Charles Buie, told me important stories. All of the Buies loved me long and hard, for which I am grateful, and listened to my stories, which was above and beyond the call of duty. Likewise all the Tysons have blessed me with love and support. Special thanks to the late Pauline Pearce, the late Dewey Tyson, the late Tommy Tyson, Earl Tyson, and Bobby Tyson for sharing family stories and being supportive over the years. I am also particularly grateful to Cheryl Tyson and Thomas Earl Tyson for their tenderness.

And the Morgans of Corapeake, all twenty-two of them, redefine the traditional connotations of the phrase "in-laws." Our bountiful matriarch, D. Morgan, has nurtured me like her own. Sam Morgan has been a steady rock. Susan Evans won a special place in my heart years ago, which only grew larger when she spent endless hours taking photographs for this book; I am obliged to write another one, if only to furnish a home for the cover shot she *will* get one day. Jason Morgan Ward sets a sterling example as a scholar, and I am grateful to his parents, Mike and Hope, for their assistance and support. As for Brooke, we'll always have Barcelona. Phil, Tom, and Leigh Morgan read parts of this manuscript, and I did find that list of typographical errors, thanks, Leigh.

My brother Vern, whom I shared a room with for many years, is a lovely man, aside from his personal habits. I want to thank him for his friendship and support, and for taking the blame for that beer Daddy found in the downstairs freezer in 1975. My deep thanks to Jessie Katherine and Thomas Tyson, two of the most important people for whom I wrote this book. Thanks to Terri, too, for greatly increasing the median IQ and personal appearance of our family. Boo, the latest Tyson to graduate from divinity school, fights for justice and mercy in Alabama, and has her own story to tell, which makes me proud. She and Lori Messinger, sister-outlaw #1, have stood by me for many years, enduring my incessant stories, and I am forever grateful. Julie Tyson, my brown-eyed soul sister, has been an angel to me and a light to the world, and I thank her from the bottom of my heart. Long live the sisteren.

My children have been perhaps the biggest blessing of my life. Samuel Hart Tyson, who has already won several games in Cameron Indoor Stadium, played hoop with me, comforted me whether Duke lost or won, made me laugh a thousand times, jumped off cliffs into cold water with me, and inspired me with his zesty embrace of the world. Hope Tyson, as noted earlier, read the manuscript in its first incarnation, and has furnished a fine example for her father by her laughter, love, and the way she makes something beautiful and useful every day. And she's brave, too, not to mention an accomplished writer herself. I love them both always.

The mother of these angels, Perri Anne Morgan, is a brilliant woman whose one large blind spot it has been my privilege to occupy for twenty years. I am sorry for all that this book has cost her, and I will try to make it up to her. I am grateful for her patient help, luminous editing, and all the years of love and friendship. Perri stitched my life together by turning our house into a juke joint—no need to choose between gospel and blues when sweet mama is at the old upright. The thrill is definitely not gone.

When I was only three years old, Mama found me on the floor with a book pulled tightly against my face, sobbing hard. When she asked me why on earth I was crying, I told her, "Because I can't get *in* the book." Now, I could not read at that age. What had happened, really, is that my mother had read so many books to me, so vividly, so beautifully, that I expected to be able to pick up the book and plunge instantly into beautiful depths of the imagination, and was disappointed that I could not. In later years, of course, I found exactly that kind of satisfaction in books, and I owe all that to Mama. Martha Buic Tyson stands like a tree beside the river of our lives, giving shade and sustenance, and teaching all of us by example. I am also grateful to her for sharing her diary, answering my endless questions, and letting me write about her family.

My father, who remains the best damn preacher who ever beat on the Book, graced my life with his passion for the word and his vision of redeeming love. Like Jacob, he has wrestled with the angels and come away walking with a limp, but he carries that vision without which the people perish. And even if he didn't, he has been the best father anyone ever had. And even if he hadn't, he has become a friend like no other, reading every draft of every sentence I ever wrote, serving as a library of eastern North Carolina lore, going with me to archives and interviews, offering excellent editorial suggestions, giving me his love and my liberty, to say nothing of lunch. This book is dedicated to Martha and Vernon, my mama and daddy, with undying gratitude for their courage and their vision and their love.

Steve Pool

ABOUT THE AUTHOR

TIMOTHY B. TYSON was born and raised in North Carolina, where he earned his Ph.D. from Duke University in 1994. He is associate professor of Afro-American Studies at the University of Wisconsin and lives in Madison with Perri Morgan and their two children. His last book, *Radio Free Dixie: Robert F. Williams and the Roots of Black Power*, won the James Rawley Prize and the Frederick Jackson Turner Prize from the Organization of American Historians. His first book, *Democracy Betrayed: The Wilmington Race Riot of 1898 and Its Legacy*, co-edited with David S. Cecelski, won the Outstanding Book Award from the Gustavus Meyers Center for the study of Human Rights in North America.